ROY MARSTEN (handwritten)

http://cran.r-project.org (handwritten)

R in Action

Data analysis and graphics with R

ROBERT I. KABACOFF

2/15/16 (handwritten)

	OS	R	XQuartz*	
desktop	10.10.5	3.2.3 / 3.0.2	2.7.11	4/30/2018
laptop	10.10.5	3.2.2	2.7.8	

MANNING
Shelter Island

In Applications folder: R.app (handwritten)
* for X11 windowing system for Mac OS-X (handwritten)

For online information and ordering of this and other Manning books, please visit
www.manning.com. The publisher offers discounts on this book when ordered in quantity.
For more information, please contact

Special Sales Department
Manning Publications Co.
20 Baldwin Road
PO Box 261
Shelter Island, NY 11964   Email: orders@manning.com

Manning Publications Co.   Development editor: Sebastian Stirling
20 Baldwin Road   Copyeditor: Liz Welch
PO Box 261   Typesetter: Composure Graphics
Shelter Island, NY 11964   Cover designer: Marija Tudor

Second, corrected printing, December 2011
ISBN: 9781935182399
Printed in the United States of America
5 6 7 8 9 10 – MAL – 16 15 14 13

brief contents

contents

preface

What is the use of a book, without pictures or conversations?
—Alice, *Alice in Wonderland*

It's wondrous, with treasures to satiate desires both subtle and gross; but it's not for the timid.
—Q, "Q Who?" *Stark Trek: The Next Generation*

When I began writing this book, I spent quite a bit of time searching for a good quote to start things off. I ended up with two. R is a wonderfully flexible platform and language for exploring, visualizing, and understanding data. I chose the quote from Alice in Wonderland to capture the flavor of statistical analysis today—an interactive process of exploration, visualization, and interpretation.

The second quote reflects the generally held notion that R is difficult to learn. What I hope to show you is that is doesn't have to be. R is broad and powerful, with so many analytic and graphic functions available (more than 50,000 at last count) that it easily intimidates both novice and experienced users alike. But there is rhyme and reason to the apparent madness. With guidelines and instructions, you can navigate the tremendous resources available, selecting the tools you need to accomplish your work with style, elegance, efficiency—and more than a little coolness.

I first encountered R several years ago, when applying for a new statistical consulting position. The prospective employer asked in the pre-interview material if I was conversant in R. Following the standard advice of recruiters, I immediately said yes, and set off to learn it. I was an experienced statistician and researcher, had

25 years experience as an SAS and SPSS programmer, and was fluent in a half dozen programming languages. How hard could it be? Famous last words.

As I tried to learn the language (as fast as possible, with an interview looming), I found either tomes on the underlying structure of the language or dense treatises on specific advanced statistical methods, written by and for subject-matter experts. The online help was written in a Spartan style that was more reference than tutorial. Every time I thought I had a handle on the overall organization and capabilities of R, I found something new that made me feel ignorant and small.

To make sense of it all, I approached R as a data scientist. I thought about what it takes to successfully process, analyze, and understand data, including

- Accessing the data (getting the data into the application from multiple sources)
- Cleaning the data (coding missing data, fixing or deleting miscoded data, transforming variables into more useful formats)
- Annotating the data (in order to remember what each piece represents)
- Summarizing the data (getting descriptive statistics to help characterize the data)
- Visualizing the data (because a picture really is worth a thousand words)
- Modeling the data (uncovering relationships and testing hypotheses)
- Preparing the results (creating publication-quality tables and graphs)

Then I tried to understand how I could use R to accomplish each of these tasks. Because I learn best by teaching, I eventually created a website (www.statmethods.net) to document what I had learned.

Then, about a year ago, Marjan Bace (the publisher) called and asked if I would like to write a book on R. I had already written 50 journal articles, 4 technical manuals, numerous book chapters, and a book on research methodology, so how hard could it be? At the risk of sounding repetitive—famous last words.

The book you're holding is the one that I wished I had so many years ago. I have tried to provide you with a guide to R that will allow you to quickly access the power of this great open source endeavor, without all the frustration and angst. I hope you enjoy it.

P.S. I was offered the job but didn't take it. However, learning R has taken my career in directions that I could never have anticipated. Life can be funny.

acknowledgments

A number of people worked hard to make this a better book. They include

- Marjan Bace, Manning publisher, who asked me to write this book in the first place.
- Sebastian Stirling, development editor, who spent many hours on the phone with me, helping me organize the material, clarify concepts, and generally make the text more interesting. He also helped me through the many steps to publication.
- Karen Tegtmeyer, review editor, who helped obtain reviewers and coordinate the review process.
- Mary Piergies, who helped shepherd this book through the production process, and her team of Liz Welch, Susan Harkins, and Rachel Schroeder.
- Pablo Domínguez Vaselli, technical proofreader, who helped uncover areas of confusion and provided an independent and expert eye for testing code.
- The peer reviewers who spent hours of their own time carefully reading through the material, finding typos and making valuable substantive suggestions: Chris Williams, Charles Malpas, Angela Staples, PhD, Daniel Reis Pereira, Dr. D. H. van Rijn, Dr. Christian Marquardt, Amos Folarin, Stuart Jefferys, Dror Berel, Patrick Breen, Elizabeth Ostrowski, PhD, Atef Ouni, Carles Fenollosa, Ricardo Pietrobon, Samuel McQuillin, Landon Cox, Austin Ziegler, Rick Wagner, Ryan Cox, Sumit Pal, Philipp K. Janert, Deepak Vohra, and Sophie Mormede.

- The many Manning Early Access Program (MEAP) participants who bought the book before it was finished, asked great questions, pointed out errors, and made helpful suggestions.

Each contributor has made this a better and more comprehensive book.

I would also like to acknowledge the many software authors that have contributed to making R such a powerful data-analytic platform. They include not only the core developers, but also the selfless individuals who have created and maintain contributed packages, extending R's capabilities greatly. Appendix F provides a list of the authors of contributed packages described in this book. In particular, I would like to mention John Fox, Hadley Wickham, Frank E. Harrell, Jr., Deepayan Sarkar, and William Revelle, whose works I greatly admire. I have tried to represent their contributions accurately, and I remain solely responsible for any errors or distortions inadvertently included in this book.

I really should have started this book by thanking my wife and partner, Carol Lynn. Although she has no intrinsic interest in statistics or programming, she read each chapter multiple times and made countless corrections and suggestions. No greater love has any person than to read multivariate statistics for another. Just as important, she suffered the long nights and weekends that I spent writing this book, with grace, support, and affection. There is no logical explanation why I should be this lucky.

There are two other people I would like to thank. One is my father, whose love of science was inspiring and who gave me an appreciation of the value of data. The other is Gary K. Burger, my mentor in graduate school. Gary got me interested in a career in statistics and teaching when I thought I wanted to be a clinician. This is all his fault.

about this book

If you picked up this book, you probably have some data that you need to collect, summarize, transform, explore, model, visualize, or present. If so, then R is for you! R has become the world-wide language for statistics, predictive analytics, and data visualization. It offers the widest range available of methodologies for understanding data, from the most basic to the most complex and bleeding edge.

As an open source project it's freely available for a range of platforms, including Windows, Mac OS X, and Linux. It's under constant development, with new procedures added daily. Additionally, R is supported by a large and diverse community of data scientists and programmers who gladly offer their help and advice to users.

Although R is probably best known for its ability to create beautiful and sophisticated graphs, it can handle just about any statistical problem. The base installation provides hundreds of data-management, statistical, and graphical functions out of the box. But some of its most powerful features come from the thousands of extensions (packages) provided by contributing authors.

This breadth comes at a price. It can be hard for new users to get a handle on what R is and what it can do. Even the most experienced R user is surprised to learn about features they were unaware of.

R in Action provides you with a guided introduction to R, giving you a 2,000-foot view of the platform and its capabilities. It will introduce you to the most important functions in the base installation and more than 90 of the most useful contributed packages. Throughout the book, the goal is practical application—how you can make sense of your data and communicate that understanding to others. When you finish, you should have a good grasp of how R works and what it can do, and where you can go to learn more. You'll be able to apply a variety of techniques for visualizing data, and you'll have the skills to tackle both basic and advanced data analytic problems.

Who should read this book

R in Action should appeal to anyone who deals with data. No background in statistical programming or the R language is assumed. Although the book is accessible to novices, there should be enough new and practical material to satisfy even experienced R mavens.

Users without a statistical background who want to use R to manipulate, summarize, and graph data should find chapters 1–6, 11, and 16 easily accessible. Chapter 7 and 10 assume a one-semester course in statistics; and readers of chapters 8, 9, and 12–15 will benefit from two semesters of statistics. But I have tried to write each chapter in such a way that both beginning and expert data analysts will find something interesting and useful.

Roadmap

This book is designed to give you a guided tour of the R platform, with a focus on those methods most immediately applicable for manipulating, visualizing, and understanding data. There are 16 chapters divided into 4 parts: "Getting started," "Basic methods," "Intermediate methods," and "Advanced methods." Additional topics are covered in eight appendices.

Chapter 1 begins with an introduction to R and the features that make it so useful as a data-analysis platform. The chapter covers how to obtain the program and how to enhance the basic installation with extensions that are available online. The remainder of the chapter is spent exploring the user interface and learning how to run programs interactively and in batches.

Chapter 2 covers the many methods available for getting data into R. The first half of the chapter introduces the data structures R uses to hold data, and how to enter data from the keyboard. The second half discusses methods for importing data into R from text files, web pages, spreadsheets, statistical packages, and databases.

Many users initially approach R because they want to create graphs, so we jump right into that topic in chapter 3. No waiting required. We review methods of creating graphs, modifying them, and saving them in a variety of formats.

Chapter 4 covers basic data management, including sorting, merging, and subsetting datasets, and transforming, recoding, and deleting variables.

Building on the material in chapter 4, chapter 5 covers the use of functions (mathematical, statistical, character) and control structures (looping, conditional execution) for data management. We then discuss how to write your own R functions and how to aggregate data in various ways.

Chapter 6 demonstrates methods for creating common univariate graphs, such as bar plots, pie charts, histograms, density plots, box plots, and dot plots. Each is useful for understanding the distribution of a single variable.

Chapter 7 starts by showing how to summarize data, including the use of descriptive statistics and cross-tabulations. We then look at basic methods for understanding relationships between two variables, including correlations, t-tests, chi-square tests, and nonparametric methods.

Chapter 8 introduces regression methods for modeling the relationship between a numeric outcome variable and a set of one or more numeric predictor variables. Methods for fitting these models, evaluating their appropriateness, and interpreting their meaning are discussed in detail.

Chapter 9 considers the analysis of basic experimental designs through the analysis of variance and its variants. Here we are usually interested in how treatment combinations or conditions affect a numerical outcome variable. Methods for assessing the appropriateness of the analyses and visualizing the results are also covered.

A detailed treatment of power analysis is provided in chapter 10. Starting with a discussion of hypothesis testing, the chapter focuses on how to determine the sample size necessary to detect a treatment effect of a given size with a given degree of confidence. This can help you to plan experimental and quasi-experimental studies that are likely to yield useful results.

Chapter 11 expands on the material in chapter 5, covering the creation of graphs that help you to visualize relationships among two or more variables. This includes various types of 2D and 3D scatter plots, scatter-plot matrices, line plots, correlograms, and mosaic plots.

Chapter 12 presents analytic methods that work well in cases where data are sampled from unknown or mixed distributions, where sample sizes are small, where outliers are a problem, or where devising an appropriate test based on a theoretical distribution is too complex and mathematically intractable. They include both resampling and bootstrapping approaches—computer-intensive methods that are easily implemented in R.

Chapter 13 expands on the regression methods in chapter 8 to cover data that are not normally distributed. The chapter starts with a discussion of generalized linear models and then focuses on cases where you're trying to predict an outcome variable that is either categorical (logistic regression) or a count (Poisson regression).

One of the challenges of multivariate data problems is simplification. Chapter 14 describes methods of transforming a large number of correlated variables into a smaller set of uncorrelated variables (principal component analysis), as well as methods for uncovering the latent structure underlying a given set of variables (factor analysis). The many steps involved in an appropriate analysis are covered in detail.

In keeping with our attempt to present practical methods for analyzing data, chapter 15 considers modern approaches to the ubiquitous problem of missing data values. R supports a number of elegant approaches for analyzing datasets that are incomplete for various reasons. Several of the best are described here, along with guidance for which ones to use when and which ones to avoid.

Chapter 16 wraps up the discussion of graphics with presentations of some of R's most advanced and useful approaches to visualizing data. This includes visual representations of very complex data using lattice graphs, an introduction to the new ggplot2 package, and a review of methods for interacting with graphs in real time.

The afterword points you to many of the best internet sites for learning more about R, joining the R community, getting questions answered, and staying current with this rapidly changing product.

Last, but not least, the eight appendices (A through H) extend the text's coverage to include such useful topics as R graphic user interfaces, customizing and upgrading an R installation, exporting data to other applications, creating publication quality output, using R for matrix algebra (à la MATLAB), and working with very large datasets.

The examples

In order to make this book as broadly applicable as possible, I have chosen examples from a range of disciplines, including psychology, sociology, medicine, biology, business, and engineering. None of these examples require a specialized knowledge of that field.

The datasets used in these examples were selected because they pose interesting questions and because they're small. This allows you to focus on the techniques described and quickly understand the processes involved. When you're learning new methods, smaller is better.

The datasets are either provided with the base installation of R or available through add-on packages that are available online. The source code for each example is available from www.manning.com/RinAction. To get the most out of this book, I recommend that you try the examples as you read them.

Finally, there is a common maxim that states that if you ask two statisticians how to analyze a dataset, you'll get three answers. The flip side of this assertion is that each answer will move you closer to an understanding of the data. I make no claim that a given analysis is the best or only approach to a given problem. Using the skills taught in this text, I invite you to play with the data and see what you can learn. R is interactive, and the best way to learn is to experiment.

Code conventions

The following typographical conventions are used throughout this book:

- A monospaced font is used for code listings that should be typed as is.
- A monospaced font is also used within the general text to denote code words or previously defined objects.
- *Italics* within code listings indicate placeholders. You should replace them with appropriate text and values for the problem at hand. For example, *path_to_my_file* would be replaced with the actual path to a file on your computer.

- R is an interactive language that indicates readiness for the next line of user input with a prompt (> by default). Many of the listings in this book capture interactive sessions. When you see code lines that start with >, don't type the prompt.
- Code annotations are used in place of inline comments (a common convention in Manning books). Additionally, some annotations appear with numbered bullets like ❶ that refer to explanations appearing later in the text.
- To save room or make text more legible, the output from interactive sessions may include additional white space or omit text that is extraneous to the point under discussion.

Author Online

Purchase of *R in Action* includes free access to a private web forum run by Manning Publications where you can make comments about the book, ask technical questions, and receive help from the author and from other users. To access the forum and subscribe to it, point your web browser to www.manning.com/RinAction. This page provides information on how to get on the forum once you're registered, what kind of help is available, and the rules of conduct on the forum.

Manning's commitment to our readers is to provide a venue where a meaningful dialog between individual readers and between readers and the author can take place. It isn't a commitment to any specific amount of participation on the part of the author, whose contribution to the AO forum remains voluntary (and unpaid). We suggest you try asking the authors some challenging questions, lest his interest stray!

The AO forum and the archives of previous discussions will be accessible from the publisher's website as long as the book is in print.

About the author

Dr. Robert Kabacoff is Vice President of Research for Management Research Group, an international organizational development and consulting firm. He has more than 20 years of experience providing research and statistical consultation to organizations in health care, financial services, manufacturing, behavioral sciences, government, and academia. Prior to joining MRG, Dr. Kabacoff was a professor of psychology at Nova Southeastern University in Florida, where he taught graduate courses in quantitative methods and statistical programming. For the past two years, he has managed Quick-R, an R tutorial website.

about the cover illustration

The figure on the cover of *R in Action* is captioned "A man from Zadar." The illustration is taken from a reproduction of an album of Croatian traditional costumes from the mid-nineteenth century by Nikola Arsenovic, published by the Ethnographic Museum in Split, Croatia, in 2003. The illustrations were obtained from a helpful librarian at the Ethnographic Museum in Split, itself situated in the Roman core of the medieval center of the town: the ruins of Emperor Diocletian's retirement palace from around AD 304. The book includes finely colored illustrations of figures from different regions of Croatia, accompanied by descriptions of the costumes and of everyday life.

Zadar is an old Roman-era town on the northern Dalmatian coast of Croatia. It's over 2,000 years old and served for hundreds of years as an important port on the trading route from Constantinople to the West. Situated on a peninsula framed by small Adriatic islands, the city is picturesque and has become a popular tourist destination with its architectural treasures of Roman ruins, moats, and old stone walls. The figure on the cover wears blue woolen trousers and a white linen shirt, over which he dons a blue vest and jacket trimmed with the colorful embroidery typical for this region. A red woolen belt and cap complete the costume.

Dress codes and lifestyles have changed over the last 200 years, and the diversity by region, so rich at the time, has faded away. It's now hard to tell apart the inhabitants of different continents, let alone of different hamlets or towns separated by only a few miles. Perhaps we have traded cultural diversity for a more varied personal life—certainly for a more varied and fast-paced technological life.

Manning celebrates the inventiveness and initiative of the computer business with book covers based on the rich diversity of regional life of two centuries ago, brought back to life by illustrations from old books and collections like this one.

Part 1

Getting started

Welcome to R in Action! R is one of the most popular platforms for data analysis and visualization currently available. It is free, open-source software, with versions for Windows, Mac OS X, and Linux operating systems. This book will provide you with the skills needed to master this comprehensive software, and apply it effectively to your own data.

The book is divided into four sections. Part I covers the basics of installing the software, learning to navigate the interface, importing data, and massaging it into a useful format for further analysis.

Chapter 1 will familiarize you with the R environment. The chapter begins with an overview of R and the features that make it such a powerful platform for modern data analysis. After briefly describing how to obtain and install the software, the user interface is explored through a series of simple examples. Next, you'll learn how to enhance the functionality of the basic installation with extensions (called contributed packages), that can be freely downloaded from online repositories. The chapter ends with an example that allows you to test your new skills.

Once you're familiar with the R interface, the next challenge is to get your data into the program. In today's information-rich world, data can come from many sources and in many formats. Chapter 2 covers the wide variety of methods available for importing data into R. The first half of the chapter introduces the data structures R uses to hold data and describes how to input data manually. The second half discusses methods for importing data from text files, web pages, spreadsheets, statistical packages, and databases.

From a workflow point of view, it would probably make sense to discuss data management and data cleaning next. However, many users approach R for the first time out of an interest in its powerful graphics capabilities. Rather than frustrating that interest and keeping you waiting, we dive right into graphics in chapter 3. The chapter reviews methods for creating graphs, customizing them, and saving them in a variety of formats. The chapter describes how to specify the colors, symbols, lines, fonts, axes, titles, labels, and legends used in a graph, and ends with a description of how to combine several graphs into a single plot.

Once you've had a chance to try out R's graphics capabilities, it is time to get back to the business of analyzing data. Data rarely comes in a readily usable format. Significant time must often be spent combining data from different sources, cleaning messy data (miscoded data, mismatched data, missing data), and creating new variables (combined variables, transformed variables, recoded variables) before the questions of interest can be addressed. Chapter 4 covers basic data management tasks in R, including sorting, merging, and subsetting datasets, and transforming, recoding, and deleting variables.

Chapter 5 builds on the material in chapter 4. It covers the use of numeric (arithmetic, trigonometric, and statistical) and character functions (string subsetting, concatenation, and substitution) in data management. A comprehensive example is used throughout this section to illustrate many of the functions described. Next, control structures (looping, conditional execution) are discussed and you will learn how to write your own R functions. Writing custom functions allows you to extend R's capabilities by encapsulating many programming steps into a single, flexible function call. Finally, powerful methods for reorganizing (reshaping) and aggregating data are discussed. Reshaping and aggregation are often useful in preparing data for further analyses.

After having completed part 1, you will be thoroughly familiar with programming in the R environment. You will have the skills needed to enter and access data, clean it up, and prepare it for further analyses. You will also have experience creating, customizing, and saving a variety of graphs.

Introduction to R

How we analyze data has changed dramatically in recent years. With the advent of personal computers and the internet, the sheer volume of data we have available has grown enormously. Companies have terabytes of data on the consumers they interact with, and governmental, academic, and private research institutions have extensive archival and survey data on every manner of research topic. Gleaning information (let alone wisdom) from these massive stores of data has become an industry in itself. At the same time, presenting the information in easily accessible and digestible ways has become increasingly challenging.

The science of data analysis (statistics, psychometrics, econometrics, machine learning) has kept pace with this explosion of data. Before personal computers and the internet, new statistical methods were developed by academic researchers who published their results as theoretical papers in professional journals. It could take years for these methods to be adapted by programmers and incorporated into the statistical packages widely available to data analysts. Today, new methodologies appear *daily*. Statistical researchers publish new and improved methods, along with the code to produce them, on easily accessible websites.

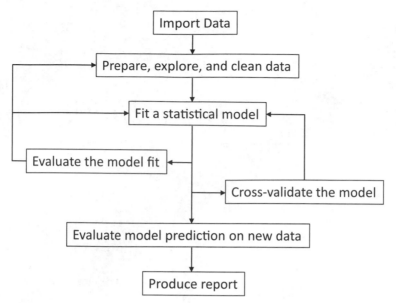

Figure 1.1   **Steps in a typical data analysis**

The advent of personal computers had another effect on the way we analyze data. When data analysis was carried out on mainframe computers, computer time was precious and difficult to come by. Analysts would carefully set up a computer run with all the parameters and options thought to be needed. When the procedure ran, the resulting output could be dozens or hundreds of pages long. The analyst would sift through this output, extracting useful material and discarding the rest. Many popular statistical packages were originally developed during this period and still follow this approach to some degree.

With the cheap and easy access afforded by personal computers, modern data analysis has shifted to a different paradigm. Rather than setting up a complete data analysis at once, the process has become highly interactive, with the output from each stage serving as the input for the next stage. An example of a typical analysis is shown in figure 1.1. At any point, the cycles may include transforming the data, imputing missing values, adding or deleting variables, and looping back through the whole process again. The process stops when the analyst believes he or she understands the data intimately and has answered all the relevant questions that can be answered.

The advent of personal computers (and especially the availability of high-resolution monitors) has also had an impact on how results are understood and presented. A picture *really can* be worth a thousand words, and human beings are very adept at extracting useful information from visual presentations. Modern data analysis increasingly relies on graphical presentations to uncover meaning and convey results.

To summarize, today's data analysts need to be able to access data from a wide range of sources (database management systems, text files, statistical packages, and spreadsheets), merge the pieces of data together, clean and annotate them, analyze them with the latest methods, present the findings in meaningful and graphically appealing ways, and incorporate the results into attractive reports that can be distributed to stakeholders and the public. As you'll see in the following pages, R is a comprehensive software package that's ideally suited to accomplish these goals.

1.1 Why use R?

R is a language and environment for statistical computing and graphics, similar to the S language originally developed at Bell Labs. It's an open source solution to data analysis that's supported by a large and active worldwide research community. But there are many popular statistical and graphing packages available (such as Microsoft Excel, SAS, IBM SPSS, Stata, and Minitab). Why turn to R?

R has many features to recommend it:

- Most commercial statistical software platforms cost thousands, if not tens of thousands of dollars. R is free! If you're a teacher or a student, the benefits are obvious.

- R is a comprehensive statistical platform, offering all manner of data analytic techniques. Just about any type of data analysis can be done in R.

- R has state-of-the-art graphics capabilities. If you want to visualize complex data, R has the most comprehensive and powerful feature set available.

- R is a powerful platform for interactive data analysis and exploration. From its inception it was designed to support the approach outlined in figure 1.1. For example, the results of any analytic step can easily be saved, manipulated, and used as input for additional analyses.

- Getting data into a usable form from multiple sources can be a challenging proposition. R can easily import data from a wide variety of sources, including text files, database management systems, statistical packages, and specialized data repositories. It can write data out to these systems as well.

- R provides an unparalleled platform for programming new statistical methods in an easy and straightforward manner. It's easily extensible and provides a natural language for quickly programming recently published methods.

- R contains advanced statistical routines not yet available in other packages. In fact, new methods become available for download on a weekly basis. If you're a SAS user, imagine getting a new SAS PROC every few days.

- If you don't want to learn a new language, a variety of graphic user interfaces (GUIs) are available, offering the power of R through menus and dialogs.

- R runs on a wide array of platforms, including Windows, Unix, and Mac OS X. It's likely to run on any computer you might have (I've even come across guides for installing R on an iPhone, which is impressive but probably not a good idea).

You can see an example of R's graphic capabilities in figure 1.2. This graph, created with a single line of code, describes the relationships between income, education, and prestige for blue-collar, white-collar, and professional jobs. Technically, it's a scatter plot matrix with groups displayed by color and symbol, two types of fit lines (linear and loess), confidence ellipses, and two types of density display (kernel density estimation, and rug plots). Additionally, the largest outlier in each scatter plot has been automatically labeled. If these terms are unfamiliar to you, don't worry. We'll cover them in later chapters. For now, trust me that they're really cool (and that the statisticians reading this are salivating).

Basically, this graph indicates the following:

- Education, income, and job prestige are linearly related.
- In general, blue-collar jobs involve lower education, income, and prestige, whereas professional jobs involve higher education, income, and prestige. White-collar jobs fall in between.

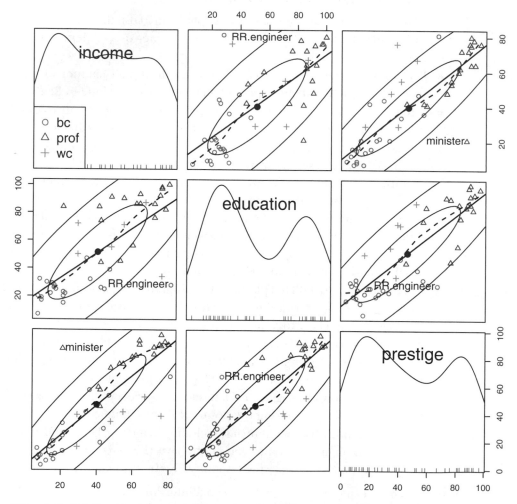

Figure 1.2   Relationships between income, education, and prestige for blue-collar (bc), white-collar (wc), and professional jobs (prof). Source: car package (`scatterplotMatrix` function) written by John Fox. Graphs like this are difficult to create in other statistical programming languages but can be created with a line or two of code in R.

- There are some interesting exceptions. Railroad Engineers have high income and low education. Ministers have high prestige and low income.
- Education and (to lesser extent) prestige are distributed bi-modally, with more scores in the high and low ends than in the middle.

Chapter 8 will have much more to say about this type of graph. The important point is that R allows you to create elegant, informative, and highly customized graphs in a simple and straightforward fashion. Creating similar plots in other statistical languages would be difficult, time consuming, or impossible.

Unfortunately, R can have a steep learning curve. Because it can do so much, the documentation and help files available are voluminous. Additionally, because much of the functionality comes from optional modules created by independent contributors, this documentation can be scattered and difficult to locate. In fact, getting a handle on all that R can do is a challenge.

The goal of this book is to make access to R quick and easy. We'll tour the many features of R, covering enough material to get you started on your data, with pointers on where to go when you need to learn more. Let's begin by installing the program.

1.2 Obtaining and installing R

R is freely available from the Comprehensive R Archive Network (CRAN) at http://cran.r-project.org. Precompiled binaries are available for Linux, Mac OS X, and Windows. Follow the directions for installing the base product on the platform of your choice. Later we'll talk about adding functionality through optional modules called packages (also available from CRAN). Appendix H describes how to update an existing R installation to a newer version.

1.3 Working with R

R is a case-sensitive, interpreted language. You can enter commands one at a time at the command prompt (>) or run a set of commands from a source file. There are a wide variety of data types, including vectors, matrices, data frames (similar to datasets), and lists (collections of objects). We'll discuss each of these data types in chapter 2.

Most functionality is provided through built-in and user-created functions, and all data objects are kept in memory during an interactive session. Basic functions are available by default. Other functions are contained in packages that can be attached to a current session as needed.

Statements consist of functions and assignments. R uses the symbol <- for assignments, rather than the typical = sign. For example, the statement

```
x <- rnorm(5)
```

creates a vector object named x containing five random deviates from a standard normal distribution.

NOTE R allows the = sign to be used for object assignments. However, you won't find many programs written that way, because it's not standard syntax, there are some situations in which it won't work, and R programmers will make fun of you. You can also reverse the assignment direction. For instance, `rnorm(5)  -> x` is equivalent to the previous statement. Again, doing so is uncommon and isn't recommended in this book.

Comments are preceded by the # symbol. Any text appearing after the # is ignored by the R interpreter.

1.3.1   *Getting started*

If you're using Windows, launch R from the Start Menu. On a Mac, double-click the R icon in the Applications folder. For Linux, type R at the command prompt of a terminal window. Any of these will start the R interface (see figure 1.3 for an example).

To get a feel for the interface, let's work through a simple contrived example. Say that you're studying physical development and you've collected the ages and weights of 10 infants in their first year of life (see table 1.1). You're interested in the distribution of the weights and their relationship to age.

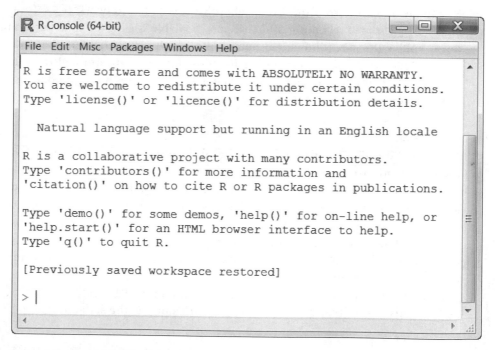

Figure 1.3   Example of the R interface on Windows

Table 1.1 The age and weights of ten infants

Age (mo.)	Weight (kg.)	Age (mo.)	Weight (kg.)
01	4.4	09	7.3
03	5.3	03	6.0
05	7.2	09	10.4
02	5.2	12	10.2
11	8.5	03	6.1

Note: These are fictional data.

You'll enter the age and weight data as vectors, using the function `c()`, which combines its arguments into a vector or list. Then you'll get the mean and standard deviation of the weights, along with the correlation between age and weight, and plot the relationship between age and weight so that you can inspect any trend visually. The `q()` function, as shown in the following listing, will end the session and allow you to quit.

Listing 1.1 A sample R session

```
> age <- c(1,3,5,2,11,9,3,9,12,3)
> weight <- c(4.4,5.3,7.2,5.2,8.5,7.3,6.0,10.4,10.2,6.1)
> mean(weight)
[1] 7.06
> sd(weight)
[1] 2.077498
> cor(age,weight)
[1] 0.9075655
> plot(age,weight)
> q()
```

You can see from listing 1.1 that the mean weight for these 10 infants is 7.06 kilograms, that the standard deviation is 2.08 kilograms, and that there is strong linear relationship between age in months and weight in kilograms (correlation = 0.91). The relationship can also be seen in the scatter plot in figure 1.4. Not surprisingly, as infants get older, they tend to weigh more.

The scatter plot in figure 1.4 is informative but somewhat utilitarian and unattractive. In later chapters, you'll see how to customize graphs to suit your needs.

TIP To get a sense of what R can do graphically, enter `demo(graphics)` at the command prompt. A sample of the graphs produced is included in figure 1.5. Other demonstrations include `demo(Hershey)`, `demo(persp)`, and `demo(image)`. To see a complete list of demonstrations, enter `demo()` without parameters.

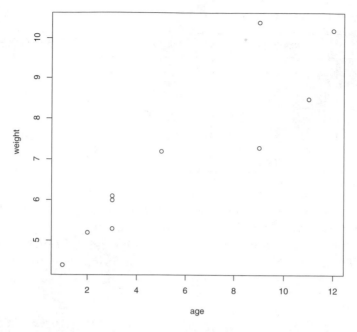

Figure 1.4   Scatter plot of infant weight (kg) by age (mo)

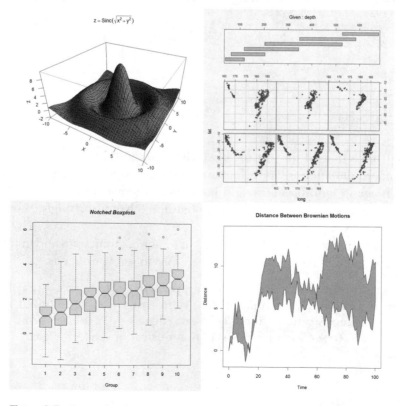

Figure 1.5   A sample of the graphs created with the `demo()` function

1.3.2　Getting help

R provides extensive help facilities, and learning to navigate them will help you significantly in your programming efforts. The built-in help system provides details, references, and examples of any function contained in a currently installed package. Help
is obtained using the functions listed in table 1.2.

Table 1.2　R help functions

Function	Action
`help.start()`	General help.
`help("foo")` or `?foo`	Help on function *foo* (the quotation marks are optional).
`help.search("foo")` or `??foo`	Search the help system for instances of the string *foo*.
`example("foo")`	Examples of function *foo* (the quotation marks are optional).
`RSiteSearch("foo")`	Search for the string *foo* in online help manuals and archived mailing lists.
`apropos("foo", mode="function")`	List all available functions with *foo* in their name.
`data()`	List all available example datasets contained in currently loaded packages.
`vignette()`	List all available vignettes for currently installed packages.
`vignette("foo")`	Display specific vignettes for topic *foo*.

The function `help.start()` opens a browser window with access to introductory
and advanced manuals, FAQs, and reference materials. The `RSiteSearch()` function
searches for a given topic in online help manuals and archives of the R-Help discussion list and returns the results in a browser window. The vignettes returned by the
`vignette()` function are practical introductory articles provided in PDF format. Not
all packages will have vignettes. As you can see, R provides extensive help facilities, and
learning to navigate them will definitely aid your programming efforts. It's a rare session that I don't use the ? to look up the features (such as options or return values) of
some function.

1.3.3　The workspace

The workspace is your current R working environment and includes any user-defined
objects (vectors, matrices, functions, data frames, or lists). At the end of an R session,
you can save an image of the current workspace that's automatically reloaded the next
time R starts. Commands are entered interactively at the R user prompt. You can use the

up and down arrow keys to scroll through your command history. Doing so allows you to select a previous command, edit it if desired, and resubmit it using the Enter key.

The current working directory is the directory R will read files from and save results to by default. You can find out what the current working directory is by using the getwd() function. You can set the current working directory by using the setwd() function. If you need to input a file that isn't in the current working directory, use the full pathname in the call. Always enclose the names of files and directories from the operating system in quote marks.

Some standard commands for managing your workspace are listed in table 1.3.

Table 1.3   Functions for managing the R workspace

Function	Action
getwd()	List the current working directory.
setwd("*mydirectory*")	Change the current working directory to *mydirectory*.
ls()	List the objects in the current workspace.
rm(*objectlist*)	Remove (delete) one or more objects.
help(options)	Learn about available options.
options()	View or set current options.
history(#)	Display your last # commands (default = 25).
savehistory("*myfile*")	Save the commands history to *myfile* (default = .Rhistory).
loadhistory("*myfile*")	Reload a command's history (default = .Rhistory).
save.image("*myfile*")	Save the workspace to myfile (default = .RData).
save(*objectlist*, file="*myfile*")	Save specific objects to a file.
load("*myfile*")	Load a workspace into the current session (default = .RData).
q()	Quit R. You'll be prompted to save the workspace.

To see these commands in action, take a look at the following listing.

Listing 1.2   An example of commands used to manage the R workspace

```
setwd("C:/myprojects/project1")
options()
options(digits=3)
x <- runif(20)
summary(x)
hist(x)
savehistory()
save.image()
q()
```

First, the current working directory is set to C:/myprojects/project1, the current option settings are displayed, and numbers are formatted to print with three digits after the decimal place. Next, a vector with 20 uniform random variates is created, and summary statistics and a histogram based on this data are generated. Finally, the command history is saved to the file .Rhistory, the workspace (including vector x) is saved to the file .RData, and the session is ended.

Note the forward slashes in the pathname of the `setwd()` command. R treats the backslash (\) as an escape character. Even when using R on a Windows platform, use forward slashes in pathnames. Also note that the `setwd()` function won't create a directory that doesn't exist. If necessary, you can use the `dir.create()` function to create a directory, and then use `setwd()` to change to its location.

It's a good idea to keep your projects in separate directories. I typically start an R session by issuing the `setwd()` command with the appropriate path to a project, followed by the `load()` command without options. This lets me start up where I left off in my last session and keeps the data and settings separate between projects. On Windows and Mac OS X platforms, it's even easier. Just navigate to the project directory and double-click on the saved image file. Doing so will start R, load the saved workspace, and set the current working directory to this location.

1.3.4 Input and output

By default, launching R starts an interactive session with input from the keyboard and output to the screen. But you can also process commands from a script file (a file containing R statements) and direct output to a variety of destinations.

INPUT

The `source("`*`filename`*`")` function submits a script to the current session. If the filename doesn't include a path, the file is assumed to be in the current working directory. For example, `source("myscript.R")` runs a set of R statements contained in file `myscript.R`. By convention, script file names end with an .R extension, but this isn't required.

TEXT OUTPUT

The `sink("`*`filename`*`")` function redirects output to the file *filename*. By default, if the file already exists, its contents are overwritten. Include the option `append=TRUE` to append text to the file rather than overwriting it. Including the option `split=TRUE` will send output to both the screen and the output file. Issuing the command `sink()` without options will return output to the screen alone.

GRAPHIC OUTPUT

Although `sink()` redirects text output, it has no effect on graphic output. To redirect graphic output, use one of the functions listed in table 1.4. Use `dev.off()` to return output to the terminal.

Table 1.4   Functions for saving graphic output

Function	Output
`pdf("filename.pdf")`	PDF file
`win.metafile("filename.wmf")`	Windows metafile
`png("filename.png")`	PBG file
`jpeg("filename.jpg")`	JPEG file
`bmp("filename.bmp")`	BMP file
`postscript("filename.ps")`	PostScript file

Let's put it all together with an example. Assume that you have three script files containing R code (script1.R, script2.R, and script3.R). Issuing the statement

```
source("script1.R")
```

will submit the R code from script1.R to the current session and the results will appear on the screen.

If you then issue the statements

```
sink("myoutput", append=TRUE, split=TRUE)
pdf("mygraphs.pdf")
source("script2.R")
```

the R code from file script2.R will be submitted, and the results will again appear on the screen. In addition, the text output will be appended to the file myoutput, and the graphic output will be saved to the file mygraphs.pdf.

Finally, if you issue the statements

```
sink()
dev.off()
source("script3.R")
```

the R code from script3.R will be submitted, and the results will appear on the screen. This time, no text or graphic output is saved to files. The sequence is outlined in figure 1.6.

R provides quite a bit of flexibility and control over where input comes from and where it goes. In section 1.5 you'll learn how to run a program in batch mode.

1.4   *Packages*

R comes with extensive capabilities right out of the box. But some of its most exciting features are available as optional modules that you can download and install. There are over 2,500 user-contributed modules called *packages* that you can download from http://cran.r-project.org/web/packages. They provide a tremendous range of new capabilities, from the analysis of geostatistical data to protein mass spectra processing to the analysis of psychological tests! You'll use many of these optional packages in this book.

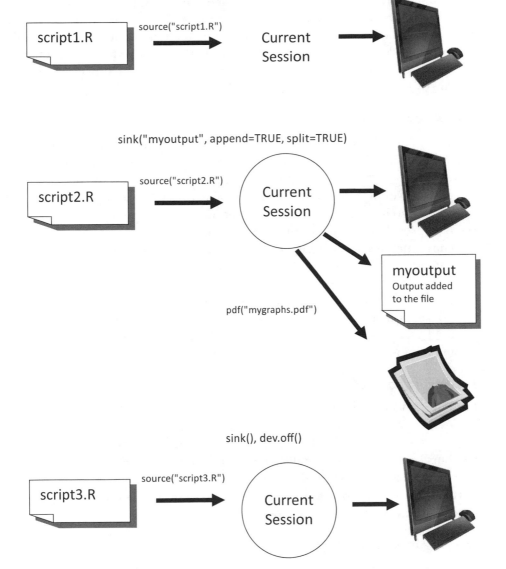

Figure 1.6 Input with the `source()` function and output with the `sink()` function

/Library/Frameworks/R.framework/Versions/3.0/Resources/library

1.4.1 What are packages?

Packages are collections of R functions, data, and compiled code in a well-defined format. The directory where packages are stored on your computer is called the library. The function `.libPaths()` shows you where your library is located, and the function `library()` shows you what packages you've saved in your library.

↳ *base   cluster   datasets   grDevices   MASS*
boot   codetools   foreign   grid   Matrix
car   compiler   graphics   KernSmooth   :
class   lattice

R comes with a standard set of packages (including `base`, `datasets`, `utils`, `grDevices`, `graphics`, `stats`, and `methods`). They provide a wide range of functions and datasets that are available by default. Other packages are available for download and installation. Once installed, they have to be loaded into the session in order to be used. The command `search()` tells you which packages are loaded and ready to use.

1.4.2   Installing a package

There are a number of R functions that let you manipulate packages. To install a package for the first time, use the `install.packages()` command. For example, `install.packages()` without options brings up a list of CRAN mirror sites. Once you select a site, you'll be presented with a list of all available packages. Selecting one will download and install it. If you know what package you want to install, you can do so directly by providing it as an argument to the function. For example, the `gclus` package contains functions for creating enhanced scatter plots. You can download and install the package with the command `install.packages("gclus")`.

You only need to install a package once. But like any software, packages are often updated by their authors. Use the command `update.packages()` to update any packages that you've installed. To see details on your packages, you can use the `installed.packages()` command. It lists the packages you have, along with their version numbers, dependencies, and other information.

1.4.3   Loading a package

Installing a package downloads it from a CRAN mirror site and places it in your library. To use it in an R session, you need to load the package using the `library()` command. For example, to use the packaged `gclus` issue the command `library(gclus)`. Of course, you must have installed a package before you can load it. You'll only have to load the package once within a given session. If desired, you can customize your startup environment to automatically load the packages you use most often. Customizing your startup is covered in appendix B.

1.4.4   Learning about a package

When you load a package, a new set of functions and datasets becomes available. Small illustrative datasets are provided along with sample code, allowing you to try out the new functionalities. The help system contains a description of each function (along with examples), and information on each dataset included. Entering `help(package="package_name")` provides a brief description of the package and an index of the functions and datasets included. Using `help()` with any of these function or dataset names will provide further details. The same information can be downloaded as a PDF manual from CRAN.

Common mistakes in R programming

There are some common mistakes made frequently by both beginning and experienced R programmers. If your program generates an error, be sure the check for the following:

- *Using the wrong case*—`help()`, `Help()`, and `HELP()` are three different functions (only the first will work).
- *Forgetting to use quote marks when they're needed*—`install.packages-("gclus")` works, whereas `install.packages(gclus)` generates an error.
- *Forgetting to include the parentheses in a function call*—for example, `help()` rather than `help`. Even if there are no options, you still need the ().
- *Using the \ in a pathname on Windows*—R sees the backslash character as an escape character. `setwd("c:\mydata")` generates an error. Use `setwd("c:/mydata")` or `setwd("c:\\mydata")` instead.
- *Using a function from a package that's not loaded*—The function `order.clusters()` is contained in the `gclus` package. If you try to use it before loading the package, you'll get an error.

The error messages in R can be cryptic, but if you're careful to follow these points, you should avoid seeing many of them.

1.5 Batch processing

Most of the time, you'll be running R interactively, entering commands at the command prompt and seeing the results of each statement as it's processed. Occasionally, you may want to run an R program in a repeated, standard, and possibly unattended fashion. For example, you may need to generate the same report once a month. You can write your program in R and run it in batch mode.

How you run R in batch mode depends on your operating system. On Linux or Mac OS X systems, you can use the following command in a terminal window:

```
R CMD BATCH options infile outfile
```

where *infile* is the name of the file containing R code to be executed, *outfile* is the name of the file receiving the output, and *options* lists options that control execution. By convention, *infile* is given the extension .R and *outfile* is given extension .Rout.

For Windows, use

```
"C:\Program Files\R\R-2.13.0\bin\R.exe" CMD BATCH
➥--vanilla --slave "c:\my projects\myscript.R"
```

adjusting the paths to match the location of your R.exe binary and your script file. For additional details on how to invoke R, including the use of command-line options, see the "Introduction to R" documentation available from CRAN (http://cran.r-project.org).

1.6   Using output as input—reusing results

One of the most useful design features of R is that the output of analyses can easily be saved and used as input to additional analyses. Let's walk through an example, using one of the datasets that comes pre-installed with R. If you don't understand the statistics involved, don't worry. We're focusing on the general principle here.

First, run a simple linear regression predicting miles per gallon (mpg) from car weight (wt), using the automotive dataset mtcars. This is accomplished with the function call:

```
lm(mpg~wt, data=mtcars)
```

The results are displayed on the screen and no information is saved.

Next, run the regression, but store the results in an object:

```
lmfit <- lm(mpg~wt, data=mtcars)
```

The assignment has created a list object called lmfit that contains extensive information from the analysis (including the predicted values, residuals, regression coefficients, and more). Although no output has been sent to the screen, the results can be both displayed and manipulated further.

Typing summary(lmfit) displays a summary of the results, and plot(lmfit) produces diagnostic plots. The statement cook<-cooks.distance(lmfit) generates influence statistics and plot(cook) graphs them. To predict miles per gallon from car weight in a new set of data, you'd use predict(lmfit, *mynewdata*).

To see what a function returns, look at the Value section of the online help for that function. Here you'd look at help(lm) or ?lm. This tells you what's saved when you assign the results of that function to an object.

1.7   Working with large datasets

Programmers frequently ask me if R can handle large data problems. Typically, they work with massive amounts of data gathered from web research, climatology, or genetics. Because R holds objects in memory, you're typically limited by the amount of RAM available. For example, on my 5-year-old Windows PC with 2 GB of RAM, I can easily handle datasets with 10 million elements (100 variables by 100,000 observations). On an iMac with 4 GB of RAM, I can usually handle 100 million elements without difficulty.

But there are two issues to consider: the size of the dataset and the statistical methods that will be applied. R can handle data analysis problems in the gigabyte to terabyte range, but specialized procedures are required. The management and analysis of very large datasets is discussed in appendix G.

1.8   Working through an example

We'll finish this chapter with an example that ties many of these ideas together. Here's the task:

1   Open the general help and look at the "Introduction to R" section.
2   Install the vcd package (a package for visualizing categorical data that we'll be using in chapter 11).

3 List the functions and datasets available in this package.
4 Load the package and read the description of the dataset `Arthritis`.
5 Print out the `Arthritis` dataset (entering the name of an object will list it).
6 Run the example that comes with the `Arthritis` dataset. Don't worry if you don't understand the results. It basically shows that arthritis patients receiving treatment improved much more than patients receiving a placebo.
7 Quit.

The code required is provided in the following listing, with a sample of the results displayed in figure 1.7.

Listing 1.3 Working with a new package

```
help.start()
install.packages("vcd")    ← need X11 for OSX.
help(package="vcd")
library(vcd)
help(Arthritis)
Arthritis
example(Arthritis)
q()
```

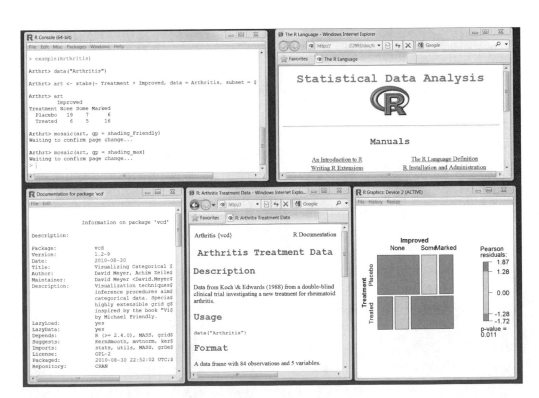

Figure 1.7 Output from listing 1.3 including (left to right) output from the arthritis example, general help, information on the vcd package, information on the Arthritis dataset, and a graph displaying the relationship between arthritis treatment and outcome

As this short exercise demonstrates, you can accomplish a great deal with a small amount of code.

1.9   Summary

In this chapter, we looked at some of the strengths that make R an attractive option for students, researchers, statisticians, and data analysts trying to understand the meaning of their data. We walked through the program's installation and talked about how to enhance R's capabilities by downloading additional packages. We explored the basic interface, running programs interactively and in batches, and produced a few sample graphs. You also learned how to save your work to both text and graphic files. Because R can be a complex program, we spent some time looking at how to access the extensive help that's available. We hope you're getting a sense of how powerful this freely available software can be.

Now that you have R up and running, it's time to get your data into the mix. In the next chapter, we'll look at the types of data R can handle and how to import them into R from text files, other programs, and database management systems.

Creating a dataset

2

This chapter covers

- Exploring R data structures
- Using data entry
- Importing data
- Annotating datasets

The first step in any data analysis is the creation of a dataset containing the information to be studied, in a format that meets your needs. In R, this task involves the following:

- Selecting a data structure to hold your data
- Entering or importing your data into the data structure

The first part of this chapter (sections 2.1–2.2) describes the wealth of structures that R can use for holding data. In particular, section 2.2 describes vectors, factors, matrices, data frames, and lists. Familiarizing yourself with these structures (and the notation used to access elements within them) will help you tremendously in understanding how R works. You might want to take your time working through this section.

The second part of this chapter (section 2.3) covers the many methods available for importing data into R. Data can be entered manually, or imported from an external source. These data sources can include text files, spreadsheets, statistical packages, and database management systems. For example, the data that I work with typically comes from SQL databases. On occasion, though, I receive data from legacy DOS systems, and from current SAS and SPSS databases. It's likely that you'll only have to use one or two of the methods described in this section, so feel free to choose those that fit your situation.

Once a dataset is created, you'll typically annotate it, adding descriptive labels for variables and variable codes. The third portion of this chapter (section 2.4) looks at annotating datasets and reviews some useful functions for working with datasets (section 2.5). Let's start with the basics.

2.1   *Understanding datasets*

A dataset is usually a rectangular array of data with rows representing observations and columns representing variables. Table 2.1 provides an example of a hypothetical patient dataset.

Table 2.1   **A patient dataset**

PatientID	AdmDate	Age	Diabetes	Status
1	10/15/2009	25	Type1	Poor
2	11/01/2009	34	Type2	Improved
3	10/21/2009	28	Type1	Excellent
4	10/28/2009	52	Type1	Poor

Different traditions have different names for the rows and columns of a dataset. Statisticians refer to them as observations and variables, database analysts call them records and fields, and those from the data mining/machine learning disciplines call them examples and attributes. We'll use the terms *observations* and *variables* throughout this book.

You can distinguish between the structure of the dataset (in this case a rectangular array) and the contents or data types included. In the dataset shown in table 2.1, PatientID is a row or case identifier, AdmDate is a date variable, Age is a continuous variable, Diabetes is a nominal variable, and Status is an ordinal variable.

R contains a wide variety of structures for holding data, including scalars, vectors, arrays, data frames, and lists. Table 2.1 corresponds to a data frame in R. This diversity of structures provides the R language with a great deal of flexibility in dealing with data.

The data types or modes that R can handle include numeric, character, logical (TRUE/FALSE), complex (imaginary numbers), and raw (bytes). In R, PatientID, AdmDate, and Age would be numeric variables, whereas Diabetes and Status would be character variables. Additionally, you'll need to tell R that PatientID is a case identifier, that AdmDate contains dates, and that Diabetes and Status are nominal and

Categorical variables are called "factors".

ordinal variables, respectively. R refers to case identifiers as <u>rownames</u> and categorical variables (nominal, ordinal) as factors. We'll cover each of these in the next section. You'll learn about dates in chapter 3.

2.2 Data structures

R has a wide variety of objects for holding data, including scalars, vectors, matrices, arrays, data frames, and lists. They differ in terms of the type of data they can hold, how they're created, their structural complexity, and the notation used to identify and access individual elements. Figure 2.1 shows a diagram of these data structures.

Let's look at each structure in turn, starting with vectors.

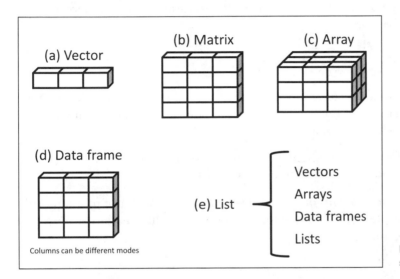

Figure 2.1 R data structures

Some definitions

There are several terms that are idiosyncratic to R, and thus confusing to new users.

In R, an *object* is anything that can be assigned to a variable. This includes constants, data structures, functions, and even graphs. Objects have a mode (which describes how the object is stored) and a class (which tells generic functions like print how to handle it).

A *data frame* is a structure in R that holds data and is similar to the datasets found in standard statistical packages (for example, SAS, SPSS, and Stata). The columns are variables and the rows are observations. <u>You can have variables of different types (for example, numeric, character) in the same data frame.</u> Data frames are the main structures you'll use to store datasets.

unlike a matrix.

Use a data frame!

> *(continued)*
> *Factors* are nominal or ordinal variables. They're stored and treated specially in R. You'll learn about factors in section 2.2.5.
>
> Most other terms should be familiar to you and follow the terminology used in statistics and computing in general.

2.2.1   Vectors

Vectors are one-dimensional arrays that can hold numeric data, character data, or logical data. The combine function c() is used to form the vector. Here are examples of each type of vector:

```
a <- c(1, 2, 5, 3, 6, -2, 4)
b <- c("one", "two", "three")
c <- c(TRUE, TRUE, TRUE, FALSE, TRUE, FALSE)
```

Here, a is numeric vector, b is a character vector, and c is a logical vector. Note that the data in a vector must only be one type or mode (numeric, character, or logical). You can't mix modes in the same vector.

NOTE   Scalars are one-element vectors. Examples include f <- 3, g <- "US" and h <- TRUE. They're used to hold constants.

You can refer to elements of a vector using a numeric vector of positions within brackets. For example, a[c(2, 4)] refers to the 2nd and 4th element of vector a. Here are additional examples:

```
> a <- c(1, 2, 5, 3, 6, -2, 4)
> a[3]
[1] 5
> a[c(1, 3, 5)]
[1] 1 5 6
> a[2:6]
[1]  2  5  3  6 -2
```

The colon operator used in the last statement is used to generate a sequence of numbers. For example, a <- c(2:6) is equivalent to a <- c(2, 3, 4, 5, 6).

2.2.2   Matrices

A matrix is a two-dimensional array where each element has the same mode (numeric, character, or logical). Matrices are created with the matrix function. The general format is

```
myymatrix <- matrix(vector, nrow=number_of_rows, ncol=number_of_columns,
                byrow=logical_value, dimnames=list(
                char_vector_rownames, char_vector_colnames))
```

where *vector* contains the elements for the matrix, nrow and ncol specify the row and column dimensions, and dimnames contains optional row and column labels stored in character vectors. The option `byrow` indicates whether the matrix should be filled in by row (`byrow=TRUE`) or by column (`byrow=FALSE`). The default is by column. The following listing demonstrates the `matrix` function.

Listing 2.1 Creating matrices

```
> y <- matrix(1:20, nrow=5, ncol=4)          ◄——❶ Create a 5x4 matrix
> y
     [,1] [,2] [,3] [,4]
[1,]    1    6   11   16
[2,]    2    7   12   17
[3,]    3    8   13   18
[4,]    4    9   14   19
[5,]    5   10   15   20
> cells    <- c(1,26,24,68)                   ◄——┐  2x2 matrix filled
> rnames   <- c("R1", "R2")                       ❷  by rows
> cnames   <- c("C1", "C2")
> mymatrix <- matrix(cells, nrow=2, ncol=2, byrow=TRUE,
                     dimnames=list(rnames, cnames))
> mymatrix
   C1 C2
R1  1 26
R2 24 68
> mymatrix <- matrix(cells, nrow=2, ncol=2, byrow=FALSE,  ◄———┐
                     dimnames=list(rnames, cnames))  2x2 matrix filled
> mymatrix                                            by columns ❸
   C1 C2
R1  1 24
R2 26 68
```

First, you create a 5x4 matrix ❶. Then you create a 2x2 matrix with labels and fill the matrix by rows ❷. Finally, you create a 2x2 matrix and fill the matrix by columns ❸.

You can identify rows, columns, or elements of a matrix by using subscripts and brackets. $X[i,]$ refers to the ith row of matrix X, $X[,j]$ refers to jth column, and $X[i, j]$ refers to the ijth element, respectively. The subscripts i and j can be numeric vectors in order to select multiple rows or columns, as shown in the following listing.

Listing 2.2 Using matrix subscripts

```
> x <- matrix(1:10, nrow=2)
> x
     [,1] [,2] [,3] [,4] [,5]
[1,]    1    3    5    7    9
[2,]    2    4    6    8   10
> x[2,]
 [1]  2  4  6  8 10
> x[,2]
[1] 3 4
> x[1,4]
[1] 7
> x[1, c(4,5)]
[1] 7 9
```

First a 2 x 5 matrix is created containing numbers 1 to 10. By default, the matrix is filled by column. Then the elements in the 2nd row are selected, followed by the elements in the 2nd column. Next, the element in the 1st row and 4th column is selected. Finally, the elements in the 1st row and the 4th and 5th columns are selected.

Matrices are two-dimensional and, like vectors, can contain only one data type. When there are more than two dimensions, you'll use arrays (section 2.2.3). When there are multiple modes of data, you'll use data frames (section 2.2.4).

2.2.3   *Arrays*

Arrays are similar to matrices but can have more than two dimensions. They're created with an array function of the following form:

```
myarray <- array(vector, dimensions, dimnames)
```

where *vector* contains the data for the array, *dimensions* is a numeric vector giving the maximal index for each dimension, and *dimnames* is an optional list of dimension labels. The following listing gives an example of creating a three-dimensional (2x3x4) array of numbers.

Listing 2.3   Creating an array

```
> dim1 <- c("A1", "A2")
> dim2 <- c("B1", "B2", "B3")
> dim3 <- c("C1", "C2", "C3", "C4")
> z <- array(1:24, c(2, 3, 4), dimnames=list(dim1, dim2, dim3))
> z
, , C1

   B1 B2 B3
A1  1  3  5
A2  2  4  6


, , C2

   B1 B2 B3
A1  7  9 11
A2  8 10 12


, , C3

   B1 B2 B3
A1 13 15 17
A2 14 16 18


, , C4

   B1 B2 B3
A1 19 21 23
A2 20 22 24
```

As you can see, arrays are a natural extension of matrices. They can be useful in programming new statistical methods. Like matrices, they must be a single mode.

Identifying elements follows what you've seen for matrices. In the previous example, the z[1,2,3] element is 15.

2.2.4 Data frames

A data frame is more general than a matrix in that different columns can contain different modes of data (numeric, character, etc.). It's similar to the datasets you'd typically see in SAS, SPSS, and Stata. Data frames are the most common data structure you'll deal with in R.

The patient dataset in table 2.1 consists of numeric and character data. Because there are multiple modes of data, you can't contain this data in a matrix. In this case, a data frame would be the structure of choice.

A data frame is created with the data.frame() function:

```
mydata <- data.frame(col1, col2, col3,…)
```

where *col1, col2, col3, …* are column vectors of any type (such as character, numeric, or logical). Names for each column can be provided with the names function. The following listing makes this clear.

Listing 2.4   Creating a data frame

```
> patientID <- c(1, 2, 3, 4)
> age <- c(25, 34, 28, 52)
> diabetes <- c("Type1", "Type2", "Type1", "Type1")
> status <- c("Poor", "Improved", "Excellent", "Poor")
> patientdata <- data.frame(patientID, age, diabetes, status)
> patientdata
  patientID age diabetes    status
1         1  25    Type1      Poor
2         2  34    Type2  Improved
3         3  28    Type1 Excellent
4         4  52    Type1      Poor
```

Each column must have only one mode, but you can put columns of different modes together to form the data frame. Because data frames are close to what analysts typically think of as datasets, we'll use the terms *columns* and *variables* interchangeably when discussing data frames.

There are several ways to identify the elements of a data frame. You can use the subscript notation you used before (for example, with matrices) or you can specify column names. Using the patientdata data frame created earlier, the following listing demonstrates these approaches.

Listing 2.5   Specifying elements of a data frame

```
> patientdata[1:2]
  patientID age
1         1  25
2         2  34
3         3  28
4         4  52
> patientdata[c("diabetes", "status")]
```

```
      diabetes    status
1       Type1       Poor
2       Type2   Improved
3       Type1  Excellent
4       Type1       Poor
> patientdata$age
[1] 25 34 28 52
```

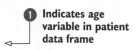

❶ Indicates age
variable in patient
data frame

The $ notation in the third example is new ❶. It's used to indicate a particular variable from a given data frame. For example, if you want to cross tabulate diabetes type by status, you could use the following code:

```
> table(patientdata$diabetes, patientdata$status)

         Excellent Improved Poor
   Type1         1        0    2
   Type2         0        1    0
```

It can get tiresome typing `patientdata$` at the beginning of every variable name, so shortcuts are available. You can use either the `attach()` and `detach()` or `with()` functions to simplify your code.

ATTACH, DETACH, AND WITH

The `attach()` function adds the data frame to the R search path. When a variable name is encountered, data frames in the search path are checked in order to locate the variable. Using the `mtcars` data frame from chapter 1 as an example, you could use the following code to obtain summary statistics for automobile mileage (`mpg`), and plot this variable against engine displacement (`disp`), and weight (`wt`):

```
summary(mtcars$mpg)
plot(mtcars$mpg, mtcars$disp)
plot(mtcars$mpg, mtcars$wt)
```

This could also be written as

```
attach(mtcars)
   summary(mpg)
   plot(mpg, disp)
   plot(mpg, wt)
detach(mtcars)
```

[handwritten margin note: attach( ) and detach( ) just for convenience!]

The `detach()` function removes the data frame from the search path. Note that `detach()` does nothing to the data frame itself. The statement is optional but is good programming practice and should be included routinely. (I'll sometimes ignore this sage advice in later chapters in order to keep code fragments simple and short.)

The limitations with this approach are evident when more than one object can have the same name. Consider the following code:

```
> mpg <- c(25, 36, 47)
> attach(mtcars)

The following object(s) are masked _by_ '.GlobalEnv':    mpg
```

```
> plot(mpg, wt)
Error in xy.coords(x, y, xlabel, ylabel, log) :
  'x' and 'y' lengths differ
> mpg
[1] 25 36 47
```

Here we already have an object named `mpg` in our environment when the `mtcars` data frame is attached. In such cases, the original object takes precedence, which isn't what you want. The `plot` statement fails because `mpg` has 3 elements and `disp` has 32 elements. The `attach()` and `detach()` functions are best used when you're analyzing a single data frame and you're unlikely to have multiple objects with the same name. In any case, be vigilant for warnings that say that objects are being masked.

An alternative approach is to use the `with()` function. You could write the previous example as

```
with(mtcars, {
  summary(mpg, disp, wt)
  plot(mpg, disp)
  plot(mpg, wt)
})
```

In this case, the statements within the `{}` brackets are evaluated with reference to the `mtcars` data frame. You don't have to worry about name conflicts here. If there's only one statement (for example, `summary(mpg)`), the `{}` brackets are optional.

The limitation of the `with()` function is that assignments will only exist within the function brackets. Consider the following:

```
> with(mtcars, {
    stats <- summary(mpg)
    stats
    })
  Min. 1st Qu.  Median    Mean 3rd Qu.    Max.
  10.40   15.43   19.20   20.09   22.80   33.90
> stats
Error: object 'stats' not found
```

If you need to create objects that will exist outside of the `with()` construct, use the special assignment operator `<<-` instead of the standard one (`<-`). It will save the object to the global environment outside of the `with()` call. This can be demonstrated with the following code:

```
> with(mtcars, {
    nokeepstats <- summary(mpg)
    keepstats <<- summary(mpg)
})
> nokeepstats
Error: object 'nokeepstats' not found
> keepstats
  Min. 1st Qu.  Median    Mean 3rd Qu.    Max.
  10.40   15.43   19.20   20.09   22.80   33.90
```

Most books on R recommend using `with()` over `attach()`. I think that ultimately the choice is a matter of preference and should be based on what you're trying to achieve and your understanding of the implications. We'll use both in this book.

CASE IDENTIFIERS

In the patient data example, `patientID` is used to identify individuals in the dataset. In R, case identifiers can be specified with a `rowname` option in the data frame function. For example, the statement

```
patientdata <- data.frame(patientID, age, diabetes, status,
    row.names=patientID)
```

specifies `patientID` as the variable to use in labeling cases on various printouts and graphs produced by R.

2.2.5 *Factors*

As you've seen, variables can be described as nominal, ordinal, or continuous. Nominal variables are categorical, without an implied order. `Diabetes` (`Type1`, `Type2`) is an example of a nominal variable. Even if `Type1` is coded as a 1 and `Type2` is coded as a 2 in the data, no order is implied. Ordinal variables imply order but not amount. `Status` (`poor`, `improved`, `excellent`) is a good example of an ordinal variable. You know that a patient with a poor status isn't doing as well as a patient with an improved status, but not by how much. Continuous variables can take on any value within some range, and both order and amount are implied. `Age` in years is a continuous variable and can take on values such as 14.5 or 22.8 and any value in between. You know that someone who is 15 is one year older than someone who is 14.

Categorical (nominal) and ordered categorical (ordinal) variables in R are called factors. Factors are crucial in R because they determine how data will be analyzed and presented visually. You'll see examples of this throughout the book.

The function `factor()` stores the categorical values as a vector of integers in the range [1... k] (where k is the number of unique values in the nominal variable), and an internal vector of character strings (the original values) mapped to these integers.

For example, assume that you have the vector

```
diabetes <- c("Type1", "Type2", "Type1", "Type1")
```

The statement `diabetes <- factor(diabetes)` stores this vector as (1, 2, 1, 1) and associates it with 1=Type1 and 2=Type2 internally (the assignment is alphabetical). Any analyses performed on the vector `diabetes` will treat the variable as nominal and select the statistical methods appropriate for this level of measurement.

For vectors representing ordinal variables, you add the parameter `ordered=TRUE` to the `factor()` function. Given the vector

```
status <- c("Poor", "Improved", "Excellent", "Poor")
```

the statement `status <- factor(status, ordered=TRUE)` will encode the vector as (3, 2, 1, 3) and associate these values internally as 1=Excellent, 2=Improved, and

3=Poor. Additionally, any analyses performed on this vector will treat the variable as ordinal and select the statistical methods appropriately.

By default, factor levels for character vectors are created in alphabetical order. This worked for the `status` factor, because the order "Excellent," "Improved," "Poor" made sense. There would have been a problem if "Poor" had been coded as "Ailing" instead, because the order would be "Ailing," "Excellent," "Improved." A similar problem exists if the desired order was "Poor," "Improved," "Excellent." For ordered factors, the alphabetical default is rarely sufficient.

You can override the default by specifying a `levels` option. For example,

```
status <- factor(status, order=TRUE,
                 levels=c("Poor", "Improved", "Excellent"))
```

would assign the levels as 1=Poor, 2=Improved, 3=Excellent. Be sure that the specified levels match your actual data values. Any data values not in the list will be set to missing.

The following listing demonstrates how specifying factors and ordered factors impact data analyses.

Listing 2.6 Using factors

```
> patientID <- c(1, 2, 3, 4)                                      ① Enter data as vectors
> age <- c(25, 34, 28, 52)
> diabetes <- c("Type1", "Type2", "Type1", "Type1")
> status <- c("Poor", "Improved", "Excellent", "Poor")
> diabetes <- factor(diabetes)
> status <- factor(status, order=TRUE)
> patientdata <- data.frame(patientID, age, diabetes, status)
> str(patientdata)                                                ② Display object
'data.frame':    4 obs. of  4 variables:                            structure
 $ patientID: num  1 2 3 4
 $ age      : num  25 34 28 52
 $ diabetes : Factor w/ 2 levels "Type1","Type2": 1 2 1 1
 $ status   : Ord.factor w/ 3 levels "Excellent"<"Improved"<..: 3 2 1 3
> summary(patientdata)                                            ③ Display object
   patientID         age          diabetes        status            summary
 Min.   :1.00   Min.   :25.00   Type1:3   Excellent:1
 1st Qu.:1.75   1st Qu.:27.25   Type2:1   Improved :1
 Median :2.50   Median :31.00             Poor     :2
 Mean   :2.50   Mean   :34.75
 3rd Qu.:3.25   3rd Qu.:38.50
 Max.   :4.00   Max.   :52.00
```

First, you enter the data as vectors ①. Then you specify that `diabetes` is a factor and `status` is an ordered factor. Finally, you combine the data into a data frame. The function `str(object)` provides information on an object in R (the data frame in this case) ②. It clearly shows that `diabetes` is a factor and `status` is an ordered factor, along with how it's coded internally. Note that the `summary()` function treats the variables differently ③. It provides the minimum, maximum, mean, and quartiles for the continuous variable age, and frequency counts for the categorical variables `diabetes` and `status`.

2.2.6   Lists

Lists are the most complex of the R data types. Basically, a list is an ordered collection of objects (components). A list allows you to gather a variety of (possibly unrelated) objects under one name. For example, a list may contain a combination of vectors, matrices, data frames, and even other lists. You create a list using the `list()` function:

```
mylist <- list(object1, object2, …)
```

where the objects are any of the structures seen so far. Optionally, you can name the objects in a list:

```
mylist <- list(name1=object1, name2=object2, …)
```

The following listing shows an example.

Listing 2.7   Creating a list

```
> g <- "My First List"
> h <- c(25, 26, 18, 39)
> j <- matrix(1:10, nrow=5)
> k <- c("one", "two", "three")
> mylist <- list(title=g, ages=h, j, k)      ⟵——— Create list
> mylist                                      ⟵——— Print entire list
$title
[1] "My First List"

$ages
[1] 25 26 18 39

[[3]]
     [,1] [,2]
[1,]    1    6
[2,]    2    7
[3,]    3    8
[4,]    4    9
[5,]    5   10

[[4]]
[1] "one"    "two"    "three"

> mylist[[2]]                    ⟵——┐ Print second
[1] 25 26 18 39                      │ component
> mylist[["ages"]]                  ─┘
[[1] 25 26 18 39
```

In this example, you create a list with four components: a string, a numeric vector, a matrix, and a character vector. You can combine any number of objects and save them as a list.

You can also specify elements of the list by indicating a component number or a name within double brackets. In this example, `mylist[[2]]` and `mylist[["ages"]]` both refer to the same four-element numeric vector. Lists are important R structures for two reasons. First, they allow you to organize and recall disparate information in a simple way. Second, the results of many R functions return lists. It's up to the analyst to pull out the components that are needed. You'll see numerous examples of functions that return lists in later chapters.

A note for programmers

Experienced programmers typically find several aspects of the R language unusual. Here are some features of the language you should be aware of:

- The period (.) has no special significance in object names. But the dollar sign ($) has a somewhat analogous meaning, identifying the parts of an object. For example, A$x refers to variable x in data frame A.
- R doesn't provide multiline or block comments. You must start each line of a multiline comment with #. For debugging purposes, you can also surround code that you want the interpreter to ignore with the statement if(FALSE){…}. Changing the FALSE to TRUE allows the code to be executed.
- Assigning a value to a nonexistent element of a vector, matrix, array, or list will expand that structure to accommodate the new value. For example, consider the following:

```
> x <- c(8, 6, 4)
> x[7] <- 10
> x
[1]  8  6  4 NA NA NA 10
```

The vector x has expanded from three to seven elements through the assignment. x <- x[1:3] would shrink it back to three elements again.
- R doesn't have scalar values. Scalars are represented as one-element vectors.
- Indices in R start at 1, not at 0. In the vector earlier, x[1] is 8.
- Variables can't be declared. They come into existence on first assignment.

To learn more, see John Cook's excellent blog post, *R programming for those coming from other languages* (www.johndcook.com/R_language_for_programmers.html).

Programmers looking for stylistic guidance may also want to check out *Google's R Style Guide* (http://google-styleguide.googlecode.com/svn/trunk/google-r-style .html).

2.3 Data input

Now that you have data structures, you need to put some data in them! As a data analyst, you're typically faced with data that comes to you from a variety of sources and in a variety of formats. Your task is to import the data into your tools, analyze the data,

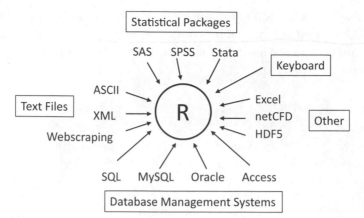

Figure 2.2   Sources of data that can be imported into R

and report on the results. R provides a wide range of tools for importing data. The definitive guide for importing data in R is the *R Data Import/Export* manual available at http://cran.r-project.org/doc/manuals/R-data.pdf.

As you can see in figure 2.2, R can import data from the keyboard, from flat files, from Microsoft Excel and Access, from popular statistical packages, from specialty formats, and from a variety of relational database management systems. Because you never know where your data will come from, we'll cover each of them here. You only need to read about the ones you're going to be using.

2.3.1   *Entering data from the keyboard*

Perhaps the simplest method of data entry is from the keyboard. The `edit()` function in R will invoke a text editor that will allow you to enter your data manually. Here are the steps involved:

1   Create an empty data frame (or matrix) with the variable names and modes you want to have in the final dataset.
2   Invoke the text editor on this data object, enter your data, and save the results back to the data object.

In the following example, you'll create a data frame named `mydata` with three variables: `age` (numeric), `gender` (character), and `weight` (numeric). You'll then invoke the text editor, add your data, and save the results.

```
mydata <- data.frame(age=numeric(0),
  gender=character(0), weight=numeric(0))
mydata <- edit(mydata)
```

Assignments like `age=numeric(0)` create a variable of a specific mode, but without actual data. Note that the result of the editing is assigned back to the object itself. The `edit()` function operates on a copy of the object. If you don't assign it a destination, all of your edits will be lost!

mydata ⟵ edit (mydata)

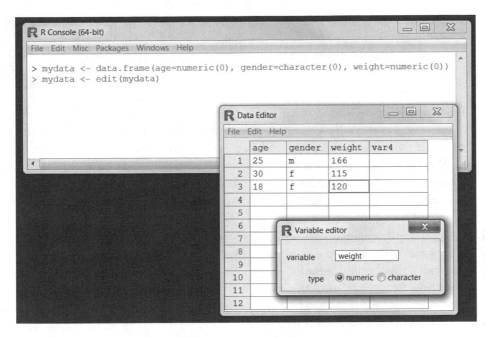

Figure 2.3   Entering data via the built-in editor on a Windows platform

The results of invoking the edit() function on a Windows platform can be seen in figure 2.3.

In this figure, I've taken the liberty of adding some data. If you click on a column title, the editor gives you the option of changing the variable name and type (numeric, character). You can add additional variables by clicking on the titles of unused columns. When the text editor is closed, the results are saved to the object assigned (mydata in this case). Invoking mydata <- edit(mydata) again allows you to edit the data you've entered and to add new data. A shortcut for mydata <- edit(mydata) is simply fix(mydata).

This method of data entry works well for small datasets. For larger datasets, you'll probably want to use the methods we'll describe next: importing data from existing text files, Excel spreadsheets, statistical packages, or database management systems.

2.3.2 *Importing data from a delimited text file*

You can import data from delimited text files using read.table(), a function that reads a file in table format and saves it as a data frame. Here's the syntax:

```
mydataframe <- read.table(file, header=logical_value,
  sep="delimiter", row.names="name")
```

where *file* is a delimited ASCII file, header is a logical value indicating whether the first row contains variable names (TRUE or FALSE), sep specifies the delimiter

need quotes around file name — see next page

separating data values, and `row.names` is an optional parameter specifying one or more variables to represent row identifiers.

For example, the statement

```
grades <- read.table("studentgrades.csv", header=TRUE, sep=",",
  row.names="STUDENTID")
```

reads a comma-delimited file named `studentgrades.csv` from the current working directory, gets the variable names from the first line of the file, specifies the variable `STUDENTID` as the row identifier, and saves the results as a data frame named `grades`.

Note that the `sep` parameter allows you to import files that use a symbol other than a comma to delimit the data values. You could read tab-delimited files with `sep="\t"`. The default is `sep=""`, which denotes one or more spaces, tabs, new lines, or carriage returns.

By default, character variables are converted to factors. This behavior may not always be desirable (for example, a variable containing respondents' comments). You can suppress this behavior in a number of ways. Including the option `stringsAsFactors=FALSE` will turn this behavior off for all character variables. Alternatively, you can use the `colClasses` option to specify a class (for example, logical, numeric, character, factor) for each column.

The `read.table()` function has many additional options for fine-tuning the data import. See `help(read.table)` for details.

NOTE   Many of the examples in this chapter import data from files that exist on the user's computer. R provides several mechanisms for accessing data via connections as well. For example, the functions `file()`, `gzfile()`, `bzfile()`, `xzfile()`, `unz()`, and `url()` can be used in place of the filename. The `file()` function allows the user to access files, the clipboard, and C-level standard input. The `gzfile()`, `bzfile()`, `xzfile()`, and `unz()` functions let the user read compressed files. The `url()` function lets you access internet files through a complete URL that includes `http://`, `ftp://`, or `file://`. For HTTP and FTP, proxies can be specified. For convenience, complete URLs (surrounded by "" marks) can usually be used directly in place of filenames as well. See `help(file)` for details.

2.3.3   *Importing data from Excel*

The best way to read an Excel file is to export it to a comma-delimited file from within Excel and import it to R using the method described earlier. On Windows systems you can also use the RODBC package to access Excel files. The first row of the spreadsheet should contain variable/column names.

First, download and install the RODBC package.

```
install.packages("RODBC")
```

You can then use the following code to import the data:

```
library(RODBC)
channel <- odbcConnectExcel("myfile.xls")
mydataframe <- sqlFetch(channel, "mysheet")
odbcClose(channel)
```

Here, `myfile.xls` is an Excel file, `mysheet` is the name of the Excel worksheet to read from the workbook, `channel` is an RODBC connection object returned by `odbcConnectExcel()`, and `mydataframe` is the resulting data frame. RODBC can also be used to import data from Microsoft Access. See `help(RODBC)` for details.

Excel 2007 uses an XLSX file format, which is essentially a zipped set of XML files. The `xlsx` package can be used to access spreadsheets in this format. Be sure to download and install it before first use. The `read.xlsx()` function imports a worksheet from an XLSX file into a data frame. The simplest format is `read.xlsx(file, n)` where *file* is the path to an Excel 2007 workbook and *n* is the number of the worksheet to be imported. For example, on a Windows platform, the code

```
library(xlsx)
workbook <- "c:/myworkbook.xlsx"
mydataframe <- read.xlsx(workbook, 1)
```

imports the first worksheet from the workbook `myworkbook.xlsx` stored on the C: drive and saves it as the data frame `mydataframe`. The `xlsx` package can do more than import worksheets. It can create and manipulate Excel XLSX files as well. Programmers who need to develop an interface between R and Excel should check out this relatively new package.

2.3.4 *Importing data from XML*

Increasingly, data is provided in the form of files encoded in XML. R has several packages for handling XML files. For example, the XML package written by Duncan Temple Lang allows users to read, write, and manipulate XML files. Coverage of XML is beyond the scope of this text. Readers interested in the accessing XML documents from within R are referred to the excellent package documentation at www.omegahat.org/RSXML.

2.3.5 *Webscraping*

In *webscraping*, the user extracts information embedded in a web page available over the internet and saves it into R structures for further analysis. One way to accomplish this is to download the web page using the `readLines()` function and manipulate it with functions such as `grep()` and `gsub()`. For complex web pages, the RCurl and XML packages can be used to extract the information desired. For more information, including examples, see "Webscraping using readLines and RCurl," available from the website *Programming with R* (www.programmingr.com).

2.3.6 *Importing data from SPSS*

SPSS datasets can be imported into R via the `read.spss()` function in the `foreign` package. Alternatively, you can use the `spss.get()` function in the `Hmisc` package. `spss.get()` is a wrapper function that automatically sets many parameters of `read.spss()` for you, making the transfer easier and more consistent with what data analysts expect as a result.

First, download and install the `Hmisc` package (the `foreign` package is already installed by default):

```
install.packages("Hmisc")
```

Then use the following code to import the data:

```
library(Hmisc)
mydataframe <- spss.get("mydata.sav", use.value.labels=TRUE)
```

In this code, `mydata.sav` is the SPSS data file to be imported, `use.value.labels=TRUE` tells the function to convert variables with value labels into R factors with those same levels, and `mydataframe` is the resulting R data frame.

2.3.7 *Importing data from SAS*

A number of functions in R are designed to import SAS datasets, including `read.ssd()` in the foreign package and `sas.get()` in the `Hmisc` package. Unfortunately, if you're using a recent version of SAS (SAS 9.1 or higher), you're likely to find that these functions don't work for you because R hasn't caught up with changes in SAS file structures. There are two solutions that I recommend.

You can save the SAS dataset as a comma-delimited text file from within SAS using `PROC EXPORT`, and read the resulting file into R using the method described in section 2.3.2. Here's an example:

SAS program:

```
proc export data=mydata
     outfile="mydata.csv"
     dbms=csv;
run;
```

R program:

```
mydata <- read.table("mydata.csv", header=TRUE, sep=",")
```

Alternatively, a commercial product called Stat Transfer (described in section 2.3.12) does an excellent job of saving SAS datasets (including any existing variable formats) as R data frames.

2.3.8 *Importing data from Stata*

Importing data from Stata to R is straightforward. The necessary code looks like this:

```
library(foreign)
mydataframe <- read.dta("mydata.dta")
```

Here, `mydata.dta` is the Stata dataset and `mydataframe` is the resulting R data frame.

2.3.9 Importing data from netCDF

Unidata's netCDF (network Common Data Form) open source software contains machine-independent data formats for the creation and distribution of array-oriented scientific data. netCDF is commonly used to store geophysical data. The `ncdf` and `ncdf4` packages provide high-level R interfaces to netCDF data files.

The `ncdf` package provides support for data files created with Unidata's netCDF library (version 3 or earlier) and is available for Windows, Mac OS X, and Linux platforms. The `ncdf4` package supports version 4 or earlier, but isn't yet available for Windows.

Consider this code:

```
library(ncdf)
nc <- nc_open("mynetCDFfile")
myarray <- get.var.ncdf(nc, myvar)
```

In this example, all the data from the variable `myvar`, contained in the netCDF file `mynetCDFfile`, is read and saved into an R array called `myarray`.

Note that both `ncdf` and `ncdf4` packages have received major recent upgrades and may operate differently than previous versions. Additionally, function names in the two packages differ. Read the online documentation for details.

2.3.10 Importing data from HDF5

HDF5 (Hierarchical Data Format) is a software technology suite for the management of extremely large and complex data collections. The `hdf5` package can be used to write R objects into a file in a form that can be read by software that understands the HDF5 format. These files can be read back into R at a later time. The package is experimental and assumes that the user has the HDF5 library (version 1.2 or higher) installed. At present, support for the HDF5 format in R is extremely limited.

2.3.11 Accessing database management systems (DBMSs)

R can interface with a wide variety of relational database management systems (DBMSs), including Microsoft SQL Server, Microsoft Access, MySQL, Oracle, PostgreSQL, DB2, Sybase, Teradata, and SQLite. Some packages provide access through native database drivers, whereas others offer access via ODBC or JDBC. Using R to access data stored in external DMBSs can be an efficient way to analyze large datasets (see appendix G), and leverages the power of both SQL and R.

THE ODBC INTERFACE

Perhaps the most popular method of accessing a DBMS in R is through the `RODBC` package, which allows R to connect to any DBMS that has an ODBC driver. This includes all of the DBMSs listed.

The first step is to install and configure the appropriate ODBC driver for your platform and database—they're not part of R. If the requisite drivers aren't already installed on your machine, an internet search should provide you with options.

Once the drivers are installed and configured for the database(s) of your choice, install the RODBC package. You can do so by using the `install.packages("RODBC")` command.

The primary functions included with the RODBC package are listed in table 2.2.

Table 2.2   RODBC functions

Function	Description
`odbcConnect(`*dsn*`,uid="",pwd="")`	Open a connection to an ODBC database
`sqlFetch(`*channel*`,`*sqltable*`)`	Read a table from an ODBC database into a data frame
`sqlQuery(`*channel*`,`*query*`)`	Submit a query to an ODBC database and return the results
`sqlSave(`*channel*`,`*mydf*`,tablename = `*sqtable*`,append=FALSE)`	Write or update (`append=TRUE`) a data frame to a table in the ODBC database
`sqlDrop(`*channel*`,`*sqtable*`)`	Remove a table from the ODBC database
`close(`*channel*`)`	Close the connection

The RODBC package allows two-way communication between R and an ODBC-connected SQL database. This means that you can not only read data from a connected database into R, but you can use R to alter the contents of the database itself. Assume that you want to import two tables (Crime and Punishment) from a DBMS into two R data frames called `crimedat` and `pundat`, respectively. You can accomplish this with code similar to the following:

```
library(RODBC)
myconn <-odbcConnect("mydsn", uid="Rob", pwd="aardvark")
crimedat <- sqlFetch(myconn, Crime)
pundat <- sqlQuery(myconn, "select * from Punishment")
close(myconn)
```

Here, you load the RODBC package and open a connection to the ODBC database through a registered data source name (`mydsn`) with a security UID (`rob`) and password (`aardvark`). The connection string is passed to `sqlFetch`, which copies the table Crime into the R data frame `crimedat`. You then run the SQL `select` statement against the table Punishment and save the results to the data frame `pundat`. Finally, you close the connection.

The `sqlQuery()` function is very powerful because any valid SQL statement can be inserted. This flexibility allows you to select specific variables, subset the data, create new variables, and recode and rename existing variables.

DBI-RELATED PACKAGES

The DBI package provides a general and consistent client-side interface to DBMS. Building on this framework, the RJDBC package provides access to DBMS via a JDBC driver. Be sure to install the necessary JDBC drivers for your platform and database. Other useful DBI-based packages include RMySQL, ROracle, RPostgreSQL, and RSQLite. These packages provide native database drivers for their respective databases but may not be available on all platforms. Check the documentation on CRAN (http://cran.r-project.org) for details.

2.3.12 *Importing data via Stat/Transfer*

Before we end our discussion of importing data, it's worth mentioning a commercial product that can make the task significantly easier. Stat/Transfer (www.stattransfer.com) is a stand-alone application that can transfer data between 34 data formats, including R (see figure 2.4).

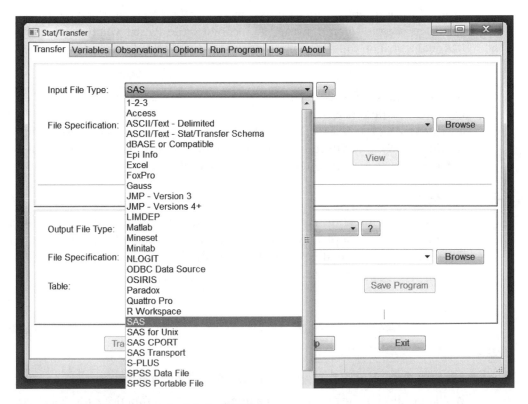

Figure 2.4   Stat/Transfer's main dialog on Windows

It's available for Windows, Mac, and Unix platforms and supports the latest versions of the statistical packages we've discussed so far, as well as ODBC-accessed DBMSs such as Oracle, Sybase, Informix, and DB/2.

2.4   Annotating datasets

Data analysts typically annotate datasets to make the results easier to interpret. Typically annotation includes adding descriptive labels to variable names and value labels to the codes used for categorical variables. For example, for the variable age, you might want to attach the more descriptive label "Age at hospitalization (in years)." For the variable gender coded 1 or 2, you might want to associate the labels "male" and "female."

2.4.1   Variable labels

Unfortunately, R's ability to handle variable labels is limited. One approach is to use the variable label as the variable's name and then refer to the variable by its position index. Consider our earlier example, where you have a data frame containing patient data. The second column, named age, contains the ages at which individuals were first hospitalized. The code

```
names(patientdata)[2] <- "Age at hospitalization (in years)"
```

renames age to "Age at hospitalization (in years)". Clearly this new name is too long to type repeatedly. Instead, you can refer to this variable as patientdata[2] and the string "Age at hospitalization (in years)" will print wherever age would've originally. Obviously, this isn't an ideal approach, and you may be better off trying to come up with better names (for example, admissionAge).

2.4.2   Value labels

The factor() function can be used to create value labels for categorical variables. Continuing our example, say that you have a variable named gender, which is coded 1 for male and 2 for female. You could create value labels with the code

```
patientdata$gender <- factor(patientdata$gender,
                             levels = c(1,2),
                             labels = c("male", "female"))
```

Here levels indicate the actual values of the variable, and labels refer to a character vector containing the desired labels.

2.5   Useful functions for working with data objects

We'll end this chapter with a brief summary of useful functions for working with data objects (see table 2.3).

Table 2.3 Useful functions for working with data objects

Function	Purpose
length(*object*)	Number of elements/components.
dim(*object*)	Dimensions of an object.
str(*object*)	Structure of an object.
class(*object*)	Class or type of an object.
mode(*object*)	How an object is stored.
names(*object*)	Names of components in an object.
c(*object, object,...*)	Combines objects into a vector.
cbind(*object, object, ...*)	Combines objects as columns.
rbind(*object, object, ...*)	Combines objects as rows.
object	Prints the object.
head(*object*)	Lists the first part of the object.
tail(*object*)	Lists the last part of the object.
ls()	Lists current objects.
rm(*object, object, ...*)	Deletes one or more objects. The statement rm(list = ls()) will remove most objects from the working environment.
newobject <- edit(*object*)	Edits object and saves as newobject.
fix(*object*)	Edits in place.

We've already discussed most of these functions. The functions head() and tail() are useful for quickly scanning large datasets. For example, head(patientdata) lists the first six rows of the data frame, whereas tail(patientdata) lists the last six. We'll cover functions such as length(), cbind(), and rbind() in the next chapter. They're gathered here as a reference.

2.6 *Summary*

One of the most challenging tasks in data analysis is data preparation. We've made a good start in this chapter by outlining the various structures that R provides for holding data and the many methods available for importing data from both keyboard and external sources. In particular, we'll use the definitions of a vector, matrix, data frame, and list again and again in later chapters. Your ability to specify elements of these structures via the bracket notation will be particularly important in selecting, subsetting, and transforming data.

As you've seen, R offers a wealth of functions for accessing external data. This includes data from flat files, web files, statistical packages, spreadsheets, and databases. Although the focus of this chapter has been on importing data into R, you can also export data from R into these external formats. Exporting data is covered in appendix C, and methods of working with large datasets (in the gigabyte to terabyte range) are covered in appendix G.

Once you get your datasets into R, it's likely that you'll have to manipulate them into a more conducive format (actually, I find guilt works well). In chapter 4, we'll explore ways of creating new variables, transforming and recoding existing variables, merging datasets, and selecting observations.

But before turning to data management tasks, let's spend some time with R graphics. Many readers have turned to R out of an interest in its graphing capabilities, and I don't want to make you wait any longer. In the next chapter, we'll jump directly into the creation of graphs. Our emphasis will be on general methods for managing and customizing graphs that can be applied throughout the remainder of this book.

Getting started with graphs

This chapter covers
- Creating and saving graphs
- Customizing symbols, lines, colors, and axes
- Annotating with text and titles
- Controlling a graph's dimensions
- Combining multiple graphs into one

On many occasions, I've presented clients with carefully crafted statistical results in the form of numbers and text, only to have their eyes glaze over while the chirping of crickets permeated the room. Yet those same clients had enthusiastic "Ah-ha!" moments when I presented the same information to them in the form of graphs. Many times I was able to see patterns in data or detect anomalies in data values by looking at graphs—patterns or anomalies that I completely missed when conducting more formal statistical analyses.

Human beings are remarkably adept at discerning relationships from visual representations. A well-crafted graph can help you make meaningful comparisons among thousands of pieces of information, extracting patterns not easily found through other methods. This is one reason why advances in the field of statistical graphics have had such a major impact on data analysis. Data analysts need to *look* at their data, and this is one area where R shines.

In this chapter, we'll review general methods for working with graphs. We'll start with how to create and save graphs. Then we'll look at how to modify the features that are found in any graph. These features include graph titles, axes, labels, colors, lines, symbols, and text annotations. Our focus will be on generic techniques that apply across graphs. (In later chapters, we'll focus on specific types of graphs.) Finally, we'll investigate ways to combine multiple graphs into one overall graph.

3.1 Working with graphs

R is an amazing platform for building graphs. I'm using the term "building" intentionally. In a typical interactive session, you build a graph one statement at a time, adding features, until you have what you want.

Consider the following five lines:

```
attach(mtcars)
plot(wt, mpg)
abline(lm(mpg~wt))
title("Regression of MPG on Weight")
detach(mtcars)
```

The first statement attaches the data frame `mtcars`. The second statement opens a graphics window and generates a scatter plot between automobile weight on the horizontal axis and miles per gallon on the vertical axis. The third statement adds a line of best fit. The fourth statement adds a title. The final statement detaches the data frame. In R, graphs are typically created in this interactive fashion (see figure 3.1).

You can save your graphs via code or through GUI menus. To save a graph via code, sandwich the statements that produce the graph between a statement that sets a destination and a statement that closes that destination. For example, the following

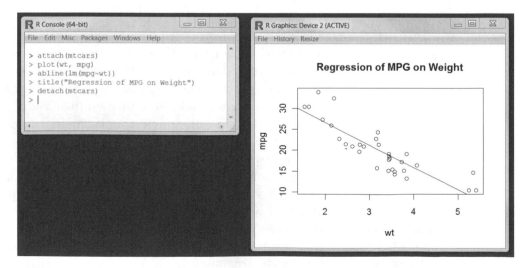

Figure 3.1   Creating a graph

will save the graph as a PDF document named `mygraph.pdf` in the current working directory:

```
pdf("mygraph.pdf")
 attach(mtcars)
 plot(wt, mpg)
 abline(lm(mpg~wt))
 title("Regression of MPG on Weight")
 detach(mtcars)
dev.off()
```

[handwritten:] ✳ this works! get pdf of graph!]

In addition to `pdf()`, you can use the functions `win.metafile()`, `png()`, `jpeg()`, `bmp()`, `tiff()`, `xfig()`, and `postscript()` to save graphs in other formats. (Note: The Windows metafile format is only available on Windows platforms.) See chapter 1, section 1.3.4 for more details on sending graphic output to files.

Saving graphs via the GUI will be platform specific. On a Windows platform, select File > Save As from the graphics window, and choose the format and location desired in the resulting dialog. On a Mac, choose File > Save As from the menu bar when the Quartz graphics window is highlighted. The only output format provided is PDF. On a Unix platform, the graphs must be saved via code. In appendix A, we'll consider alternative GUIs for each platform that will give you more options.

Creating a new graph by issuing a high-level plotting command such as `plot()`, `hist()` (for histograms), or `boxplot()` will typically overwrite a previous graph. How can you create more than one graph and still have access to each? There are several methods.

First, you can open a new graph window *before* creating a new graph:

```
dev.new()
 statements to create graph 1
dev.new()
 statements to create a graph 2
etc.
```

Each new graph will appear in the most recently opened window.

Second, you can access multiple graphs via the GUI. On a Mac platform, you can step through the graphs at any time using Back and Forward on the Quartz menu. On a Windows platform, you must use a two-step process. After opening the *first* graph window, choose History > Recording. Then use the Previous and Next menu items to step through the graphs that are created.

Third and finally, you can use the functions `dev.new()`, `dev.next()`, `dev.prev()`, `dev.set()`, and `dev.off()` to have multiple graph windows open at one time and choose which output are sent to which windows. This approach works on any platform. See `help(dev.cur)` for details on this approach.

R will create attractive graphs with a minimum of input on our part. But you can also use graphical parameters to specify fonts, colors, line styles, axes, reference lines, and annotations. This flexibility allows for a wide degree of customization.

In this chapter, we'll start with a simple graph and explore the ways you can modify and enhance it to meet your needs. Then we'll look at more complex examples that illustrate additional customization methods. The focus will be on techniques that you can apply to a wide range of the graphs that you'll create in R. The methods discussed here will work on all the graphs described in this book, with the exception of those created with the lattice package in chapter 16. (The lattice package has its own methods for customizing a graph's appearance.) In other chapters, we'll explore each specific type of graph and discuss where and when they're most useful.

3.2   A simple example

Let's start with the simple fictitious dataset given in table 3.1. It describes patient response to two drugs at five dosage levels.

Table 3.1   Patient response to two drugs at five dosage levels

Dosage	Response to Drug A	Response to Drug B
20	16	15
30	20	18
40	27	25
45	40	31
60	60	40

You can input this data using this code:

```
dose  <- c(20, 30, 40, 45, 60)
drugA <- c(16, 20, 27, 40, 60)
drugB <- c(15, 18, 25, 31, 40)
```

A simple line graph relating dose to response for drug A can be created using

```
plot(dose, drugA, type="b")
```

plot() is a generic function that plots objects in R (its output will vary according to the type of object being plotted). In this case, plot(x, y, type="b") places x on the horizontal axis and y on the vertical axis, plots the (x, y) data points, and connects them with line segments. The option type="b" indicates that both points and lines should be plotted. Use help(plot) to view other options. The graph is displayed in figure 3.2.

Line plots are covered in detail in chapter 11. Now let's modify the appearance of this graph.

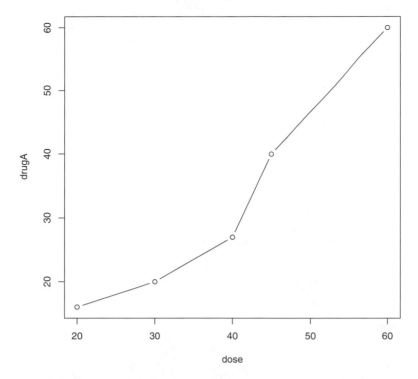

Figure 3.2   Line plot of dose vs. response for drug A

3.3   *Graphical parameters*

You can customize many features of a graph (fonts, colors, axes, titles) through options called *graphical parameters.*

One way is to specify these options through the par() function. Values set in this manner will be in effect for the rest of the session or until they're changed. The format is par(*optionname=value, optionname=value, ...*). Specifying par() without parameters produces a list of the current graphical settings. Adding the no.readonly=TRUE option produces a list of current graphical settings that can be modified.

Continuing our example, let's say that you'd like to use a solid triangle rather than an open circle as your plotting symbol, and connect points using a dashed line rather than a solid line. You can do so with the following code:

```
opar <- par(no.readonly=TRUE)
par(lty=2, pch=17)
plot(dose, drugA, type="b")
par(opar)
```

The resulting graph is shown in figure 3.3.

The first statement makes a copy of the current settings. The second statement changes the default line type to dashed (lty=2) and the default symbol for plotting

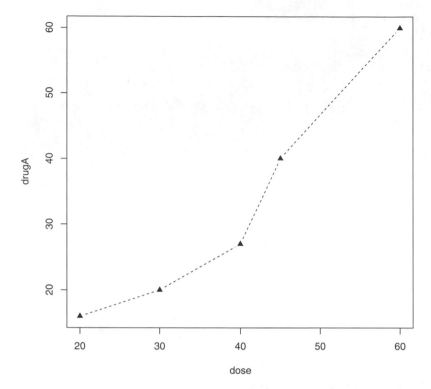

Figure 3.3   Line plot of dose vs. response for drug A with modified line type and symbol

points to a solid triangle (`pch=17`). You then generate the plot and restore the original settings. Line types and symbols are covered in section 3.3.1.

You can have as many `par()` functions as desired, so `par(lty=2, pch=17)` could also have been written as

```
par(lty=2)
par(pch=17)
```

A second way to specify graphical parameters is by providing the *optionname=value* pairs directly to a high-level plotting function. In this case, the options are only in effect for that specific graph. You could've generated the same graph with the code

```
plot(dose, drugA, type="b", lty=2, pch=17)
```

Not all high-level plotting functions allow you to specify all possible graphical parameters. See the help for a specific plotting function (such as `?plot`, `?hist`, or `?boxplot`) to determine which graphical parameters can be set in this way. The remainder of section 3.3 describes many of the important graphical parameters that you can set.

3.3.1   *Symbols and lines*

As you've seen, you can use graphical parameters to specify the plotting symbols and lines used in your graphs. The relevant parameters are shown in table 3.2.

Table 3.2 Parameters for specifying symbols and lines

Parameter	Description
pch	Specifies the symbol to use when plotting points (see figure 3.4).
cex	Specifies the symbol size. cex is a number indicating the amount by which plotting symbols should be scaled relative to the default. 1=default, 1.5 is 50% larger, 0.5 is 50% smaller, and so forth.
lty	Specifies the line type (see figure 3.5).
lwd	Specifies the line width. lwd is expressed relative to the default (default=1). For example, lwd=2 generates a line twice as wide as the default.

The pch= option specifies the symbols to use when plotting points. Possible values are shown in figure 3.4.

For symbols 21 through 25 you can also specify the border (col=) and fill (bg=) colors.

Use lty= to specify the type of line desired. The option values are shown in figure 3.5.

Taking these options together, the code

```
plot(dose, drugA, type="b", lty=3, lwd=3, pch=15, cex=2)
```

would produce a plot with a dotted line that was three times wider than the default width, connecting points displayed as filled squares that are twice as large as the default symbol size. The results are displayed in figure 3.6.

Next, let's look at specifying colors.

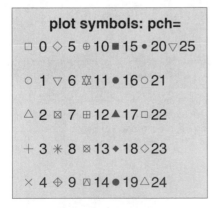

Figure 3.4 Plotting symbols specified with the pch parameter

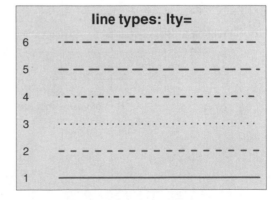

Figure 3.5 Line types specified with the lty parameter

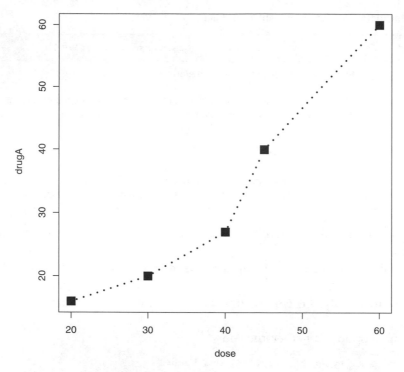

Figure 3.6   Line plot of dose vs. response for drug A with modified line type, line width, symbol, and symbol width

3.3.2   Colors

There are several color-related parameters in R. Table 3.3 shows some of the common ones.

Table 3.3   Parameters for specifying color

Parameter	Description
col	Default plotting color. Some functions (such as lines and pie) accept a vector of values that are recycled. For example, if col=c("red", "blue") and three lines are plotted, the first line will be red, the second blue, and the third red.
col.axis	Color for axis text.
col.lab	Color for axis labels.
col.main	Color for titles.
col.sub	Color for subtitles.
fg	The plot's foreground color.
bg	The plot's background color.

You can specify colors in R by index, name, hexadecimal, RGB, or HSV. For example, `col=1`, `col="white"`, `col="#FFFFFF"`, `col=rgb(1,1,1)`, and `col=hsv(0,0,1)` are equivalent ways of specifying the color white. The function `rgb()` creates colors based on red-green-blue values, whereas `hsv()` creates colors based on hue-saturation values. See the help feature on these functions for more details.

The function `colors()` returns all available color names. Earl F. Glynn has created an excellent online chart of R colors, available at http://research.stowers-institute. org/efg/R/Color/Chart. R also has a number of functions that can be used to create vectors of contiguous colors. These include `rainbow()`, `heat.colors()`, `terrain. colors()`, `topo.colors()`, and `cm.colors()`. For example, `rainbow(10)` produces 10 contiguous "rainbow" colors. Gray levels are generated with the `gray()` function. In this case, you specify gray levels as a vector of numbers between 0 and 1. `gray(0:10/10)` would produce 10 gray levels. Try the code

```
n <- 10
mycolors <- rainbow(n)
pie(rep(1, n), labels=mycolors, col=mycolors)
mygrays <- gray(0:n/n)
pie(rep(1, n), labels=mygrays, col=mygrays)
```

to see how this works. You'll see examples that use color parameters throughout this chapter.

3.3.3 Text characteristics

Graphic parameters are also used to specify text size, font, and style. Parameters controlling text size are explained in table 3.4. Font family and style can be controlled with font options (see table 3.5).

Table 3.4 Parameters specifying text size

Parameter	Description
`cex`	Number indicating the amount by which plotted text should be scaled relative to the default. 1=default, 1.5 is 50% larger, 0.5 is 50% smaller, etc.
`cex.axis`	Magnification of axis text relative to `cex`.
`cex.lab`	Magnification of axis labels relative to `cex`.
`cex.main`	Magnification of titles relative to `cex`.
`cex.sub`	Magnification of subtitles relative to `cex`.

For example, all graphs created after the statement

```
par(font.lab=3, cex.lab=1.5, font.main=4, cex.main=2)
```

will have italic axis labels that are 1.5 times the default text size, and bold italic titles that are twice the default text size.

Table 3.5   Parameters specifying font family, size, and style

Parameter	Description
font	Integer specifying font to use for plotted text.. 1=plain, 2=bold, 3=italic, 4=bold italic, 5=symbol (in Adobe symbol encoding).
font.axis	Font for axis text.
font.lab	Font for axis labels.
font.main	Font for titles.
font.sub	Font for subtitles.
ps	Font point size (roughly 1/72 inch). The text size = ps*cex.
family	Font family for drawing text. Standard values are serif, sans, and mono.

Whereas font size and style are easily set, font family is a bit more complicated. This is because the mapping of serif, sans, and mono are device dependent. For example, on Windows platforms, mono is mapped to TT Courier New, serif is mapped to TT Times New Roman, and sans is mapped to TT Arial (TT stands for True Type). If you're satisfied with this mapping, you can use parameters like family="serif" to get the results you want. If not, you need to create a new mapping. On Windows, you can create this mapping via the windowsFont() function. For example, after issuing the statement

```
windowsFonts(
  A=windowsFont("Arial Black"),
  B=windowsFont("Bookman Old Style"),
  C=windowsFont("Comic Sans MS")
)
```

you can use A, B, and C as family values. In this case, par(family="A") will specify an Arial Black font. (Listing 3.2 in section 3.4.2 provides an example of modifying text parameters.) Note that the windowsFont() function only works for Windows. On a Mac, use quartzFonts() instead.

If graphs will be output in PDF or PostScript format, changing the font family is relatively straightforward. For PDFs, use names(pdfFonts()) to find out which fonts are available on your system and pdf(file="*myplot*.pdf", family="*fontname*") to generate the plots. For graphs that are output in PostScript format, use names(postscriptFonts()) and postscript(file="*myplot*.ps", family="*fontname*"). See the online help for more information.

3.3.4   *Graph and margin dimensions*

Finally, you can control the plot dimensions and margin sizes using the parameters listed in table 3.6.

Table 3.6   Parameters for graph and margin dimensions

Parameter	Description
pin	Plot dimensions (width, height) in inches.
mai	Numerical vector indicating margin size where c(bottom, left, top, right) is expressed in inches.
mar	Numerical vector indicating margin size where c(bottom, left, top, right) is expressed in lines. The default is c(5, 4, 4, 2) + 0.1.

The code

```
par(pin=c(4,3), mai=c(1,.5, 1, .2))
```

produces graphs that are 4 inches wide by 3 inches tall, with a 1-inch margin on the bottom and top, a 0.5-inch margin on the left, and a 0.2-inch margin on the right. For a complete tutorial on margins, see Earl F. Glynn's comprehensive online tutorial (http://research.stowers-institute.org/efg/R/Graphics/Basics/mar-oma/).

Let's use the options we've covered so far to enhance our simple example. The code in the following listing produces the graphs in figure 3.7.

Listing 3.1   Using graphical parameters to control graph appearance

```
dose  <- c(20, 30, 40, 45, 60)
drugA <- c(16, 20, 27, 40, 60)
drugB <- c(15, 18, 25, 31, 40)
opar <- par(no.readonly=TRUE)
par(pin=c(2, 3))
par(lwd=2, cex=1.5)
par(cex.axis=.75, font.axis=3)
plot(dose, drugA, type="b", pch=19, lty=2, col="red")
plot(dose, drugB, type="b", pch=23, lty=6, col="blue", bg="green")
par(opar)
```

First you enter your data as vectors, then save the current graphical parameter settings (so that you can restore them later). You modify the default graphical parameters so that graphs will be 2 inches wide by 3 inches tall. Additionally, lines will be twice the default width and symbols will be 1.5 times the default size. Axis text will be set to italic and scaled to 75 percent of the default. The first plot is then created using filled red circles and dashed lines. The second plot is created using filled green filled diamonds and a blue border and blue dashed lines. Finally, you restore the original graphical parameter settings.

Note that parameters set with the par() function apply to both graphs, whereas parameters specified in the plot functions only apply to that specific graph. Looking at figure 3.7 you can see some limitations in your presentation. The graphs lack titles and the vertical axes are not on the same scale, limiting your ability to compare the two drugs directly. The axis labels could also be more informative.

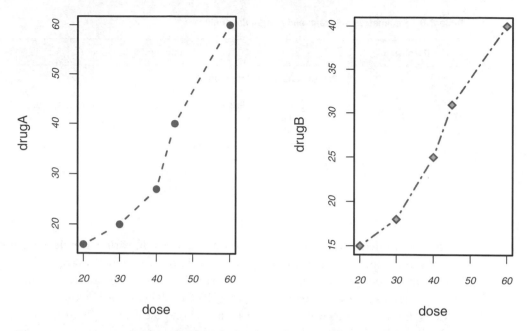

Figure 3.7   Line plot of dose vs. response for both drug A and drug B

In the next section, we'll turn to the customization of text annotations (such as titles and labels) and axes. For more information on the graphical parameters that are available, take a look at `help(par)`.

3.4   *Adding text, customized axes, and legends*

Many high-level plotting functions (for example, `plot`, `hist`, `boxplot`) allow you to include axis and text options, as well as graphical parameters. For example, the following adds a title (`main`), subtitle (`sub`), axis labels (`xlab`, `ylab`), and axis ranges (`xlim`, `ylim`). The results are presented in figure 3.8:

```
plot(dose, drugA, type="b",
    col="red", lty=2, pch=2, lwd=2,
    main="Clinical Trials for Drug A",
    sub="This is hypothetical data",
    xlab="Dosage", ylab="Drug Response",
    xlim=c(0, 60), ylim=c(0, 70))
```

Again, not all functions allow you to add these options. See the help for the function of interest to see what options are accepted. For finer control and for modularization, you can use the functions described in the remainder of this section to control titles, axes, legends, and text annotations.

> **NOTE**   Some high-level plotting functions include default titles and labels. You can remove them by adding `ann=FALSE` in the `plot()` statement or in a separate `par()` statement.

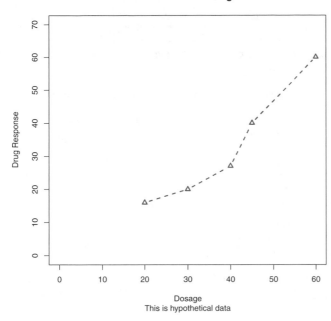

Clinical Trials for Drug A

Figure 3.8 **Line plot of dose versus response for drug A with title, subtitle, and modified axes**

3.4.1 *Titles*

Use the `title()` function to add title and axis labels to a plot. The format is

```
title(main="main title", sub="sub-title",
      xlab="x-axis label", ylab="y-axis label")
```

Graphical parameters (such as text size, font, rotation, and color) can also be specified in the `title()` function. For example, the following produces a red title and a blue subtitle, and creates green x and y labels that are 25 percent smaller than the default text size:

```
title(main="My Title", col.main="red",
      sub="My Sub-title", col.sub="blue",
      xlab="My X label", ylab="My Y label",
      col.lab="green", cex.lab=0.75)
```

3.4.2 *Axes*

Rather than using R's default axes, you can create custom axes with the `axis()` function. The format is

```
axis(side, at=, labels=, pos=, lty=, col=, las=, tck=, ...)
```

where each parameter is described in table 3.7.

When creating a custom axis, you should suppress the axis automatically generated by the high-level plotting function. The option `axes=FALSE` suppresses all axes (including all axis frame lines, unless you add the option `frame.plot=TRUE`). The options `xaxt="n"` and `yaxt="n"` suppress the x- and y-axis, respectively (leaving the frame

Table 3.7   Axis options

Option	Description
side	An integer indicating the side of the graph to draw the axis (1=bottom, 2=left, 3=top, 4=right).
at	A numeric vector indicating where tick marks should be drawn.
labels	A character vector of labels to be placed at the tick marks (if NULL, the at values will be used).
pos	The coordinate at which the axis line is to be drawn (that is, the value on the other axis where it crosses).
lty	Line type.
col	The line and tick mark color.
las	Labels are parallel (=0) or perpendicular (=2) to the axis.
tck	Length of tick mark as a fraction of the plotting region (a negative number is outside the graph, a positive number is inside, 0 suppresses ticks, 1 creates gridlines); the default is –0.01.
(...)	Other graphical parameters.

lines, without ticks). The following listing is a somewhat silly and overblown example that demonstrates each of the features we've discussed so far. The resulting graph is presented in figure 3.9.

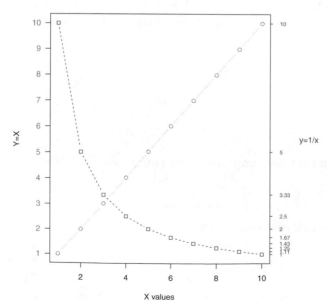

Figure 3.9   A demonstration of axis options

Listing 3.2 An example of custom axes

```
x <- c(1:10)                        ◁—— Specify data
y <- x
z <- 10/x

opar <- par(no.readonly=TRUE)

par(mar=c(5, 4, 4, 8) + 0.1)              ◁—— Increase margins

plot(x, y, type="b",                          ◁—— Plot x versus y
     pch=21, col="red",
     yaxt="n", lty=3, ann=FALSE)

                                              ┌ Add x versus
lines(x, z, type="b", pch=22, col="blue", lty=2)   ◁—┘ l/x line

axis(2, at=x, labels=x, col.axis="red", las=2)   ◁—— Draw your axes

axis(4, at=z, labels=round(z, digits=2),
     col.axis="blue", las=2, cex.axis=0.7, tck=-.01)

mtext("y=1/x", side=4, line=3, cex.lab=1, las=2, col="blue")   ◁┐ Add titles
                                                               └ and text
title("An Example of Creative Axes",
      xlab="X values",
      ylab="Y=X")

par(opar)
```

At this point, we've covered everything in listing 3.2 except for the `line()` and the `mtext()` statements. A `plot()` statement starts a new graph. By using the `line()` statement instead, you can add new graph elements to an *existing* graph. You'll use it again when you plot the response of drug A and drug B on the same graph in section 3.4.4. The `mtext()` function is used to add text to the margins of the plot. The `mtext()` function is covered in section 3.4.5, and the `line()` function is covered more fully in chapter 11.

MINOR TICK MARKS

Notice that each of the graphs you've created so far have major tick marks but not minor tick marks. To create minor tick marks, you'll need the `minor.tick()` function in the `Hmisc` package. If you don't already have `Hmisc` installed, be sure to install it first (see chapter 1, section 1.4.2). You can add minor tick marks with the code

```
library(Hmisc)
minor.tick(nx=n, ny=n, tick.ratio=n)
```

where nx and ny specify the number of intervals in which to divide the area between major tick marks on the x-axis and y-axis, respectively. `tick.ratio` is the size of the minor tick mark relative to the major tick mark. The current length of the major tick mark can be retrieved using `par("tck")`. For example, the following statement will add one tick mark between each major tick mark on the x-axis and two tick marks between each major tick mark on the y-axis:

```
minor.tick(nx=2, ny=3, tick.ratio=0.5)
```

The length of the tick marks will be 50 percent as long as the major tick marks. An example of minor tick marks is given in the next section (listing 3.3 and figure 3.10).

3.4.3 Reference lines

The `abline()` function is used to add reference lines to our graph. The format is

```
abline(h=yvalues, v=xvalues)
```

Other graphical parameters (such as line type, color, and width) can also be specified in the `abline()` function. For example:

```
abline(h=c(1,5,7))
```

adds solid horizontal lines at y = 1, 5, and 7, whereas the code

```
abline(v=seq(1, 10, 2), lty=2, col="blue")
```

adds dashed blue vertical lines at x = 1, 3, 5, 7, and 9. Listing 3.3 creates a reference line for our drug example at y = 30. The resulting graph is displayed in figure 3.10.

3.4.4 Legend

When more than one set of data or group is incorporated into a graph, a legend can help you to identify what's being represented by each bar, pie slice, or line. A legend can be added (not surprisingly) with the `legend()` function. The format is

```
legend(location, title, legend, ...)
```

The common options are described in table 3.8.

Table 3.8 Legend options

Option	Description
location	There are several ways to indicate the location of the legend. You can give an x,y coordinate for the upper-left corner of the legend. You can use `locator(1)`, in which case you use the mouse to indicate the location of the legend. You can also use the keywords `bottom`, `bottomleft`, `left`, `topleft`, `top`, `topright`, `right`, `bottomright`, or `center` to place the legend in the graph. If you use one of these keywords, you can also use `inset=` to specify an amount to move the legend into the graph (as fraction of plot region).
title	A character string for the legend title (optional).
legend	A character vector with the labels.

Table 3.8 Legend options (*continued*)

Option	Description
. . .	Other options. If the legend labels colored lines, specify `col=` and a vector of colors. If the legend labels point symbols, specify `pch=` and a vector of point symbols. If the legend labels line width or line style, use `lwd=` or `lty=` and a vector of widths or styles. To create colored boxes for the legend (common in bar, box, or pie charts), use `fill=` and a vector of colors.

Other common legend options include `bty` for box type, `bg` for background color, `cex` for size, and `text.col` for text color. Specifying `horiz=TRUE` sets the legend horizontally rather than vertically. For more on legends, see `help(legend)`. The examples in the help file are particularly informative.

Let's take a look at an example using our drug data (listing 3.3). Again, you'll use a number of the features that we've covered up to this point. The resulting graph is presented in figure 3.10.

Listing 3.3 Comparing Drug A and Drug B response by dose

```
dose  <- c(20, 30, 40, 45, 60)
drugA <- c(16, 20, 27, 40, 60)
drugB <- c(15, 18, 25, 31, 40)

opar <- par(no.readonly=TRUE)

par(lwd=2, cex=1.5, font.lab=2)            Increase line, text,
                                           symbol, label size

plot(dose, drugA, type="b",                Generate graph
     pch=15, lty=1, col="red", ylim=c(0, 60),
     main="Drug A vs. Drug B",
     xlab="Drug Dosage", ylab="Drug Response")

lines(dose, drugB, type="b",
      pch=17, lty=2, col="blue")

abline(h=c(30), lwd=1.5, lty=2, col="gray")

library(Hmisc)                             Add minor tick
minor.tick(nx=3, ny=3, tick.ratio=0.5)     marks

legend("topleft", inset=.05, title="Drug Type", c("A","B"),    Add legend
       lty=c(1, 2), pch=c(15, 17), col=c("red", "blue"))

par(opar)
```

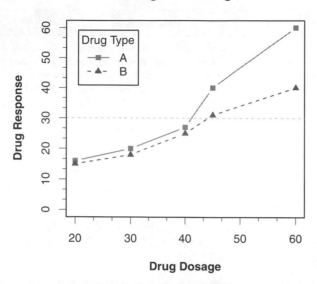

Figure 3.10   An annotated comparison of Drug A and Drug B

Almost all aspects of the graph in figure 3.10 can be modified using the options discussed in this chapter. Additionally, there are many ways to specify the options desired. The final annotation to consider is the addition of text to the plot itself. This topic is covered in the next section.

3.4.5   Text annotations

Text can be added to graphs using the `text()` and `mtext()` functions. `text()` places text within the graph whereas `mtext()` places text in one of the four margins. The formats are

```
text(location, "text to place", pos, ...)
mtext("text to place", side, line=n, ...)
```

and the common options are described in table 3.9.

Table 3.9   Options for the `text()` and `mtext()` functions

Option	Description
location	Location can be an x,y coordinate. Alternatively, the text can be placed interactively via mouse by specifying location as `locator(1)`.
pos	Position relative to location. 1 = below, 2 = left, 3 = above, 4 = right. If you specify `pos`, you can specify `offset=` in percent of character width.
side	Which margin to place text in, where 1 = bottom, 2 = left, 3 = top, 4 = right. You can specify `line=` to indicate the line in the margin starting with 0 (closest to the plot area) and moving out. You can also specify `adj=0` for left/bottom alignment or `adj=1` for top/right alignment.

Other common options are cex, col, and font (for size, color, and font style, respectively).

The text() function is typically used for labeling points as well as for adding other text annotations. Specify location as a set of x, y coordinates and specify the text to place as a vector of labels. The x, y, and label vectors should all be the same length. An example is given next and the resulting graph is shown in figure 3.11.

```
attach(mtcars)
plot(wt, mpg,
     main="Mileage vs. Car Weight",
     xlab="Weight", ylab="Mileage",
     pch=18, col="blue")
text(wt, mpg,
     row.names(mtcars),
     cex=0.6, pos=4, col="red")
detach(mtcars)
```

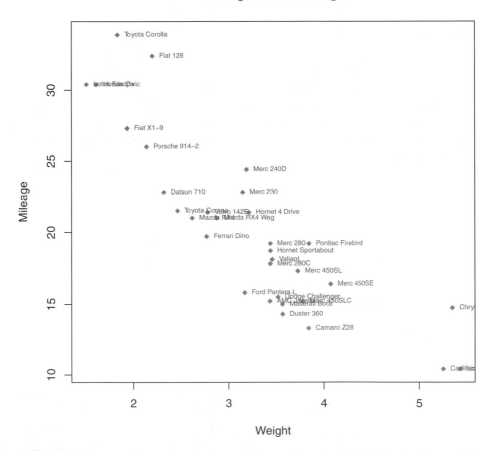

Figure 3.11 Example of a scatter plot (car weight vs. mileage) with labeled points (car make)

Here we've plotted car mileage versus car weight for the 32 automobile makes provided in the `mtcars` data frame. The `text()` function is used to add the car makes to the right of each data point. The point labels are shrunk by 40 percent and presented in red.

As a second example, the following code can be used to display font families:

```
opar <- par(no.readonly=TRUE)
par(cex=1.5)
plot(1:7,1:7,type="n")
text(3,3,"Example of default text")
text(4,4,family="mono","Example of mono-spaced text")
text(5,5,family="serif","Example of serif text")
par(opar)
```

The results, produced on a Windows platform, are shown in figure 3.12. Here the `par()` function was used to increase the font size to produce a better display.

The resulting plot will differ from platform to platform, because plain, mono, and serif text are mapped to different font families on different systems. What does it look like on yours?

MATH ANNOTATIONS

Finally, you can add mathematical symbols and formulas to a graph using TEX-like rules. See `help(plotmath)` for details and examples. You can also try `demo(plotmath)` to see this in action. A portion of the results is presented in figure 3.13. The `plotmath()` function can be used to add mathematical symbols to titles, axis labels, or text annotation in the body or margins of the graph.

You can often gain greater insight into your data by comparing several graphs at one time. So, we'll end this chapter by looking at ways to combine more than one graph into a single image.

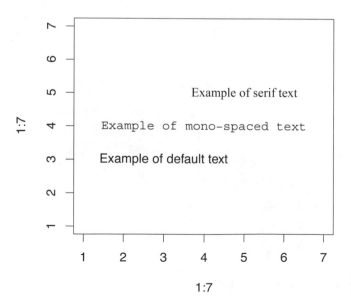

1:7

Figure 3.12   Examples of font families on a Windows platform

Arithmetic Operators		Radicals	
x + y	x + y	sqrt(x)	$\sqrt{x}$
x – y	x – y	sqrt(x, y)	$\sqrt[y]{x}$
x * y	xy	Relations	
x/y	x/y	x == y	x = y
x %+-% y	x ± y	x != y	x ↑ y
x%/%y	x√y	x < y	x < y
x %*% y	x × y	x <= y	x " y
x %.% y	x · y	x > y	x > y
–x	– x	x >= y	x ≥ y
+x	+ x	x %~~% y	x ⊕ y
Sub/Superscripts		x %=~% y	x ≅ y
x[i]	x_i	x %==% y	x ≡ y
x^2	x^2	x %prop% y	x ∝ y
Juxtaposition		Typeface	
x * y	xy	plain(x)	x
paste(x, y, z)	xyz	italic(x)	*x*
Lists		bold(x)	**x**
list(x, y, z)	x, y, z	bolditalic(x)	***x***
		underline(x)	x̲

Figure 3.13 Partial results from `demo(plotmath)`

3.5   *Combining graphs*

R makes it easy to combine several graphs into one overall graph, using either the `par()` or `layout()` function. At this point, don't worry about the specific types of graphs being combined; our focus here is on the general methods used to combine them. The creation and interpretation of each graph type is covered in later chapters.

With the `par()` function, you can include the graphical parameter mfrow=c(*nrows*, *ncols*) to create a matrix of *nrows* x *ncols* plots that are filled in by row. Alternatively, you can use mfcol=c(*nrows, ncols*) to fill the matrix by columns.

For example, the following code creates four plots and arranges them into two rows and two columns:

```
attach(mtcars)
opar <- par(no.readonly=TRUE)
par(mfrow=c(2,2))
plot(wt,mpg, main="Scatterplot of wt vs. mpg")
plot(wt,disp, main="Scatterplot of wt vs disp")
hist(wt, main="Histogram of wt")
```

```
boxplot(wt, main="Boxplot of wt")
par(opar)
detach(mtcars)
```

The results are presented in figure 3.14.

As a second example, let's arrange 3 plots in 3 rows and 1 column. Here's the code:

```
attach(mtcars)
opar <- par(no.readonly=TRUE)
par(mfrow=c(3,1))
hist(wt)
hist(mpg)
hist(disp)
par(opar)
detach(mtcars)
```

The graph is displayed in figure 3.15. Note that the high-level function `hist()` includes a default title (use `main=""` to suppress it, or `ann=FALSE` to suppress all titles and labels).

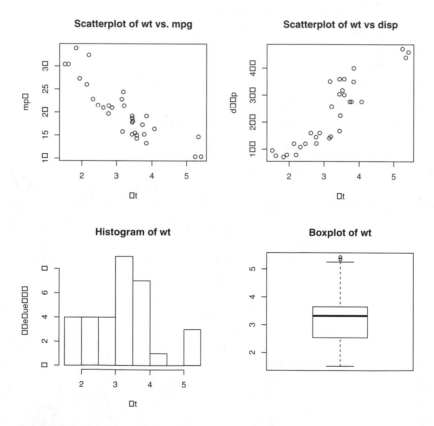

Figure 3.14 Graph combining four figures through `par(mfrow=c(2,2))`

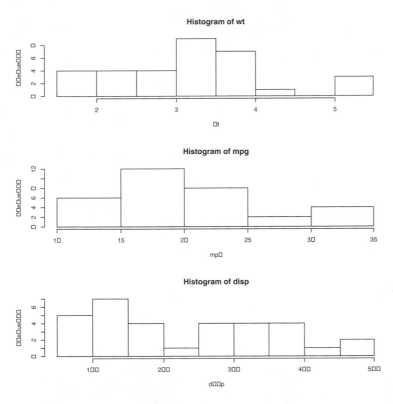

Figure 3.15 **Graph combining with three figures through `par(mfrow=c(3,1))`**

The `layout()` function has the form `layout(mat)` where *mat* is a matrix object specifying the location of the multiple plots to combine. In the following code, one figure is placed in row 1 and two figures are placed in row 2:

```
attach(mtcars)
layout(matrix(c(1,1,2,3), 2, 2, byrow = TRUE))
hist(wt)
hist(mpg)
hist(disp)
detach(mtcars)
```

The resulting graph is presented in figure 3.16.

Optionally, you can include `widths=` and `heights=` options in the `layout()` function to control the size of each figure more precisely. These options have the form

　　`widths` = a vector of values for the widths of columns

　　`heights` = a vector of values for the heights of rows

Relative widths are specified with numeric values. Absolute widths (in centimeters) are specified with the `lcm()` function.

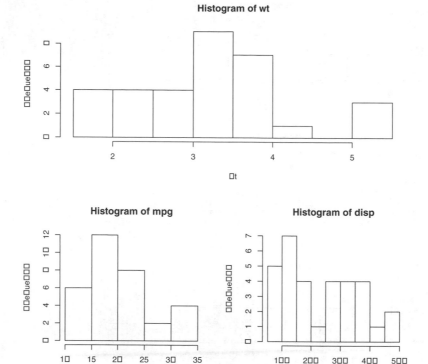

Figure 3.16   Graph combining three figures using the `layout()` function with default widths

In the following code, one figure is again placed in row 1 and two figures are placed in row 2. But the figure in row 1 is one-third the height of the figures in row 2. Additionally, the figure in the bottom-right cell is one-fourth the width of the figure in the bottom-left cell:

```
attach(mtcars)
layout(matrix(c(1, 1, 2, 3), 2, 2, byrow = TRUE),
       widths=c(3, 1), heights=c(1, 2))
hist(wt)
hist(mpg)
hist(disp)
detach(mtcars)
```

The graph is presented in figure 3.17.

As you can see, the `layout()` function gives you easy control over both the number and placement of graphs in a final image and the relative sizes of these graphs. See `help(layout)` for more details.

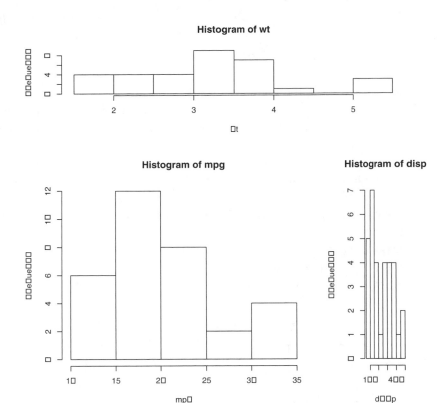

Figure 3.17 Graph combining three figures using the `layout()` function with specified widths

3.5.1 *Creating a figure arrangement with fine control*

There are times when you want to arrange or superimpose several figures to create a single meaningful plot. Doing so requires fine control over the placement of the figures. You can accomplish this with the `fig=` graphical parameter. In the following listing, two box plots are added to a scatter plot to create a single enhanced graph. The resulting graph is shown in figure 3.18.

Listing 3.4 Fine placement of figures in a graph

```
opar <- par(no.readonly=TRUE)
par(fig=c(0, 0.8, 0, 0.8))              ⟵—— Set up scatter plot
plot(mtcars$wt, mtcars$mpg,
     xlab="Miles Per Gallon",
     ylab="Car Weight")

par(fig=c(0, 0.8, 0.55, 1), new=TRUE)    ⟵—— Add box plot above
boxplot(mtcars$wt, horizontal=TRUE, axes=FALSE)
```

```
par(fig=c(0.65, 1, 0, 0.8), new=TRUE)                    ⟵—— Add box plot to right
boxplot(mtcars$mpg, axes=FALSE)
```

```
mtext("Enhanced Scatterplot", side=3, outer=TRUE, line=-3)
par(opar)
```

To understand how this graph was created, think of the full graph area as going from (0,0) in the lower-left corner to (1,1) in the upper-right corner. Figure 3.19 will help you visualize this. The format of the `fig=` parameter is a numerical vector of the form `c(x1, x2, y1, y2)`.

The first `fig=` sets up the scatter plot going from 0 to 0.8 on the x-axis and 0 to 0.8 on the y-axis. The top box plot goes from 0 to 0.8 on the x-axis and 0.55 to 1 on the y-axis. The right-hand box plot goes from 0.65 to 1 on the x-axis and 0 to 0.8 on the y-axis. `fig=` starts a new plot, so when adding a figure to an existing graph, include the `new=TRUE` option.

I chose 0.55 rather than 0.8 so that the top figure would be pulled closer to the scatter plot. Similarly, I chose 0.65 to pull the right-hand box plot closer to the scatter plot. You have to experiment to get the placement right.

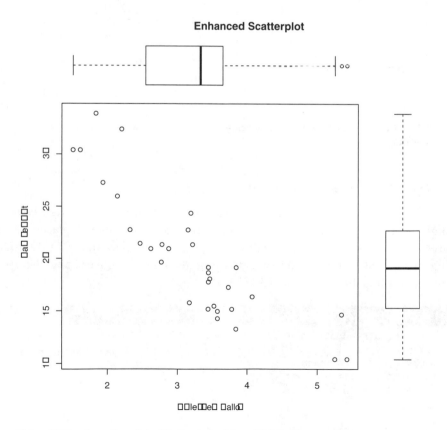

Figure 3.18   A scatter plot with two box plots added to the margins

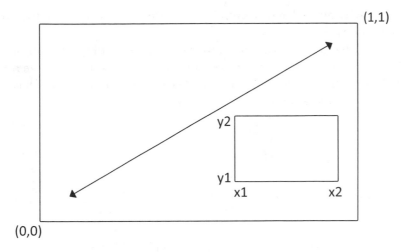

Figure 3.19 Specifying locations using the `fig=` graphical parameter

NOTE The amount of space needed for individual subplots can be device dependent. If you get "Error in plot.new(): figure margins too large," try varying the area given for each portion of the overall graph.

You can use `fig=` graphical parameter to combine several plots into any arrangement within a single graph. With a little practice, this approach gives you a great deal of flexibility when creating complex visual presentations.

3.6 *Summary*

In this chapter, we reviewed methods for creating graphs and saving them in a variety of formats. The majority of the chapter was concerned with modifying the default graphs produced by R, in order to arrive at more useful or attractive plots. You learned how to modify a graph's axes, fonts, symbols, lines, and colors, as well as how to add titles, subtitles, labels, plotted text, legends, and reference lines. You saw how to specify the size of the graph and margins, and how to combine multiple graphs into a single useful image.

Our focus in this chapter was on general techniques that you can apply to all graphs (with the exception of lattice graphs in chapter 16). Later chapters look at specific types of graphs. For example, chapter 7 covers methods for graphing a single variable. Graphing relationships between variables will be described in chapter 11. In chapter 16, we discuss advanced graphic methods, including lattice graphs (graphs that display the relationship between variables, for each level of other variables) and interactive graphs. Interactive graphs let you use the mouse to dynamically explore the plotted relationships.

In other chapters, we'll discuss methods of visualizing data that are particularly useful for the statistical approaches under consideration. Graphs are a central part of modern data analysis, and I'll endeavor to incorporate them into each of the statistical approaches we discuss.

In the previous chapter we discussed a range of methods for inputting or importing data into R. Unfortunately, in the real world your data is rarely usable in the format in which you first get it. In the next chapter we look at ways to transform and massage our data into a state that's more useful and conducive to analysis.

Basic data management 4

This chapter covers
- Manipulating dates and missing values
- Understanding data type conversions
- Creating and recoding variables
- Sorting, merging, and subsetting datasets
- Selecting and dropping variables

In chapter 2, we covered a variety of methods for importing data into R. Unfortunately, getting our data in the rectangular arrangement of a matrix or data frame is the first step in preparing it for analysis. To paraphrase Captain Kirk in the Star Trek episode "A Taste of Armageddon" (and proving my geekiness once and for all): "Data is a messy business—a very, very messy business." In my own work, as much as 60 percent of the time I spend on data analysis is focused on preparing the data for analysis. I'll go out a limb and say that the same is probably true in one form or another for most real-world data analysts. Let's take a look at an example.

4.1 A working example

One of the topics that I study in my current job is how men and women differ in the ways they lead their organizations. Typical questions might be

- Do men and women in management positions differ in the degree to which they defer to superiors?

- Does this vary from country to country, or are these gender differences universal?

One way to address these questions is to have bosses in multiple countries rate their managers on deferential behavior, using questions like the following:

This manager asks my opinion before making personnel decisions.

1	2	3	4	5
strongly disagree	disagree	neither agree nor disagree	agree	strongly agree

The resulting data might resemble those in table 4.1. Each row represents the ratings given to a manager by his or her boss.

Table 4.1 Gender differences in leadership behavior

Manager	Date	Country	Gender	Age	q1	q2	q3	q4	q5
1	10/24/08	US	M	32	5	4	5	5	5
2	10/28/08	US	F	45	3	5	2	5	5
3	10/01/08	UK	F	25	3	5	5	5	2
4	10/12/08	UK	M	39	3	3	4		
5	05/01/09	UK	F	99	2	2	1	2	1

Here, each manager is rated by their boss on five statements (q1 to q5) related to deference to authority. For example, manager 1 is a 32-year-old male working in the US and is rated deferential by his boss, while manager 5 is a female of unknown age (99 probably indicates missing) working in the UK and is rated low on deferential behavior. The date column captures when the ratings were made.

Although a dataset might have dozens of variables and thousands of observations, we've only included 10 columns and 5 rows to simplify the examples. Additionally, we've limited the number of items pertaining to the managers' deferential behavior to 5. In a real-world study, you'd probably use 10–20 such items to improve the reliability and validity of the results. You can create a data frame containing the data in table 4.1 using the following code.

Listing 4.1 Creating the leadership data frame

```
manager <- c(1, 2, 3, 4, 5)
date <- c("10/24/08", "10/28/08", "10/1/08", "10/12/08", "5/1/09")
country <- c("US", "US", "UK", "UK", "UK")
gender <- c("M", "F", "F", "M", "F")
age <- c(32, 45, 25, 39, 99)
q1 <- c(5, 3, 3, 3, 2)
q2 <- c(4, 5, 5, 3, 2)
q3 <- c(5, 2, 5, 4, 1)
q4 <- c(5, 5, 5, NA, 2)
q5 <- c(5, 5, 2, NA, 1)
leadership <- data.frame(manager, date, country, gender, age,
                         q1, q2, q3, q4, q5, stringsAsFactors=FALSE)
```

In order to address the questions of interest, we must first address several data management issues. Here's a partial list:

- The five ratings (q1 to q5) will need to be combined, yielding a single mean deferential score from each manager.
- In surveys, respondents often skip questions. For example, the boss rating manager 4 skipped questions 4 and 5. We'll need a method of handling incomplete data. We'll also need to recode values like 99 for age to missing.
- There may be hundreds of variables in a dataset, but we may only be interested in a few. To simplify matters, we'll want to create a new dataset with only the variables of interest.
- Past research suggests that leadership behavior may change as a function of the manager's age. To examine this, we may want to recode the current values of age into a new categorical age grouping (for example, young, middle-aged, elder).
- Leadership behavior may change over time. We might want to focus on deferential behavior during the recent global financial crisis. To do so, we may want to limit the study to data gathered during a specific period of time (say, January 1, 2009 to December 31, 2009).

We'll work through each of these issues in the current chapter, as well as other basic data management tasks such as combining and sorting datasets. Then in chapter 5 we'll look at some advanced topics.

4.2 Creating new variables

In a typical research project, you'll need to create new variables and transform existing ones. This is accomplished with statements of the form

```
variable <- expression
```

A wide array of operators and functions can be included in the `expression` portion of the statement. Table 4.2 lists R's arithmetic operators. Arithmetic operators are used when developing formulas.

Table 4.2 Arithmetic operators

Operator	Description
+	Addition
−	Subtraction
*	Multiplication
/	Division
^ or **	Exponentiation
x%%y	Modulus (x mod y) 5%%2 is 1
x%/%y	Integer division 5%/%2 is 2

Let's say that you have a data frame named `mydata`, with variables x1 and x2, and you want to create a new variable `sumx` that adds these two variables and a new variable called `meanx` that averages the two variables. If you use the code

```
sumx  <-  x1 + x2
meanx <- (x1 + x2)/2
```

you'll get an error, because R doesn't know that x1 and x2 are from data frame `mydata`. If you use this code instead

```
sumx  <-  mydata$x1 + mydata$x2
meanx <- (mydata$x1 + mydata$x2)/2
```

the statements will succeed but you'll end up with a data frame (`mydata`) and two separate vectors (`sumx` and `meanx`). This is probably not what you want. Ultimately, you want to incorporate new variables into the original data frame. The following listing provides three separate ways to accomplish this goal. The one you choose is up to you; the results will be the same.

Listing 4.2   Creating new variables

```
mydata<-data.frame(x1 = c(2, 2, 6, 4),
                   x2 = c(3, 4, 2, 8))

mydata$sumx  <-  mydata$x1 + mydata$x2
mydata$meanx <- (mydata$x1 + mydata$x2)/2


attach(mydata)
mydata$sumx  <-  x1 + x2
mydata$meanx <- (x1 + x2)/2
detach(mydata)

mydata <- transform(mydata,
                    sumx  =  x1 + x2,
                    meanx = (x1 + x2)/2)
```

Personally, I prefer the third method, exemplified by the use of the `transform()` function. It simplifies inclusion of as many new variables as desired and saves the results to the data frame.

4.3   Recoding variables

Recoding involves creating new values of a variable conditional on the existing values of the same and/or other variables. For example, you may want to

- Change a continuous variable into a set of categories
- Replace miscoded values with correct values
- Create a pass/fail variable based on a set of cutoff scores

To recode data, you can use one or more of R's logical operators (see table 4.3). Logical operators are expressions that return TRUE or FALSE.

Table 4.3 Logical operators

Operator	Description
<	Less than
<=	Less than or equal to
>	Greater than
>=	Greater than or equal to
==	Exactly equal to
!=	Not equal to
!x	Not x
x | y	x or y
x & y	x and y
isTRUE(x)	Test if x is TRUE

Let's say that you want to recode the ages of the managers in our leadership dataset from the continuous variable age to the categorical variable agecat (Young, Middle Aged, Elder). First, you must recode the value 99 for age to missing with code such as

```
leadership$age[leadership$age  == 99]      <- NA
```

The statement variable[condition] <- expression will only make the assignment when condition is TRUE.

Once missing values for age have been specified, you can then use the following code to create the agecat variable:

```
leadership$agecat[leadership$age  > 75]    <- "Elder"
leadership$agecat[leadership$age >= 55 &
                  leadership$age <= 75]    <- "Middle Aged"
leadership$agecat[leadership$age  < 55]    <- "Young"
```

banding.

You include the data frame names in leadership$agecat to ensure that the new variable is saved back to the data frame. You define middle aged as 55 to 75 so that I won't feel so old. Note that if you hadn't recoded 99 as missing for age first, manager 5 would've erroneously been given the value "Elder" for agecat.

This code can be written more compactly as

```
leadership <- within(leadership,{
                agecat <- NA
                agecat[age > 75]          <- "Elder"
                agecat[age >= 55 & age <= 75] <- "Middle Aged"
                agecat[age < 55]          <- "Young" })
```

The within() function is similar to the with() function (section 2.2.4), but allows you to modify the data frame. First, the variable agecat variable is created and set to missing for each row of the data frame. Then the remaining statements within the braces are executed in order. Remember that `agecat` is a character variable; you're likely to want to turn it into an ordered factor, as explained in section 2.2.5.

Several packages offer useful recoding functions; in particular, the `car` package's `recode()` function recodes numeric and character vectors and factors very simply. The package `doBy` offers `recodevar()`, another popular function. Finally, R ships with `cut()`, which allows you to divide the range of a numeric variable into intervals, returning a factor.

4.4   Renaming variables

If you're not happy with your variable names, you can change them interactively or programmatically. Let's say that you want to change the variables `manager` to `managerID` and `date` to `testDate`. You can use the statement

```
fix(leadership)
```

to invoke an interactive editor, click on the variable names, and rename them in the dialogs that are presented (see figure 4.1).

Programmatically, the `reshape` package has a `rename()` function that's useful for altering the names of variables. The format of the `rename()` function is

```
rename(dataframe, c(oldname="newname", oldname="newname",…))
```

Here's an example:

```
library(reshape)
leadership <- rename(leadership,
                    c(manager="managerID", date="testDate")
)
```

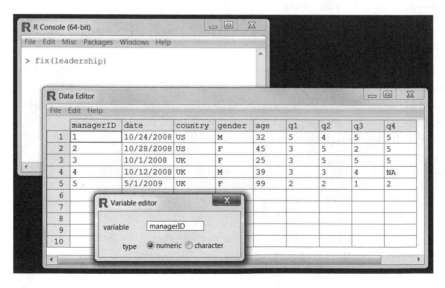

Figure 4.1   Renaming variables interactively using the `fix()` function

The `reshape` package isn't installed by default, so you'll need to install it on first use using the `install.packages("reshape")` command. The `reshape` package has a powerful set of functions for altering the structure of a dataset. We'll explore several in chapter 5.

Finally, you can rename variables via the `names()` function. For example:

```
names(leadership)[2] <- "testDate"
```

would rename `date` to `testDate` as demonstrated in the following code:

```
> names(leadership)
 [1] "manager" "date"    "country" "gender" "age"    "q1"    "q2"
 [8] "q3"      "q4"      "q5"
> names(leadership)[2] <- "testDate"
> leadership
  manager testDate country gender age q1 q2 q3 q4 q5
1       1 10/24/08      US       M  32  5  4  5  5  5
2       2 10/28/08      US       F  45  3  5  2  5  5
3       3  10/1/08      UK       F  25  3  5  5  5  2
4       4 10/12/08      UK       M  39  3  3  4 NA NA
5       5   5/1/09      UK       F  99  2  2  1  2  1
```

In a similar fashion,

```
names(leadership)[6:10] <- c("item1", "item2", "item3", "item4", "item5")
```

would rename `q1` through `q5` to `item1` through `item5`.

4.5 Missing values

In a project of any size, data is likely to be incomplete because of missed questions, faulty equipment, or improperly coded data. In R, missing values are represented by the symbol NA (not available). Impossible values (for example, dividing by 0) are represented by the symbol NaN (not a number). Unlike programs such as SAS, R uses the same missing values symbol for character and numeric data.

R provides a number of functions for identifying observations that contain missing values. The function `is.na()` allows you to test for the presence of missing values. Assume that you have a vector:

```
y <- c(1, 2, 3, NA)
```

then the function

```
is.na(y)
```

returns `c(FALSE, FALSE, FALSE, TRUE)`.

Notice how the `is.na()` function works on an object. It returns an object of the same size, with the entries replaced by TRUE if the element is a missing value, and FALSE if the element is not a missing value. Listing 4.3 applies this to our leadership example.

Listing 4.3   Applying the `is.na()` function

```
> is.na(leadership[,6:10])
        q1    q2    q3    q4    q5
[1,] FALSE FALSE FALSE FALSE FALSE
[2,] FALSE FALSE FALSE FALSE FALSE
[3,] FALSE FALSE FALSE FALSE FALSE
[4,] FALSE FALSE FALSE  TRUE  TRUE
[5,] FALSE FALSE FALSE FALSE FALSE
```

Here, `leadership[,6:10]` limited the data frame to columns 6 to 10, and `is.na()` identified which values are missing.

> **NOTE**   Missing values are considered noncomparable, even to themselves. This means that you can't use comparison operators to test for the presence of missing values. For example, the logical test `myvar == NA` is never `TRUE`. Instead, you have to use missing values functions, like those in this section, to identify the missing values in R data objects.

4.5.1   *Recoding values to missing*

As demonstrated in section 4.3, you can use assignments to recode values to missing. In our leadership example, missing age values were coded as 99. Before analyzing this dataset, you must let R know that the value 99 means missing in this case (otherwise the mean age for this sample of bosses will be way off!). You can accomplish this by recoding the variable:

```
leadership$age[leadership$age == 99] <- NA
```

Any value of age that's equal to 99 is changed to NA. Be sure that any missing data is properly coded as missing before analyzing the data or the results will be meaningless.

4.5.2   *Excluding missing values from analyses*

Once you've identified the missing values, you need to eliminate them in some way before analyzing your data further. The reason is that arithmetic expressions and functions that contain missing values yield missing values. For example, consider the following code:

```
x <- c(1, 2, NA, 3)
y <- x[1] + x[2] + x[3] + x[4]
z <- sum(x)
```

Both `y` and `z` will be `NA` (missing) because the third element of `x` is missing.

Luckily, most numeric functions have a `na.rm=TRUE` option that removes missing values prior to calculations and applies the function to the remaining values:

```
x <- c(1, 2, NA, 3)
y <- sum(x, na.rm=TRUE)
```

Here, `y` is equal to 6.

When using functions with incomplete data, be sure to check how that function handles missing data by looking at its online help (for example, `help(sum)`). The sum() function is only one of many functions we'll consider in chapter 5. Functions allow you to transform data with flexibility and ease.

You can remove *any* observation with missing data by using the na.omit() function. na.omit() deletes any rows with missing data. Let's apply this to our leadership dataset in the following listing.

Listing 4.4 Using `na.omit()` to delete incomplete observations

```
> leadership                                           ⟵─┐  Data frame with
  manager     date country gender age q1 q2 q3 q4 q5     │  missing data
1       1 10/24/08      US      M  32  5  4  5  5  5
2       2 10/28/08      US      F  40  3  5  2  5  5
3       3 10/01/08      UK      F  25  3  5  5  5  2
4       4 10/12/08      UK      M  39  3  3  4 NA NA
5       5 05/01/09      UK      F  99  2  2  1  2  1

> newdata <- na.omit(leadership)                       ⟵─┐  Data frame with
> newdata                                                 │  complete cases only
  manager     date country gender age q1 q2 q3 q4 q5
1       1 10/24/08      US      M  32  5  4  5  5  5
2       2 10/28/08      US      F  40  3  5  2  5  5
3       3 10/01/08      UK      F  25  3  5  5  5  2
5       5 05/01/09      UK      F  99  2  2  1  2  1
```

Any rows containing missing data are deleted from leadership before the results are saved to newdata.

Deleting all observations with missing data (called listwise deletion) is one of several methods of handling incomplete datasets. If there are only a few missing values or they're concentrated in a small number of observations, listwise deletion can provide a good solution to the missing values problem. But if missing values are spread throughout the data, or there's a great deal of missing data in a small number of variables, listwise deletion can exclude a substantial percentage of your data. We'll explore several more sophisticated methods of dealing with missing values in chapter 15. Next, let's take a look at dates.

4.6   *Date values*

Dates are typically entered into R as character strings and then translated into date variables that are stored numerically. The function as.Date() is used to make this translation. The syntax is as.Date(*x*, "*input_format*"), where *x* is the character data and *input_format* gives the appropriate format for reading the date (see table 4.4).

Table 4.4   Date formats

Symbol	Meaning	Example
%d	Day as a number (0–31)	01–31
%a	Abbreviated weekday	Mon
%A	Unabbreviated weekday	Monday
%m	Month (00–12)	00–12

Table 4.4   Date formats *(continued)*

Symbol	Meaning	Example
%b	Abbreviated month	Jan
%B	Unabbreviated month	January
%y	2-digit year	07
%Y	4-digit year	2007

The default format for inputting dates is yyyy-mm-dd. The statement

```
mydates <- as.Date(c("2007-06-22", "2004-02-13"))
```

converts the character data to dates using this default format. In contrast,

```
strDates <- c("01/05/1965", "08/16/1975")
dates <- as.Date(strDates, "%m/%d/%Y")
```

reads the data using a mm/dd/yyyy format.

In our leadership dataset, date is coded as a character variable in mm/dd/yy format. Therefore:

```
myformat <- "%m/%d/%y"
leadership$date <- as.Date(leadership$date, myformat)
```

uses the specified format to read the character variable and replace it in the data frame as a date variable. Once the variable is in date format, you can analyze and plot the dates using the wide range of analytic techniques covered in later chapters.

Two functions are especially useful for time-stamping data. Sys.Date() returns today's date and date() returns the current date and time. As I write this, it's December 1, 2010 at 4:28pm. So executing those functions produces

```
> Sys.Date()
[1] "2010-12-01"
> date()
[1] "Wed Dec 01 16:28:21 2010"
```

You can use the format(x, format="*output_format*") function to output dates in a specified format, and to extract portions of dates:

```
> today <- Sys.Date()
> format(today, format="%B %d %Y")
[1] "December 01 2010"
> format(today, format="%A")
[1] "Wednesday"
```

The format() function takes an argument (a date in this case) and applies an output format (in this case, assembled from the symbols in table 4.4). The important result here is that there are only two more days until the weekend!

When R stores dates internally, they're represented as the number of days since January 1, 1970, with negative values for earlier dates. That means you can perform arithmetic operations on them. For example:

```
> startdate <- as.Date("2004-02-13")
> enddate   <- as.Date("2011-01-22")
```

```
> days        <- enddate - startdate
> days
Time difference of 2535 days
```

displays the number of days between February 13, 2004 and January 22, 2011.

Finally, you can also use the function `difftime()` to calculate a time interval and express it as seconds, minutes, hours, days, or weeks. Let's assume that I was born on October 12, 1956. How old am I?

```
> today <- Sys.Date()
> dob   <- as.Date("1956-10-12")
> difftime(today, dob, units="weeks")
Time difference of 2825 weeks
```

Apparently, I am 2825 weeks old. Who knew? Final test: On which day of the week was I born?

4.6.1 Converting dates to character variables

Although less commonly used, you can also convert date variables to character variables. Date values can be converted to character values using the `as.character()` function:

```
strDates <- as.character(dates)
```

The conversion allows you to apply a range of character functions to the data values (subsetting, replacement, concatenation, etc.). We'll cover character functions in detail in chapter 5.

4.6.2 Going further

To learn more about converting character data to dates, take a look at `help(as.Date)` and `help(strftime)`. To learn more about formatting dates and times, see `help(ISOdatetime)`. The `lubridate` package contains a number of functions that simplify working with dates, including functions to identify and parse date-time data, extract date-time components (for example, years, months, days, etc.), and perform arithmetic calculations on date-times. If you need to do complex calculations with dates, the `fCalendar` package can also help. It provides a myriad of functions for dealing with dates, can handle multiple time zones at once, and provides sophisticated calendar manipulations that recognize business days, weekends, and holidays.

4.7 Type conversions

In the previous section, we discussed how to convert character data to date values, and vice versa. R provides a set of functions to identify an object's data type and convert it to a different data type.

Type conversions in R work in a similar fashion to those in other statistical programming languages. For example, adding a character string to a numeric vector converts all the elements in the vector to character values. You can use the functions listed in table 4.5 to test for a data type and to convert it to a given type.

Table 4.5   Type conversion functions

Test	Convert
is.numeric()	as.numeric()
is.character()	as.character()
is.vector()	as.vector()
is.matrix()	as.matrix()
is.data.frame()	as.data.frame()
is.factor()	as.factor()
is.logical()	as.logical()

Functions of the form is.*datatype*() return TRUE or FALSE, whereas as.*datatype*() converts the argument to that type. The following listing provides an example.

Listing 4.5   Converting from one data type to another

```
> a <- c(1,2,3)
> a
[1] 1 2 3
> is.numeric(a)
[1] TRUE
> is.vector(a)
[1] TRUE

> a <- as.character(a)
> a
[1] "1" "2" "3"
> is.numeric(a)
[1] FALSE
> is.vector(a)
[1] TRUE
> is.character(a)
[1] TRUE
```

When combined with the flow controls (such as if-then) that we'll discuss in chapter 5, the is.*datatype*() function can be a powerful tool, allowing you to handle data in different ways, depending on its type. Additionally, some R functions require data of a specific type (character or numeric, matrix or data frame) and the as.*datatype*() will let you transform your data into the format required prior to analyses.

4.8   Sorting data

Sometimes, viewing a dataset in a sorted order can tell you quite a bit about the data. For example, which managers are most deferential? To sort a data frame in R, use the order() function. By default, the sorting order is ascending. Prepend the sorting variable with a minus sign to indicate a descending order. The following examples illustrate sorting with the leadership data frame.

The statement

```
newdata <- leadership[order(leadership$age),]
```

creates a new dataset containing rows sorted from youngest manager to oldest manager. The statement

```
attach(leadership)
newdata <- leadership[order(gender, age),]
detach(leadership)
```

sorts the rows into female followed by male, and youngest to oldest within each gender. Finally,

```
attach(leadership)
newdata <-leadership[order(gender, -age),]
detach(leadership)
```

sorts the rows by gender, and then from oldest to youngest manager within each gender.

4.9   Merging datasets

If your data exist in multiple locations, you'll need to combine them before moving forward. This section shows you how to add columns (variables) and rows (observations) to a data frame.

4.9.1   Adding columns

To merge two data frames (datasets) horizontally, you use the merge() function. In most cases, two data frames are joined by one or more common key variables (that is an inner join). For example:

```
total <- merge(dataframeA, dataframeB, by="ID")
```

merges dataframeA and dataframeB by ID. Similarly,

```
total <- merge(dataframeA, dataframeB, by=c("ID","Country"))
```

merges the two data frames by ID and Country. Horizontal joins like this are typically used to add variables to a data frame.

> **NOTE**   If you're joining two matrices or data frames horizontally and don't need to specify a common key, you can use the cbind() function:
>
> ```
> total <- cbind(A, B)
> ```
>
> This function will horizontally concatenate the objects A and B. For the function to work properly, each object has to have the same number of rows and be sorted in the same order.

4.9.2 Adding rows

To join two data frames (datasets) vertically, use the `rbind()` function:

```
total <- rbind(dataframeA, dataframeB)
```

how resolved?

The two data frames must have the same variables, but they don't have to be in the same order. If `dataframeA` has variables that `dataframeB` doesn't, then before joining them do one of the following:

- Delete the extra variables in `dataframeA`
- Create the additional variables in `dataframeB` and set them to `NA` (missing)

Vertical concatenation is typically used to add observations to a data frame.

4.10 Subsetting datasets

R has powerful indexing features for accessing the elements of an object. These features can be used to select and exclude variables, observations, or both. The following sections demonstrate several methods for keeping or deleting variables and observations.

4.10.1 Selecting (keeping) variables

It's a common practice to create a new dataset from a limited number of variables chosen from a larger dataset. In chapter 2, you saw that the elements of a data frame are accessed using the notation *dataframe[row indices, column indices]*. You can use this to select variables. For example:

```
newdata <- leadership[, c(6:10)]
```

selects variables q1, q2, q3, q4, and q5 from the `leadership` data frame and saves them to the data frame `newdata`. Leaving the row indices blank (,) selects all the rows by default.

The statements

```
myvars <- c("q1", "q2", "q3", "q4", "q5")
newdata <-leadership[myvars]
```

accomplish the same variable selection. Here, variable names (in quotes) have been entered as column indices, thereby selecting the same columns.

Finally, you could've used

```
myvars <- paste("q", 1:5, sep="")
newdata <- leadership[myvars]
```

This example uses the `paste()` function to create the same character vector as in the previous example. The `paste()` function will be covered in chapter 5.

4.10.2 Excluding (dropping) variables

There are many reasons to exclude variables. For example, if a variable has several missing values, you may want to drop it prior to further analyses. Let's look at some methods of excluding variables.

You could exclude variables q3 and q4 with the statements

```
myvars <- names(leadership) %in% c("q3", "q4")
newdata <- leadership[!myvars]
```

In order to understand why this works, you need to break it down:

1 `names(leadership)` produces a character vector containing the variable names. `c("managerID","testDate","country","gender","age","q1",` `"q2","q3","q4","q5")`.

2 `names(leadership) %in% c("q3", "q4")` returns a logical vector with `TRUE` for each element in `names(leadership)` that matches q3 or q4 and `FALSE` otherwise. `c(FALSE, FALSE, FALSE, FALSE, FALSE, FALSE, FALSE, TRUE, TRUE, FALSE)`.

3 The not (`!`) operator reverses the logical values `c(TRUE, TRUE, TRUE, TRUE, TRUE, TRUE, TRUE, FALSE, FALSE, TRUE)`.

4 `leadership[c(TRUE, TRUE, TRUE, TRUE, TRUE, TRUE, TRUE, FALSE, FALSE, TRUE)]` selects columns with `TRUE` logical values, so q3 and q4 are excluded.

Knowing that q3 and q4 are the 8th and 9th variable, you could exclude them with the statement

```
newdata <- leadership[c(-8,-9)]
```

This works because prepending a column index with a minus sign (`-`) excludes that column.

Finally, the same deletion can be accomplished via

```
leadership$q3 <- leadership$q4 <- NULL
```

Here you set columns q3 and q4 to undefined (`NULL`). Note that `NULL` isn't the same as `NA` (missing).

Dropping variables is the converse of keeping variables. The choice will depend on which is easier to code. If there are many variables to drop, it may be easier to keep the ones that remain, or vice versa.

4.10.3 *Selecting observations*

Selecting or excluding observations (rows) is typically a key aspect of successful data preparation and analysis. Several examples are given in the following listing.

Listing 4.6 Selecting observations

```
newdata <- leadership[1:3,]

newdata <- leadership[which(leadership$gender=="M" &
                            leadership$age > 30),]


attach(leadership)
newdata <- leadership[which(gender=='M' & age > 30),]
detach(leadership)
```

In each of these examples, you provide the row indices and leave the column indices blank (therefore choosing all columns). In the first example, you ask for rows 1 through 3 (the first three observations).

In the second example, you select all men over 30. Let's break down this line of code in order to understand it:

1 The logical comparison `leadership$gender=="M"` produces the vector `c(TRUE, FALSE, FALSE, TRUE, FALSE)`.

2 The logical comparison `leadership$age > 30` produces the vector `c(TRUE, TRUE, FALSE, TRUE, TRUE)`.

3 The logical comparison `c(TRUE, FALSE, FALSE, TRUE, FALSE) & c(TRUE, TRUE, FALSE, TRUE, TRUE)` produces the vector `c(TRUE, FALSE, FALSE, TRUE, FALSE)`.

4 The function `which()` gives the indices of a vector that are `TRUE`. Thus, `which(c(TRUE, FALSE, FALSE, TRUE, FALSE))` produces the vector `c(1, 4)`.

5 `leadership[c(1,4),]` selects the first and fourth observations from the data frame. This meets our selection criteria (men over 30).

In the third example, the `attach()` function is used so that you don't have to prepend the variable names with the data frame names.

At the beginning of this chapter, I suggested that you might want to limit your analyses to observations collected between January 1, 2009 and December 31, 2009. How can you do this? Here's one solution:

```
leadership$date <- as.Date(leadership$date, "%m/%d/%y")
startdate <- as.Date("2009-01-01")
enddate   <- as.Date("2009-10-31")
newdata <- leadership[which(leadership$date >= startdate &
leadership$date <= enddate),]
```

Convert the date values read in originally as character values to date values using the format mm/dd/yy. Then, create starting and ending dates. Because the default for the `as.Date()` function is yyyy-mm-dd, you don't have to supply it here. Finally, select cases meeting your desired criteria as you did in the previous example.

4.10.4 *The subset() function*

The examples in the previous two sections are important because they help describe the ways in which logical vectors and comparison operators are interpreted within R. Understanding how these examples work will help you to interpret R code in general. Now that you've done things the hard way, let's look at a shortcut.

The `subset` function is probably the easiest way to select variables and observations. Here are two examples:

```
newdata <- subset(leadership, age >= 35 | age < 24,
                  select=c(q1, q2, q3, q4))

newdata <- subset(leadership, gender=="M" & age > 25,
                  select=gender:q4)
```

In the first example, you select all rows that have a value of age greater than or equal to 35 *or* age less than 24. You keep the variables q1 through q4. In the second example, you select all men over the age of 25 and you keep variables gender through q4 (gender, q4, and all columns between them). You've seen the colon operator from:to in chapter 2. Here, it provides all variables in a data frame between the from variable and the to variable, inclusive.

4.10.5 Random samples

Sampling from larger datasets is a common practice in data mining and machine learning. For example, you may want to select two random samples, creating a predictive model from one and validating its effectiveness on the other. The sample() function enables you to take a random sample (with or without replacement) of size *n* from a dataset.

You could take a random sample of size 3 from the leadership dataset using the statement

```
mysample <- leadership[sample(1:nrow(leadership), 3, replace=FALSE),]
```

The first argument to the sample() function is a vector of elements to choose from. Here, the vector is 1 to the number of observations in the data frame. The second argument is the number of elements to be selected, and the third argument indicates sampling without replacement. The sample() function returns the randomly sampled elements, which are then used to select rows from the data frame.

GOING FURTHER

R has extensive facilities for sampling, including drawing and calibrating survey samples (see the sampling package) and analyzing complex survey data (see the survey package). Other methods that rely on sampling, including bootstrapping and resampling statistics, are described in chapter 11.

4.11 Using SQL statements to manipulate data frames

Until now, you've been using R statements to manipulate data. But many data analysts come to R well versed in Structured Query Language (SQL). It would be a shame to lose all that accumulated knowledge. Therefore, before we end, let me briefly mention the existence of the sqldf package. (If you're unfamiliar with SQL, please feel free to skip this section.)

After downloading and installing the package (install.packages("sqldf")), you can use the sqldf() function to apply SQL SELECT statements to data frames. Two examples are given in the following listing.

Listing 4.7 Using SQL statements to manipulate data frames

```
> library(sqldf)
> newdf <- sqldf("select * from mtcars where carb=1 order by mpg",
                 row.names=TRUE)
> newdf
```

```
                 mpg cyl  disp  hp drat   wt qsec vs am gear carb
Valiant          18.1   6 225.0 105 2.76 3.46 20.2  1  0    3    1
Hornet 4 Drive 21.4   6 258.0 110 3.08 3.21 19.4  1  0    3    1
Toyota Corona  21.5   4 120.1  97 3.70 2.46 20.0  1  0    3    1
Datsun 710     22.8   4 108.0  93 3.85 2.32 18.6  1  1    4    1
Fiat X1-9      27.3   4  79.0  66 4.08 1.94 18.9  1  1    4    1
Fiat 128       32.4   4  78.7  66 4.08 2.20 19.5  1  1    4    1
Toyota Corolla 33.9   4  71.1  65 4.22 1.83 19.9  1  1    4    1

> sqldf("select avg(mpg) as avg_mpg, avg(disp) as avg_disp, gear
            from mtcars where cyl in (4, 6) group by gear")
  avg_mpg avg_disp gear
1    20.3      201    3
2    24.5      123    4
3    25.4      120    5
```

In the first example, you selected all the variables (columns) from the data frame mt-cars, kept only automobiles (rows) with one carburetor (carb), sorted the automobiles in ascending order by mpg, and saved the results as the data frame newdf. The option row.names=TRUE carried the row names from the original data frame over to the new one. In the second example, you printed the mean mpg and disp within each level of gear for automobiles with four or six cylinders (cyl).

Experienced SQL users will find the sqldf package a useful adjunct to data management in R. See the project home page (http://code.google.com/p/sqldf/) for more details.

4.12 *Summary*

We covered a great deal of ground in this chapter. We looked at the way R stores missing and date values and explored various ways of handling them. You learned how to determine the data type of an object and how to convert it to other types. You used simple formulas to create new variables and recode existing variables. I showed you how to sort your data and rename your variables. You learned how to merge your data with other datasets both horizontally (adding variables) and vertically (adding observations). Finally, we discussed how to keep or drop variables and how to select observations based on a variety of criteria.

In the next chapter, we'll look at the myriad of arithmetic, character, and statistical functions that R makes available for creating and transforming variables. After exploring ways of controlling program flow, you'll see how to write your own functions. We'll also explore how you can use these functions to aggregate and summarize your data.

By the end of chapter 5 you'll have most of the tools necessary to manage complex datasets. (And you'll be the envy of data analysts everywhere!)

Advanced data management

In chapter 4, we reviewed the basic techniques used for managing datasets within R. In this chapter, we'll focus on advanced topics. The chapter is divided into three basic parts. In the first part we'll take a whirlwind tour of R's many functions for mathematical, statistical, and character manipulation. To give this section relevance, we begin with a data management problem that can be solved using these functions. After covering the functions themselves, we'll look at one possible solution to the data management problem.

Next, we cover how to write your own functions to accomplish data management and analysis tasks. First, you'll explore ways of controlling program flow, including looping and conditional statement execution. Then we'll investigate the structure of user-written functions and how to invoke them once created.

Then, we'll look at ways of aggregating and summarizing data, along with methods of reshaping and restructuring datasets. When aggregating data, you can specify the use of any appropriate built-in or user-written function to accomplish the summarization, so the topics you learned in the first two parts of the chapter will provide a real benefit.

5.1   *A data management challenge*

To begin our discussion of numerical and character functions, let's consider a data management problem. A group of students have taken exams in Math, Science, and English. You want to combine these scores in order to determine a single performance indicator for each student. Additionally, you want to assign an A to the top 20 percent of students, a B to the next 20 percent, and so on. Finally, you want to sort the students alphabetically. The data are presented in table 5.1.

Table 5.1   Student exam data

Student	Math	Science	English
John Davis	502	95	25
Angela Williams	600	99	22
Bullwinkle Moose	412	80	18
David Jones	358	82	15
Janice Markhammer	495	75	20
Cheryl Cushing	512	85	28
Reuven Ytzrhak	410	80	15
Greg Knox	625	95	30
Joel England	573	89	27
Mary Rayburn	522	86	18

Looking at this dataset, several obstacles are immediately evident. First, scores on the three exams aren't comparable. They have widely different means and standard deviations, so averaging them doesn't make sense. You must transform the exam scores into comparable units before combining them. Second, you'll need a method of determining a student's percentile rank on this score in order to assign a grade. Third, there's a single field for names, complicating the task of sorting students. You'll need to break apart their names into first name and last name in order to sort them properly.

Each of these tasks can be accomplished through the judicious use of R's numerical and character functions. After working through the functions described in the next section, we'll consider a possible solution to this data management challenge.

5.2 Numerical and character functions

In this section, we'll review functions in R that can be used as the basic building blocks for manipulating data. They can be divided into numerical (mathematical, statistical, probability) and character functions. After we review each type, I'll show you how to apply functions to the columns (variables) and rows (observations) of matrices and data frames (see section 5.2.6).

5.2.1 Mathematical functions

Table 5.2 lists common mathematical functions along with short examples.

Table 5.2 Mathematical functions

Function	Description
abs(x)	Absolute value abs(-4) returns 4.
sqrt(x)	Square root sqrt(25) returns 5. This is the same as 25^(0.5).
ceiling(x)	Smallest integer not less than x ceiling(3.475) returns 4.
floor(x)	Largest integer not greater than x floor(3.475) returns 3.
trunc(x)	Integer formed by truncating values in x toward 0 trunc(5.99) returns 5.
round(x, digits=n)	Round x to the specified number of decimal places round(3.475, digits=2) returns 3.48.
signif(x, digits=n)	Round x to the specified number of significant digits signif(3.475, digits=2) returns 3.5.
cos(x), sin(x), tan(x)	Cosine, sine, and tangent cos(2) returns –0.416.
acos(x), asin(x), atan(x)	Arc-cosine, arc-sine, and arc-tangent acos(-0.416) returns 2.
cosh(x), sinh(x), tanh(x)	Hyperbolic cosine, sine, and tangent sinh(2) returns 3.627.
acosh(x), asinh(x), atanh(x)	Hyperbolic arc-cosine, arc-sine, and arc-tangent asinh(3.627) returns 2.
log(x,base=n) log(x) log10(x)	Logarithm of x to the base n For convenience log(x) is the natural logarithm. log10(x) is the common logarithm. log(10) returns 2.3026. log10(10) returns 1.

(handwritten note: } differ on negatives!)

(handwritten note: floor (-3.5) = -4   trunc (-3.5) = -3)

Table 5.2   Mathematical functions *(continued)*

Function	Description
`exp(x)`	Exponential function `exp(2.3026)` returns 10.

Data transformation is one of the primary uses for these functions. For example, you often transform positively skewed variables such as income to a log scale before further analyses. Mathematical functions will also be used as components in formulas, in plotting functions (for example, `x versus sin(x)`) and in formatting numerical values prior to printing.

The examples in table 5.2 apply mathematical functions to scalars (individual numbers). When these functions are applied to numeric vectors, matrices, or data frames, they operate on each individual value. For example, `sqrt(c(4, 16, 25))` returns `c(2, 4, 5)`.

5.2.2   Statistical functions

Common statistical functions are presented in table 5.3. Many of these functions have optional parameters that affect the outcome. For example:

```
y <- mean(x)
```

provides the arithmetic mean of the elements in object x, and

```
z <- mean(x, trim = 0.05, na.rm=TRUE)
```

provides the trimmed mean, dropping the highest and lowest 5 percent of scores and any missing values. Use the `help()` function to learn more about each function and its arguments.

Table 5.3   Statistical functions

Function	Description
`mean(x)`	Mean `mean(c(1,2,3,4))` returns 2.5.
`median(x)`	Median `median(c(1,2,3,4))` returns 2.5.
`sd(x)`	Standard deviation `sd(c(1,2,3,4))` returns 1.29.
`var(x)`	Variance `var(c(1,2,3,4))` returns 1.67.
`mad(x)`	Median absolute deviation `mad(c(1,2,3,4))` returns 1.48.

Table 5.3 Statistical functions *(continued)*

Function	Description

quantile(*x*, *probs*)	Quantiles where x is the numeric vector where quantiles are desired and *probs* is a numeric vector with probabilities in [0,1].
	`# 30th and 84th percentiles of x`
	`y <- quantile(x, c(.3,.84))`

range(*x*)	Range `x <- c(1,2,3,4)` `range(x)` returns c(1,4). `diff(range(x))` returns 3.
sum(*x*)	Sum `sum(c(1,2,3,4))` returns 10.
diff(*x*, lag=*n*)	Lagged differences, with `lag` indicating which lag to use. The default lag is 1. `x<- c(1, 5, 23, 29)` `diff(x)` returns c(4, 18, 6).
min(*x*)	Minimum `min(c(1,2,3,4))` returns 1.
max(*x*)	Maximum `max(c(1,2,3,4))` returns 4.
scale(*x*, center=TRUE, scale=TRUE)	Column center (`center=TRUE`) or standardize (`center=TRUE`, `scale=TRUE`) data object x. An example is given in listing 5.6.

To see these functions in action, look at the next listing. This listing demonstrates two ways to calculate the mean and standard deviation of a vector of numbers.

Listing 5.1 Calculating the mean and standard deviation

```
> x <- c(1,2,3,4,5,6,7,8)

> mean(x)                        <—— Short way
[1] 4.5
> sd(x)
[1] 2.449490

> n <- length(x)                 <—— Long way
> meanx <- sum(x)/n
> css <- sum((x - meanx)^2)
> sdx <- sqrt(css / (n-1))
> meanx
[1] 4.5
> sdx
[1] 2.449490
```

It's instructive to view how the corrected sum of squares (`css`) is calculated in the second approach:

1 x equals c(1, 2, 3, 4, 5, 6, 7, 8) and mean x equals 4.5 (length(x)
   returns the number of elements in x).
2 (x - meanx) subtracts 4.5 from each element of x, resulting in
   c(-3.5, -2.5, -1.5, -0.5, 0.5, 1.5, 2.5, 3.5).
3 (x - meanx)^2 squares each element of (x - meanx), resulting in
   c(12.25, 6.25, 2.25, 0.25, 0.25, 2.25, 6.25, 12.25).
4 sum((x - meanx)^2) sums each of the elements of (x - meanx)^2,
   resulting in 42.

Writing formulas in R has much in common with matrix manipulation languages such as MATLAB (we'll look more specifically at solving matrix algebra problems in appendix E).

STANDARDIZING DATA

By default, the scale() function standardizes the specified columns of a matrix or data frame to a mean of 0 and a standard deviation of 1:

```
newdata <- scale(mydata)
```

To standardize each column to an arbitrary mean and standard deviation, you can use code similar to the following:

```
newdata <- scale(mydata)*SD + M
```

where M is the desired mean and SD is the desired standard deviation. Using the scale() function on non-numeric columns will produce an error. To standardize a specific column rather than an entire matrix or data frame, you can use code such as

```
newdata <- transform(mydata, myvar = scale(myvar)*10+50)
```

This code standardizes the variable myvar to a mean of 50 and standard deviation of 10. We'll use the scale() function in the solution to the data management challenge in section 5.3.

5.2.3   *Probability functions*

You may wonder why probability functions aren't listed with the statistical functions (it was really bothering you, wasn't it?). Although probability functions are statistical by definition, they're unique enough to deserve their own section. Probability functions are often used to generate simulated data with known characteristics and to calculate probability values within user-written statistical functions.

In R, probability functions take the form

```
[dpqr]distribution_abbreviation()
```

where the first letter refers to the aspect of the *distribution* returned:

d = density
p = distribution function
q = quantile function
r = random generation (random deviates)

The common probability functions are listed in table 5.4.

Table 5.4 **Probability distributions**

Distribution	Abbreviation	Distribution	Abbreviation
Beta	`beta`	Logistic	`logis`
Binomial	`binom`	Multinomial	`multinom`
Cauchy	`cauchy`	Negative binomial	`nbinom`
Chi-squared (noncentral)	`chisq`	Normal	`norm`
Exponential	`exp`	Poisson	`pois`
F	`f`	Wilcoxon Signed Rank	`signrank`
Gamma	`gamma`	T	`t`
Geometric	`geom`	Uniform	`unif`
Hypergeometric	`hyper`	Weibull	`weibull`
Lognormal	`lnorm`	Wilcoxon Rank Sum	`wilcox`

To see how these work, let's look at functions related to the normal distribution. If you don't specify a mean and a standard deviation, the standard normal distribution is assumed (mean=0, sd=1). Examples of the density (`dnorm`), distribution (`pnorm`), quantile (`qnorm`) and random deviate generation (`rnorm`) functions are given in table 5.5.

Table 5.5 **Normal distribution functions**

Problem	Solution
| Plot the standard normal curve on the interval [–3,3] (see below) 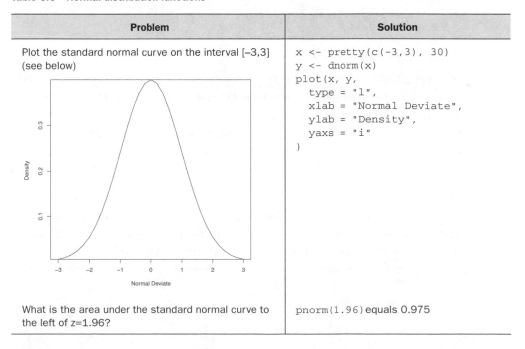 | ```
x <- pretty(c(-3,3), 30)
y <- dnorm(x)
plot(x, y,
    type = "l",
    xlab = "Normal Deviate",
    ylab = "Density",
    yaxs = "i"
)
``` |
| What is the area under the standard normal curve to the left of z=1.96? | `pnorm(1.96)` equals 0.975 |
```

Table 5.5   Normal distribution functions *(continued)*

Problem	Solution
What is the value of the 90th percentile of a normal distribution with a mean of 500 and a standard deviation of 100?	`qnorm(.9, mean=500, sd=100)` equals 628.16
Generate 50 random normal deviates with a mean of 50 and a standard deviation of 10.	`rnorm(50, mean=50, sd=10)`

Don't worry if the plot function options are unfamiliar. They're covered in detail in chapter 11; `pretty()` is explained in table 5.7 later in this chapter.

SETTING THE SEED FOR RANDOM NUMBER GENERATION

Each time you generate pseudo-random deviates, a different seed, and therefore different results, are produced. To make your results reproducible, you can specify the seed explicitly, using the `set.seed()` function. An example is given in the next listing. Here, the `runif()` function is used to generate pseudo-random numbers from a uniform distribution on the interval 0 to 1.

Listing 5.2   Generating pseudo-random numbers from a uniform distribution

```
> runif(5)
[1] 0.8725344 0.3962501 0.6826534 0.3667821 0.9255909
> runif(5)
[1] 0.4273903 0.2641101 0.3550058 0.3233044 0.6584988
> set.seed(1234)
> runif(5)
[1] 0.1137034 0.6222994 0.6092747 0.6233794 0.8609154
> set.seed(1234)
> runif(5)
[1] 0.1137034 0.6222994 0.6092747 0.6233794 0.8609154
```

By setting the seed manually, you're able to reproduce your results. This ability can be helpful in creating examples you can access at a future time and share with others.

GENERATING MULTIVARIATE NORMAL DATA

In simulation research and Monte Carlo studies, you often want to draw data from multivariate normal distribution with a given mean vector and covariance matrix. The `mvrnorm()` function in the MASS package makes this easy. The function call is

`mvrnorm(n, mean, sigma)`

where *n* is the desired sample size, *mean* is the vector of means, and *sigma* is the variance-covariance (or correlation) matrix. In listing 5.3 you'll sample 500 observations from a three-variable multivariate normal distribution with

Mean Vector	230.7	146.7	3.6
Covariance Matrix	15360.8	6721.2	-47.1
	6721.2	4700.9	-16.5
	-47.1	-16.5	0.3

Listing 5.3 Generating data from a multivariate normal distribution

```
> library(MASS)
> options(digits=3)
> set.seed(1234)          ◄——❶ Set random number seed

> mean <- c(230.7, 146.7, 3.6)                   ◄——
> sigma <- matrix(c(15360.8, 6721.2, -47.1,          ❷ Specify mean vector,
                    6721.2, 4700.9, -16.5,             covariance matrix
                    -47.1,  -16.5,   0.3), nrow=3, ncol=3)

> mydata <- mvrnorm(500, mean, sigma)     ◄——❸ Generate data
> mydata <- as.data.frame(mydata)
> names(mydata) <- c("y","x1","x2")

> dim(mydata)                ◄——❹ View results
[1] 500 3
> head(mydata, n=10)
        y    x1   x2
1    98.8  41.3 4.35
2   244.5 205.2 3.57
3   375.7 186.7 3.69
4   -59.2  11.2 4.23
5   313.0 111.0 2.91
6   288.8 185.1 4.18
7   134.8 165.0 3.68
8   171.7  97.4 3.81
9   167.3 101.0 4.01
10  121.1  94.5 3.76
```

In listing 5.3, you set a random number seed so that you can reproduce the results at a later time ❶. You specify the desired mean vector and variance-covariance matrix ❷, and generate 500 pseudo-random observations ❸. For convenience, the results are converted from a matrix to a data frame, and the variables are given names. Finally, you confirm that you have 500 observations and 3 variables, and print out the first 10 observations ❹. Note that because a correlation matrix is also a covariance matrix, you could've specified the correlations structure directly.

The probability functions in R allow you to generate simulated data, sampled from distributions with known characteristics. Statistical methods that rely on simulated data have grown exponentially in recent years, and you'll see several examples of these in later chapters.

5.2.4 Character functions

Although mathematical and statistical functions operate on numerical data, character functions extract information from textual data, or reformat textual data for printing and reporting. For example, you may want to concatenate a person's first name and last name, ensuring that the first letter of each is capitalized. Or you may want to count the instances of obscenities in open-ended feedback. Some of the most useful character functions are listed in table 5.6.

Table 5.6   Character functions

Function	Description
`nchar(x)`	Counts the number of characters of x `x <- c("ab", "cde", "fghij")` `length(x)` returns 3 (see table 5.7). `nchar(x[3])` returns 5.
`substr(x, start, stop)`	Extract or replace substrings in a character vector. `x <- "abcdef"` `substr(x, 2, 4)` returns "bcd". `substr(x, 2, 4) <- "222` `"` (x is now `"a222ef"`).
`grep(pattern, x, ignore.case=FALSE, fixed=FALSE)`	Search for pattern in x. If `fixed=FALSE`, then *pattern* is a regular expression. If `fixed=TRUE`, then *pattern* is a text string. Returns matching indices. `grep("A", c("b","A","c"), fixed=TRUE)` returns 2.
`sub(pattern, replacement, x, ignore.case=FALSE, fixed=FALSE)`	Find *pattern* in x and substitute with *replacement* text. If `fixed=FALSE` then *pattern* is a regular expression. If `fixed=TRUE` then *pattern* is a text string. `sub("\\s",".","Hello There")` returns `Hello.There`. Note `"\s"` is a regular expression for finding whitespace; use `"\\s"` instead because `"\"` is R's escape character (see section 1.3.3).
`strsplit(x, split, fixed=FALSE)`	Split the elements of character vector x at *split*. If `fixed=FALSE`, then *pattern* is a regular expression. If `fixed=TRUE`, then *pattern* is a text string. `y <- strsplit("abc", "")` returns a 1-component, 3-element list containing `"a" "b" "c"`. `unlist(y)[2]` and `sapply(y, "[", 2)` both return "b".
`paste(..., sep="")`	Concatenate strings after using `sep` string to separate them. `paste("x", 1:3, sep="")` returns `c("x1", "x2", "x3")`. `paste("x",1:3,sep="M")` returns `c("xM1","xM2" "xM3")`. `paste("Today is", date())` returns `Today is Thu Jun 25 14:17:32 2011` (I changed the date to appear more current.)
`toupper(x)`	Uppercase `toupper("abc")` returns "ABC".
`tolower(x)`	Lowercase `tolower("ABC")` returns "abc".

Note that the functions `grep()`, `sub()`, and `strsplit()` can search for a text string (`fixed=TRUE`) or a regular expression (`fixed=FALSE`) (`FALSE` is the default). Regular expressions provide a clear and concise syntax for matching a pattern of text. For example, the regular expression

```
^[hc]?at
```

matches any string that starts with 0 or one occurrences of h or c, followed by at. The expression therefore matches hat, cat, and at, but not bat. To learn more, see the *regular expression* entry in Wikipedia.

5.2.5 Other useful functions

The functions in table 5.7 are also quite useful for data management and manipulation, but they don't fit cleanly into the other categories.

Table 5.7 Other useful functions

Function	Description
length(x)	Length of object x. `x <- c(2, 5, 6, 9)` `length(x)` returns 4.
seq(from, to, by)	Generate a sequence. `indices <- seq(1,10,2)` `indices` is c(1, 3, 5, 7, 9).
rep(x, n)	Repeat x n times. `y <- rep(1:3, 2)` `y` is c(1, 2, 3, 1, 2, 3).
cut(x, n)	Divide continuous variable x into factor with n levels. To create an ordered factor, include the option `ordered_result = TRUE`.
pretty(x, n)	Create pretty breakpoints. Divides a continuous variable x into n intervals, by selecting n+1 equally spaced rounded values. Often used in plotting.

cat(… , file = "myfile", append = FALSE)	Concatenates the objects in … and outputs them to the screen or to a file (if one is declared) .
	`firstname <- c("Jane")`
	`cat("Hello" , firstname, "\n").`

The last example in the table demonstrates the use of escape characters in printing. Use \n for new lines, \t for tabs, \' for a single quote, \b for backspace, and so forth (type `?Quotes` for more information). For example, the code

```
name <- "Bob"
cat( "Hello", name, "\b.\n", "Isn\'t R", "\t", "GREAT?\n")
```

produces

```
Hello Bob.
 Isn't R        GREAT?
```

Note that the second line is indented one space. When `cat` concatenates objects for output, it separates each by a space. That's why you include the backspace (`\b`) escape character before the period. Otherwise it would have produced "Hello Bob ."

How you apply the functions you've covered so far to numbers, strings, and vectors is intuitive and straightforward, but how do you apply them to matrices and data frames? That's the subject of the next section.

5.2.6   *Applying functions to matrices and data frames*

One of the interesting features of R functions is that they can be applied to a variety of data objects (scalars, vectors, matrices, arrays, and data frames). The following listing provides an example.

Listing 5.4   Applying functions to data objects

```
> a <- 5
> sqrt(a)
[1] 2.236068
> b <- c(1.243, 5.654, 2.99)
> round(b)
[1] 1 6 3
> c <- matrix(runif(12), nrow=3)
> c
        [,1]  [,2]  [,3]  [,4]
[1,] 0.4205 0.355 0.699 0.323
[2,] 0.0270 0.601 0.181 0.926
[3,] 0.6682 0.319 0.599 0.215
> log(c)
        [,1]   [,2]   [,3]   [,4]
[1,] -0.866 -1.036 -0.358 -1.130
[2,] -3.614 -0.508 -1.711 -0.077
[3,] -0.403 -1.144 -0.513 -1.538
> mean(c)
[1] 0.444
```

Notice that the mean of matrix c in listing 5.4 results in a scalar (0.444). The `mean()` function took the average of all 12 elements in the matrix. But what if you wanted the 3 row means or the 4 column means?

R provides a function, `apply()`, that allows you to `apply` an arbitrary function to any dimension of a matrix, array, or data frame. The format for the apply function is

```
apply(x, MARGIN, FUN, ...)
```

where *x* is the data object, *MARGIN* is the dimension index, *FUN* is a function you specify, and `...` are any parameters you want to pass to *FUN*. In a matrix or data frame `MARGIN=1` indicates rows and `MARGIN=2` indicates columns. Take a look at the examples in listing 5.5.

Listing 5.5   Applying a function to the rows (columns) of a matrix

```
> mydata <- matrix(rnorm(30), nrow=6)                      ◄── ❶ Generate data
> mydata
          [,1]    [,2]     [,3]     [,4]     [,5]
[1,]   0.71298   1.368  -0.8320  -1.234  -0.790
[2,]  -0.15096  -1.149  -1.0001  -0.725   0.506
[3,]  -1.77770   0.519  -0.6675   0.721  -1.350
[4,]  -0.00132  -0.308   0.9117  -1.391   1.558
[5,]  -0.00543   0.378  -0.0906  -1.485  -0.350
[6,]  -0.52178  -0.539  -1.7347   2.050   1.569
> apply(mydata, 1, mean)                                   ◄── ❷ Calculate row means
[1] -0.155 -0.504 -0.511  0.154 -0.310  0.165
> apply(mydata, 2, mean)                                   ◄── ❸ Calculate column means
[1] -0.2907  0.0449 -0.5688 -0.3442  0.1906
> apply(mydata, 2, mean, trim=0.2)                         ◄──┐ Calculate trimmed
[1] -0.1699  0.0127 -0.6475 -0.6575  0.2312                 ❹ column means
```

You start by generating a 6 x 5 matrix containing random normal variates ❶. Then you calculate the 6 row means ❷, and 5 column means ❸. Finally, you calculate trimmed column means (in this case, means based on the middle 60 percent of the data, with the bottom 20 percent and top 20 percent of values discarded) ❹.

Because *FUN* can be any R function, including a function that you write yourself (see section 5.4), apply() is a powerful mechanism. While apply() applies a function over the margins of an array, lapply() and sapply() apply a function over a list. You'll see an example of sapply (which is a user-friendly version of lapply) in the next section.

You now have all the tools you need to solve the data challenge in section 5.1, so let's give it a try.

5.3   *A solution for our data management challenge*

Your challenge from section 5.1 is to combine subject test scores into a single performance indicator for each student, grade each student from A to F based on their relative standing (top 20 percent, next 20 percent, etc.), and sort the roster by students' last name, followed by first name. A solution is given in the following listing.

Listing 5.6   A solution to the learning example

```
> options(digits=2)

> Student <- c("John Davis", "Angela Williams", "Bullwinkle Moose",
               "David Jones", "Janice Markhammer", "Cheryl Cushing",
               "Reuven Ytzrhak", "Greg Knox", "Joel England",
               "Mary Rayburn")
> Math <- c(502, 600, 412, 358, 495, 512, 410, 625, 573, 522)
> Science <- c(95, 99, 80, 82, 75, 85, 80, 95, 89, 86)
> English <- c(25, 22, 18, 15, 20, 28, 15, 30, 27, 18)
> roster <- data.frame(Student, Math, Science, English,
                       stringsAsFactors=FALSE)

> z <- scale(roster[,2:4])                                 ◄──┐ Obtain performance
> score <- apply(z, 1, mean)                                 │ scores
> roster <- cbind(roster, score)
```

```
> y <- quantile(score, c(.8,.6,.4,.2))                        ⟵── Grade students
> roster$grade[score >= y[1]] <- "A"
> roster$grade[score < y[1] & score >= y[2]] <- "B"
> roster$grade[score < y[2] & score >= y[3]] <- "C"
> roster$grade[score < y[3] & score >= y[4]] <- "D"
> roster$grade[score < y[4]] <- "F"

> name <- strsplit((roster$Student), " ")          ⟵──┐ Extract last and
> lastname <- sapply(name, "[", 2)                      │ first names
> firstname <- sapply(name, "[", 1)
> roster <- cbind(firstname,lastname, roster[,-1])

> roster <- roster[order(lastname,firstname),]     ⟵──┐ Sort by last and
                                                         │ first names
> roster
      Firstname    Lastname Math Science English score grade
6        Cheryl     Cushing  512      85      28  0.35     C
1          John       Davis  502      95      25  0.56     B
9          Joel     England  573      89      27  0.70     B
4         David       Jones  358      82      15 -1.16     F
8          Greg        Knox  625      95      30  1.34     A
5        Janice  Markhammer  495      75      20 -0.63     D
3    Bullwinkle       Moose  412      80      18 -0.86     D
10         Mary     Rayburn  522      86      18 -0.18     C
2        Angela    Williams  600      99      22  0.92     A
7        Reuven     Ytzrhak  410      80      15 -1.05     F
```

see → p. 106

The code is dense so let's walk through the solution step by step:

Step 1. The original student roster is given. The options(digits=2) limits the number of digits printed after the decimal place and makes the printouts easier to read.

```
> options(digits=2)
> roster
             Student Math Science English
1        John Davis   502      95      25
2    Angela Williams  600      99      22
3    Bullwinkle Moose 412      80      18
4       David Jones   358      82      15
5   Janice Markhammer 495      75      20
6     Cheryl Cushing  512      85      28
7     Reuven Ytzrhak  410      80      15
8          Greg Knox  625      95      30
9       Joel England  573      89      27
10      Mary Rayburn  522      86      18
```

Step 2. Because the Math, Science, and English tests are reported on different scales (with widely differing means and standard deviations), you need to make them comparable before combining them. One way to do this is to standardize the variables so that each test is reported in standard deviation units, rather than in their original scales. You can do this with the scale() function:

```
> z <- scale(roster[,2:4])
> z
        Math Science English
```

```
 [1,]   0.013   1.078   0.587
 [2,]   1.143   1.591   0.037
 [3,]  -1.026  -0.847  -0.697
 [4,]  -1.649  -0.590  -1.247
 [5,]  -0.068  -1.489  -0.330
 [6,]   0.128  -0.205   1.137
 [7,]  -1.049  -0.847  -1.247
 [8,]   1.432   1.078   1.504
 [9,]   0.832   0.308   0.954
[10,]   0.243  -0.077  -0.697
```

Step 3. You can then get a performance score for each student by calculating the row means using the mean() function and adding it to the roster using the cbind() function:

```
> score <- apply(z, 1, mean)
> roster <- cbind(roster, score)
> roster
             Student  Math Science English   score
1          John Davis  502      95      25   0.559
2     Angela Williams  600      99      22   0.924
3     Bullwinkle Moose  412      80      18  -0.857
4         David Jones  358      82      15  -1.162
5   Janice Markhammer  495      75      20  -0.629
6      Cheryl Cushing  512      85      28   0.353
7      Reuven Ytzrhak  410      80      15  -1.048
8           Greg Knox  625      95      30   1.338
9        Joel England  573      89      27   0.698
10      Mary Rayburn  522      86      18  -0.177
```

Step 4. The quantile() function gives you the percentile rank of each student's performance score. You see that the cutoff for an A is 0.74, for a B is 0.44, and so on.

```
> y <- quantile(roster$score, c(.8,.6,.4,.2))
> y
  80%    60%    40%    20%
 0.74   0.44  -0.36  -0.89
```

Step 5. Using logical operators, you can recode students' percentile ranks into a new categorical grade variable. This creates the variable grade in the roster data frame.

```
> roster$grade[score >= y[1]] <- "A"
> roster$grade[score < y[1] & score >= y[2]] <- "B"
> roster$grade[score < y[2] & score >= y[3]] <- "C"
> roster$grade[score < y[3] & score >= y[4]] <- "D"
> roster$grade[score < y[4]] <- "F"
> roster
             Student Math Science English   score grade
1          John Davis  502      95      25   0.559     B
2     Angela Williams  600      99      22   0.924     A
3     Bullwinkle Moose  412      80      18  -0.857     D
4         David Jones  358      82      15  -1.162     F
5   Janice Markhammer  495      75      20  -0.629     D
6      Cheryl Cushing  512      85      28   0.353     C
7      Reuven Ytzrhak  410      80      15  -1.048     F
8           Greg Knox  625      95      30   1.338     A
```

```
9        Joel England  573      89      27  0.698      B
10       Mary Rayburn  522      86      18 -0.177      C
```

Step 6. You'll use the `strsplit()` function to break student names into first name and last name at the space character. Applying `strsplit()` to a vector of strings returns a list:

```
> name <- strsplit((roster$Student), " ")
> name

[[1]]
[1] "John"  "Davis"

[[2]]
[1] "Angela"    "Williams"

[[3]]
[1] "Bullwinkle" "Moose"

[[4]]
[1] "David" "Jones"

[[5]]
[1] "Janice"      "Markhammer"

[[6]]
[1] "Cheryl"  "Cushing"

[[7]]
[1] "Reuven"  "Ytzrhak"

[[8]]
[1] "Greg" "Knox"

[[9]]
[1] "Joel"     "England"

[[10]]
[1] "Mary"     "Rayburn"
```

Step 7. You can use the `sapply()` function to take the first element of each component and put it in a firstname vector, and the second element of each component and put it in a lastname vector. `"["` is a function that extracts part of an object—here the first or second component of the list `name`. You'll use `cbind()` to add them to the roster. Because you no longer need the student variable, you'll drop it (with the −1 in the roster index).

```
> Firstname <- sapply(name, "[", 1)
> Lastname <- sapply(name, "[", 2)
> roster <- cbind(Firstname, Lastname, roster[,-1])
> roster
    Firstname   Lastname Math Science English  score grade
1        John      Davis  502      95      25  0.559     B
2      Angela   Williams  600      99      22  0.924     A
3  Bullwinkle      Moose  412      80      18 -0.857     D
```

```
4        David      Jones   358      82     15 -1.162    F
5       Janice Markhammer   495      75     20 -0.629    D
6       Cheryl    Cushing   512      85     28  0.353    C
7       Reuven    Ytzrhak   410      80     15 -1.048    F
8         Greg       Knox   625      95     30  1.338    A
9         Joel    England   573      89     27  0.698    B
10        Mary    Rayburn   522      86     18 -0.177    C
```

Step 8. Finally, you can sort the dataset by first and last name using the order() function:

```
> roster[order(Lastname,Firstname),]
      Firstname    Lastname  Math  Science  English  score  grade
6        Cheryl     Cushing   512       85       28   0.35      C
1          John       Davis   502       95       25   0.56      B
9          Joel     England   573       89       27   0.70      B
4         David       Jones   358       82       15  -1.16      F
8          Greg        Knox   625       95       30   1.34      A
5        Janice  Markhammer   495       75       20  -0.63      D
3     Bullwinkle       Moose   412       80       18  -0.86      D
10         Mary     Rayburn   522       86       18  -0.18      C
2        Angela    Williams   600       99       22   0.92      A
7        Reuven     Ytzrhak   410       80       15  -1.05      F
```

Voilà! Piece of cake!

There are many other ways to accomplish these tasks, but this code helps capture the flavor of these functions. Now it's time to look at control structures and user-written functions.

5.4 Control flow

In the normal course of events, the statements in an R program are executed sequentially from the top of the program to the bottom. But there are times that you'll want to execute some statements repetitively, while only executing other statements if certain conditions are met. This is where control-flow constructs come in.

R has the standard control structures you'd expect to see in a modern programming language. First you'll go through the constructs used for conditional execution, followed by the constructs used for looping.

For the syntax examples throughout this section, keep the following in mind:

- *statement* is a single R statement or a compound statement (a group of R statements enclosed in curly braces { } and separated by semicolons).
- *cond* is an expression that resolves to true or false.
- *expr* is a statement that evaluates to a number or character string.
- *seq* is a sequence of numbers or character strings.

After we discuss control-flow constructs, you'll learn how to write your functions.

5.4.1 Repetition and looping

Looping constructs repetitively execute a statement or series of statements until a condition isn't true. These include the for and while structures.

FOR

The `for` loop executes a statement repetitively until a variable's value is no longer contained in the sequence `seq`. The syntax is

```
for (var in seq) statement
```

In this example

```
for (i in 1:10)  print("Hello")
```

the word Hello is printed 10 times.

WHILE

A `while` loop executes a statement repetitively until the condition is no longer true. The syntax is

```
while (cond) statement
```

In a second example, the code

```
i <- 10
while (i > 0) {print("Hello"); i <- i - 1}
```

once again prints the word Hello 10 times. Make sure that the statements inside the brackets modify the `while` condition so that sooner or later it's no longer true—otherwise the loop will never end! In the previous example, the statement

```
i <- i - 1
```

subtracts 1 from object i on each loop, so that after the tenth loop it's no longer larger than 0. If you instead added 1 on each loop, R would never stop saying Hello. This is why `while` loops can be more dangerous than other looping constructs.

Looping in R can be inefficient and time consuming when you're processing the rows or columns of large datasets. Whenever possible, it's better to use R's built-in numerical and character functions in conjunction with the `apply` family of functions.

5.4.2 *Conditional execution*

In conditional execution, a statement or statements are only executed if a specified condition is met. These constructs include `if-else`, `ifelse`, and `switch`.

IF-ELSE

The `if-else` control structure executes a statement if a given condition is true. Optionally, a different statement is executed if the condition is false. The syntax is

```
if (cond) statement
if (cond) statement1 else statement2
```

Here are examples:

```
if (is.character(grade)) grade <- as.factor(grade)
if (!is.factor(grade)) grade <- as.factor(grade) else print("Grade already
    is a factor")
```

In the first instance, if grade is a character vector, it's converted into a factor. In the second instance, one of two statements is executed. If grade isn't a factor (note the ! symbol), it's turned into one. If it is a factor, then the message is printed.

IFELSE

The `ifelse` construct is a compact and vectorized version of the `if-else` construct. The syntax is

```
ifelse(cond, statement1, statement2)
```

The first statement is executed if *cond* is TRUE. If *cond* is FALSE, the second statement is executed. Here are examples:

```
ifelse(score > 0.5, print("Passed"), print("Failed"))
outcome <- ifelse (score > 0.5, "Passed", "Failed")
```

Use `ifelse` when you want to take a binary action or when you want to input and output vectors from the construct.

SWITCH

`switch` chooses statements based on the value of an expression. The syntax is

```
switch(expr, ...)
```

where . . . represents statements tied to the possible outcome values of *expr*. It's easiest to understand how `switch` works by looking at the example in the following listing.

Listing 5.7 A `switch` example

```
> feelings <- c("sad", "afraid")
> for (i in feelings)
    print(
      switch(i,
        happy  = "I am glad you are happy",
        afraid = "There is nothing to fear",
        sad    = "Cheer up",
        angry  = "Calm down now"
      )
    )

[1] "Cheer up"
[1] "There is nothing to fear"
```

This is a silly example but shows the main features. You'll learn how to use `switch` in user-written functions in the next section.

5.5 *User-written functions*

One of R's greatest strengths is the user's ability to add functions. In fact, many of the functions in R are functions of existing functions. The structure of a function looks like this:

```
myfunction <- function(arg1, arg2, ... ){
  statements
  return(object)
}
```

Objects in the function are local to the function. The object returned can be any data type, from scalar to list. Let's take a look at an example.

Say you'd like to have a function that calculates the central tendency and spread of data objects. The function should give you a choice between parametric (mean and standard deviation) and nonparametric (median and median absolute deviation) statistics. The results should be returned as a named list. Additionally, the user should have the choice of automatically printing the results, or not. Unless otherwise specified, the function's default behavior should be to calculate parametric statistics and not print the results. One solution is given in the following listing.

Listing 5.8   `mystats()`: a user-written function for summary statistics

```
mystats <- function(x, parametric=TRUE, print=FALSE) {
  if (parametric) {
    center <- mean(x); spread <- sd(x)
  } else {
    center <- median(x); spread <- mad(x)
  }
  if (print & parametric) {
    cat("Mean=", center, "\n", "SD=", spread, "\n")
  } else if (print & !parametric) {
    cat("Median=", center, "\n", "MAD=", spread, "\n")
  }
  result <- list(center=center, spread=spread)
  return(result)
}
```

To see your function in action, first generate some data (a random sample of size 500 from a normal distribution):

```
set.seed(1234)
x <- rnorm(500)
```

After executing the statement

```
y <- mystats(x)
```

`y$center` will contain the mean (0.00184) and `y$spread` will contain the standard deviation (1.03). No output is produced. If you execute the statement

```
y <- mystats(x, parametric=FALSE, print=TRUE)
```

`y$center` will contain the median (–0.0207) and `y$spread` will contain the median absolute deviation (1.001). In addition, the following output is produced:

```
Median= -0.0207
MAD= 1
```

Next, let's look at a user-written function that uses the `switch` construct. This function gives the user a choice regarding the format of today's date. Values that are assigned to parameters in the function declaration are taken as defaults. In the `mydate()` function, `long` is the default format for dates if `type` isn't specified:

```
mydate <- function(type="long") {
  switch(type,
    long =  format(Sys.time(), "%A %B %d %Y"),
    short = format(Sys.time(), "%m-%d-%y"),
    cat(type, "is not a recognized type\n")
    )
}
```

Here's the function in action:

```
> mydate("long")
[1] "Thursday December 02 2010"
> mydate("short")
[1] "12-02-10"
> mydate()
[1] "Thursday December 02 2010"
> mydate("medium")
medium is not a recognized type
```

Note that the cat() function is only executed if the entered type doesn't match "long" or "short". It's usually a good idea to have an expression that catches user-supplied arguments that have been entered incorrectly.

Several functions are available that can help add error trapping and correction to your functions. You can use the function warning() to generate a warning message, message() to generate a diagnostic message, and stop() to stop execution of the current expression and carry out an error action. See each function's online help for more details.

> **TIP** Once you start writing functions of any length and complexity, access to good debugging tools becomes important. R has a number of useful built-in functions for debugging, and user-contributed packages are available that provide additional functionality. An excellent resource on this topic is Duncan Murdoch's "Debugging in R" (http://www.stats.uwo.ca/faculty/murdoch/software/debuggingR).

After creating your own functions, you may want to make them available in every session. Appendix B describes how to customize the R environment so that user-written functions are loaded automatically at startup. We'll look at additional examples of user-written functions in chapters 6 and 8.

You can accomplish a great deal using the basic techniques provided in this section. If you'd like to explore the subtleties of function writing, or want to write professional-level code that you can distribute to others, I recommend two excellent books that you'll find in the References section at the end of this book: Venables & Ripley (2000) and Chambers (2008). Together, they provide a significant level of detail and breadth of examples.

Now that we've covered user-written functions, we'll end this chapter with a discussion of data aggregation and reshaping.

5.6   Aggregation and restructuring

R provides a number of powerful methods for aggregating and reshaping data. When you aggregate data, you replace groups of observations with summary statistics based on those observations. When you reshape data, you alter the structure (rows and columns) determining how the data is organized. This section describes a variety of methods for accomplishing these tasks.

In the next two subsections, we'll use the `mtcars` data frame that's included with the base installation of R. This dataset, extracted from *Motor Trend* magazine (1974), describes the design and performance characteristics (number of cylinders, displacement, horsepower, mpg, and so on) for 34 automobiles. To learn more about the dataset, see `help(mtcars)`.

5.6.1   Transpose

The transpose (reversing rows and columns) is perhaps the simplest method of reshaping a dataset. Use the `t()` function to transpose a matrix or a data frame. In the latter case, row names become variable (column) names. An example is presented in the next listing.

Listing 5.9   Transposing a dataset

```
> cars <- mtcars[1:5,1:4]
> cars
                   mpg cyl disp  hp
Mazda RX4         21.0   6  160 110
Mazda RX4 Wag     21.0   6  160 110
Datsun 710        22.8   4  108  93
Hornet 4 Drive    21.4   6  258 110
Hornet Sportabout 18.7   8  360 175
> t(cars)
     Mazda RX4 Mazda RX4 Wag Datsun 710 Hornet 4 Drive Hornet Sportabout
mpg         21            21       22.8           21.4              18.7
cyl          6             6        4.0            6.0               8.0
disp       160           160      108.0          258.0             360.0
hp         110           110       93.0          110.0             175.0
```

Listing 5.9 uses a subset of the `mtcars` dataset in order to conserve space on the page. You'll see a more flexible way of transposing data when we look at the `shape` package later in this section.

5.6.2   Aggregating data

It's relatively easy to collapse data in R using one or more `by` variables and a defined function. The format is

```
aggregate(x, by, FUN)
```

where *x* is the data object to be collapsed, *by* is a list of variables that will be crossed to form the new observations, and *FUN* is the scalar function used to calculate summary statistics that will make up the new observation values.

As an example, we'll aggregate the `mtcars` data by number of cylinders and gears, returning means on each of the numeric variables (see the next listing).

Listing 5.10   Aggregating data

```
> options(digits=3)
> attach(mtcars)
> aggdata <-aggregate(mtcars, by=list(cyl,gear), FUN=mean, na.rm=TRUE)
> aggdata
  Group.1 Group.2  mpg cyl disp  hp drat   wt qsec  vs   am gear carb
1       4       3 21.5   4  120  97 3.70 2.46 20.0 1.0 0.00    3 1.00
2       6       3 19.8   6  242 108 2.92 3.34 19.8 1.0 0.00    3 1.00
3       8       3 15.1   8  358 194 3.12 4.10 17.1 0.0 0.00    3 3.08
4       4       4 26.9   4  103  76 4.11 2.38 19.6 1.0 0.75    4 1.50
5       6       4 19.8   6  164 116 3.91 3.09 17.7 0.5 0.50    4 4.00
6       4       5 28.2   4  108 102 4.10 1.83 16.8 0.5 1.00    5 2.00
7       6       5 19.7   6  145 175 3.62 2.77 15.5 0.0 1.00    5 6.00
8       8       5 15.4   8  326 300 3.88 3.37 14.6 0.0 1.00    5 6.00
```

In these results, Group.1 represents the number of cylinders (4, 6, or 8) and Group.2 represents the number of gears (3, 4, or 5). For example, cars with 4 cylinders and 3 gears have a mean of 21.5 miles per gallon (mpg).

When you're using the `aggregate()` function, the `by` variables must be in a list (even if there's only one). You can declare a custom name for the groups from within the list, for instance, using `by=list(Group.cyl=cyl, Group.gears=gear)`. The function specified can be any built-in or user-provided function. This gives the aggregate command a great deal of power. But when it comes to power, nothing beats the `reshape` package.

5.6.3   *The reshape package*

The `reshape` package is a tremendously versatile approach to both restructuring and aggregating datasets. Because of this versatility, it can be a bit challenging to learn. We'll go through the process slowly and use a small dataset so that it's clear what's happening. Because `reshape` isn't included in the standard installation of R, you'll need to install it one time, using `install.packages("reshape")`.

Basically, you'll "melt" data so that each row is a unique ID-variable combination. Then you'll "cast" the melted data into any shape you desire. During the cast, you can aggregate the data with any function you wish.

The dataset you'll be working with is shown in table 5.8.

In this dataset, the *measurements* are the values in the last two columns (5, 6, 3, 5, 6, 1, 2, and 4). Each measurement is uniquely identified by a combination of ID variables (in this case ID, Time, and whether the measurement is on X1 or X2). For example, the measured value 5 in the first row is

Table 5.8   The original dataset (`mydata`)

ID	Time	X1	X2
1	1	5	6
1	2	3	5
2	1	6	1
2	2	2	4

uniquely identified by knowing that it's from observation (ID) 1, at Time 1, and on variable X1.

MELTING

When you melt a dataset, you restructure it into a format where each measured variable is in its own row, along with the ID variables needed to uniquely identify it. If you melt the data from table 5.8, using the following code

```
library(reshape)
md <- melt(mydata, id=(c("id", "time")))
```

you end up with the structure shown in table 5.9.

Note that you must specify the variables needed to uniquely identify each measurement (ID and Time) and that the variable indicating the measurement variable names (X1 or X2) is created for you automatically.

Now that you have your data in a melted form, you can recast it into any shape, using the cast() function.

Table 5.9   The melted dataset

ID	Time	Variable	Value
1	1	X1	5
1	2	X1	3
2	1	X1	6
2	2	X1	2
1	1	X2	6
1	2	X2	5
2	1	X2	1
2	2	X2	4

CASTING

The cast() function starts with melted data and reshapes it using a formula that you provide and an (optional) function used to aggregate the data. The format is

```
newdata <- cast(md, formula, FUN)
```

where *md* is the melted data, *formula* describes the desired end result, and *FUN* is the (optional) aggregating function. The formula takes the form

```
rowvar1 + rowvar2 + … ~ colvar1 + colvar2 + …
```

In this formula, *rowvar1 + rowvar2 +* ... define the set of crossed variables that define the rows, and *colvar1 + colvar2 +* ... define the set of crossed variables that define the columns. See the examples in figure 5.1.

Because the formulas on the right side (d, e, and f) don't include a function, the data is reshaped. In contrast, the examples on the left side (a, b, and c) specify the mean as an aggregating function. Thus the data are not only reshaped but aggregated as well. For example, (a) gives the means on X1 and X2 averaged over time for each observation. Example (b) gives the mean scores of X1 and X2 at Time 1 and Time 2, averaged over observations. In (c) you have the mean score for each observation at Time 1 and Time 2, averaged over X1 and X2.

As you can see, the flexibility provided by the melt() and cast() functions is amazing. There are many times when you'll have to reshape or aggregate your data prior to analysis. For example, you'll typically need to place your data in what's called

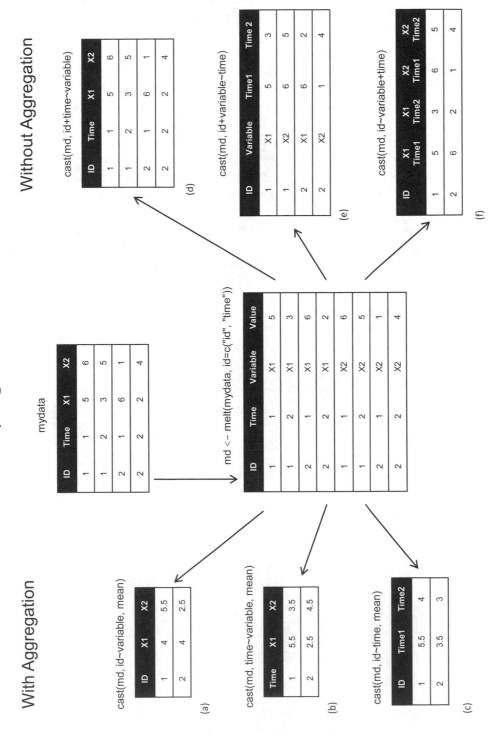

Figure 5.1 Reshaping data with the melt() and cast() functions

"long format" resembling table 5.9 when analyzing repeated measures data (data where multiple measures are recorded for each observation). See section 9.6 for an example.

5.7   *Summary*

This chapter reviewed dozens of mathematical, statistical, and probability functions that are useful for manipulating data. We saw how to apply these functions to a wide range of data objects, including vectors, matrices, and data frames. We learned to use control-flow constructs for looping and branching to execute some statements repetitively and execute other statements only when certain conditions are met. You then had a chance to write your own functions and apply them to data. Finally, we explored ways of collapsing, aggregating, and restructuring your data.

Now that you've gathered the tools you need to get your data into shape (no pun intended), we're ready to bid part 1 goodbye and enter the exciting world of data analysis! In upcoming chapters, we'll begin to explore the many statistical and graphical methods available for turning data into information.

Part 2

Basic methods

In part 1, we explored the R environment and discussed how to input data from a wide variety of sources, combine and transform it, and prepare it for further analyses. Once your data has been input and cleaned up, the next step is typically to explore each variable one at a time. This provides you with information about the distribution of each variable, which is useful in understanding the characteristics of the sample, identifying unexpected or problematic values, and selecting appropriate statistical methods. Next, a subset of variables is typically studied two at a time. This step can help you to uncover basic relationships among variables, and is a useful first step in developing more complex models.

Part 2 focuses on graphical and statistical techniques for obtaining basic information about data. Chapter 6 describes methods for visualizing the distribution of individual variables. For categorical variables, this includes bar plots, pie charts, and the newer fan plot. For numeric variables, this includes histograms, density plots, box plots, dot plots, and the less well-known violin plot. Each type of graph is useful for understanding the distribution of a single variable.

Chapter 7 describes statistical methods for summarizing individual variables and bivariate relationships. This chapter starts with coverage of descriptive statistics for numerical data based on the dataset as a whole, and on subgroups of interest. Next, the use of frequency tables and cross-tabulations for summarizing categorical data is described. The chapter ends with coverage of basic inferential methods for understanding relationships between two variables at a time, including bivariate correlations, chi-square tests, t-tests, and nonparametric methods.

When you have finished part 2, you will be able to use basic graphical and statistical methods available in R to describe your data, explore group differences, and identify significant relationships among variables.

Basic graphs

Whenever we analyze data, the first thing that we should do is *look* at it. For each variable, what are the most common values? How much variability is present? Are there any unusual observations? R provides a wealth of functions for visualizing data. In this chapter, we'll look at graphs that help you understand a single categorical or continuous variable. This topic includes

- Visualizing the distribution of variable
- Comparing groups on an outcome variable

In both cases, the variable could be continuous (for example, car mileage as miles per gallon) or categorical (for example, treatment outcome as none, some, or marked). In later chapters, we'll explore graphs that display bivariate and multivariate relationships among variables.

In the following sections, we'll explore the use of bar plots, pie charts, fan charts, histograms, kernel density plots, box plots, violin plots, and dot plots. Some of these may be familiar to you, whereas others (such as fan plots or violin plots) may be new

119

to you. Our goal, as always, is to understand your data better and to communicate this understanding to others.

Let's start with bar plots.

6.1 Bar plots

Bar plots display the distribution (frequencies) of a categorical variable through vertical or horizontal bars. In its simplest form, the format of the `barplot()` function is

```
barplot(height)
```

where *height* is a vector or matrix.

In the following examples, we'll plot the outcome of a study investigating a new treatment for rheumatoid arthritis. The data are contained in the `Arthritis` data frame distributed with the vcd package. Because the vcd package isn't included in the default R installation, be sure to download and install it before first use (`install.packages("vcd")`).

Note that the vcd package isn't needed to create bar plots. We're loading it in order to gain access to the `Arthritis` dataset. But we'll need the vcd package when creating spinogram, which are described in section 6.1.5.

6.1.1 Simple bar plots

If *height* is a vector, the values determine the heights of the bars in the plot and a vertical bar plot is produced. Including the option `horiz=TRUE` produces a horizontal bar chart instead. You can also add annotating options. The `main` option adds a plot title, whereas the `xlab` and `ylab` options add x-axis and y-axis labels, respectively.

In the Arthritis study, the variable `Improved` records the patient outcomes for individuals receiving a placebo or drug.

```
> library(vcd)
> counts <- table(Arthritis$Improved)
> counts

  None   Some Marked
    42     14     28
```

Here, we see that 28 patients showed marked improvement, 14 showed some improvement, and 42 showed no improvement. We'll discuss the use of the `table()` function to obtain cell counts more fully in chapter 7.

You can graph the variable `counts` using a vertical or horizontal bar plot. The code is provided in the following listing and the resulting graphs are displayed in figure 6.1.

Listing 6.1   Simple bar plots

```
barplot(counts,                                          ←— Simple bar plot
        main="Simple Bar Plot",
        xlab="Improvement", ylab="Frequency")

barplot(counts,                                          ←┐ Horizontal
        main="Horizontal Bar Plot",                       │ bar plot
        xlab="Frequency", ylab="Improvement",
        horiz=TRUE)
```

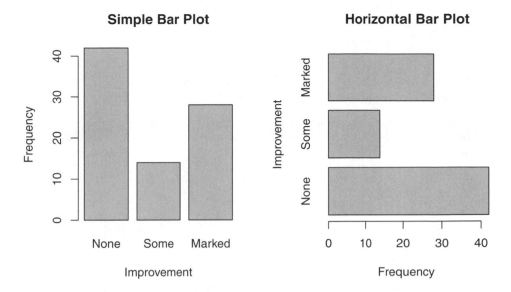

Figure 6.1 Simple vertical and horizontal bar charts

> **TIP** If the categorical variable to be plotted is a factor or ordered factor, you can create a vertical bar plot quickly with the `plot()` function. Because `Arthritis$Improved` is a factor, the code

```
plot(Arthritis$Improved, main="Simple Bar Plot",
    xlab="Improved", ylab="Frequency")
plot(Arthritis$Improved, horiz=TRUE, main="Horizontal Bar Plot",
    xlab="Frequency", ylab="Improved")
```

will generate the same bar plots as those in listing 6.1, but without the need to tabulate values with the `table()` function.

What happens if you have long labels? In section 6.1.4, you'll see how to tweak labels so that they don't overlap.

6.1.2 Stacked and grouped bar plots

If height is a matrix rather than a vector, the resulting graph will be a stacked or grouped bar plot. If `beside=FALSE` (the default), then each column of the matrix produces a bar in the plot, with the values in the column giving the heights of stacked "sub-bars." If `beside=TRUE`, each column of the matrix represents a group, and the values in each column are juxtaposed rather than stacked.

Consider the cross-tabulation of treatment type and improvement status:

```
> library(vcd)
> counts <- table(Arthritis$Improved, Arthritis$Treatment)
> counts
        Treatment
```

```
Improved Placebo Treated
   None         29      13
   Some          7       7
   Marked        7      21
```

You can graph the results as either a stacked or a grouped bar plot (see the next listing). The resulting graphs are displayed in figure 6.2.

Listing 6.2   Stacked and grouped bar plotsw

```
barplot(counts,                                      ⟵── Stacked bar plot
        main="Stacked Bar Plot",
        xlab="Treatment", ylab="Frequency",
        col=c("red", "yellow","green"),
        legend=rownames(counts))

barplot(counts,                                      ⟵── Grouped bar plot
        main="Grouped Bar Plot",
        xlab="Treatment", ylab="Frequency",
        col=c("red", "yellow", "green"),
        legend=rownames(counts), beside=TRUE)
```

The first `barplot` function produces a stacked bar plot, whereas the second produces a grouped bar plot. We've also added the `col` option to add color to the bars plotted. The `legend.text` parameter provides bar labels for the legend (which are only useful when `height` is a matrix).

In chapter 3, we covered ways to format and place the legend to maximum benefit. See if you can rearrange the legend to avoid overlap with the bars.

6.1.3 *Mean bar plots*

Bar plots needn't be based on counts or frequencies. You can create bar plots that represent means, medians, standard deviations, and so forth by using the aggregate

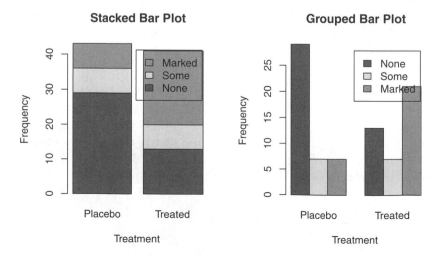

Figure 6.2   Stacked and grouped bar plots

function and passing the results to the barplot() function. The following listing shows an example, which is displayed in figure 6.3.

Listing 6.3 Bar plot for sorted mean values

```
> states <- data.frame(state.region, state.x77)
> means <- aggregate(states$Illiteracy, by=list(state.region), FUN=mean)
> means
        Group.1    x
1      Northeast 1.00
2          South 1.74
3 North Central 0.70
4           West 1.02
> means <- means[order(means$x),]          ◄─┐  Means sorted
> means                                    ❶  smallest to
        Group.1    x                          largest
3 North Central 0.70
1      Northeast 1.00
4           West 1.02
2          South 1.74
> barplot(means$x, names.arg=means$Group.1)
> title("Mean Illiteracy Rate")           ◄─❷  Title added
```

Listing 6.3 sorts the means from smallest to largest ❶. Also note that use of the title() function ❷ is equivalent to adding the main option in the plot call. means$x is the vector containing the heights of the bars, and the option names.arg=means$Group.1 is added to provide labels.

    'You can take this example further. The bars can be connected with straight line segments using the lines() function. You can also create mean bar plots with superimposed confidence intervals using the barplot2() function in the gplots package. See "barplot2: Enhanced Bar Plots" on the R Graph Gallery website (http://addictedtor.free.fr/graphiques) for an example.

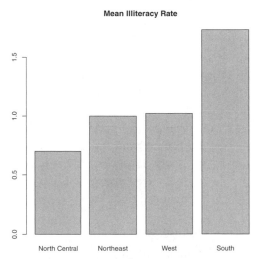

Figure 6.3 Bar plot of mean illiteracy rates for US regions sorted by rate

6.1.4 *Tweaking bar plots*

There are several ways to tweak the appearance of a bar plot. For example, with many bars, bar labels may start to overlap. You can decrease the font size using the cex. names option. Specifying values smaller than 1 will shrink the size of the labels. Optionally, the names.arg argument allows you to specify a character vector of names used to label the bars. You can also use graphical parameters to help text spacing. An example is given in the following listing with the output displayed in figure 6.4.

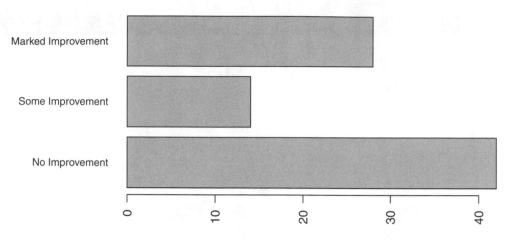

Figure 6.4   Horizontal bar plot with tweaked labels

Listing 6.4   Fitting labels in a bar plot

```
par(mar=c(5,8,4,2))
par(las=2)
counts <- table(Arthritis$Improved)

barplot(counts,
        main="Treatment Outcome",
        horiz=TRUE, cex.names=0.8,
      names.arg=c("No Improvement", "Some Improvement",
                    "Marked Improvement"))
```

In this example, we've rotated the bar labels (with `las=2`), changed the label text, and both increased the size of the y margin (with `mar`) and decreased the font size in order to fit the labels comfortably (using `cex.names=0.8`). The `par()` function allows you to make extensive modifications to the graphs that R produces by default. See chapter 3 for more details.

6.1.5   *Spinograms*

Before finishing our discussion of bar plots, let's take a look at a specialized version called a *spinogram*. In a spinogram, a stacked bar plot is rescaled so that the height of each bar is 1 and the segment heights represent proportions. Spinograms are created through the `spine()` function of the vcd package. The following code produces a simple spinogram:

```
library(vcd)
attach(Arthritis)
counts <- table(Treatment, Improved)
spine(counts, main="Spinogram Example")
detach(Arthritis)
```

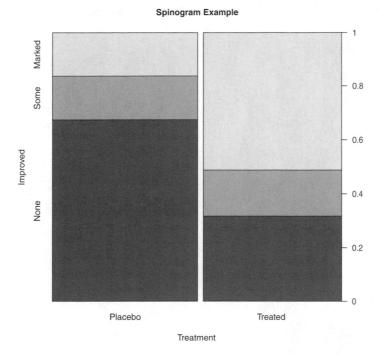

Figure 6.5 **Spinogram of arthritis treatment outcome**

The output is provided in figure 6.5. The larger percentage of patients with marked improvement in the Treated condition is quite evident when compared with the Placebo condition.

In addition to bar plots, pie charts are a popular vehicle for displaying the distribution of a categorical variable. We consider them next.

6.2 *Pie charts*

Whereas pie charts are ubiquitous in the business world, they're denigrated by most statisticians, including the authors of the R documentation. They recommend bar or dot plots over pie charts because people are able to judge length more accurately than volume. Perhaps for this reason, the pie chart options in R are quite limited when compared with other statistical software.

Pie charts are created with the function

```
pie(x, labels)
```

where *x* is a non-negative numeric vector indicating the area of each slice and *labels* provides a character vector of slice labels. Four examples are given in the next listing; the resulting plots are provided in figure 6.6.

Simple Pie Chart

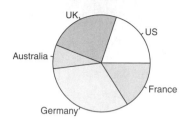

Pie Chart with Percentages

3D Pie Chart

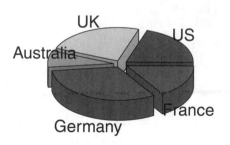

**Pie Chart from a Table
(with sample sizes)**

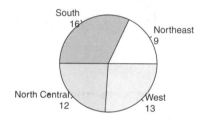

Figure 6.6　Pie chart examples

Listing 6.5　Pie charts

```
par(mfrow=c(2, 2))
slices <- c(10, 12,4, 16, 8)                                    ❶ Combine four
lbls <- c("US", "UK", "Australia", "Germany", "France")           graphs into one

pie(slices, labels = lbls,
    main="Simple Pie Chart")

pct <- round(slices/sum(slices)*100)                           ❷ Add
lbls2 <- paste(lbls, " ", pct, "%", sep="")                       percentages
pie(slices, labels=lbls2, col=rainbow(length(lbls2)),             to pie chart
    main="Pie Chart with Percentages")

library(plotrix)
pie3D(slices, labels=lbls,explode=0.1,
      main="3D Pie Chart ")

mytable <- table(state.region)                                 ❸ Create chart
lbls3 <- paste(names(mytable), "\n", mytable, sep="")             from table
pie(mytable, labels = lbls3,
    main="Pie Chart from a Table\n (with sample sizes)")
```

First you set up the plot so that four graphs are combined into one ❶. (Combining multiple graphs is covered in chapter 3.) Then you input the data that will be used for the first three graphs.

For the second pie chart ❷, you convert the sample sizes to percentages and add the information to the slice labels. The second pie chart also defines the colors of the slices using the `rainbow()` function, described in chapter 3. Here `rainbow(length(lbls2))` resolves to `rainbow(5)`, providing five colors for the graph.

The third pie chart is a 3D chart created using the `pie3D()` function from the `plotrix` package. Be sure to download and install this package before using it for the first time. If statisticians dislike pie charts, they positively despise 3D pie charts (although they may secretly find them pretty). This is because the 3D effect adds no additional insight into the data and is considered distracting eye candy.

The fourth pie chart demonstrates how to create a chart from a table ❸. In this case, you count the number of states by US region, and append the information to the labels before producing the plot.

Pie charts make it difficult to compare the values of the slices (unless the values are appended to the labels). For example, looking at the simple pie chart, can you tell how the US compares to Germany? (If you can, you're more perceptive than I am.) In an attempt to improve on this situation, a variation of the pie chart, called a fan plot, has been developed. The fan plot (Lemon & Tyagi, 2009) provides the user with a way to display both relative quantities and differences. In R, it's implemented through the `fan.plot()` function in the `plotrix` package.

Consider the following code and the resulting graph (figure 6.7):

```
library(plotrix)
slices <- c(10, 12,4, 16, 8)
lbls <- c("US", "UK", "Australia", "Germany", "France")
fan.plot(slices, labels = lbls, main="Fan Plot")
```

In a fan plot, the slices are rearranged to overlap each other and the radii have been modified so that each slice is visible. Here you can see that Germany is the largest slice and that the US slice is roughly 60 percent as large. France appears to be half as large

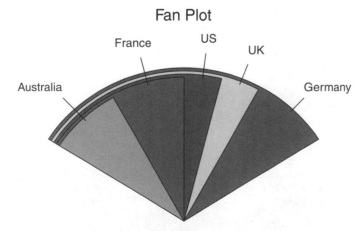

Figure 6.7 A fan plot of the country data

as Germany and twice as large as Australia. Remember that the `width` of the slice and not the radius is what's important here.

As you can see, it's much easier to determine the relative sizes of the slice in a fan plot than in a pie chart. Fan plots haven't caught on yet, but they're new. Now that we've covered pie and fan charts, let's move on to histograms. Unlike bar plots and pie charts, histograms describe the distribution of a continuous variable.

6.3   *Histograms*

Histograms display the distribution of a continuous variable by dividing up the range of scores into a specified number of bins on the x-axis and displaying the frequency of scores in each bin on the y-axis. You can create histograms with the function

```
hist(x)
```

where *x* is a numeric vector of values. The option `freq=FALSE` creates a plot based on probability densities rather than frequencies. The `breaks` option controls the number of bins. The default produces equally spaced breaks when defining the cells of the histogram. Listing 6.6 provides the code for four variations of a histogram; the results are plotted in figure 6.8.

Listing 6.6   Histograms

```
par(mfrow=c(2,2))

hist(mtcars$mpg)                                    ◄─── ❶ Simple histogram

hist(mtcars$mpg,                                    ◄─┐  With specified
     breaks=12,                                       ❷ bins and color
     col="red",
     xlab="Miles Per Gallon",
     main="Colored histogram with 12 bins")

hist(mtcars$mpg,                                    ◄─── ❸ With rug plot
     freq=FALSE,
     breaks=12,
     col="red",
     xlab="Miles Per Gallon",
     main="Histogram, rug plot, density curve")
rug(jitter(mtcars$mpg))
lines(density(mtcars$mpg), col="blue", lwd=2)       ❷

x <- mtcars$mpg                                     ◄─┐  With normal curve
h<-hist(x,                                            ❹ and frame
        breaks=12,
        col="red",
        xlab="Miles Per Gallon",
        main="Histogram with normal curve and box")
xfit<-seq(min(x), max(x), length=40)
yfit<-dnorm(xfit, mean=mean(x), sd=sd(x))
yfit <- yfit*diff(h$mids[1:2])*length(x)
lines(xfit, yfit, col="blue", lwd=2)
box()
```

The first histogram ❶ demonstrates the default plot when no options are specified. In this case, five bins are created, and the default axis labels and titles are printed. For the second histogram ❷, you've specified 12 bins, a red fill for the bars, and more attractive and informative labels and title.

The third histogram ❸ maintains the colors, bins, labels, and titles as the previous plot, but adds a density curve and rug plot overlay. The density curve is a kernel density estimate and is described in the next section. It provides a smoother description of the distribution of scores. You use the `lines()` function to overlay this curve in a blue color and a width that's twice the default thickness for lines. Finally, a rug plot is a one-dimensional representation of the actual data values. If there are many tied values, you can jitter the data on the rug plot using code like the following:

```
rug(jitter(mtcars$mpag, amount=0.01))
```

This will add a small random value to each data point (a uniform random variate between ±amount), in order to avoid overlapping points.

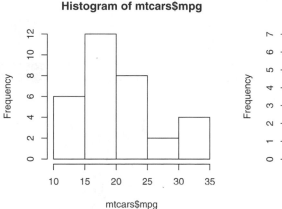

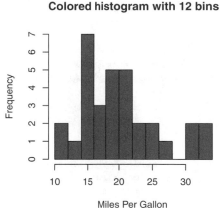

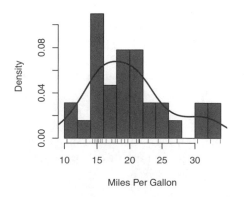

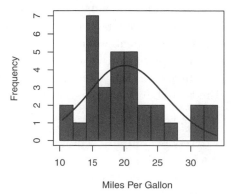

Figure 6.8   Histograms examples

The fourth histogram ❹ is similar to the second but has a superimposed normal curve and a box around the figure. The code for superimposing the normal curve comes from a suggestion posted to the R-help mailing list by Peter Dalgaard. The surrounding box is produced by the box() function.

6.4 Kernel density plots

In the previous section, you saw a kernel density plot superimposed on a histogram. Technically, kernel density estimation is a nonparametric method for estimating the probability density function of a random variable. Although the mathematics are beyond the scope of this text, in general kernel density plots can be an effective way to view the distribution of a continuous variable. The format for a density plot (that's not being superimposed on another graph) is

```
plot(density(x))
```

where *x* is a numeric vector. Because the plot() function begins a new graph, use the lines() function (listing 6.6) when superimposing a density curve on an existing graph.

Two kernel density examples are given in the next listing, and the results are plotted in figure 6.9.

Listing 6.7   Kernel density plots

see p. 65 2 graphs

```
par(mfrow=c(2,1))
d <- density(mtcars$mpg)

plot(d)

d <- density(mtcars$mpg)
plot(d, main="Kernel Density of Miles Per Gallon")
polygon(d, col="red", border="blue")
rug(mtcars$mpg, col="brown")
```

In the first plot, you see the minimal graph created with all the defaults in place. In the second plot, you add a title, color the curve blue, fill the area under the curve with solid red, and add a brown rug. The polygon() function draws a polygon whose vertices are given by x and y (provided by the density() function in this case).

Kernel density plots can be used to compare groups. This is a highly underutilized approach, probably due to a general lack of easily accessible software. Fortunately, the sm package fills this gap nicely.

The sm.density.compare() function in the sm package allows you to superimpose the kernel density plots of two or more groups. The format is

```
sm.density.compare(x, factor)
```

where x is a numeric vector and factor is a grouping variable. Be sure to install the sm package before first use. An example comparing the mpg of cars with 4, 6, or 8 cylinders is provided in listing 6.8.

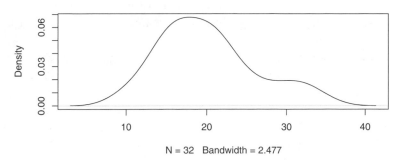

density.default(x = mtcars$mpg)

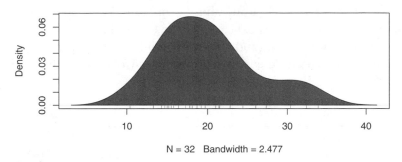

Kernel Density of Miles Per Gallon

Figure 6.9   Kernel density plots

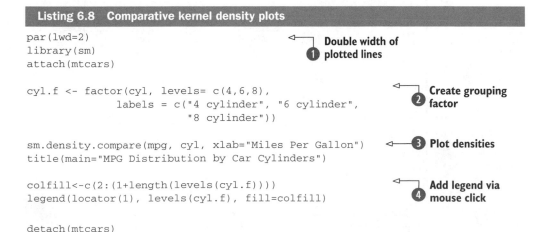

Listing 6.8   Comparative kernel density plots

```
par(lwd=2)                                              ← ❶ Double width of
library(sm)                                                 plotted lines
attach(mtcars)

cyl.f <- factor(cyl, levels= c(4,6,8),                  ← ❷ Create grouping
          labels = c("4 cylinder", "6 cylinder",             factor
                     "8 cylinder"))

sm.density.compare(mpg, cyl, xlab="Miles Per Gallon")   ← ❸ Plot densities
title(main="MPG Distribution by Car Cylinders")

colfill<-c(2:(1+length(levels(cyl.f))))                 ← ❹ Add legend via
legend(locator(1), levels(cyl.f), fill=colfill)              mouse click

detach(mtcars)
```

The `par()` function is used to double the width of the plotted lines (`lwd=2`) so that they'd be more readable in this book ❶. The `sm` packages is loaded and the `mtcars` data frame is attached.

In the `mtcars` data frame ❷, the variable `cyl` is a numeric variable coded 4, 6, or 8. `cyl` is transformed into a factor, named `cyl.f`, in order to provide value labels for the plot. The `sm.density.compare()` function creates the plot ❸ and a `title()` statement adds a main title.

Finally, you add a legend to improve interpretability ❹. (Legends are covered in chapter 3.) First, a vector of colors is created. Here `colfill` is `c(2, 3, 4)`. Then a legend is added to the plot via the `legend()` function. The `locator(1)` option indicates that you'll place the legend interactively by clicking on the graph where you want the legend to appear. The second option provides a character vector of the labels. The third option assigns a color from the vector `colfill` to each level of `cyl.f`. The results are displayed in figure 6.10.

As you can see, overlapping kernel density plots can be a powerful way to compare groups of observations on an outcome variable. Here you can see both the shapes of the distribution of scores for each group and the amount of overlap between groups. (The moral of the story is that my next car will have four cylinders—or a battery.)

Box plots are also a wonderful (and more commonly used) graphical approach to visualizing distributions and differences among groups. We'll discuss them next.

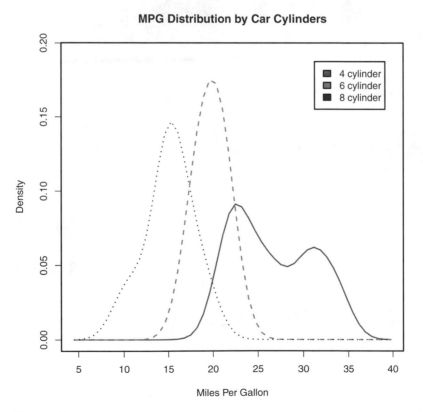

Figure 6.10   Kernel density plots of mpg by number of cylinders

6.5   Box plots

A "box-and-whiskers" plot describes the distribution of a continuous variable by plotting its five-number summary: the minimum, lower quartile (25th percentile), median (50th percentile), upper quartile (75th percentile), and maximum. It can also display observations that may be outliers (values outside the range of ± 1.5*IQR, where IQR is the interquartile range defined as the upper quartile minus the lower quartile). For example:

```
boxplot(mtcars$mpg, main="Box plot", ylab="Miles per Gallon")
```

produces the plot shown in figure 6.11. I added annotations by hand to illustrate the components.

By default, each whisker extends to the most extreme data point, which is no more than the 1.5 times the interquartile range for the box. Values outside this range are depicted as dots (not shown here).

For example, in our sample of cars the median mpg is 19.2, 50 percent of the scores fall between 15.3 and 22.8, the smallest value is 10.4, and the largest value is 33.9. How did I read this so precisely from the graph? Issuing `boxplot.stats(mtcars$mpg)`

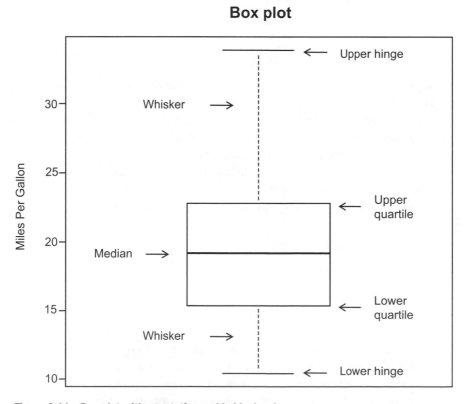

Figure 6.11   Box plot with annotations added by hand

prints the statistics used to build the graph (in other words, I cheated). There doesn't appear to be any outliers, and there is a mild positive skew (the upper whisker is longer than the lower whisker).

6.5.1 Using parallel box plots to compare groups

Box plots can be created for individual variables or for variables by group. The format is

```
boxplot(formula, data=dataframe)
```

where *formula* is a formula and *dataframe* denotes the data frame (or list) providing the data. An example of a formula is y ~ A, where a separate box plot for numeric variable y is generated for each value of categorical variable A. The formula y ~ A*B would produce a box plot of numeric variable y, for each combination of levels in categorical variables A and B.

Adding the option varwidth=TRUE will make the box plot widths proportional to the square root of their sample sizes. Add horizontal=TRUE to reverse the axis orientation.

In the following code, we revisit the impact of four, six, and eight cylinders on auto mpg with parallel box plots. The plot is provided in figure 6.12.

```
boxplot(mpg ~ cyl, data=mtcars,
        main="Car Mileage Data",
        xlab="Number of Cylinders",
        ylab="Miles Per Gallon")
```

You can see in figure 6.12 that there's a good separation of groups based on gas mileage. You can also see that the distribution of mpg for six-cylinder cars is more symmetrical than for the other two car types. Cars with four cylinders show the greatest spread (and positive skew) of mpg scores, when compared with six- and eight-cylinder cars. There's also an outlier in the eight-cylinder group.

Box plots are very versatile. By adding notch=TRUE, you get *notched* box plots. If two boxes' notches don't overlap, there's strong evidence that their medians differ (Chambers et al., 1983, p. 62). The following code will create notched box plots for our mpg example:

```
boxplot(mpg ~ cyl, data=mtcars,
        notch=TRUE,
        varwidth=TRUE,
        col="red",
        main="Car Mileage Data",
        xlab="Number of Cylinders",
        ylab="Miles Per Gallon")
```

The col option fills the box plots with a red color, and varwidth=TRUE produces box plots with widths that are proportional to their sample sizes.

You can see in figure 6.13 that the median car mileage for four-, six-, and eight-cylinder cars differ. Mileage clearly decreases with number of cylinders.

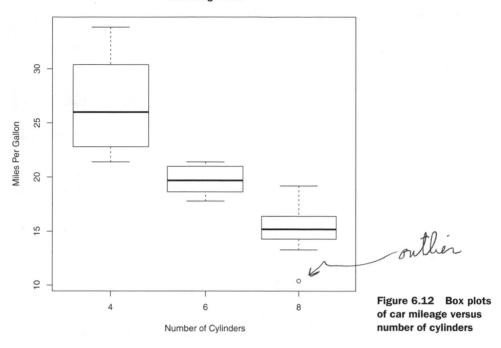

Figure 6.12 Box plots of car mileage versus number of cylinders

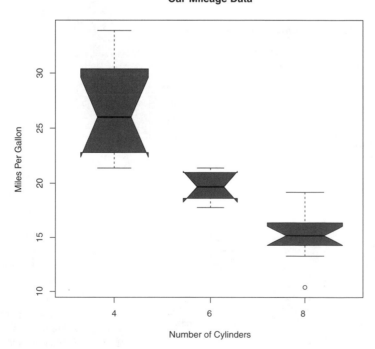

Figure 6.13 Notched box plots for car mileage versus number of cylinders

Finally, you can produce box plots for more than one grouping factor. Listing 6.9 provides box plots for mpg versus the number of cylinders and transmission type in an automobile. Again, you use the col option to fill the box plots with color. Note that colors recycle. In this case, there are six box plots and only two specified colors, so the colors repeat three times.

Listing 6.9   Box plots for two crossed factors

```
mtcars$cyl.f <- factor(mtcars$cyl,                    ◁───┐  Create factor for # of
                   levels=c(4,6,8),                        │  cylinders
                   labels=c("4","6","8"))

mtcars$am.f <- factor(mtcars$am,                      ◁───┐  Create factor for
                   levels=c(0,1),                          │  transmission type
                   labels=c("auto", "standard"))

boxplot(mpg ~ am.f *cyl.f,                            ◁───── Generate box plot
        data=mtcars,
        varwidth=TRUE,
        col=c("gold","darkgreen"),
        main="MPG Distribution by Auto Type",
        xlab="Auto Type")
```

The plot is provided in figure 6.14.

From figure 6.14 it's again clear that median mileage decreases with cylinder number. For four- and six-cylinder cars, mileage is higher for standard transmissions. But for eight-cylinder cars there doesn't appear to be a difference. You can also see from the

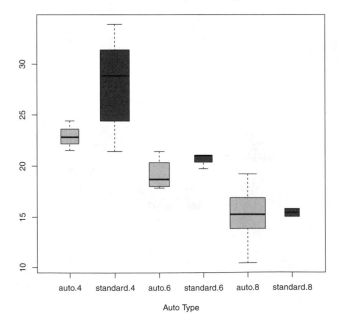

Figure 6.14   Box plots for car mileage versus transmission type and number of cylinders

widths of the box plots that standard four-cylinder and automatic eight-cylinder cars are the most common in this dataset.

6.5.2   Violin plots

Before we end our discussion of box plots, it's worth examining a variation called a violin plot. A violin plot is a combination of a box plot and a kernel density plot. You can create one using the `vioplot()` function from the `vioplot` package. Be sure to install the `vioplot` package before first use.

The format for the `vioplot()` function is

```
vioplot(x1, x2, … , names=, col=)
```

where *x1*, *x2*, … represent one or more numeric vectors to be plotted (one violin plot will be produced for each vector). The `names` parameter provides a character vector of labels for the violin plots, and `col` is a vector specifying the colors for each violin plot. An example is given in the following listing.

Listing 6.10   Violin plots

```
library(vioplot)
x1 <- mtcars$mpg[mtcars$cyl==4]
x2 <- mtcars$mpg[mtcars$cyl==6]
x3 <- mtcars$mpg[mtcars$cyl==8]
vioplot(x1, x2, x3,
        names=c("4 cyl", "6 cyl", "8 cyl"),
        col="gold")
title("Violin Plots of Miles Per Gallon")
```

Note that the `vioplot()` function requires you to separate the groups to be plotted into separate variables. The results are displayed in figure 6.15.

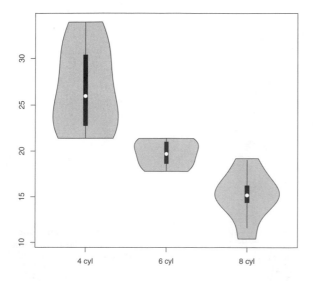

Figure 6.15   Violin plots of mpg versus number of cylinders

Violin plots are basically kernel density plots superimposed in a mirror image fashion over box plots. Here, the white dot is the median, the black boxes range from the lower to the upper quartile, and the thin black lines represent the whiskers. The outer shape provides the kernel density plots. Violin plots haven't really caught on yet. Again, this may be due to a lack of easily accessible software. Time will tell.

We'll end this chapter with a look at dot plots. Unlike the graphs you've seen previously, dot plots plot every value for a variable.

6.6   Dot plots

Dot plots provide a method of plotting a large number of labeled values on a simple horizontal scale. You create them with the `dotchart()` function, using the format

```
dotchart(x, labels=)
```

where *x* is a numeric vector and `labels` specifies a vector that labels each point. You can add a `groups` option to designate a factor specifying how the elements of *x* are grouped. If so, the option `gcolor` controls the color of the groups label and `cex` controls the size of the labels. Here's an example with the `mtcars` dataset:

```
dotchart(mtcars$mpg, labels=row.names(mtcars), cex=.7,
        main="Gas Mileage for Car Models",
        xlab="Miles Per Gallon")
```

The resulting plot is given in figure 6.16.

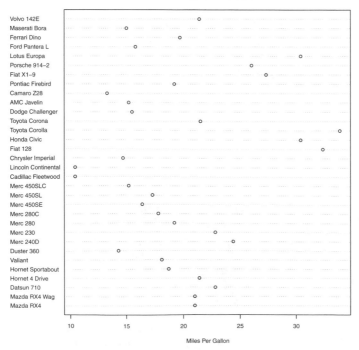

Gas Milage for Car Models

all the different cars.

Figure 6.16   Dot plot of mpg for each car model

1 number for many different cases.

The graph in figure 6.16 allows you to see the mpg for each make of car on the same horizontal axis. Dot plots typically become most interesting when they're sorted and grouping factors are distinguished by symbol and color. An example is given in the following listing.

Listing 6.11 Dot plot grouped, sorted, and colored

```
x <- mtcars[order(mtcars$mpg),]
x$cyl <- factor(x$cyl)
x$color[x$cyl==4] <- "red"
x$color[x$cyl==6] <- "blue"
x$color[x$cyl==8] <- "darkgreen"
dotchart(x$mpg,
         labels = row.names(x),
         cex=.7,
         groups = x$cyl,
         gcolor = "black",
         color = x$color,
         pch=19,
         main = "Gas Mileage for Car Models\ngrouped by cylinder",
         xlab = "Miles Per Gallon")
```

In this example, the data frame `mtcars` is sorted by mpg (lowest to highest) and saved as data frame x. The numeric vector `cyl` is transformed into a factor. A character vector (`color`) is added to data frame x and contains the values `"red"`, `"blue"`, or `"darkgreen"` depending on the value of `cyl`. In addition, the labels for the data points are taken from the row names of the data frame (car makes). Data points are grouped by number of cylinders. The numbers 4, 6, and 8 are printed in black. The color of the points and labels are derived from the `color` vector, and points are represented by filled circles. The code produces the graph in figure 6.17.

In figure 6.17, a number of features become evident for the first time. Again, you see an increase in gas mileage as the number of cylinders decrease. But you also see exceptions. For example, the Pontiac Firebird, with eight cylinders, gets higher gas mileage than the Mercury 280C and the Valiant, each with six cylinders. The Hornet 4 Drive, with six cylinders, gets the same miles per gallon as the Volvo 142E, which has four cylinders. It's also clear that the Toyota Corolla gets the best gas mileage by far, whereas the Lincoln Continental and Cadillac Fleetwood are outliers on the low end.

You can gain significant insight from a dot plot in this example because each point is labeled, the value of each point is inherently meaningful, and the points are arranged in a manner that promotes comparisons. But as the number of data points increase, the utility of the dot plot decreases.

NOTE There are many variations of the dot plot. Jacoby (2006) provides a very informative discussion of the dot plot and provides R code for innovative applications. Additionally, the `Hmisc` package offers a dot plot function (aptly named `dotchart2`) with a number of additional features.

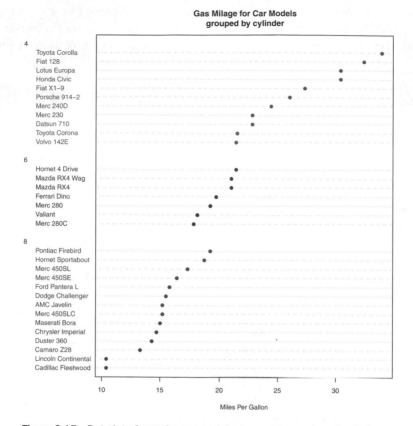

Figure 6.17   Dot plot of mpg for car models grouped by number of cylinders

6.7   Summary

In this chapter, we learned how to describe continuous and categorical variables. We saw how bar plots and (to a lesser extent) pie charts can be used to gain insight into the distribution of a categorical variable, and how stacked and grouped bar charts can help us understand how groups differ on a categorical outcome. We also explored how histograms, kernel density plots, box plots, rug plots, and dot plots can help us visualize the distribution of continuous variables. Finally, we explored how overlapping kernel density plots, parallel box plots, and grouped dot plots can help you visualize group differences on a continuous outcome variable.

In later chapters, we'll extend this univariate focus to include bivariate and multivariate graphical methods. You'll see how to visually depict relationships among many variables at once, using such methods as scatter plots, multigroup line plots, mosaic plots, correlograms, lattice graphs, and more.

In the next chapter, we'll look at basic statistical methods for describing distributions and bivariate relationships numerically, as well as inferential methods for evaluating whether relationships among variables exist or are due to sampling error.

Basic statistics

In previous chapters, you learned how to import data into R and use a variety of functions to organize and transform the data into a useful format. We then reviewed basic methods for visualizing data.

Once your data is properly organized and you've begun to explore the data visually, the next step will typically be to describe the distribution of each variable numerically, followed by an exploration of the relationships among selected variables two at a time. The goal is to answer questions like these:

- What kind of mileage are cars getting these days? Specifically, what's the distribution of miles per gallon (mean, standard deviation, median, range, etc.) in a survey of automobile makes?
- After a new drug trial, what's the outcome (no improvement, some improvement, marked improvement) for drug versus placebo groups? Does the gender of the participants have an impact on the outcome?

141

- What's the correlation between income and life expectancy? Is it significantly different from zero?
- Are you more likely to receive imprisonment for a crime in different regions of the United States? Are the differences between regions statistically significant?

In this chapter we'll review R functions for generating basic descriptive and inferential statistics. First we'll look at measures of location and scale for quantitative variables. Then we'll learn how to generate frequency and contingency tables (and associated chi-square tests) for categorical variables. Next, we'll examine the various forms of correlation coefficients available for continuous and ordinal variables. Finally, we'll turn to the study of group differences through parametric (t-tests) and nonparametric (Mann–Whitney U test, Kruskal–Wallis test) methods. Although our focus is on numerical results, we'll refer to graphical methods for visualizing these results throughout.

The statistical methods covered in this chapter are typically taught in a first-year undergraduate statistics course. If these methodologies are unfamiliar to you, two excellent references are McCall (2000) and Snedecor & Cochran (1989). Alternatively, there are many informative online resources available (such as Wikipedia) for each of the topics covered.

7.1   *Descriptive statistics*

In this section, we'll look at measures of central tendency, variability, and distribution shape for continuous variables. For illustrative purposes, we'll use several of the variables from the Motor Trend Car Road Tests (mtcars) dataset you first saw in chapter 1. Our focus will be on miles per gallon (mpg), horsepower (hp), and weight (wt).

```
> vars <- c("mpg", "hp", "wt")
> head(mtcars[vars])
                   mpg  hp   wt
Mazda RX4          21.0 110 2.62
Mazda RX4 Wag      21.0 110 2.88
Datsun 710         22.8  93 2.32
Hornet 4 Drive     21.4 110 3.21
Hornet Sportabout  18.7 175 3.44
Valiant            18.1 105 3.46
```

First we'll look at descriptive statistics for all 32 cars. Then we'll examine descriptive statistics by transmission type (am) and number of cylinders (cyl). Transmission type is a dichotomous variable coded 0=automatic, 1=manual, and the number of cylinders can be 4, 5, or 6.

7.1.1   *A menagerie of methods*

When it comes to calculating descriptive statistics, R has an embarrassment of riches. Let's start with functions that are included in the base installation. Then we'll look at extensions that are available through the use of user-contributed packages.

In the base installation, you can use the summary() function to obtain descriptive statistics. An example is presented in the following listing.

head() first part of object. see p. 43

Listing 7.1 Descriptive statistics via `summary()`

```
> summary(mtcars[vars])
      mpg                hp               wt
 Min.   :10.4    Min.   : 52.0    Min.   :1.51
 1st Qu.:15.4    1st Qu.: 96.5    1st Qu.:2.58
 Median :19.2    Median :123.0    Median :3.33
 Mean   :20.1    Mean   :146.7    Mean   :3.22
 3rd Qu.:22.8    3rd Qu.:180.0    3rd Qu.:3.61
 Max.   :33.9    Max.   :335.0    Max.   :5.42
```

The `summary()` function provides the minimum, maximum, quartiles, and the mean for numerical variables and frequencies for factors and logical vectors. You can use the `apply()` or `sapply()` function from chapter 5 to provide any descriptive statistics you choose. For the `sapply()` function, the format is

`sapply(x, FUN, options)`

where *x* is your data frame (or matrix) and *FUN* is an arbitrary function. If *options* are present, they're passed to *FUN*. Typical functions that you can plug in here are `mean`, `sd`, `var`, `min`, `max`, `median`, `length`, `range`, and `quantile`. The function `fivenum()` returns Tukey's five-number summary (minimum, lower-hinge, median, upper-hinge, and maximum).

Surprisingly, the base installation doesn't provide functions for skew and kurtosis, but you can add your own. The example in the next listing provides several descriptive statistics, including skew and kurtosis.

Listing 7.2 Descriptive statistics via `sapply()`

```
> mystats <- function(x, na.omit=FALSE){
              if (na.omit)
                  x <- x[!is.na(x)]
              m <- mean(x)
              n <- length(x)
              s <- sd(x)
              skew <- sum((x-m)^3/s^3)/n
              kurt <- sum((x-m)^4/s^4)/n - 3
              return(c(n=n, mean=m, stdev=s, skew=skew, kurtosis=kurt))

            }

> sapply(mtcars[vars], mystats)
              mpg      hp       wt
n         32.000  32.000  32.0000
mean      20.091 146.688   3.2172
stdev      6.027  68.563   0.9785
skew       0.611   0.726   0.4231
kurtosis  -0.373  -0.136  -0.0227
```

For cars in this sample, the mean mpg is 20.1, with a standard deviation of 6.0. The distribution is skewed to the right (+0.61) and somewhat flatter than a normal distribution (–0.37). This will be most evident if you graph the data. Note that if you'd wanted to omit missing values, you would have used `sapply(mtcars[vars],` `mystats, na.omit=TRUE)`.

EXTENSIONS

Several user-contributed packages offer functions for descriptive statistics, including `Hmisc`, `pastecs`, and `psych`. Because these packages aren't included in the base distribution, you'll need to install them on first use (see chapter 1, section 1.4).

The `describe()` function in the `Hmisc` package returns the number of variables and observations, the number of missing and unique values, the mean, quantiles, and the five highest and lowest values. An example is provided in the following listing.

Listing 7.3   Descriptive statistics via `describe()` in the `Hmisc` package()

```
> library(Hmisc)
> describe(mtcars[vars])

 3  Variables      32  Observations
---------------------------------------------------------------------------
mpg
n missing  unique  Mean    .05    .10    .25    .50    .75    .90    .95
32       0      25  20.09  12.00  14.34  15.43  19.20  22.80  30.09  31.30

lowest : 10.4 13.3 14.3 14.7 15.0, highest: 26.0 27.3 30.4 32.4 33.9
---------------------------------------------------------------------------
hp
n missing  unique   Mean    .05    .10    .2     .50    .75    .90     .95
32       0      22   146.7  63.65  66.00 96.50 123.00 180.00 243.50 253.55

lowest :  52  62  65  66  91, highest: 215 230 245 264 335
---------------------------------------------------------------------------
wt
n missing  unique   Mean    .05    .10    .25    .50    .75    .90    .95
32       0      29   3.217  1.736  1.956  2.581  3.325  3.610  4.048 5.293

lowest : 1.513 1.615 1.835 1.935 2.140, highest: 3.845 4.070 5.250 5.345
5.424
---------------------------------------------------------------------------
```

The `pastecs` package includes a function named `stat.desc()` that provides a wide range of descriptive statistics. The format is

```
stat.desc(x, basic=TRUE, desc=TRUE, norm=FALSE, p=0.95)
```

where x is a data frame or time series. If `basic=TRUE` (the default), the number of values, null values, missing values, minimum, maximum, range, and sum are provided. If `desc=TRUE` (also the default), the median, mean, standard error of the mean, 95 percent confidence interval for the mean, variance, standard deviation, and coefficient of variation are also provided. Finally, if `norm=TRUE` (not the default), normal distribution statistics are returned, including skewness and kurtosis (and their statistical significance), and the Shapiro–Wilk test of normality. A p-value option is used to calculate the confidence interval for the mean (.95 by default). Listing 7.4 gives an example.

Listing 7.4   Descriptive statistics via `stat.desc()` in the `pastecs` package

```
> library(pastecs)
> stat.desc(mtcars[vars])
                 mpg       hp       wt
nbr.val        32.00   32.000   32.000
nbr.null        0.00    0.000    0.000
nbr.na          0.00    0.000    0.000
min            10.40   52.000    1.513
max            33.90  335.000    5.424
range          23.50  283.000    3.911
sum           642.90 4694.000  102.952
median         19.20  123.000    3.325
mean           20.09  146.688    3.217
SE.mean         1.07   12.120    0.173
CI.mean.0.95    2.17   24.720    0.353
var            36.32 4700.867    0.957
std.dev         6.03   68.563    0.978
coef.var        0.30    0.467    0.304
```

As if this isn't enough, the `psych` package also has a function called `describe()` that provides the number of nonmissing observations, mean, standard deviation, median, trimmed mean, median absolute deviation, minimum, maximum, range, skew, kurtosis, and standard error of the mean. You can see an example in the following listing.

Listing 7.5   Descriptive statistics via `describe()` in the `psych` package

```
> library(psych)

Attaching package: 'psych'
        The following object(s) are masked from package:Hmisc :
          describe

> describe(mtcars[vars])
     var  n   mean    sd median trimmed   mad   min    max
mpg    1 32  20.09  6.03  19.20   19.70  5.41 10.40  33.90
hp     2 32 146.69 68.56 123.00  141.19 77.10 52.00 335.00
wt     3 32   3.22  0.98   3.33    3.15  0.77  1.51   5.42
     range skew kurtosis    se
mpg  23.50 0.61    -0.37  1.07
hp  283.00 0.73    -0.14 12.12
wt    3.91 0.42    -0.02  0.17
```

I told you that it was an embarrassment of riches!

> **NOTE** In the previous examples, the packages `psych` and `Hmisc` both provided functions named `describe()`. How does R know which one to use? Simply put, the package last loaded takes precedence, as seen in listing 7.5. Here, `psych` is loaded after `Hmisc`, and a message is printed indicating that the `describe()` function in `Hmisc` is masked by the function in `psych`. When you type in the `describe()` function and R searches for it, R comes to the `psych` package first and executes it. If you want the `Hmisc` version instead, you can type `Hmisc::describe(mt)`. The function is still there. You have to give R more information to find it.

Now that you know how to generate descriptive statistics for the data as a whole, let's review how to obtain statistics for subgroups of the data.

7.1.2 *Descriptive statistics by group*

When comparing groups of individuals or observations, the focus is usually on the descriptive statistics of each group, rather than the total sample. Again, there are several ways to accomplish this in R. We'll start by getting descriptive statistics for each level of transmission type.

In chapter 5, we discussed methods of aggregating data. You can use the `aggregate()` function (section 5.6.2) to obtain descriptive statistics by group, as shown in the following listing.

Listing 7.6   Descriptive statistics by group using `aggregate()`

```
> aggregate(mtcars[vars], by=list(am=mtcars$am), mean)
  am  mpg  hp   wt
1  0 17.1 160 3.77
2  1 24.4 127 2.41
> aggregate(mtcars[vars], by=list(am=mtcars$am), sd)
  am  mpg   hp    wt
1  0 3.83 53.9 0.777
2  1 6.17 84.1 0.617
```

Note the use of `list(am=mtcars$am)`. If you had used `list(mtcars$am)`, the am column would have been labeled `Group.1` rather than `am`. You use the assignment to provide a more useful column label. If you have more than one grouping variable, you can use code like `by=list(name1=groupvar1, name2=groupvar2, ... , groupvarN)`.

Unfortunately, `aggregate()` only allows you to use single value functions such as mean, standard deviation, and the like in each call. It won't return several statistics at once. For that task, you can use the `by()` function. The format is

```
by(data, INDICES, FUN)
```

where *data* is a data frame or matrix, *INDICES* is a factor or list of factors that define the groups, and *FUN* is an arbitrary function. This next listing provides an example.

Listing 7.7   Descriptive statistics by group using `by()`

```
> dstats <- function(x)(c(mean=mean(x), sd=sd(x)))
> by(mtcars[vars], mtcars$am, dstats)

mtcars$am: 0
mean.mpg  mean.hp  mean.wt   sd.mpg    sd.hp    sd.wt
  17.147  160.263    3.769    3.834   53.908    0.777
------------------------------------------------
mtcars$am: 1
mean.mpg  mean.hp  mean.wt   sd.mpg    sd.hp    sd.wt
  24.392  126.846    2.411    6.167   84.062    0.617
```

am is transmission type (automatic, manual)

EXTENSIONS

The doBy package and the psych package also provide functions for descriptive statistics by group. Again, they aren't distributed in the base installation and must be installed before first use. The summaryBy() function in the doBy package has the format

```
summaryBy(formula, data=dataframe, FUN=function)
```

where the formula takes the form

```
var1 + var2 + var3 + ... + varN ~ groupvar1 + groupvar2 + ... + groupvarN
```

Variables on the left of the ~ are the numeric variables to be analyzed and variables on the right are categorical grouping variables. The *function* can be any built-in or user-created R function. An example using the mystats() function you created in section 7.2.1 is shown in the following listing.

Listing 7.8 Summary statistics by group using summaryBy() in the doBy package

```
> library(doBy)
> summaryBy(mpg+hp+wt~am, data=mtcars, FUN=mystats)
  am mpg.n mpg.mean mpg.stdev mpg.skew mpg.kurtosis hp.n hp.mean hp.stdev
1  0    19     17.1      3.83   0.0140       -0.803   19     160     53.9
2  1    13     24.4      6.17   0.0526       -1.455   13     127     84.1
  hp.skew hp.kurtosis wt.n wt.mean wt.stdev wt.skew wt.kurtosis
1 -0.0142      -1.210   19    3.77    0.777   0.976       0.142
2  1.3599       0.563   13    2.41    0.617   0.210      -1.174
```

The describe.by() function contained in the psych package provides the same descriptive statistics as describe, stratified by one or more grouping variables, as you can see in the following listing.

Listing 7.9 Summary statistics by group using describe.by() in the psych package

```
> library(psych)
> describe.by(mtcars[vars], mtcars$am)
group: 0
     var  n    mean     sd median trimmed    mad    min     max
mpg    1 19   17.15   3.83  17.30   17.12   3.11  10.40   24.40
hp     2 19  160.26  53.91 175.00  161.06  77.10  62.00  245.00
wt     3 19    3.77   0.78   3.52    3.75   0.45   2.46    5.42
      range   skew kurtosis     se
mpg   14.00   0.01    -0.80   0.88
hp   183.00  -0.01    -1.21  12.37
wt     2.96   0.98     0.14   0.18
-------------------------------------------------

group: 1
     var  n    mean     sd median trimmed    mad    min     max
mpg    1 13   24.39   6.17  22.80   24.38   6.67  15.00   33.90
hp     2 13  126.85  84.06 109.00  114.73  63.75  52.00  335.00
wt     3 13    2.41   0.62   2.32    2.39   0.68   1.51    3.57
      range  skew kurtosis     se
```

```
mpg  18.90 0.05    -1.46  1.71
hp  283.00 1.36     0.56 23.31
wt    2.06 0.21    -1.17  0.17
```

Unlike the previous example, the `describe.by()` function doesn't allow you to specify an arbitrary function, so it's less generally applicable. If there's more than one grouping variable, you can write them as `list(`*groupvar1*`,` *groupvar2*`,` … `,` *groupvarN*`)`. But this will only work if there are no empty cells when the grouping variables are crossed.

Finally, you can use the `reshape` package described in section 5.6.3 to derive descriptive statistics by group in a flexible way. (If you haven't read that section, I suggest you review it before continuing.) First, you melt the data frame using

```
dfm <- melt(dataframe, measure.vars=y, id.vars=g)
```

where *dataframe* contains the data, *y* is a vector indicating the numeric variables to be summarized (the default is to use all), and *g* is a vector of one or more grouping variables. You then cast the data using

```
cast(dfm, groupvar1 + groupvar2 + … + variable ~ ., FUN)
```

where the grouping variables are separated by + signs, the word `variable` is entered exactly as is, and *FUN* is an arbitrary function.

In the final example of this section, we'll apply the reshape approach to obtaining descriptive statistics for each subgroup formed by transmission type and number of cylinders. For descriptive statistics, we'll get the sample size, mean, and standard deviation. The code and results are shown in the following listing.

Listing 7.10 Summary statistics by group via the `reshape` package

```
> library(reshape)
> dstats <- function(x)(c(n=length(x), mean=mean(x), sd=sd(x)))
> dfm <- melt(mtcars, measure.vars=c("mpg", "hp", "wt"),
              id.vars=c("am", "cyl"))
> cast(dfm, am + cyl + variable ~ ., dstats)


   am cyl variable   n    mean      sd
1   0   4      mpg   3   22.90   1.453
2   0   4       hp   3   84.67  19.655
3   0   4       wt   3    2.94   0.408
4   0   6      mpg   4   19.12   1.632
5   0   6       hp   4  115.25   9.179
6   0   6       wt   4    3.39   0.116
7   0   8      mpg  12   15.05   2.774
8   0   8       hp  12  194.17  33.360
9   0   8       wt  12    4.10   0.768
10  1   4      mpg   8   28.07   4.484
11  1   4       hp   8   81.88  22.655
12  1   4       wt   8    2.04   0.409
```

```
13  1  6      mpg  3  20.57  0.751
14  1  6       hp  3 131.67 37.528
15  1  6       wt  3   2.75  0.128
16  1  8      mpg  2  15.40  0.566
17  1  8       hp  2 299.50 50.205
18  1  8       wt  2   3.37  0.283
```

Personally, I find this approach the most compact and appealing. Data analysts have their own preferences for which descriptive statistics to display and how they like to see them formatted. This is probably why there are many variations available. Choose the one that works best for you, or create your own!

7.1.3 Visualizing results

Numerical summaries of a distribution's characteristics are important, but they're no substitute for a visual representation. For quantitative variables you have histograms (section 6.3), density plots (section 6.4), box plots (section 6.5), and dot plots (section 6.6). They can provide insights that are easily missed by reliance on a small set of descriptive statistics.

The functions considered so far provide summaries of quantitative variables. The functions in the next section allow you to examine the distributions of categorical variables.

7.2   Frequency and contingency tables

In this section, we'll look at frequency and contingency tables from categorical variables, along with tests of independence, measures of association, and methods for graphically displaying results. We'll be using functions in the basic installation, along with functions from the vcd and gmodels package. In the following examples, assume that A, B, and C represent categorical variables.

The data for this section come from the Arthritis dataset included with the vcd package. The data are from Kock & Edward (1988) and represent a double-blind clinical trial of new treatments for rheumatoid arthritis. Here are the first few observations:

```
> library(vcd)
> head(Arthritis)
  ID Treatment  Sex Age Improved
1 57   Treated Male  27     Some
2 46   Treated Male  29     None
3 77   Treated Male  30     None
4 17   Treated Male  32   Marked
5 36   Treated Male  46   Marked
6 23   Treated Male  58   Marked
```

Treatment (Placebo, Treated), Sex (Male, Female), and Improved (None, Some, Marked) are all categorical factors. In the next section, we'll create frequency and contingency tables (cross-classifications) from the data.

7.2.1 *Generating frequency tables*

R provides several methods for creating frequency and contingency tables. The most important functions are listed in table 7.1.

Table 7.1   Functions for creating and manipulating contingency tables

Function	Description
`table(var1, var2, …, varN)`	Creates an N-way contingency table from N categorical variables (factors)
`xtabs(formula, data)`	Creates an N-way contingency table based on a formula and a matrix or data frame
`prop.table(table, margins)`	Expresses table entries as fractions of the marginal table defined by the *margins*
`margin.table(table, margins)`	Computes the sum of table entries for a marginal table defined by the *margins*
`addmargins(table, margins)`	Puts summary *margins* (sums by default) on a table
`ftable(table)`	Creates a compact "flat" contingency table

In the following sections, we'll use each of these functions to explore categorical variables. We'll begin with simple frequencies, followed by two-way contingency tables, and end with multiway contingency tables. The first step is to create a table using either the `table()` or the `xtabs()` function, then manipulate it using the other functions.

ONE-WAY TABLES

You can generate simple frequency counts using the `table()` function. Here's an example:

```
> mytable <- with(Arthritis, table(Improved))
> mytable
Improved
  None   Some Marked
    42     14     28
```

You can turn these frequencies into proportions with `prop.table()`:

```
> prop.table(mytable)
Improved
  None   Some Marked
 0.500  0.167  0.333
```

or into percentages, using `prop.table()*100`:

```
> prop.table(mytable)*100
Improved
  None   Some Marked
  50.0   16.7   33.3
```

Here you can see that 50 percent of study participants had some or marked improvement (16.7 + 33.3).

TWO-WAY TABLES

For two-way tables, the format for the `table()` function is

```
mytable <- table(A, B)
```

where *A* is the row variable, and *B* is the column variable. Alternatively, the `xtabs()` function allows you to create a contingency table using formula style input. The format is

```
mytable <- xtabs(~ A + B, data=mydata)
```

where *mydata* is a matrix or data frame. In general, the variables to be cross-classified appear on the right of the formula (that is, to the right of the ~) separated by + signs. If a variable is included on the left side of the formula, it's assumed to be a vector of frequencies (useful if the data have already been tabulated).

For the `Arthritis` data, you have

```
> mytable <- xtabs(~ Treatment+Improved, data=Arthritis)
> mytable
          Improved
Treatment None Some Marked
   Placebo   29    7      7
   Treated   13    7     21
```

row sum
43
41

col sum
42 14 28

You can generate marginal frequencies and proportions using the `margin.table()` and `prop.table()` functions, respectively. For row sums and row proportions, you have

```
> margin.table(mytable, 1)
Treatment
Placebo Treated
     43      41
> prop.table(mytable, 1)
          Improved
Treatment   None   Some Marked
   Placebo 0.674  0.163  0.163
   Treated 0.317  0.171  0.512
```

$.674 = \dfrac{29}{43}$ *share of row sum*

The index (1) refers to the first variable in the `table()` statement. Looking at the table, you can see that 51 percent of treated individuals had marked improvement, compared to 16 percent of those receiving a placebo.

For column sums and column proportions, you have

```
> margin.table(mytable, 2)
Improved
  None   Some Marked
    42     14     28
> prop.table(mytable, 2)
          Improved
Treatment   None   Some Marked
```

```
   Placebo 0.690 0.500   0.250
   Treated 0.310 0.500   0.750
```

Here, the `index (2)` refers to the second variable in the `table()` statement. Cell proportions are obtained with this statement:

```
> prop.table(mytable)
           Improved
Treatment   None    Some Marked
   Placebo 0.3452 0.0833 0.0833
   Treated 0.1548 0.0833 0.2500
```

cell probs

share of column sum

You can use the `addmargins()` function to add marginal sums to these tables. For example, the following code adds a sum row and column:

```
> addmargins(mytable)
           Improved
Treatment None Some Marked Sum
   Placebo   29    7      7  43
   Treated   13    7     21  41
   Sum       42   14     28  84
> addmargins(prop.table(mytable))
           Improved
Treatment   None    Some Marked    Sum
   Placebo 0.3452 0.0833 0.0833 0.5119
   Treated 0.1548 0.0833 0.2500 0.4881
   Sum     0.5000 0.1667 0.3333 1.0000
```

When using `addmargins()`, the default is to create sum margins for all variables in a table. In contrast:

```
> addmargins(prop.table(mytable, 1), 2)
           Improved
Treatment  None  Some Marked    Sum
   Placebo 0.674 0.163  0.163 1.000
   Treated 0.317 0.171  0.512 1.000
```

adds a sum column alone. Similarly,

```
> addmargins(prop.table(mytable, 2), 1)
           Improved
Treatment  None  Some Marked
   Placebo 0.690 0.500  0.250
   Treated 0.310 0.500  0.750
   Sum     1.000 1.000  1.000
```

adds a sum row. In the table, you see that 25 percent of those patients with marked improvement received a placebo.

> **NOTE** The `table()` function ignores missing values (NAs) by default. To include NA as a valid category in the frequency counts, include the table option `useNA="ifany"`.

A third method for creating two-way tables is the `CrossTable()` function in the `gmodels` package. The `CrossTable()` function produces two-way tables modeled after `PROC FREQ` in SAS or `CROSSTABS` in SPSS. See listing 7.11 for an example.

Listing 7.11 Two-way table using `CrossTable`

```
> library(gmodels)
> CrossTable(Arthritis$Treatment, Arthritis$Improved)


   Cell Contents
|-----------------------|
|                     N |
| Chi-square contribution |
|           N / Row Total |
|           N / Col Total |
|         N / Table Total |
|-----------------------|
```

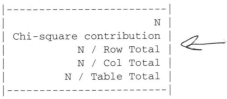

```
Total Observations in Table:   84


                       | Arthritis$Improved
Arthritis$Treatment |     None  |     Some  |   Marked  | Row Total |
--------------------|-----------|-----------|-----------|-----------|
           Placebo  |       29  |        7  |        7  |       43  |
                    |    2.616  |    0.004  |    3.752  |           |
                    |    0.674  |    0.163  |    0.163  |    0.512  |
                    |    0.690  |    0.500  |    0.250  |           |
                    |    0.345  |    0.083  |    0.083  |           |
--------------------|-----------|-----------|-----------|-----------|
           Treated  |       13  |        7  |       21  |       41  |
                    |    2.744  |    0.004  |    3.935  |           |
                    |    0.317  |    0.171  |    0.512  |    0.488  |
                    |    0.310  |    0.500  |    0.750  |           |
                    |    0.155  |    0.083  |    0.250  |           |
--------------------|-----------|-----------|-----------|-----------|
      Column Total  |       42  |       14  |       28  |       84  |
                    |    0.500  |    0.167  |    0.333  |           |
--------------------|-----------|-----------|-----------|-----------|
```

The `CrossTable()` function has options to report percentages (row, column, cell); specify decimal places; produce chi-square, Fisher, and McNemar tests of independence; report expected and residual values (Pearson, standardized, adjusted standardized); include missing values as valid; annotate with row and column titles; and format as SAS or SPSS style output. See `help(CrossTable)` for details.

If you have more than two categorical variables, you're dealing with multidimensional tables. We'll consider these next.

MULTIDIMENSIONAL TABLES

Both `table()` and `xtabs()` can be used to generate multidimensional tables based on three or more categorical variables. The `margin.table()`, `prop.table()`, and `addmargins()` functions extend naturally to more than two dimensions. Additionally, the `ftable()` function can be used to print multidimensional tables in a compact and attractive manner. An example is given in listing 7.12.

Listing 7.12   Three-way contingency table

```
> mytable <- xtabs(~ Treatment+Sex+Improved, data=Arthritis)        ◄──┐ ❶ Cell
> mytable                                                               frequencies
, , Improved = None


        Sex
Treatment Female Male
  Placebo     19   10
  Treated      6    7

, , Improved = Some


        Sex
Treatment Female Male
  Placebo      7    0
  Treated      5    2

, , Improved = Marked


        Sex
Treatment Female Male
  Placebo      6    1
  Treated     16    5


> ftable(mytable)
                Sex Female Male
Treatment Improved
Placebo   None             19   10
          Some              7    0
          Marked            6    1
Treated   None              6    7
          Some              5    2
          Marked           16    5


> margin.table(mytable, 1)                          ◄──┐ ❷ Marginal
Treatment                                              frequencies
Placebo Treated
     43      41
> margin.table(mytable, 2)
Sex
Female   Male
    59     25
> margin.table(mytable, 3)
Improved
  None  Some Marked
    42    14     28
> margin.table(mytable, c(1, 3))                    ◄──┐ Treatment x
        Improved                                       Improved marginal
Treatment None Some Marked                          ❸ frequencies
  Placebo   29    7      7
  Treated   13    7     21
> ftable(prop.table(mytable, c(1, 2)))              ◄──┐ Improve
                Improved  None   Some Marked            proportions for
Treatment Sex                                       ❹ Treatment x Sex
```

```
Placebo   Female              0.594 0.219  0.188
          Male                0.909 0.000  0.091
Treated   Female              0.222 0.185  0.593
          Male                0.500 0.143  0.357

> ftable(addmargins(prop.table(mytable, c(1, 2)), 3))
                  Improved None  Some Marked   Sum
Treatment Sex
Placebo   Female              0.594 0.219  0.188 1.000
          Male                0.909 0.000  0.091 1.000
Treated   Female              0.222 0.185  0.593 1.000
          Male                0.500 0.143  0.357 1.000
```

The code in ❶ produces cell frequencies for the three-way classification. The code also demonstrates how the `ftable()` function can be used to print a more compact and attractive version of the table.

The code in ❷ produces the marginal frequencies for Treatment, Sex, and Improved. Because you created the table with the formula `~Treatement+Sex+Improve`, `Treatment` is referred to by index 1, `Sex` is referred to by index 2, and `Improve` is referred to by index 3.

The code in ❸ produces the marginal frequencies for the Treatment x Improved classification, summed over Sex. The proportion of patients with `None`, `Some`, and `Marked` improvement for each `Treatment` x `Sex` combination is provided in ❹. Here you see that 36 percent of treated males had marked improvement, compared to 59 percent of treated females. In general, the proportions will add to one over the indices not included in the `prop.table()` call (the third index, or `Improve` in this case). You can see this in the last example, where you add a sum margin over the third index.

If you want percentages instead of proportions, you could multiply the resulting table by 100. For example:

```
ftable(addmargins(prop.table(mytable, c(1, 2)), 3)) * 100
```

would produce this table:

```
                    Sex Female  Male    Sum
Treatment Improved
Placebo   None           65.5  34.5  100.0
          Some          100.0   0.0  100.0
          Marked         85.7  14.3  100.0
Treated   None           46.2  53.8  100.0
          Some           71.4  28.6  100.0
          Marked         76.2  23.8  100.0
```

While contingency tables tell you the frequency or proportions of cases for each combination of the variables that comprise the table, you're probably also interested in whether the variables in the table are related or independent. Tests of independence are covered in the next section.

7.2.2 *Tests of independence*

R provides several methods of testing the independence of the categorical variables. The three tests described in this section are the chi-square test of independence, the Fisher exact test, and the Cochran-Mantel–Haenszel test.

CHI-SQUARE TEST OF INDEPENDENCE

You can apply the function `chisq.test()` to a two-way table in order to produce a chi-square test of independence of the row and column variables. See this next listing for an example.

Listing 7.13 Chi-square test of independence

```
> library(vcd)
> mytable <- xtabs(~Treatment+Improved, data=Arthritis)
> chisq.test(mytable)

        Pearson's Chi-squared test                        ❶ Treatment and
                                                             Improved not
data:  mytable                                               independent
X-squared = 13.1, df = 2, p-value = 0.001463

> mytable <- xtabs(~Improved+Sex, data=Arthritis)
> chisq.test(mytable)

        Pearson's Chi-squared test                        ❷ Gender and
                                                             Improved
data:  mytable                                               independent
X-squared = 4.84, df = 2, p-value = 0.0889

Warning message:
In chisq.test(mytable) : Chi-squared approximation may be incorrect
```

From the results ❶, there appears to be a relationship between treatment received and level of improvement ($p < .01$). But there doesn't appear to be a relationship ❷ between patient sex and improvement ($p > .05$). The p-values are the probability of obtaining the sampled results assuming independence of the row and column variables in the population. Because the probability is small for ❶, you reject the hypothesis that treatment type and outcome are independent. Because the probability for ❷ isn't small, it's not unreasonable to assume that outcome and gender are independent. The warning message in listing 7.13 is produced because one of the six cells in the table (male-some improvement) has an expected value less than five, which may invalidate the chi-square approximation.

FISHER'S EXACT TEST

You can produce a Fisher's exact test via the `fisher.test()` function. Fisher's exact test evaluates the null hypothesis of independence of rows and columns in a contingency table with fixed marginals. The format is `fisher.test(mytable)`, where *mytable* is a two-way table. Here's an example:

```
> mytable <- xtabs(~Treatment+Improved, data=Arthritis)
> fisher.test(mytable)
```

```
       Fisher's Exact Test for Count Data
data:  mytable
p-value = 0.001393
alternative hypothesis: two.sided
```

In contrast to many statistical packages, the `fisher.test()` function can be applied to any two-way table with two or more rows and columns, not a 2x2 table.

COCHRAN–MANTEL–HAENSZEL TEST

The `mantelhaen.test()` function provides a Cochran–Mantel–Haenszel chi-square test of the null hypothesis that two nominal variables are conditionally independent in each stratum of a third variable. The following code tests the hypothesis that Treatment and Improved variables are independent within each level Sex. The test assumes that there's no three-way (Treatment x Improved x Sex) interaction.

```
> mytable <- xtabs(~Treatment+Improved+Sex, data=Arthritis)
> mantelhaen.test(mytable)

        Cochran-Mantel-Haenszel test

data:  mytable
Cochran-Mantel-Haenszel M^2 = 14.6, df = 2, p-value = 0.0006647
```

The results suggest that the treatment received and the improvement reported aren't independent within each level of sex (that is, treated individuals improved more than those receiving placebos when controlling for sex).

7.2.3 *Measures of association*

The significance tests in the previous section evaluated whether or not sufficient evidence existed to reject a null hypothesis of independence between variables. If you can reject the null hypothesis, your interest turns naturally to measures of association in order to gauge the strength of the relationships present. The `assocstats()` function in the vcd package can be used to calculate the phi coefficient, contingency coefficient, and Cramer's V for a two-way table. An example is given in the following listing.

Listing 7.14 Measures of association for a two-way table

```
> library(vcd)
> mytable <- xtabs(~Treatment+Improved, data=Arthritis)
> assocstats(mytable)

                    X^2 df  P(> X^2)
Likelihood Ratio 13.530  2 0.0011536
Pearson          13.055  2 0.0014626

Phi-Coefficient   : 0.394
Contingency Coeff.: 0.367
Cramer's V        : 0.394
```

In general, larger magnitudes indicated stronger associations. The vcd package also provides a `kappa()` function that can calculate Cohen's kappa and weighted kappa for a confusion matrix (for example, the degree of agreement between two judges classifying a set of objects into categories).

7.2.4 Visualizing results

R has mechanisms for visually exploring the relationships among categorical variables that go well beyond those found in most other statistical platforms. You typically use bar charts to visualize frequencies in one dimension (see chapter 6, section 6.1). The vcd package has excellent functions for visualizing relationships among categorical variables in multidimensional datasets using mosaic and association plots (see chapter 11, section 11.4). Finally, correspondence analysis functions in the ca package allow you to visually explore relationships between rows and columns in contingency tables using various geometric representations (Nenadic and Greenacre, 2007).

7.2.5 Converting tables to flat files

We'll end this section with a topic that's rarely covered in books on R but that can be very useful. What happens if you have a table but need the original raw data? For example, say you have the following:

```
                   Sex Female Male
Treatment Improved
Placebo   None             19   10
          Some              7    0
          Marked            6    1
Treated   None              6    7
          Some              5    2
          Marked           16    5
```

but you need this:

```
   ID Treatment  Sex Age Improved
1 57    Treated Male  27     Some
2 46    Treated Male  29     None
3 77    Treated Male  30     None
4 17    Treated Male  32   Marked
5 36    Treated Male  46   Marked
6 23    Treated Male  58   Marked
[78 more rows go here]
```

There are many statistical functions in R that expect the latter format rather than the former. You can use the function provided in the following listing to convert an R table back into a flat data file.

Listing 7.15 Converting a table into a flat file via `table2flat`

```
table2flat <- function(mytable) {
  df <- as.data.frame(mytable)
  rows  <- dim(df)[1]
  cols  <- dim(df)[2]
  x <- NULL
  for (i in 1:rows){
    for (j in 1:df$Freq[i]){
```

```
      row <- df[i,c(1:(cols-1))]
      x <- rbind(x,row)
   }
 }
 row.names(x)<-c(1:dim(x)[1])
 return(x)
}
```

This function takes an R table (with any number of rows and columns) and returns a data frame in flat file format. You can also use this function to input tables from published studies. For example, let's say that you came across table 7.2 in a journal and wanted to save it into R as a flat file.

Table 7.2 Contingency table for treatment versus improvement from the `Arthritis` dataset

	Improved		
Treatment	**None**	**Some**	**Marked**
Placebo	29	7	7
Treated	13	17	21

This next listing describes a method that would do the trick.

Listing 7.16 Using the `table2flat()` function with published data

```
> treatment <- rep(c("Placebo", "Treated"), times=3)
> improved <- rep(c("None", "Some", "Marked"), each=2)
> Freq <- c(29,13,7,17,7,21)
> mytable <- as.data.frame(cbind(treatment, improved, Freq))
> mydata <- table2flat(mytable)
> head(mydata)
  treatment improved
1   Placebo     None
2   Placebo     None
3   Placebo     None
4   Treated     None
5   Placebo     Some
6   Placebo     Some
[12 more rows go here]
```

This ends the discussion of contingency tables, until we take up more advanced topics in chapters 11 and 15. Next, let's look at various types of correlation coefficients.

7.3 Correlations

Correlation coefficients are used to describe relationships among quantitative variables. The sign ± indicates the direction of the relationship (positive or inverse) and the magnitude indicates the strength of the relationship (ranging from 0 for no relationship to 1 for a perfectly predictable relationship).

In this section, we'll look at a variety of correlation coefficients, as well as tests of significance. We'll use the `state.x77` dataset available in the base R installation. It provides data on the population, income, illiteracy rate, life expectancy, murder rate, and high school graduation rate for the 50 US states in 1977. There are also temperature and land area measures, but we'll drop them to save space. Use `help(state.x77)` to learn more about the file. In addition to the base installation, we'll be using the `psych` and `ggm` packages.

7.3.1   *Types of correlations*

R can produce a variety of correlation coefficients, including Pearson, Spearman, Kendall, partial, polychoric, and polyserial. Let's look at each in turn.

PEARSON, SPEARMAN, AND KENDALL CORRELATIONS

The Pearson product moment correlation assesses the degree of linear relationship between two quantitative variables. Spearman's Rank Order correlation coefficient assesses the degree of relationship between two rank-ordered variables. Kendall's Tau is also a nonparametric measure of rank correlation.

The `cor()` function produces all three correlation coefficients, whereas the `cov()` function provides covariances. There are many options, but a simplified format for producing correlations is

```
cor(x, use= , method= )
```

The options are described in table 7.3.

Table 7.3   `cor/cov` options

Option	Description
x	Matrix or data frame.
use	Specifies the handling of missing data. The options are `all.obs` (assumes no missing data—missing data will produce an error), `everything` (any correlation involving a case with missing values will be set to `missing`), `complete.obs` (listwise deletion), and `pairwise.complete.obs` (pairwise deletion).
method	Specifies the type of correlation. The options are `pearson`, `spearman`, or `kendall`.

The default options are `use="everything"` and `method="pearson"`. You can see an example in the following listing.

Listing 7.17   Covariances and correlations

```
> states<- state.x77[,1:6]
> cov(states)
           Population Income Illiteracy Life Exp  Murder  HS Grad
Population   19931684 571230    292.868 -407.842 5663.52 -3551.51
Income         571230 377573   -163.702  280.663 -521.89  3076.77
Illiteracy        293   -164      0.372   -0.482    1.58    -3.24
Life Exp         -408    281     -0.482    1.802   -3.87     6.31
Murder           5664   -522      1.582   -3.869   13.63   -14.55
HS Grad         -3552   3077     -3.235    6.313  -14.55    65.24
```

```
> cor(states)
          Population Income Illiteracy Life Exp Murder HS Grad
Population    1.0000  0.208      0.108   -0.068  0.344 -0.0985
Income        0.2082  1.000     -0.437    0.340 -0.230  0.6199
Illiteracy    0.1076 -0.437      1.000   -0.588  0.703 -0.6572
Life Exp     -0.0681  0.340     -0.588    1.000 -0.781  0.5822
Murder        0.3436 -0.230      0.703   -0.781  1.000 -0.4880
HS Grad      -0.0985  0.620     -0.657    0.582 -0.488  1.0000

> cor(states, method="spearman")
          Population Income Illiteracy Life Exp Murder HS Grad
Population     1.000  0.125      0.313   -0.104  0.346  -0.383
Income         0.125  1.000     -0.315    0.324 -0.217   0.510
Illiteracy     0.313 -0.315      1.000   -0.555  0.672  -0.655
Life Exp      -0.104  0.324     -0.555    1.000 -0.780   0.524
Murder         0.346 -0.217      0.672   -0.780  1.000  -0.437
HS Grad       -0.383  0.510     -0.655    0.524 -0.437   1.000
```

The first call produces the variances and covariances. The second provides Pearson Product Moment correlation coefficients, whereas the third produces Spearman Rank Order correlation coefficients. You can see, for example, that a strong positive correlation exists between income and high school graduation rate and that a strong negative correlation exists between illiteracy rates and life expectancy.

Notice that you get square matrices by default (all variables crossed with all other variables). You can also produce nonsquare matrices; see the following example:

```
> x <- states[,c("Population", "Income", "Illiteracy", "HS Grad")]
> y <- states[,c("Life Exp", "Murder")]
> cor(x,y)
           Life Exp Murder
Population   -0.068  0.344
Income        0.340 -0.230
Illiteracy   -0.588  0.703
HS Grad       0.582 -0.488
```

This version of the function is particularly useful when you're interested in the relationships between one set of variables and another. Notice that the results don't tell you if the correlations differ significantly from 0 (that is, whether there's sufficient evidence based on the sample data to conclude that the population correlations differ from 0). For that, you need tests of significance (described in section 7.3.2).

PARTIAL CORRELATIONS

A *partial* correlation is a correlation between two quantitative variables, <u>controlling for</u> one or more other quantitative variables. You can use the pcor() function in the ggm package to provide partial correlation coefficients. The ggm package isn't installed by default, so be sure to install it on first use. The format is

pcor(u, S)

where u is a vector of numbers, with the first two numbers the indices of the variables to be correlated, and the remaining numbers the indices of the conditioning variables (that is, the variables being partialed out). *S* is the covariance matrix among the variables. An example will help clarify this:

```
> library(ggm)
> # partial correlation of population and murder rate, controlling
> # for income, illiteracy rate, and HS graduation rate
> pcor(c(1,5,2,3,6), cov(states))
[1] 0.346
```

In this case, 0.346 is the correlation between population and murder rate, controlling for the influence of income, illiteracy rate, and HS graduation rate. The use of partial correlations is common in the social sciences.

OTHER TYPES OF CORRELATIONS

The `hetcor()` function in the `polycor` package can compute a heterogeneous correlation matrix containing Pearson product-moment correlations between numeric variables, polyserial correlations between numeric and ordinal variables, polychoric correlations between ordinal variables, and tetrachoric correlations between two dichotomous variables. Polyserial, polychoric, and tetrachoric correlations assume that the ordinal or dichotomous variables are derived from underlying normal distributions. See the documentation that accompanies this package for more information.

7.3.2 *Testing correlations for significance*

Once you've generated correlation coefficients, how do you test them for statistical significance? The typical null hypothesis is no relationship (that is, the correlation in the population is 0). You can use the `cor.test()` function to test an individual Pearson, Spearman, and Kendall correlation coefficient. A simplified format is

```
cor.test(x, y, alternative = , method = )
```

where *x* and *y* are the variables to be correlated, `alternative` specifies a two-tailed or one-tailed test (`"two.side"`, `"less"`, or `"greater"`) and `method` specifies the type of correlation (`"pearson"`, `"kendall"`, or `"spearman"`) to compute. Use `alternative="less"` when the research hypothesis is that the population correlation is less than 0. Use `alternative="greater"` when the research hypothesis is that the population correlation is greater than 0. By default, `alternative="two.side"` (population correlation isn't equal to 0) is assumed. See the following listing for an example.

Listing 7.18 Testing a correlation coefficient for significance

```
> cor.test(states[,3], states[,5])

        Pearson's product-moment correlation

data:  states[, 3] and states[, 5]
t = 6.85, df = 48, p-value = 1.258e-08
alternative hypothesis: true correlation is not equal to 0
95 percent confidence interval:
 0.528 0.821
sample estimates:
  cor
0.703
```

This code tests the null hypothesis that the Pearson correlation between life expectancy and murder rate is 0. Assuming that the population correlation is 0, you'd expect to see a sample correlation as large as 0.703 less than 1 time out of 10 million (that is, p = 1.258e-08). Given how unlikely this is, you reject the null hypothesis in favor of the research hypothesis, that the population correlation between life expectancy and murder rate is *not* 0.

Unfortunately, you can test only one correlation at a time using cor.test. Luckily, the corr.test() function provided in the psych package allows you to go further. The corr.test() function produces correlations and significance levels for matrices of Pearson, Spearman, or Kendall correlations. An example is given in the following listing.

Listing 7.19   Correlation matrix and tests of significance via corr.test

```
> library(psych)
> corr.test(states, use="complete")

Call:corr.test(x = states, use = "complete")
Correlation matrix
           Population Income Illiteracy Life Exp Murder HS Grad
Population      1.00    0.21       0.11    -0.07   0.34   -0.10
Income          0.21    1.00      -0.44     0.34  -0.23    0.62
Illiteracy      0.11   -0.44       1.00    -0.59   0.70   -0.66
Life Exp       -0.07    0.34      -0.59     1.00  -0.78    0.58
Murder          0.34   -0.23       0.70    -0.78   1.00   -0.49
HS Grad        -0.10    0.62      -0.66     0.58  -0.49    1.00

Sample Size
[1] 50
Probability value
           Population Income Illiteracy Life Exp Murder HS Grad
Population      0.00    0.15       0.46     0.64   0.01     0.5
Income          0.15    0.00       0.00     0.02   0.11     0.0
Illiteracy      0.46    0.00       0.00     0.00   0.00     0.0
Life Exp        0.64    0.02       0.00     0.00   0.00     0.0
Murder          0.01    0.11       0.00     0.00   0.00     0.0
HS Grad         0.50    0.00       0.00     0.00   0.00     0.0
```

The use= options can be "pairwise" or "complete" (for pairwise or listwise deletion of missing values, respectively). The method= option is "pearson" (the default), "spearman", or "kendall". Here you see that the correlation between population size and high school graduation rate (–0.10) is not significantly different from 0 (p = 0.5).

OTHER TESTS OF SIGNIFICANCE

In section 7.4.1, we looked at partial correlations. The pcor.test() function in the psych package can be used to test the conditional independence of two variables controlling for one or more additional variables, assuming multivariate normality. The format is

```
pcor.test(r, q, n)
```

where *r* is the partial correlation produced by the pcor() function, *q* is the number of variables being controlled, and *n* is the sample size.

Before leaving this topic, it should be mentioned that the `r.test()` function in the psych package also provides a number of useful significance tests. The function can be used to test the following:

- The significance of a correlation coefficient
- The difference between two independent correlations
- The difference between two dependent correlations sharing one single variable
- The difference between two dependent correlations based on completely different variables

See `help(r.test)` for details.

7.3.3   Visualizing correlations

The bivariate relationships underlying correlations can be visualized through scatter plots and scatter plot matrices, whereas correlograms provide a unique and powerful method for comparing a large numbers of correlation coefficients in a meaningful way. Each is covered in chapter 11.

7.4   t-tests

The most common activity in research is the comparison of two groups. Do patients receiving a new drug show greater improvement than patients using an existing medication? Does one manufacturing process produce fewer defects than another? Which of two teaching methods is most cost-effective? If your outcome variable is categorical, you can use the methods described in section 7.3. Here, we'll focus on group comparisons, where the outcome variable is continuous and assumed to be distributed normally.

For this illustration, we'll use the `UScrime` dataset distributed with the MASS package. It contains information on the effect of punishment regimes on crime rates in 47 US states in 1960. The outcome variables of interest will be `Prob` (the probability of imprisonment), `U1` (the unemployment rate for urban males ages 14–24) and `U2` (the unemployment rate for urban males ages 35–39). The categorical variable `So` (an indicator variable for Southern states) will serve as the grouping variable. The data have been rescaled by the original authors. (Note: I considered naming this section "Crime and Punishment in the Old South," but cooler heads prevailed.)

7.4.1   Independent t-test

Are you more likely to be imprisoned if you commit a crime in the South? The comparison of interest is Southern versus non-Southern states and the dependent variable is the probability of incarceration. A two-group independent t-test can be used to test the hypothesis that the two population means are equal. Here, you assume that the two groups are independent and that the data are sampled from normal populations. The format is either

```
t.test(y ~ x, data)
```

where y is numeric and x is a dichotomous variable, or

```
t.test(y1, y2)
```

where y1 and y2 are numeric vectors (the outcome variable for each group). The optional data argument refers to a matrix or data frame containing the variables. In contrast to most statistical packages, the default test assumes unequal variance and applies the Welsh degrees of freedom modification. You can add a var.equal=TRUE option to specify equal variances and a pooled variance estimate. By default, a two-tailed alternative is assumed (that is, the means differ but the direction isn't specified). You can add the option alternative="less" or alternative="greater" to specify a directional test.

In the following code, you compare Southern (group 1) and non-Southern (group 0) states on the probability of imprisonment using a two-tailed test without the assumption of equal variances:

```
> library(MASS)
> t.test(Prob ~ So, data=UScrime)

        Welch Two Sample t-test

data:  Prob by So
t = -3.8954, df = 24.925, p-value = 0.0006506
alternative hypothesis: true difference in means is not equal to 0
95 percent confidence interval:
 -0.03852569 -0.01187439
sample estimates:
mean in group 0 mean in group 1
     0.03851265      0.06371269
```

You can reject the hypothesis that Southern states and non-Southern states have equal probabilities of imprisonment ($p < .001$).

> **NOTE**   Because the outcome variable is a proportion, you might try to transform it to normality before carrying out the t-test. In the current case, all reasonable transformations of the outcome variable (Y/1-Y, log(Y/1-Y), arcsin(Y), arcsin(sqrt(Y))) would've led to the same conclusions. Transformations are covered in detail in chapter 8.

7.4.2 *Dependent t-test*

As a second example, you might ask if unemployment rate for younger males (14–24) is greater than for older males (35–39). In this case, the two groups aren't independent. You wouldn't expect the unemployment rate for younger and older males in Alabama to be unrelated. When observations in the two groups are related, you have a dependent groups design. Pre-post or repeated measures designs also produce dependent groups.

A dependent t-test assumes that the difference between groups is normally distributed. In this case, the format is

```
t.test(y1, y2, paired=TRUE)
```

where *y1* and *y2* are the numeric vectors for the two dependent groups. The results are as follows:

```
> library(MASS)
> sapply(UScrime[c("U1","U2")], function(x)(c(mean=mean(x),sd=sd(x))))
        U1    U2
mean 95.5 33.98
sd   18.0  8.45

> with(UScrime, t.test(U1, U2, paired=TRUE))

        Paired t-test

data:  U1 and U2
t = 32.4066, df = 46, p-value < 2.2e-16
alternative hypothesis: true difference in means is not equal to 0
95 percent confidence interval:
 57.67003 65.30870
sample estimates:
mean of the differences
               61.48936
```

The mean difference (61.5) is large enough to warrant rejection of the hypothesis that the mean unemployment rate for older and younger males is the same. Younger males have a higher rate. In fact, the probability of obtaining a sample difference this large if the population means are equal is less than 0.00000000000000022 (that is, 2.2e–16).

7.4.3   *When there are more than two groups*

What do you do if you want to compare more than two groups? If you can assume that the data are independently sampled from normal populations, you can use analysis of variance (ANOVA). ANOVA is a comprehensive methodology that covers many experimental and quasi-experimental designs. As such, it has earned its own chapter. Feel free to abandon this section and jump to chapter 9 at any time.

7.5   *Nonparametric tests of group differences*

If you're unable to meet the parametric assumptions of a t-test or ANOVA, you can turn to nonparametric approaches. For example, if the outcome variables are severely skewed or ordinal in nature, you may wish to use the techniques in this section.

7.5.1   *Comparing two groups*

If the two groups are independent, you can use the Wilcoxon rank sum test (more popularly known as the Mann–Whitney U test) to assess whether the observations are sampled from the same probability distribution (that is, whether the probability of obtaining higher scores is greater in one population than the other). The format is either

```
wilcox.test(y ~ x, data)
```

where y is numeric and x is a dichotomous variable, or

```
wilcox.test(y1, y2)
```

where $y1$ and $y2$ are the outcome variables for each group. The optional `data` argument refers to a matrix or data frame containing the variables. The default is a two-tailed test. You can add the option `exact` to produce an exact test, and `alternative="less"` or `alternative="greater"` to specify a directional test.

If you apply the Mann–Whitney U test to the question of incarceration rates from the previous section, you'll get these results:

```
> with(UScrime, by(Prob, So, median))

So: 0
[1] 0.0382
--------------------
So: 1
[1] 0.0556

> wilcox.test(Prob ~ So, data=UScrime)

        Wilcoxon rank sum test

data:  Prob by So
W = 81, p-value = 8.488e-05

alternative hypothesis: true location shift is not equal to 0
```

Again, you can reject the hypothesis that incarceration rates are the same in Southern and non-Southern states ($p < .001$).

The Wilcoxon signed rank test provides a nonparametric alternative to the dependent sample t-test. It's appropriate in situations where the groups are paired and the assumption of normality is unwarranted. The format is identical to the Mann–Whitney U test, but you add the `paired=TRUE` option. Let's apply it to the unemployment question from the previous section:

```
> sapply(UScrime[c("U1","U2")], median)
U1 U2
92 34

> with(UScrime, wilcox.test(U1, U2, paired=TRUE))

        Wilcoxon signed rank test with continuity correction

data:  U1 and U2
V = 1128, p-value = 2.464e-09
alternative hypothesis: true location shift is not equal to 0
```

Again, you'd reach the same conclusion reached with the paired t-test.

In this case, the parametric t-tests and their nonparametric equivalents reach the same conclusions. When the assumptions for the t-tests are reasonable, the parametric tests will be more powerful (more likely to find a difference if it exists). The nonparametric tests are more appropriate when the assumptions are grossly unreasonable (for example, rank ordered data).

7.5.2   *Comparing more than two groups*

When there are more than two groups to be compared, you must turn to other methods. Consider the `state.x77` dataset from section 7.4. It contains population, income, illiteracy rate, life expectancy, murder rate, and high school graduation rate data for US states. What if you want to compare the illiteracy rates in four regions of the country (Northeast, South, North Central, and West)? This is called a one-way design, and there are both parametric and nonparametric approaches available to address the question.

If you can't meet the assumptions of ANOVA designs, you can use nonparametric methods to evaluate group differences. If the groups are independent, a Kruskal–Wallis test will provide you with a useful approach. If the groups are dependent (for example, repeated measures or randomized block design), the Friedman test is more appropriate.

The format for the Kruskal–Wallis test is

```
kruskal.test(y ~ A, data)
```

where y is a numeric outcome variable and A is a grouping variable with two or more levels (if there are two levels, it's equivalent to the Mann–Whitney U test). For the Friedman test, the format is

```
friedman.test(y ~ A | B, data)
```

where y is the numeric outcome variable, A is a grouping variable, and B is a blocking variable that identifies matched observations. In both cases, *data* is an option argument specifying a matrix or data frame containing the variables.

Let's apply the Kruskal–Wallis test to the illiteracy question. First, you'll have to add the region designations to the dataset. These are contained in the dataset `state. region` distributed with the base installation of R.

```
states <- as.data.frame(cbind(state.region, state.x77))
```

Now you can apply the test:

```
> kruskal.test(Illiteracy ~ state.region, data=states)

        Kruskal-Wallis rank sum test

data:  states$Illiteracy by states$state.region
Kruskal-Wallis chi-squared = 22.7, df = 3, p-value = 4.726e-05
```

The significance test suggests that the illiteracy rate isn't the same in each of the four regions of the country (p <.001).

Although you can reject the null hypothesis of no difference, the test doesn't tell you *which* regions differ significantly from each other. To answer this question, you could compare groups two at a time using the Mann–Whitney U test. A more elegant approach is to apply a simultaneous multiple comparisons procedure that makes all pairwise comparisons, while controlling the type I error rate (the probability of finding a difference that isn't there). The npmc package provides the nonparametric multiple comparisons you need.

To be honest, I'm stretching the definition of *basic* in the chapter title quite a bit, but because it fits well here, I hope you'll bear with me. First, be sure to install the npmc package. The npmc() function in this package expects input to be a two-column data frame with a column named var (the dependent variable) and class (the grouping variable). The following listing contains the code you can use to accomplish this.

Listing 7.20   Nonparametric multiple comparisons

```
> class <- state.region
> var <- state.x77[,c("Illiteracy")]
> mydata <- as.data.frame(cbind(class, var))
> rm(class, var)
> library(npmc)
> summary(npmc(mydata), type="BF")

$'Data-structure'
              group.index    class.level nobs
Northeast               1      Northeast    9
South                   2          South   16
North Central           3  North Central   12
West                    4           West   13

$'Results of the multiple Behrens-Fisher-Test'
  cmp effect lower.cl upper.cl p.value.1s p.value.2s
1 1-2 0.8750  0.66149   1.0885   0.000665    0.00135
2 1-3 0.1898 -0.13797   0.5176   0.999999    0.06547
3 1-4 0.3974 -0.00554   0.8004   0.998030    0.92004
4 2-3 0.0104 -0.02060   0.0414   1.000000    0.00000
5 2-4 0.1875 -0.07923   0.4542   1.000000    0.02113
6 3-4 0.5641  0.18740   0.9408   0.797198    0.98430

> aggregate(mydata, by=list(mydata$class), median)
  Group.1 class  var
1       1     1 1.10
2       2     2 1.75
3       3     3 0.70
4       4     4 0.60
```

① Pairwise group comparisons

② Median illiteracy by class

The npmc call generates six statistical comparisons (Northeast versus South, Northeast versus North Central, Northeast versus West, South versus North Central, South versus West, and North Central versus West) ①. You can see from the two-sided p-values (p.value.2s) that the South differs significantly from the other three regions, and that the other three regions don't differ from each other. In ② you see that the South has a higher median illiteracy rate. Note that npmc uses randomized values for integral calculations, so results differ slightly from call to call.

7.6　*Visualizing group differences*

In sections 7.4 and 7.5, we looked at statistical methods for comparing groups. Examining group differences visually is also a crucial part of a comprehensive data analysis strategy. It allows you to assess the magnitude of the differences, identify any distributional characteristics that influence the results (such as skew, bimodality, or outliers), and evaluate the appropriateness of the test assumptions. R provides a wide range of graphical methods for comparing groups, including box plots (simple, notched, and violin), covered in section 6.5; overlapping kernel density plots, covered in section 6.4.1; and graphical methods of assessing test assumptions, discussed in chapter 9.

7.7　*Summary*

In this chapter, we reviewed the functions in R that provide basic statistical summaries and tests. We looked at sample statistics and frequency tables, tests of independence and measures of association for categorical variables, correlations between quantitative variables (and their associated significance tests), and comparisons of two or more groups on a quantitative outcome variable.

In the next chapter, we'll explore simple and multiple regression, where the focus is on understanding relationships between one (simple) or more than one (multiple) predictor variables and a predicted or criterion variable. Graphical methods will help you diagnose potential problems, evaluate and improve the fit of your models, and uncover unexpected gems of information in your data.

Part 3

Intermediate methods

While part 2 covered basic graphical and statistical methods, section 3 offers coverage of intermediate methods. We move from describing the relationship between two variables, to modeling the relationship between a numerical outcome variable and a set of numeric and/or categorical predictor variables.

Chapter 8 introduces regression methods for modeling the relationship between a numeric outcome variable and a set of one or more predictor variables. Modeling data is typically a complex, multistep, interactive process. Chapter 8 provides step-by-step coverage of the methods available for fitting linear models, evaluating their appropriateness, and interpreting their meaning.

Chapter 9 considers the analysis of basic experimental and quasi-experimental designs through the analysis of variance and its variants. Here we're interested in how treatment combinations or conditions affect a numerical outcome variable. The chapter introduces the functions in R that are used to perform an analysis of variance, analysis of covariance, repeated measures analysis of variance, multifactor analysis of variance, and multivariate analysis of variance. Methods for assessing the appropriateness of these analyses, and visualizing the results are also discussed.

In designing experimental and quasi-experimental studies, it's important to determine if the sample size is adequate for detecting the effects of interest (power analysis). Otherwise, why conduct the study? A detailed treatment of power analysis is provided in chapter 10. Starting with a discussion of hypothesis testing, the presentation focuses on how to use R functions to determine the sample size necessary to detect a treatment effect of a given size with a given degree of confidence. This can help you to plan studies that are likely to yield useful results.

Chapter 11 expands on the material in chapter 5 by covering the creation of graphs that help you to visualize relationships among two or more variables. This includes the various types of two- and three-dimensional scatter plots, scatter plot matrices, line plots, and bubble plots. It also introduces the useful, but less well-known, correlograms and mosaic plots.

The linear models described in chapters 8 and 9 assume that the outcome or response variable is not only numeric, but also randomly sampled from a normal distribution. There are situations where this distributional assumption is untenable. Chapter 12 presents analytic methods that work well in cases where data are sampled from unknown or mixed distributions, where sample sizes are small, where outliers are a problem, or where devising an appropriate test based on a theoretical distribution is mathematically intractable. They include both resampling and bootstrapping approaches—computer intensive methods that are powerfully implemented in R. The methods described in this chapter will allow you to devise hypothesis tests for data that do not fit traditional parametric assumptions.

After completing part 3, you'll have the tools to analyze most common data analytic problems encountered in practice. And you will be able to create some gorgeous graphs!

Regression

This chapter covers
- Fitting and interpreting linear models
- Evaluating model assumptions
- Selecting among competing models

In many ways, regression analysis lives at the heart of statistics. It's a broad term for a set of methodologies used to predict a response variable (also called a dependent, criterion, or outcome variable) from one or more predictor variables (also called independent or explanatory variables). In general, regression analysis can be used to *identify* the explanatory variables that are related to a response variable, to *describe* the form of the relationships involved, and to provide an equation for *predicting* the response variable from the explanatory variables.

For example, an exercise physiologist might use regression analysis to develop an equation for predicting the expected number of calories a person will burn while exercising on a treadmill. The response variable is the number of calories burned (calculated from the amount of oxygen consumed), and the predictor variables might include duration of exercise (minutes), percentage of time spent at their target heart rate, average speed (mph), age (years), gender, and body mass index (BMI).

From a theoretical point of view, the analysis will help answer such questions as these:

- What's the relationship between exercise duration and calories burned? Is it linear or curvilinear? For example, does exercise have less impact on the number of calories burned after a certain point?
- How does effort (the percentage of time at the target heart rate, the average walking speed) factor in?
- Are these relationships the same for young and old, male and female, heavy and slim?

From a practical point of view, the analysis will help answer such questions as the following:

- How many calories can a 30-year-old man with a BMI of 28.7 expect to burn if he walks for 45 minutes at an average speed of 4 miles per hour and stays within his target heart rate 80 percent of the time?
- What's the minimum number of variables you need to collect in order to accurately predict the number of calories a person will burn when walking?
- How accurate will your prediction tend to be?

Because regression analysis plays such a central role in modern statistics, we'll cover it in some depth in this chapter. First, we'll look at how to fit and interpret regression models. Next, we'll review a set of techniques for identifying potential problems with these models and how to deal with them. Third, we'll explore the issue of variable selection. Of all the potential predictor variables available, how do you decide which ones to include in your final model? Fourth, we'll address the question of generalizability. How well will your model work when you apply it in the real world? Finally, we'll look at the issue of relative importance. Of all the predictors in your model, which one is the most important, the second most important, and the least important?

As you can see, we're covering a lot of ground. Effective regression analysis is an interactive, holistic process with many steps, and it involves more than a little skill. Rather than break it up into multiple chapters, I've opted to present this topic in a single chapter in order to capture this flavor. As a result, this will be the longest and most involved chapter in the book. Stick with it to the end and you'll have all the tools you need to tackle a wide variety of research questions. Promise!

8.1 The many faces of regression

The term *regression* can be confusing because there are so many specialized varieties (see table 8.1). In addition, R has powerful and comprehensive features for fitting regression models, and the abundance of options can be confusing as well. For example, in 2005, Vito Ricci created a list of over 205 functions in R that are used to generate regression analyses (http://cran.r-project.org/doc/contrib/Ricci-refcard-regression.pdf).

Table 8.1 Varieties of regression analysis

Type of regression	Typical use
Simple linear	Predicting a quantitative response variable from a quantitative explanatory variable
Polynomial	Predicting a quantitative response variable from a quantitative explanatory variable, where the relationship is modeled as an nth order polynomial
Multiple linear	Predicting a quantitative response variable from two or more explanatory variables
Multivariate	Predicting more than one response variable from one or more explanatory variables
Logistic	Predicting a categorical response variable from one or more explanatory variables
Poisson	Predicting a response variable representing counts from one or more explanatory variables
Cox proportional hazards	Predicting time to an event (death, failure, relapse) from one or more explanatory variables
Time-series	Modeling time-series data with correlated errors
Nonlinear	Predicting a quantitative response variable from one or more explanatory variables, where the form of the model is nonlinear
Nonparametric	Predicting a quantitative response variable from one or more explanatory variables, where the form of the model is derived from the data and not specified a priori
Robust	Predicting a quantitative response variable from one or more explanatory variables using an approach that's resistant to the effect of influential observations

In this chapter, we'll focus on regression methods that fall under the rubric of ordinary least squares (OLS) regression, including simple linear regression, polynomial regression, and multiple linear regression. OLS regression is the most common variety of statistical analysis today. Other types of regression models (including logistic regression and Poisson regression) will be covered in chapter 13.

8.1.1 Scenarios for using OLS regression

In OLS regression, a quantitative dependent variable is predicted from a weighted sum of predictor variables, where the weights are parameters estimated from the data. Let's take a look at a concrete example (no pun intended), loosely adapted from Fwa (2006).

An engineer wants to identify the most important factors related to bridge deterioration (such as age, traffic volume, bridge design, construction materials and methods, construction quality, and weather conditions) and determine the mathematical form of these relationships. She collects data on each of these variables from a representative sample of bridges and models the data using OLS regression.

The approach is highly interactive. She fits a series of models, checks their compliance with underlying statistical assumptions, explores any unexpected or aberrant findings, and finally chooses the "best" model from among many possible models. If successful, the results will help her to

- Focus on important variables, by determining which of the many collected variables are useful in predicting bridge deterioration, along with their relative importance.
- Look for bridges that are likely to be in trouble, by providing an equation that can be used to predict bridge deterioration for new cases (where the values of the predictor variables are known, but the degree of bridge deterioration isn't).
- Take advantage of serendipity, by identifying unusual bridges. If she finds that some bridges deteriorate much faster or slower than predicted by the model, a study of these "outliers" may yield important findings that could help her to understand the mechanisms involved in bridge deterioration.

Bridges may hold no interest for you. I'm a clinical psychologist and statistician, and I know next to nothing about civil engineering. But the general principles apply to an amazingly wide selection of problems in the physical, biological, and social sciences. Each of the following questions could also be addressed using an OLS approach:

- What's the relationship between surface stream salinity and paved road surface area (Montgomery, 2007)?
- What aspects of a user's experience contribute to the overuse of massively multiplayer online role playing games (MMORPGs) (Hsu, Wen, & Wu, 2009)?
- Which qualities of an educational environment are most strongly related to higher student achievement scores?
- What's the form of the relationship between blood pressure, salt intake, and age? Is it the same for men and women?
- What's the impact of stadiums and professional sports on metropolitan area development (Baade & Dye, 1990)?
- What factors account for interstate differences in the price of beer (Culbertson & Bradford, 1991)? (That one got your attention!)

Our primary limitation is our ability to formulate an interesting question, devise a useful response variable to measure, and gather appropriate data.

8.1.2   *What you need to know*

For the remainder of this chapter I'll describe how to use R functions to fit OLS regression models, evaluate the fit, test assumptions, and select among competing models. It's assumed that the reader has had exposure to least squares regression as typically taught in a second semester undergraduate statistics course. However, I've made efforts to keep the mathematical notation to a minimum and focus on practical rather than theoretical issues. A number of excellent texts are available that cover the statistical material outlined in this chapter. My favorites are John Fox's *Applied Regression Analysis and Generalized Linear Models* (for theory) and *An R and S-Plus Companion to Applied Regression* (for application). They both served as major sources for this chapter. A good nontechnical overview is provided by Licht (1995).

8.2 OLS regression

For most of this chapter, we'll be predicting the response variable from a set of predictor variables (also called "regressing" the response variable on the predictor variables—hence the name) using OLS. OLS regression fits models of the form

$$\hat{Y}_i = \hat{\beta}_0 + \hat{\beta}_1 X_{1i} + \cdots + \hat{\beta}_k X_{ki} \quad i = 1 \cdots n$$

where n is the number of observations and k is the number of predictor variables. (Although I've tried to keep equations out of our discussions, this is one of the few places where it simplifies things.) In this equation:

$\hat{Y}_i$	is the predicted value of the dependent variable for observation i (specifically, it's the estimated mean of the Y distribution, conditional on the set of predictor values)
X_{ji}	is the jth predictor value for the ith observation
$\hat{\beta}_0$	is the intercept (the predicted value of Y when all the predictor variables equal zero)
$\hat{\beta}_j$	is the regression coefficient for the jth predictor (slope representing the change in Y for a unit change in X_j)

Our goal is to select model parameters (intercept and slopes) that minimize the difference between actual response values and those predicted by the model. Specifically, model parameters are selected to minimize the sum of squared residuals

$$\sum_{1}^{n} \left(Y_i - \hat{Y}_i \right)^2 = \sum_{1}^{n} \left(Y_i - \left(\hat{\beta}_0 + \hat{\beta}_1 X_{1i} + \cdots + \hat{\beta}_k X_{ki} \right) \right)^2 = \sum_{1}^{n} \varepsilon^2$$

To properly interpret the coefficients of the OLS model, you must satisfy a number of statistical assumptions:

- *Normality*—For fixed values of the independent variables, the dependent variable is normally distributed.
- *Independence*—The Yi values are independent of each other.
- *Linearity*—The dependent variable is linearly related to the independent variables.
- *Homoscedasticity*—The variance of the dependent variable doesn't vary with the levels of the independent variables. We could call this constant variance, but saying homoscedasticity makes me feel smarter.

If you violate these assumptions, your statistical significance tests and confidence intervals may not be accurate. Note that OLS regression also assumes that the independent variables are fixed and measured without error, but this assumption is typically relaxed in practice.

8.2.1   *Fitting regression models with lm()*

In R, the basic function for fitting a linear model is `lm()`. The format is

```
myfit <- lm(formula, data)
```

where `formula` describes the model to be fit and `data` is the data frame containing the data to be used in fitting the model. The resulting object (`myfit` in this case) is a list that contains extensive information about the fitted model. The formula is typically written as

```
Y ~ X1 + X2 + … + Xk
```

where the ~ separates the response variable on the left from the predictor variables on the right, and the predictor variables are separated by + signs. Other symbols can be used to modify the formula in various ways (see table 8.2).

Table 8.2   Symbols commonly used in R formulas

Symbol	Usage
~	Separates response variables on the left from the explanatory variables on the right. For example, a prediction of y from x, z, and w would be coded `y ~ x + z + w`.
+	Separates predictor variables.
:	Denotes an interaction between predictor variables. A prediction of y from x, z, and the interaction between x and z would be coded `y ~ x + z + x:z`.
*	A shortcut for denoting all possible interactions. The code `y ~ x * z * w` expands to `y ~ x + z + w + x:z + x:w + z:w + x:z:w`.
^	Denotes interactions up to a specified degree. The code `y ~ (x + z + w)^2` expands to `y ~ x + z + w + x:z + x:w + z:w`.
.	A place holder for all other variables in the data frame except the dependent variable. For example, if a data frame contained the variables x, y, z, and w, then the code `y ~ .` would expand to `y ~ x + z + w`.
-	A minus sign removes a variable from the equation. For example, `y ~ (x + z + w)^2 - x:w` expands to `y ~ x + z + w + x:z + z:w`.
-1	Suppresses the intercept. For example, the formula `y ~ x -1` fits a regression of y on x, and forces the line through the origin at x=0.
I()	Elements within the parentheses are interpreted arithmetically. For example, `y ~ x + (z + w)^2` would expand to `y ~ x + z + w + z:w`. In contrast, the code `y ~ x + I((z + w)^2)` would expand to `y ~ x + h`, where h is a new variable created by squaring the sum of z and w.
function	Mathematical functions can be used in formulas. For example, `log(y) ~ x + z + w` would predict `log(y)` from x, z, and w.

important! →

In addition to `lm()`, table 8.3 lists several functions that are useful when generating a simple or multiple regression analysis. Each of these functions is applied to the object returned by `lm()` in order to generate additional information based on that fitted model.

Table 8.3 Other functions that are useful when fitting linear models

Function	Action
`summary()`	Displays detailed results for the fitted model
`coefficients()`	Lists the model parameters (intercept and slopes) for the fitted model
`confint()`	Provides confidence intervals for the model parameters (95 percent by default)
`fitted()`	Lists the predicted values in a fitted model
`residuals()`	Lists the residual values in a fitted model
`anova()`	Generates an ANOVA table for a fitted model, or an ANOVA table comparing two or more fitted models
`vcov()`	Lists the covariance matrix for model parameters
`AIC()`	Prints Akaike's Information Criterion
`plot()`	Generates diagnostic plots for evaluating the fit of a model
`predict()`	Uses a fitted model to predict response values for a new dataset

When the regression model contains one dependent variable and one independent variable, we call the approach simple linear regression. When there's one predictor variable but powers of the variable are included (for example, X, X^2, X^3), we call it polynomial regression. When there's more than one predictor variable, you call it multiple linear regression. We'll start with an example of a simple linear regression, then progress to examples of polynomial and multiple linear regression, and end with an example of multiple regression that includes an interaction among the predictors.

8.2.2 Simple linear regression

Let's take a look at the functions in table 8.3 through a simple regression example. The dataset women in the base installation provides the height and weight for a set of 15 women ages 30 to 39. We want to predict weight from height. Having an equation for predicting weight from height can help us to identify overweight or underweight individuals. The analysis is provided in the following listing, and the resulting graph is shown in figure 8.1.

Listing 8.1 Simple linear regression

```
> fit <- lm(weight ~ height, data=women)
> summary(fit)
```

```
Call:
lm(formula=weight ~ height, data=women)

Residuals:
   Min    1Q Median    3Q    Max
-1.733 -1.133 -0.383  0.742  3.117

Coefficients:
              Estimate Std. Error t value Pr(>|t|)
(Intercept)  -87.5167     5.9369   -14.7  1.7e-09 ***
height         3.4500     0.0911    37.9  1.1e-14 ***
---
Signif. codes:  0 '***' 0.001 '**' 0.01 '*' 0.05 '.' 0.1 ' ' 1

Residual standard error: 1.53 on 13 degrees of freedom
Multiple R-squared: 0.991      Adjusted R-squared: 0.99
F-statistic: 1.43e+03 on 1 and 13 DF,  p-value: 1.09e-14

> women$weight

 [1] 115 117 120 123 126 129 132 135 139 142 146 150 154 159 164

> fitted(fit)

     1      2      3      4      5      6      7      8      9
112.58 116.03 119.48 122.93 126.38 129.83 133.28 136.73 140.18
    10     11     12     13     14     15
143.63 147.08 150.53 153.98 157.43 160.88

> residuals(fit)

    1     2     3     4     5     6     7     8     9    10    11
 2.42  0.97  0.52  0.07 -0.38 -0.83 -1.28 -1.73 -1.18 -1.63 -1.08
   12    13    14    15
-0.53  0.02  1.57  3.12

> plot(women$height,women$weight,
    xlab="Height (in inches)",
    ylab="Weight (in pounds)")
> abline(fit)
```

Handwritten annotations: $\hat{\beta}_0$　$\hat{\beta}_1$　3 stars is a code meaning .001

From the output, you see that the prediction equation is

$$\overline{\text{Weight}} = -87.52 + 3.45 \times Height$$

Because a height of 0 is impossible, you wouldn't try to give a physical interpretation to the intercept. It merely becomes an adjustment constant. From the Pr(>|t|) column, you see that the regression coefficient (3.45) is significantly different from zero ($p < 0.001$) and indicates that there's an expected increase of 3.45 pounds of weight for every 1 inch increase in height. The multiple R-squared (0.991) indicates that the model accounts for 99.1 percent of the variance in weights. The multiple R-squared is also the squared correlation between the actual and predicted value (that is, $R^2 = r_{\hat{Y}Y}^2$). The residual standard error (1.53 lbs.) can be thought of as the average error in

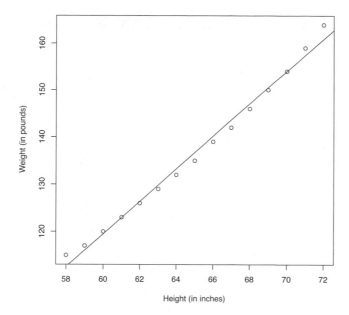

Figure 8.1 Scatter plot with regression line for weight predicted from height

predicting weight from height using this model. The F statistic tests whether the predictor variables taken together, predict the response variable above chance levels. Because there's only one predictor variable in simple regression, in this example the F test is equivalent to the t-test for the regression coefficient for height.

For demonstration purposes, we've printed out the actual, predicted, and residual values. Evidently, the largest residuals occur for low and high heights, which can also be seen in the plot (figure 8.1).

The plot suggests that you might be able to improve on the prediction by using a line with one bend. For example, a model of the form $\hat{Y} = \beta_0 + \beta_1 X + \beta_2 X^2$ may provide a better fit to the data. Polynomial regression allows you to predict a response variable from an explanatory variable, where the form of the relationship is an nth degree polynomial.

8.2.3 Polynomial regression

The plot in figure 8.1 suggests that you might be able to improve your prediction using a regression with a quadratic term (that is, X^2).

You can fit a quadratic equation using the statement

```
fit2 <- lm(weight ~ height + I(height^2), data=women)
```

The new term `I(height^2)` requires explanation. `height^2` adds a height-squared term to the prediction equation. The `I` function treats the contents within the parentheses as an R regular expression. You need this because the `^` operator has a special meaning in formulas that you don't want to invoke here (see table 8.2).

Listing 8.2 shows the results of fitting the quadratic equation.

Listing 8.2   Polynomial regression

```
> fit2 <- lm(weight ~ height + I(height^2), data=women)
> summary(fit2)

Call:
lm(formula=weight ~ height + I(height^2), data=women)

Residuals:
    Min      1Q  Median      3Q     Max
-0.5094 -0.2961 -0.0094  0.2862  0.5971

Coefficients:
             Estimate Std. Error t value Pr(>|t|)
(Intercept) 261.87818   25.19677   10.39 2.4e-07 ***
height       -7.34832    0.77769   -9.45 6.6e-07 ***
I(height^2)   0.08306    0.00598   13.89 9.3e-09 ***
---
Signif. codes:  0 '***' 0.001 '**' 0.01 '*' 0.05 '.' 0.1 ' ' 1

Residual standard error: 0.384 on 12 degrees of freedom
Multiple R-squared: 0.999,     Adjusted R-squared: 0.999
F-statistic: 1.14e+04 on 2 and 12 DF,  p-value: <2e-16

> plot(women$height,women$weight,
    xlab="Height (in inches)",
    ylab="Weight (in lbs)")
> lines(women$height,fitted(fit2))
```

From this new analysis, the prediction equation is

$$\widehat{Weight} = 261.88 - 7.35 \times Height + 0.083 \times Height^2$$

and both regression coefficients are significant at the $p < 0.0001$ level. The amount of variance accounted for has increased to 99.9 percent. The significance of the squared term ($t = 13.89$, $p < .001$) suggests that inclusion of the quadratic term improves the model fit. If you look at the plot of fit2 (figure 8.2) you can see that the curve does indeed provides a better fit.

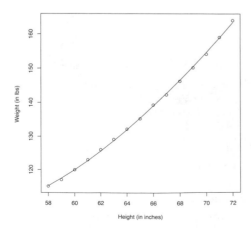

Figure 8.2   Quadratic regression for weight predicted by height

Linear versus nonlinear models

Note that this polynomial equation still fits under the rubric of linear regression. It's linear because the equation involves a weighted sum of predictor variables (height and height-squared in this case). Even a model such as

$$\hat{Y}_i = \hat{\beta}_0 + \hat{\beta}_1 \times \log X_1 + \hat{\beta}_2 \times \sin X_2$$

would be considered a linear model (linear in terms of the parameters) and fit with the formula

$$Y \sim \log(X1) + \sin(X2)$$

In contrast, here's an example of a truly nonlinear model:

$$Y_i = \hat{\beta}_0 + \hat{\beta}_1 e^{\frac{X}{\beta_2}}$$

Nonlinear models of this form can be fit with the `nls()` function.

In general, an nth degree polynomial produces a curve with n-1 bends. To fit a cubic polynomial, you'd use

```
fit3 <- lm(weight ~ height + I(height^2) +I(height^3), data=women)
```

Although higher polynomials are possible, I've rarely found that terms higher than cubic are necessary.

Before we move on, I should mention that the `scatterplot()` function in the `car` package provides a simple and convenient method of plotting a bivariate relationship. The code

```
library(car)
scatterplot(weight ~ height,
  data=women,
  spread=FALSE, lty.smooth=2,
  pch=19,
  main="Women Age 30-39",
  xlab="Height (inches)",
  ylab="Weight (lbs.)")
```

produces the graph in figure 8.3.

This enhanced plot provides the scatter plot of weight with height, box plots for each variable in their respective margins, the linear line of best fit, and a smoothed (loess) fit line. The `spread=FALSE` options suppress spread and asymmetry information. The `lty.smooth=2` option specifies that the loess fit be rendered as a dashed line. The

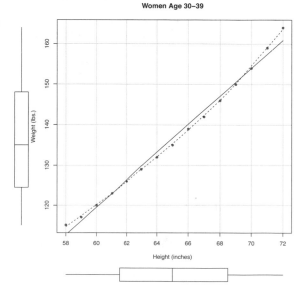

Figure 8.3 Scatter plot of height by weight, with linear and smoothed fits, and marginal box plots

pch=19 options display points as filled circles (the default is open circles). You can tell at a glance that the two variables are roughly symmetrical and that a curved line will fit the data points better than a straight line.

8.2.4   *Multiple linear regression*

When there's more than one predictor variable, simple linear regression becomes multiple linear regression, and the analysis grows more involved. Technically, polynomial regression is a special case of multiple regression. Quadratic regression has two predictors (X and X^2), and cubic regression has three predictors (X, X^2, and X^3). Let's look at a more general example.

We'll use the state.x77 dataset in the base package for this example. We want to explore the relationship between a state's murder rate and other characteristics of the state, including population, illiteracy rate, average income, and frost levels (mean number of days below freezing).

Because the lm() function requires a data frame (and the state.x77 dataset is contained in a matrix), you can simplify your life with the following code:

```
states <- as.data.frame(state.x77[,c("Murder", "Population",
          "Illiteracy", "Income", "Frost")])
```

This code creates a data frame called states, containing the variables we're interested in. We'll use this new data frame for the remainder of the chapter.

A good first step in multiple regression is to examine the relationships among the variables two at a time. The bivariate correlations are provided by the cor() function, and scatter plots are generated from the scatterplotMatrix() function in the car package (see the following listing and figure 8.4).

Listing 8.3   Examining bivariate relationships

```
> cor(states)
            Murder Population Illiteracy Income Frost
Murder        1.00       0.34       0.70  -0.23 -0.54
Population     0.34       1.00       0.11   0.21 -0.33
Illiteracy     0.70       0.11       1.00  -0.44 -0.67
Income        -0.23       0.21      -0.44   1.00  0.23
Frost         -0.54      -0.33      -0.67   0.23  1.00

> library(car)
> scatterplotMatrix(states, spread=FALSE, lty.smooth=2,
    main="Scatter Plot Matrix")
```

By default, the scatterplotMatrix() function provides scatter plots of the variables with each other in the off-diagonals and superimposes smoothed (loess) and linear fit lines on these plots. The principal diagonal contains density and rug plots for each variable.

You can see that murder rate may be bimodal and that each of the predictor variables is skewed to some extent. Murder rates rise with population and illiteracy, and fall with higher income levels and frost. At the same time, colder states have lower illiteracy rates and population and higher incomes.

Scatterplot Matrix

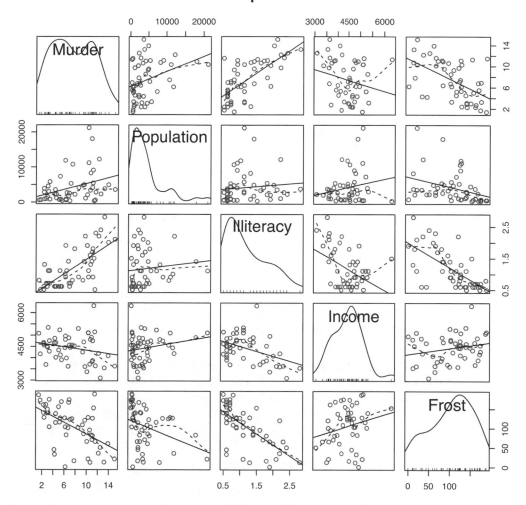

Figure 8.4 Scatter plot matrix of dependent and independent variables for the states data, including linear and smoothed fits, and marginal distributions (kernel density plots and rug plots)

Now let's fit the multiple regression model with the `lm()` function (see the following listing).

Listing 8.4   Multiple linear regression

```
> fit <- lm(Murder ~ Population + Illiteracy + Income + Frost,
            data=states)
> summary(fit)

Call:
lm(formula=Murder ~ Population + Illiteracy + Income + Frost,
    data=states)
```

```
Residuals:
     Min      1Q   Median       3Q      Max
 -4.7960 -1.6495  -0.0811   1.4815   7.6210

Coefficients:
              Estimate Std. Error t value Pr(>|t|)
 (Intercept)  1.23e+00    3.87e+00    0.32    0.751
 Population   2.24e-04    9.05e-05    2.47    0.017 *
 Illiteracy   4.14e+00    8.74e-01    4.74  2.2e-05 ***
 Income       6.44e-05    6.84e-04    0.09    0.925
 Frost        5.81e-04    1.01e-02    0.06    0.954
 ---
 Signif. codes:  0 '***' 0.001 '**' 0.01 '*' 0.05 '.v 0.1 'v' 1

 Residual standard error: 2.5 on 45 degrees of freedom
 Multiple R-squared: 0.567,        Adjusted R-squared: 0.528
 F-statistic: 14.7 on 4 and 45 DF,  p-value: 9.13e-08
```

When there's more than one predictor variable, the regression coefficients indicate the increase in the dependent variable for a unit change in a predictor variable, holding all other predictor variables constant. For example, the regression coefficient for Illiteracy is 4.14, suggesting that an increase of 1 percent in illiteracy is associated with a 4.14 percent increase in the murder rate, controlling for population, income, and temperature. The coefficient is significantly different from zero at the $p < .0001$ level. On the other hand, the coefficient for Frost isn't significantly different from zero ($p = 0.954$) suggesting that Frost and Murder aren't linearly related when controlling for the other predictor variables. Taken together, the predictor variables account for 57 percent of the variance in murder rates across states.

Up to this point, we've assumed that the predictor variables don't interact. In the next section, we'll consider a case in which they do.

8.2.5 *Multiple linear regression with interactions*

Some of the most interesting research findings are those involving interactions among predictor variables. Consider the automobile data in the mtcars data frame. Let's say that you're interested in the impact of automobile weight and horse power on mileage. You could fit a regression model that includes both predictors, along with their interaction, as shown in the next listing.

Listing 8.5   Multiple linear regression with a significant interaction term

```
> fit <- lm(mpg ~ hp + wt + hp:wt, data=mtcars)
> summary(fit)

Call:
lm(formula=mpg ~ hp + wt + hp:wt, data=mtcars)

Residuals:
    Min      1Q  Median      3Q     Max
 -3.063  -1.649  -0.736   1.421   4.551
```

```
Coefficients:
            Estimate Std. Error t value Pr(>|t|)
(Intercept) 49.80842    3.60516   13.82 5.0e-14 ***
hp          -0.12010    0.02470   -4.86 4.0e-05 ***
wt          -8.21662    1.26971   -6.47 5.2e-07 ***
hp:wt        0.02785    0.00742    3.75 0.00081 ***
---
Signif. codes:  0 '***' 0.001 '**' 0.01 '*' 0.05 '.' 0.1 ' ' 1

Residual standard error: 2.1 on 28 degrees of freedom
Multiple R-squared: 0.885,      Adjusted R-squared: 0.872
F-statistic: 71.7 on 3 and 28 DF,  p-value: 2.98e-13
```

You can see from the `Pr(>|t|)` column that the interaction between horse power and car weight is significant. What does this mean? A significant interaction between two predictor variables tells you that the relationship between one predictor and the response variable depends on the level of the other predictor. Here it means that the relationship between miles per gallon and horse power varies by car weight.

Our model for predicting `mpg` is $\widehat{mpg} = 49.81 - 0.12 \times hp - 8.22 \times wt + 0.03 \times hp \times wt$. To interpret the interaction, you can plug in various values of `wt` and simplify the equation. For example, you can try the mean of `wt` (3.2) and one standard deviation below and above the mean (2.2 and 4.2, respectively). For `wt=2.2`, the equation simplifies to $\widehat{mpg} = 49.81 - 0.12 \times hp - 8.22 \times (2.2) + 0.03 \times hp \times (2.2) = 31.41 - 0.06 \times hp$. For `wt=3.2`, this becomes $\widehat{mpg} = 23.37 - 0.03 \times hp$. Finally, for `wt=4.2` the equation becomes $\widehat{mpg} = 15.33 - 0.003 \times hp$. You see that as weight increases (2.2, 3.2, 4.2), the expected change in `mpg` from a unit increase in `hp` decreases (0.06, 0.03, 0.003).

You can visualize interactions using the `effect()` function in the `effects` package. The format is

```
plot(effect(term, mod, xlevels),
   multiline=TRUE)
```

where `term` is the quoted model term to plot, `mod` is the fitted model returned by `lm()`, and `xlevels` is a list specifying the variables to be set to constant values and the values to employ. The `multiline=TRUE` option superimposes the lines being plotted. For the previous model, this becomes

```
library(effects)
plot(effect("hp:wt", fit,
   list(wt=c(2.2,3.2,4.2))),
   multiline=TRUE)
```

The resulting graph is displayed in figure 8.5.

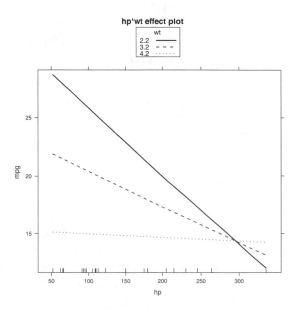

Figure 8.5 Interaction plot for hp*wt. This plot displays the relationship between mpg and hp at 3 values of wt.

You can see from this graph that as the weight of the car increases, the relationship between horse power and miles per gallon weakens. For wt=4.2, the line is almost horizontal, indicating that as hp increases, mpg doesn't change.

Unfortunately, fitting the model is only the first step in the analysis. Once you fit a regression model, you need to evaluate whether you've met the statistical assumptions underlying your approach before you can have confidence in the inferences you draw. This is the topic of the next section.

8.3 *Regression diagnostics*

In the previous section, you used the lm() function to fit an OLS regression model and the summary() function to obtain the model parameters and summary statistics. Unfortunately, there's nothing in this printout that tells you if the model you have fit is appropriate. Your confidence in inferences about regression parameters depends on the degree to which you've met the statistical assumptions of the OLS model. Although the summary() function in listing 8.4 describes the model, it provides no information concerning the degree to which you've satisfied the statistical assumptions *underlying* the model.

Why is this important? Irregularities in the data or misspecifications of the relationships between the predictors and the response variable can lead you to settle on a model that's wildly inaccurate. On the one hand, you may conclude that a predictor and response variable are unrelated when, in fact, they are. On the other hand, you may conclude that a predictor and response variable are related when, in fact, they aren't! You may also end up with a model that makes poor predictions when applied in real-world settings, with significant and unnecessary error.

Let's look at the output from the confint() function applied to the states multiple regression problem in section 8.2.4.

```
> fit <- lm(Murder ~ Population + Illiteracy + Income + Frost, data=states)
> confint(fit)
                   2.5 %     97.5 %
(Intercept) -6.55e+00   9.021318
Population   4.14e-05   0.000406
Illiteracy   2.38e+00   5.903874
Income      -1.31e-03   0.001441
Frost       -1.97e-02   0.020830
```

(handwritten annotation) ← 95% interval

(handwritten annotation) [2.38, 5.90]

The results suggest that you can be 95 percent confident that the interval [2.38, 5.90] contains the true change in murder rate for a 1 percent change in illiteracy rate. Additionally, because the confidence interval for Frost contains 0, you can conclude that a change in temperature is unrelated to murder rate, holding the other variables constant. But your faith in these results is only as strong as the evidence that you have that your data satisfies the statistical assumptions underlying the model.

A set of techniques called *regression diagnostics* provides you with the necessary tools for evaluating the appropriateness of the regression model and can help you to uncover and correct problems. First, we'll start with a standard approach that uses functions that come with R's base installation. Then we'll look at newer, improved methods available through the car package.

8.3.1 A typical approach

R's base installation provides numerous methods for evaluating the statistical assumptions in a regression analysis. The most common approach is to apply the plot() function to the object returned by the lm(). Doing so produces four graphs that are useful for evaluating the model fit. Applying this approach to the simple linear regression example

```
fit <- lm(weight ~ height, data=women)
par(mfrow=c(2,2))
plot(fit)
```

produces the graphs shown in figure 8.6. The par(mfrow=c(2,2)) statement is used to combine the four plots produced by the plot() function into one large 2x2 graph. The par() function is described in chapter 3.

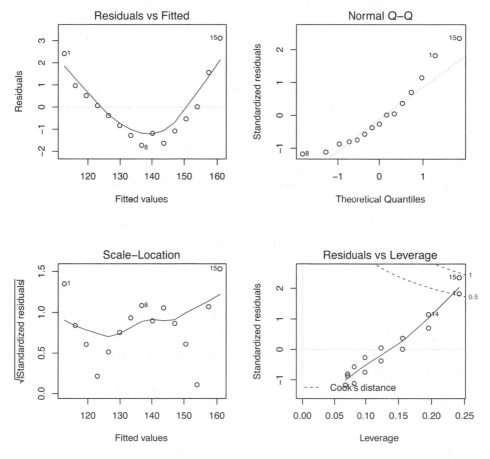

Figure 8.6 Diagnostic plots for the regression of weight on height

To understand these graphs, consider the assumptions of OLS regression:

- *Normality*—If the dependent variable is normally distributed for a fixed set of predictor values, then the residual values should be normally distributed with a mean of 0. The Normal Q-Q plot (upper right) is a probability plot of the standardized residuals against the values that would be expected under normality. If you've met the normality assumption, the points on this graph should fall on the straight 45-degree line. Because they don't, you've clearly violated the normality assumption.

- *Independence*—You can't tell if the dependent variable values are independent from these plots. You have to use your understanding of how the data were collected. There's no a priori reason to believe that one woman's weight influences another woman's weight. If you found out that the data were sampled from families, you may have to adjust your assumption of independence.

- *Linearity*—If the dependent variable is linearly related to the independent variables, there should be no systematic relationship between the residuals and the predicted (that is, fitted) values. In other words, the model should capture all the systematic variance present in the data, leaving nothing but random noise. In the Residuals versus Fitted graph (upper left), you see clear evidence of a curved relationship, which suggests that you may want to add a quadratic term to the regression.

- *Homoscedasticity*—If you've met the constant variance assumption, the points in the Scale-Location graph (bottom left) should be a random band around a horizontal line. You seem to meet this assumption.

Finally, the Residual versus Leverage graph (bottom right) provides information on individual observations that you may wish to attend to. The graph identifies outliers, high-leverage points, and influential observations. Specifically:

- An *outlier* is an observation that isn't predicted well by the fitted regression model (that is, has a large positive or negative residual).

- An observation with a high *leverage* value has an unusual combination of predictor values. That is, it's an outlier in the predictor space. The dependent variable value isn't used to calculate an observation's leverage.

- An *influential observation* is an observation that has a disproportionate impact on the determination of the model parameters. Influential observations are identified using a statistic called Cook's distance, or Cook's D.

To be honest, I find the Residual versus Leverage plot difficult to read and not useful. You'll see better representations of this information in later sections.

To complete this section, let's look at the diagnostic plots for the quadratic fit. The necessary code is

```
fit2 <- lm(weight ~ height + I(height^2), data=women)
par(mfrow=c(2,2))
plot(fit2)
```

and the resulting graph is provided in figure 8.7.

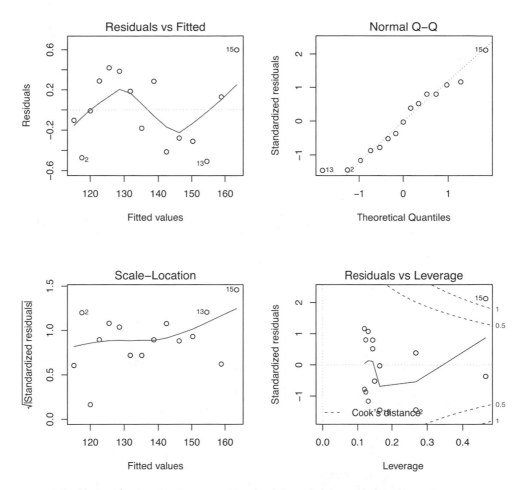

Figure 8.7	**Diagnostic plots for the regression of weight on height and height-squared**

This second set of plots suggests that the polynomial regression provides a better fit with regard to the linearity assumption, normality of residuals (except for observation 13), and homoscedasticity (constant residual variance). Observation 15 appears to be influential (based on a large Cook's D value), and deleting it has an impact on the parameter estimates. In fact, dropping both observation 13 and 15 produces a better model fit. To see this, try

```
newfit <- lm(weight~ height + I(height^2), data=women[-c(13,15),])
```

for yourself. But you need to be careful when deleting data. Your models should fit your data, not the other way around!

Finally, let's apply the basic approach to the states multiple regression problem:

```
fit <- lm(Murder ~ Population + Illiteracy + Income + Frost, data=states)
par(mfrow=c(2,2))
plot(fit)
```

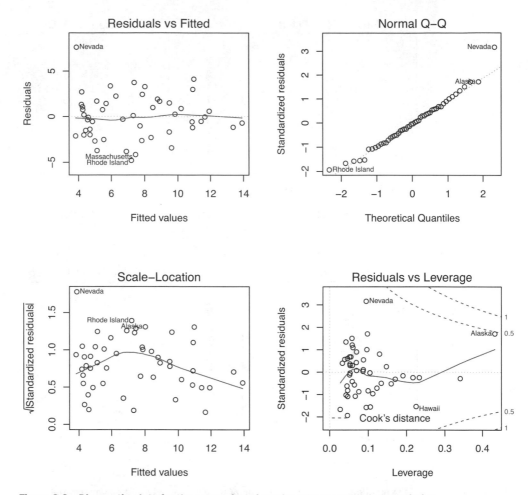

Figure 8.8 Diagnostic plots for the regression of murder rate on state characteristics

The results are displayed in figure 8.8. As you can see from the graph, the model assumptions appear to be well satisfied, with the exception that Nevada is an outlier.

Although these standard diagnostic plots are helpful, better tools are now available in R and I recommend their use over the plot(fit) approach.

8.3.2 *An enhanced approach*

The car package provides a number of functions that significantly enhance your ability to fit and evaluate regression models (see table 8.4).

Table 8.4   Useful functions for regression diagnostics (`car` package)

Function	Purpose
`qqPlot()`	Quantile comparisons plot
`durbinWatsonTest()`	Durbin–Watson test for autocorrelated errors
`crPlots()`	Component plus residual plots
`ncvTest()`	Score test for nonconstant error variance
`spreadLevelPlot()`	Spread-level plot
`outlierTest()`	Bonferroni outlier test
`avPlots()`	Added variable plots
`influencePlot()`	Regression influence plot
`scatterplot()`	Enhanced scatter plot
`scatterplotMatrix()`	Enhanced scatter plot matrix
`vif()`	Variance inflation factors

It's important to note that there are many changes between version 1.x and version 2.x of the `car` package, including changes in function names and behavior. This chapter is based on version 2.

In addition, the `gvlma` package provides a global test for linear model assumptions. Let's look at each in turn, by applying them to our multiple regression example.

NORMALITY

The `qqPlot()` function provides a more accurate method of assessing the normality assumption than provided by the `plot()` function in the base package. It plots the *studentized residuals* (also called *studentized deleted residuals* or *jackknifed residuals*) against a *t* distribution with n-p-1 degrees of freedom, where n is the sample size and p is the number of regression parameters (including the intercept). The code follows:

```
library(car)
fit <- lm(Murder ~ Population + Illiteracy + Income + Frost, data=states)
qqPlot(fit, labels=row.names(states), id.method="identify",
  simulate=TRUE, main="Q-Q Plot")
```

The `qqPlot()` function generates the probability plot displayed in figure 8.9. The option `id.method="identify"` makes the plot interactive—after the graph is drawn, mouse clicks on points within the graph will label them with values specified in the `labels` option of the function. Hitting the Esc key, selecting Stop from the graph's drop-down menu, or right-clicking on the graph will turn off this interactive mode. Here, I identified Nevada. When `simulate=TRUE`, a 95 percent confidence envelope is produced using a parametric bootstrap. (Bootstrap methods are considered in chapter 12.)

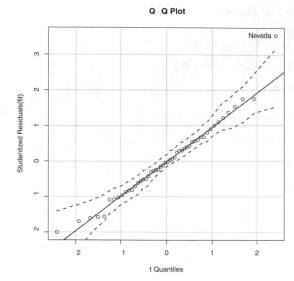

Figure 8.9   Q-Q plot for studentized residuals

With the exception of Nevada, all the points fall close to the line and are within the confidence envelope, suggesting that you've met the normality assumption fairly well. But you should definitely look at Nevada. It has a large positive residual (actual-predicted), indicating that the model underestimates the murder rate in this state. Specifically:

```
> states["Nevada",]

         Murder Population Illiteracy Income Frost
Nevada    11.5        590        0.5   5149   188

> fitted(fit)["Nevada"]

  Nevada
3.878958

> residuals(fit)["Nevada"]

  Nevada
7.621042

> rstudent(fit)["Nevada"]

  Nevada
3.542929
```

Here you see that the murder rate is 11.5 percent, but the model predicts a 3.9 percent murder rate.

The question that you need to ask is, "Why does Nevada have a higher murder rate than predicted from population, income, illiteracy, and temperature?" Anyone (who hasn't see *Goodfellas*) want to guess?

For completeness, here's another way of visualizing errors. Take a look at the code in the next listing. The `residplot()` function generates a histogram of the studentized residuals and superimposes a normal curve, kernel density curve, and rug plot. It doesn't require the `car` package.

Listing 8.6　Function for plotting studentized residuals

```
residplot <- function(fit, nbreaks=10) {
            z <- rstudent(fit)
            hist(z, breaks=nbreaks, freq=FALSE,
            xlab="Studentized Residual",
            main="Distribution of Errors")
            rug(jitter(z), col="brown")
            curve(dnorm(x, mean=mean(z), sd=sd(z)),
                add=TRUE, col="blue", lwd=2)
            lines(density(z)$x, density(z)$y,
                col="red", lwd=2, lty=2)
            legend("topright",
                legend = c( "Normal Curve", "Kernel Density Curve"),
                lty=1:2, col=c("blue","red"), cex=.7)
        }

residplot(fit)
```

The results are displayed in figure 8.10.

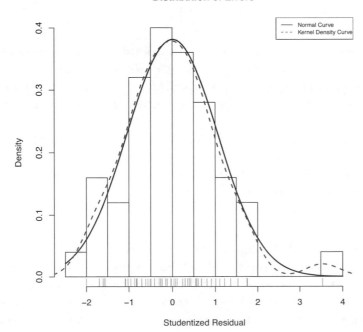

Figure 8.10　Distribution of studentized residuals using the `residplot()` function

As you can see, the errors follow a normal distribution quite well, with the exception of a large outlier. Although the Q-Q plot is probably more informative, I've always found it easier to gauge the skew of a distribution from a histogram or density plot than from a probability plot. Why not use both?

INDEPENDENCE OF ERRORS

As indicated earlier, the best way to assess whether the dependent variable values (and thus the residuals) are independent is from your knowledge of how the data were collected. For example, time series data will often display autocorrelation—observations collected closer in time will be more correlated with each other than with observations distant in time. The car package provides a function for the Durbin–Watson test to detect such serially correlated errors. You can apply the Durbin–Watson test to the multiple regression problem with the following code:

```
> durbinWatsonTest(fit)
 lag Autocorrelation D-W Statistic p-value
   1          -0.201          2.32   0.282
 Alternative hypothesis: rho != 0
```

The nonsignificant p-value (p=0.282) suggests a lack of autocorrelation, and conversely an independence of errors. The lag value (1 in this case) indicates that each observation is being compared with the one next to it in the dataset. Although appropriate for time-dependent data, the test is less applicable for data that isn't clustered in this fashion. Note that the durbinWatsonTest() function uses bootstrapping (see chapter 12) to derive p-values. Unless you add the option simulate=FALSE, you'll get a slightly different value each time you run the test.

LINEARITY

You can look for evidence of nonlinearity in the relationship between the dependent variable and the independent variables by using *component plus residual plots* (also known as *partial residual plots*). The plot is produced by crPlots() function in the car package. You're looking for any systematic departure from the linear model that you've specified.

To create a component plus residual plot for variable X_j, you plot the points $\varepsilon_i + (\hat{\beta}_j * X_{ji})$ vs. X_{ji}, where the residuals (ε_i) are based on the full model, and i =1…n. The straight line in each graph is given by $(\hat{\beta}_j * X_{ji})$ vs. X_{ji}. Loess fit lines are described in chapter 11. The code to produce these plots is as follows:

```
> library(car)
> crPlots(fit)
```

The resulting plots are provided in figure 8.11. Nonlinearity in any of these plots suggests that you may not have adequately modeled the functional form of that predictor in the regression. If so, you may need to add curvilinear components such as polynomial terms, transform one or more variables (for example, use log(X) instead of X), or abandon linear regression in favor of some other regression variant. Transformations are discussed later in this chapter.

Component + Residual Plots

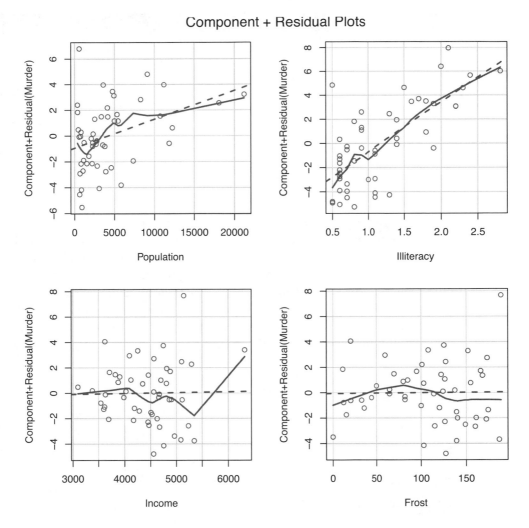

Figure 8.11 Component plus residual plots for the regression of murder rate on state characteristics

The component plus residual plots confirm that you've met the linearity assumption. The form of the linear model seems to be appropriate for this dataset. *?*

HOMOSCEDASTICITY

The car package also provides two useful functions for identifying non-constant error variance. The ncvTest() function produces a score test of the hypothesis of constant error variance against the alternative that the error variance changes with the level of the fitted values. A significant result suggests heteroscedasticity (nonconstant error variance).

The spreadLevelPlot() function creates a scatter plot of the absolute standardized residuals versus the fitted values, and superimposes a line of best fit. Both functions are demonstrated in listing 8.7.

? 8.11 looks terrible!
If this is good, what does bad look like?

Listing 8.7   Assessing homoscedasticity

```
> library(car)
> ncvTest(fit)

Non-constant Variance Score Test
Variance formula: ~ fitted.values
Chisquare=1.7     Df=1      p=0.19

> spreadLevelPlot(fit)

Suggested power transformation:   1.2
```

The score test is nonsignificant (p = 0.19), suggesting that you've met the constant variance assumption. You can also see this in the spread-level plot (figure 8.12). The points form a random horizontal band around a horizontal line of best fit. If you'd violated the assumption, you'd expect to see a nonhorizontal line. The suggested power transformation in listing 8.7 is the suggested power p (Y^p) that would stabilize the nonconstant error variance. For example, if the plot showed a nonhorizontal trend and the suggested power transformation was 0.5, then using $\sqrt{Y}$ rather than Y in the regression equation might lead to a model that satisfies homoscedasticity. If the suggested power was 0, you'd use a log transformation. In the current example, there's no evidence of heteroscedasticity and the suggested power is close to 1 (no transformation required).

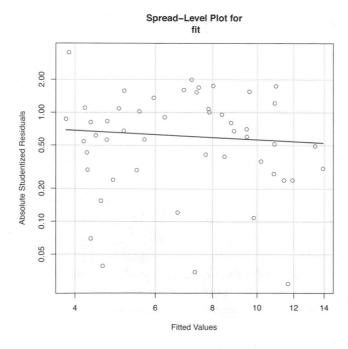

Figure 8.12   Spread-level plot for assessing constant error variance

8.3.3 Global validation of linear model assumption

Finally, let's examine the `gvlma()` function in the `gvlma` package. Written by Pena and Slate (2006), the `gvlma()` function performs a global validation of linear model assumptions as well as separate evaluations of skewness, kurtosis, and heteroscedasticity. In other words, it provides a single omnibus (go/no go) test of model assumptions. The following listing applies the test to the states data.

Listing 8.8   Global test of linear model assumptions

```
> library(gvlma)
> gvmodel <- gvlma(fit)
> summary(gvmodel)

ASSESSMENT OF THE LINEAR MODEL ASSUMPTIONS
USING THE GLOBAL TEST ON 4 DEGREES-OF-FREEDOM:
Level of Significance= 0.05

Call:
 gvlma(x=fit)

                     Value p-value                   Decision
Global Stat          2.773   0.597 Assumptions acceptable.
Skewness             1.537   0.215 Assumptions acceptable.
Kurtosis             0.638   0.425 Assumptions acceptable.
Link Function        0.115   0.734 Assumptions acceptable.
Heteroscedasticity 0.482   0.487 Assumptions acceptable.
```

You can see from the printout (the Global Stat line) that the data meet all the statistical assumptions that go with the OLS regression model ($p = 0.597$). If the decision line had indicated that the assumptions were violated (say, $p < 0.05$), you'd have had to explore the data using the previous methods discussed in this section to determine which assumptions were the culprit.

8.3.4 Multicollinearity

Before leaving this section on regression diagnostics, let's focus on a problem that's not directly related to statistical assumptions but is important in allowing you to interpret multiple regression results.

Imagine you're conducting a study of grip strength. Your independent variables include date of birth (DOB) and age. You regress grip strength on DOB and age and find a significant overall F test at $p < .001$. But when you look at the individual regression coefficients for DOB and age, you find that they're both nonsignificant (that is, there's no evidence that either is related to grip strength). What happened?

The problem is that DOB and age are perfectly correlated within rounding error. A regression coefficient measures the impact of one predictor variable on the response variable, holding all other predictor variables constant. This amounts to looking at the relationship of grip strength and age, holding age constant. The problem is called *multicollinearity*. It leads to large confidence intervals for your model parameters and makes the interpretation of individual coefficients difficult.

Multicollinearity can be detected using a statistic called the *variance inflation factor* (VIF). For any predictor variable, the square root of the VIF indicates the degree to which the confidence interval for that variable's regression parameter is expanded relative to a model with uncorrelated predictors (hence the name). VIF values are provided by the vif() function in the car package. As a general rule, $\sqrt{vif} > 2$ indicates a multicollinearity problem. The code is provided in the following listing. The results indicate that multicollinearity isn't a problem with our predictor variables.

Listing 8.9   Evaluating multicollinearity

```
>library(car)
> vif(fit)

Population Illiteracy      Income      Frost
      1.2         2.2         1.3        2.1

> sqrt(vif(fit)) > 2 # problem?
Population Illiteracy      Income      Frost
     FALSE       FALSE       FALSE      FALSE
```

8.4   *Unusual observations*

A comprehensive regression analysis will also include a screening for unusual observations—namely outliers, high-leverage observations, and influential observations. These are data points that warrant further investigation, either because they're different than other observations in some way, or because they exert a disproportionate amount of influence on the results. Let's look at each in turn.

8.4.1   *Outliers*

Outliers are observations that aren't predicted well by the model. They have either unusually large positive or negative residuals $(Y_i - \widehat{Y}_i)$. Positive residuals indicate that the model is underestimating the response value, while negative residuals indicate an overestimation.

You've already seen one way to identify outliers. Points in the Q-Q plot of figure 8.9 that lie outside the confidence band are considered outliers. A rough rule of thumb is that standardized residuals that are larger than 2 or less than –2 are worth attention.

The car package also provides a statistical test for outliers. The outlierTest() function reports the Bonferroni adjusted p-value for the largest absolute studentized residual:

```
> library(car)
> outlierTest(fit)

       rstudent unadjusted p-value Bonferonni p
Nevada      3.5            0.00095        0.048
```

Here, you see that Nevada is identified as an outlier (p = 0.048). Note that this function tests the single largest (positive or negative) residual for significance as an outlier. If it isn't significant, there are no outliers in the dataset. If it is significant, you must delete it and rerun the test to see if others are present.

8.4.2 High leverage points

Observations that have high leverage are outliers with regard to the other predictors. In other words, they have an unusual combination of predictor values. The response value isn't involved in determining leverage.

Observations with high leverage are identified through the *hat statistic*. For a given dataset, the average hat value is p/n, where p is the number of parameters estimated in the model (including the intercept) and n is the sample size. Roughly speaking, an observation with a hat value greater than 2 or 3 times the average hat value should be examined. The code that follows plots the hat values:

```
hat.plot <- function(fit) {
            p <- length(coefficients(fit))
            n <- length(fitted(fit))
            plot(hatvalues(fit), main="Index Plot of Hat Values")
            abline(h=c(2,3)*p/n, col="red", lty=2)
            identify(1:n, hatvalues(fit), names(hatvalues(fit)))
         }
hat.plot(fit)
```

define hat value?

The resulting graph is shown in figure 8.13.

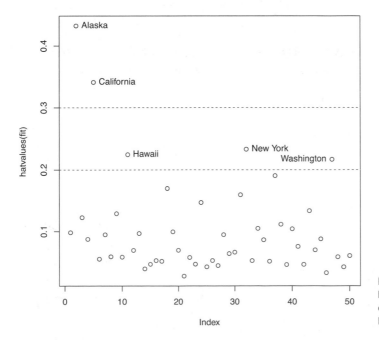

Index Plot of Hat Values

$$avg\ hat = \frac{p}{n}$$
$$= \frac{5}{50}$$
$$= 1/10$$

Figure 8.13   Index plot of hat values for assessing observations with high leverage

Horizontal lines are drawn at 2 and 3 times the average hat value. The locator function places the graph in interactive mode. Clicking on points of interest labels them until the user presses Esc, selects Stop from the graph drop-down menu, or right-clicks on the graph. Here you see that Alaska and California are particularly unusual when it comes to their predictor values. Alaska has a much higher income than other states, while having a lower population and temperature. California has a much higher population than other states, while having a higher income and higher temperature. These states are atypical compared with the other 48 observations.

High leverage observations may or may not be influential observations. That will depend on whether they're also outliers.

8.4.3   Influential observations

Influential observations are observations that have a disproportionate impact on the values of the model parameters. Imagine finding that your model changes dramatically with the removal of a single observation. It's this concern that leads you to examine your data for influential points.

There are two methods for identifying influential observations: Cook's distance, or D statistic and *added variable* plots. Roughly speaking, Cook's D values greater than $4/(n\text{-}k\text{-}1)$, where n is the sample size and k is the number of predictor variables, indicate influential observations. You can create a Cook's D plot (figure 8.14) with the following code:

```
cutoff <- 4/(nrow(states)-length(fit$coefficients)-2)
plot(fit, which=4, cook.levels=cutoff)
abline(h=cutoff, lty=2, col="red")
```

The graph identifies Alaska, Hawaii, and Nevada as influential observations. Deleting these states will have a notable impact on the values of the intercept and slopes in the

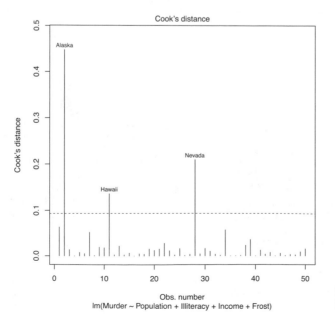

Figure 8.14   Cook's D plot for identifying influential observations

$$\frac{4}{n-k-1} =$$

$$\frac{4}{50-4-1} =$$

$$\frac{4}{45} = .0\overline{8}$$

regression model. Note that although it's useful to cast a wide net when searching for influential observations, I tend to find a cutoff of 1 more generally useful than 4/(n-k-1). Given a criterion of D=1, none of the observations in the dataset would appear to be influential.

Cook's D plots can help identify influential observations, but they don't provide information on how these observations affect the model. Added-variable plots can help in this regard. For one response variable and k predictor variables, you'd create k added-variable plots as follows.

For each predictor X_k, plot the residuals from regressing the response variable on the other k-1 predictors versus the residuals from regressing X_k on the other k-1 predictors. Added-variable plots can be created using the avPlots() function in the car package:

```
library(car)
avPlots(fit, ask=FALSE, onepage=TRUE, id.method="identify")
```

The resulting graphs are provided in figure 8.15. The graphs are produced one at a time, and users can click on points to identify them. Press Esc, choose Stop from the graph's menu, or right-click to move on to the next plot. Here, I've identified Alaska in the bottom-left plot.

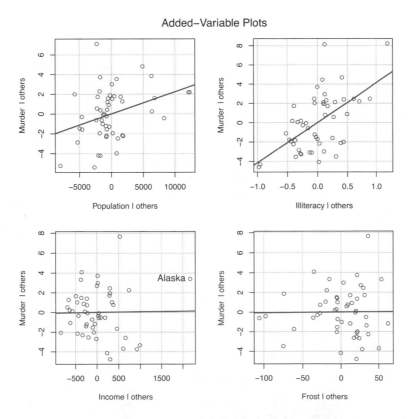

Figure 8.15 Added-variable plots for assessing the impact of influential observations

The straight line in each plot is the actual regression coefficient for that predictor variable. You can see the impact of influential observations by imagining how the line would change if the point representing that observation was deleted. For example, look at the graph of Murder | others versus Income | others in the lower-left corner. You can see that eliminating the point labeled Alaska would move the line in a negative direction. In fact, deleting Alaska changes the regression coefficient for Income from positive (.00006) to negative (−.00085).

You can combine the information from outlier, leverage, and influence plots into one highly informative plot using the `influencePlot()` function from the `car` package:

```
library(car)
influencePlot(fit, id.method="identify", main="Influence Plot",
              sub="Circle size is proportional to Cook's distance")
```

The resulting plot (figure 8.16) shows that Nevada and Rhode Island are outliers; New York, California, Hawaii, and Washington have high leverage; and Nevada, Alaska, and Hawaii are influential observations.

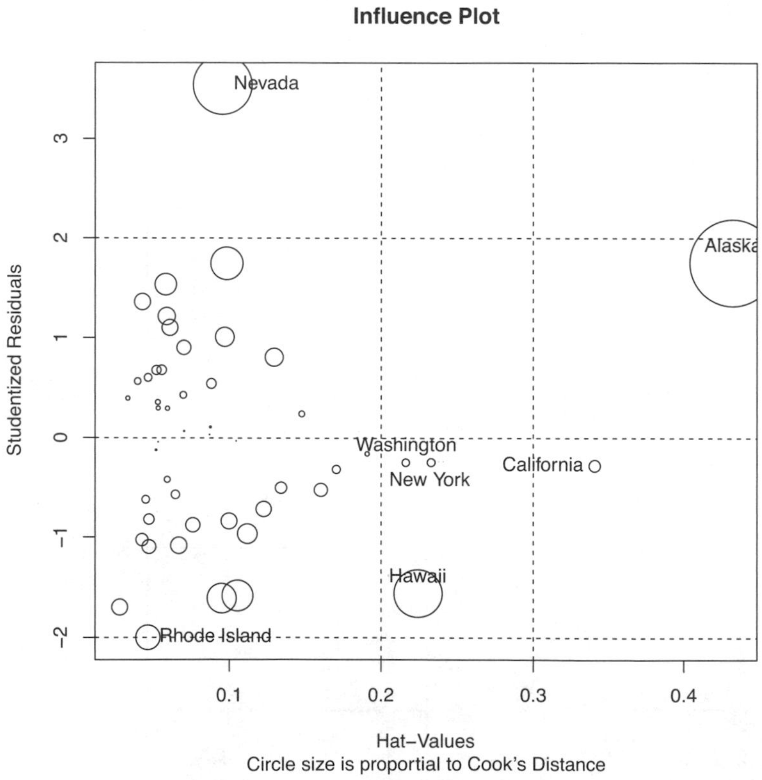

Figure 8.16   Influence plot. States above +2 or below −2 on the vertical axis are considered outliers. States above 0.2 or 0.3 on the horizontal axis have high leverage (unusual combinations of predictor values). Circle size is proportional to influence. Observations depicted by large circles may have disproportionate influence on the parameters estimates of the model.

8.5 Corrective measures

Having spent the last 20 pages learning about regression diagnostics, you may ask, "What do you do if you identify problems?" There are four approaches to dealing with violations of regression assumptions:

- Deleting observations
- Transforming variables
- Adding or deleting variables
- Using another regression approach

Let's look at each in turn.

8.5.1 Deleting observations

Deleting outliers can often improve a dataset's fit to the normality assumption. Influential observations are often deleted as well, because they have an inordinate impact on the results. The largest outlier or influential observation is deleted, and the model is refit. If there are still outliers or influential observations, the process is repeated until an acceptable fit is obtained.

Again, I urge caution when considering the deletion of observations. Sometimes, you can determine that the observation is an outlier because of data errors in recording, or because a protocol wasn't followed, or because a test subject misunderstood instructions. In these cases, deleting the offending observation seems perfectly reasonable.

In other cases, the unusual observation may be the most interesting thing about the data you've collected. Uncovering why an observation differs from the rest can contribute great insight to the topic at hand, and to other topics you might not have thought of. Some of our greatest advances have come from the serendipity of noticing that something doesn't fit our preconceptions (pardon the hyperbole).

8.5.2 Transforming variables

When models don't meet the normality, linearity, or homoscedasticity assumptions, transforming one or more variables can often improve or correct the situation. Transformations typically involve replacing a variable Y with Y^λ. Common values of λ and their interpretations are given in table 8.5.

If Y is a proportion, a logit transformation [ln (Y/1-Y)] is often used.

Table 8.5 Common transformations

	−2	−1	−0.5	0	0.5	1	2
Transformation	$1/Y^2$	$1/Y$	$1/\sqrt{Y}$	log(Y)	$\sqrt{Y}$	None	Y^2

When the model violates the normality assumption, you typically attempt a transformation of the response variable. You can use the `powerTransform()` function in the car package to generate a maximum-likelihood estimation of the power λ most likely to normalize the variable X^λ. In the next listing, this is applied to the states data.

Listing 8.10   Box–Cox transformation to normality

```
> library(car)
> summary(powerTransform(states$Murder))

bcPower Transformation to Normality

              Est.Power Std.Err. Wald Lower Bound Wald Upper Bound
states$Murder   0.6       0.26        0.088              1.1

Likelihood ratio tests about transformation parameters
                   LRT df  pval
LR test, lambda=(0) 5.7  1 0.017
LR test, lambda=(1) 2.1  1 0.145
```

The results suggest that you can normalize the variable Murder by replacing it with Murder$^{0.6}$. Because 0.6 is close to 0.5, you could try a square root transformation to improve the model's fit to normality. But in this case the hypothesis that $\lambda=1$ can't be rejected (p = 0.145), so there's no strong evidence that a transformation is actually needed in this case. This is consistent with the results of the Q-Q plot in figure 8.9.

When the assumption of linearity is violated, a transformation of the predictor variables can often help. The `boxTidwell()` function in the car package can be used to generate maximum-likelihood estimates of predictor powers that can improve linearity. An example of applying the Box–Tidwell transformations to a model that predicts state murder rates from their population and illiteracy rates follows:

```
> library(car)
> boxTidwell(Murder~Population+Illiteracy,data=states)

           Score Statistic p-value MLE of lambda
Population        -0.32      0.75       0.87
Illiteracy         0.62      0.54       1.36
```

The results suggest trying the transformations Population$^{.87}$ and Population$^{1.36}$ to achieve greater linearity. But the score tests for Population (p = .75) and Illiteracy (p = .54) suggest that neither variable needs to be transformed. Again, these results are consistent with the component plus residual plots in figure 8.11.

Finally, transformations of the response variable can help in situations of heteroscedasticity (nonconstant error variance). You saw in listing 8.7 that the `spreadLevelPlot()` function in the car package offers a power transformation for improving homoscedasticity. Again, in the case of the states example, the constant error variance assumption is met and no transformation is necessary.

> ### A caution concerning transformations
>
> There's an old joke in statistics: If you can't prove A, prove B and pretend it was A. (For statisticians, that's pretty funny.) The relevance here is that if you transform your variables, your interpretations must be based on the transformed variables, not the original variables. If the transformation makes sense, such as the log of income or the inverse of distance, the interpretation is easier. But how do you interpret the relationship between the frequency of suicidal ideation and the cube root of depression? If a transformation doesn't make sense, you should avoid it.

8.5.3 Adding or deleting variables

Changing the variables in a model will impact the fit of a model. Sometimes, adding an important variable will correct many of the problems that we've discussed. Deleting a troublesome variable can do the same thing.

Deleting variables is a particularly important approach for dealing with multicollinearity. If your only goal is to make predictions, then multicollinearity isn't a problem. But if you want to make interpretations about individual predictor variables, then you must deal with it. The most common approach is to delete one of the variables involved in the multicollinearity (that is, one of the variables with a $\sqrt{vif} > 2$). An alternative is to use ridge regression, a variant of multiple regression designed to deal with multicollinearity situations.

8.5.4 Trying a different approach

As you've just seen, one approach to dealing with multicollinearity is to fit a different type of model (ridge regression in this case). If there are outliers and/or influential observations, you could fit a robust regression model rather than an OLS regression. If you've violated the normality assumption, you can fit a nonparametric regression model. If there's significant nonlinearity, you can try a nonlinear regression model. If you've violated the assumptions of independence of errors, you can fit a model that specifically takes the error structure into account, such as time-series models or multi-level regression models. Finally, you can turn to generalized linear models to fit a wide range of models in situations where the assumptions of OLS regression don't hold.

We'll discuss some of these alternative approaches in chapter 13. The decision regarding when to try to improve the fit of an OLS regression model and when to try a different approach, is a complex one. It's typically based on knowledge of the subject matter and an assessment of which approach will provide the best result.

Speaking of best results, let's turn now to the problem of deciding which predictor variables to include in our regression model.

8.6 Selecting the "best" regression model

When developing a regression equation, you're implicitly faced with a selection of many possible models. Should you include all the variables under study, or drop ones that don't make a significant contribution to prediction? Should you add polynomial and/or interaction terms to improve the fit? The selection of a final regression model always involves a compromise between predictive accuracy (a model that fits the data as well as possible) and parsimony (a simple and replicable model). All things being equal, if you have two models with approximately equal predictive accuracy, you favor the simpler one. This section describes methods for choosing among competing models. The word "best" is in quotation marks, because there's no single criterion you can use to make the decision. The final decision requires judgment on the part of the investigator. (Think of it as job security.)

8.6.1 Comparing models

You can compare the fit of two nested models using the `anova()` function in the base installation. A nested model is one whose terms are completely included in the other model. In our `states` multiple regression model, we found that the regression coefficients for Income and Frost were nonsignificant. You can test whether a model without these two variables predicts as well as one that includes them (see the following listing).

Listing 8.11   Comparing nested models using the `anova()` function

```
> fit1 <- lm(Murder ~ Population + Illiteracy + Income + Frost,
          data=states)
> fit2 <- lm(Murder ~ Population + Illiteracy, data=states)
> anova(fit2, fit1)

Analysis of Variance Table

Model 1: Murder ~ Population + Illiteracy
Model 2: Murder ~ Population + Illiteracy + Income + Frost
  Res.Df     RSS  Df   Sum of Sq      F Pr(>F)
1     47 289.246
2     45 289.167   2     0.079 0.0061        0.994
```

Here, model 1 is nested within model 2. The `anova()` function provides a simultaneous test that Income and Frost add to linear prediction above and beyond Population and Illiteracy. Because the test is nonsignificant ($p = .994$), we conclude that they don't add to the linear prediction and we're justified in dropping them from our model.

The Akaike Information Criterion (AIC) provides another method for comparing models. The index takes into account a model's statistical fit and the number of parameters needed to achieve this fit. Models with *smaller* AIC values—indicating adequate fit with fewer parameters—are preferred. The criterion is provided by the `AIC()` function (see the following listing).

Listing 8.12   Comparing models with the AIC

```
> fit1 <- lm(Murder ~ Population + Illiteracy + Income + Frost,
          data=states)
> fit2 <- lm(Murder ~ Population + Illiteracy, data=states)
```

```
> AIC(fit1,fit2)

     df     AIC
fit1  6 241.6429
fit2  4 237.6565
```

The AIC values suggest that the model without Income and Frost is the better model. Note that although the ANOVA approach requires nested models, the AIC approach doesn't.

Comparing two models is relatively straightforward, but what do you do when there are four, or ten, or a hundred possible models to consider? That's the topic of the next section.

8.6.2 *Variable selection*

Two popular approaches to selecting a final set of predictor variables from a larger pool of candidate variables are stepwise methods and all-subsets regression.

STEPWISE REGRESSION

In stepwise selection, variables are added to or deleted from a model one at a time, until some stopping criterion is reached. For example, in *forward stepwise* regression you add predictor variables to the model one at a time, stopping when the addition of variables would no longer improve the model. In *backward stepwise* regression, you start with a model that includes all predictor variables, and then delete them one at a time until removing variables would degrade the quality of the model. In *stepwise stepwise* regression (usually called stepwise to avoid sounding silly), you combine the forward and backward stepwise approaches. Variables are entered one at a time, but at each step, the variables in the model are reevaluated, and those that don't contribute to the model are deleted. A predictor variable may be added to, and deleted from, a model several times before a final solution is reached.

The implementation of stepwise regression methods vary by the criteria used to enter or remove variables. The stepAIC() function in the MASS package performs stepwise model selection (forward, backward, stepwise) using an exact AIC criterion. In the next listing, we apply backward stepwise regression to the multiple regression problem.

Listing 8.13   Backward stepwise selection

```
> library(MASS)
> fit1 <- lm(Murder ~ Population + Illiteracy + Income + Frost,
         data=states)
> stepAIC(fit, direction="backward")

Start:  AIC=97.75
Murder ~ Population + Illiteracy + Income + Frost

             Df Sum of Sq    RSS    AIC
- Frost       1      0.02 289.19  95.75
- Income      1      0.06 289.22  95.76
```

```
<none>                       289.17  97.75
- Population   1     39.24 328.41 102.11
- Illiteracy   1    144.26 433.43 115.99

Step:  AIC=95.75
Murder ~ Population + Illiteracy + Income

              Df Sum of Sq    RSS    AIC
- Income       1      0.06 289.25  93.76
<none>                       289.19  95.75
- Population   1     43.66 332.85 100.78
- Illiteracy   1    236.20 525.38 123.61

Step:  AIC=93.76
Murder ~ Population + Illiteracy

              Df Sum of Sq    RSS    AIC
<none>                       289.25  93.76
- Population   1     48.52 337.76  99.52
- Illiteracy   1    299.65 588.89 127.31

Call:
lm(formula=Murder ~ Population + Illiteracy, data=states)

Coefficients:
(Intercept)    Population    Illiteracy
  1.6515497     0.0002242     4.0807366
```

You start with all four predictors in the model. For each step, the AIC column provides the model AIC resulting from the deletion of the variable listed in that row. The AIC value for <none> is the model AIC if no variables are removed. In the first step, Frost is removed, decreasing the AIC from 97.75 to 95.75. In the second step, Income is removed, decreasing the AIC to 93.76. Deleting any more variables would increase the AIC, so the process stops.

Stepwise regression is controversial. Although it may find a good model, there's no guarantee that it will find the best model. This is because not every possible model is evaluated. An approach that attempts to overcome this limitation is *all subsets regression*.

ALL SUBSETS REGRESSION

In all subsets regression, every possible model is inspected. The analyst can choose to have all possible results displayed, or ask for the *nbest* models of each subset size (one predictor, two predictors, etc.). For example, if nbest=2, the two best one-predictor models are displayed, followed by the two best two-predictor models, followed by the two best three-predictor models, up to a model with all predictors.

All subsets regression is performed using the regsubsets() function from the leaps package. You can choose R-squared, Adjusted R-squared, or Mallows Cp statistic as your criterion for reporting "best" models.

As you've seen, R-squared is the amount of variance accounted for in the response variable by the predictors variables. Adjusted R-squared is similar, but takes into account the number of parameters in the model. R-squared always increases with the addition of predictors. When the number of predictors is large compared to the sample size, this can lead to significant overfitting. The Adjusted R-squared is an attempt to provide a more honest estimate of the population R-squared—one that's less likely to take advantage of chance variation in the data. The Mallows Cp statistic is also used as a stopping rule in stepwise regression. It has been widely suggested that a good model is one in which the Cp statistic is close to the number of model parameters (including the intercept).

In listing 8.14, we'll apply all subsets regression to the `states` data. The results can be plotted with either the `plot()` function in the `leaps` package or the `subsets()` function in the `car` package. An example of the former is provided in figure 8.17, and an example of the latter is given in figure 8.18.

Listing 8.14 All subsets regression

```
library(leaps)
leaps <-regsubsets(Murder ~ Population + Illiteracy + Income +
  Frost, data=states, nbest=4)
plot(leaps, scale="adjr2")

library(car)
subsets(leaps, statistic="cp",
  main="Cp Plot for All Subsets Regression")
abline(1,1,lty=2,col="red")
```

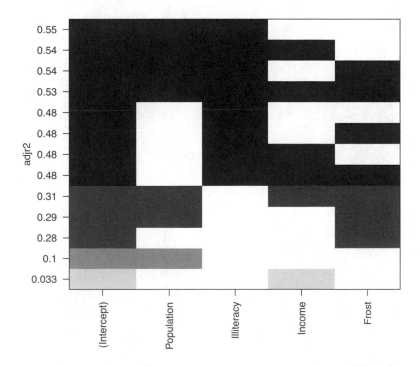

Figure 8.17 Best four models for each subset size based on Adjusted R-square

Figure 8.17 can be confusing to read. Looking at the first row (starting at the bottom), you can see that a model with the intercept and Income has an adjusted R-square of 0.33. A model with the intercept and Population has an adjusted R-square of 0.1. Jumping to the 12th row, you see that a model with the intercept, Population, Illiteracy, and Income has an adjusted R-square of 0.54, whereas one with the intercept, Population, and Illiteracy alone has an adjusted R-square of 0.55. Here you see that a model with fewer predictors has a larger adjusted R-square (something that can't happen with an unadjusted R-square). The graph suggests that the two-predictor model (Population and Illiteracy) is the best.

In figure 8.18, you see the best four models for each subset size based on the Mallows Cp statistic. Better models will fall close to a line with intercept 1 and slope 1. The plot suggests that you consider a two-predictor model with Population and Illiteracy; a three-predictor model with Population, Illiteracy, and Frost, *or* Population, Illiteracy and Income (they overlap on the graph and are hard to read); or a four-predictor model with Population, Illiteracy, Income, and Frost. You can reject the other possible models.

In most instances, all subsets regression is preferable to stepwise regression, because more models are considered. However, when the number of predictors is large, the

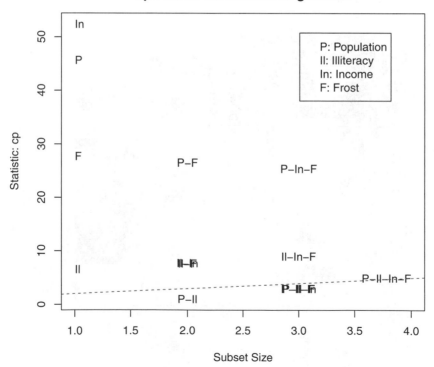

Cp Plot for All Subsets Regression

Figure 8.18   **Best four models for each subset size based on the Mallows Cp statistic**

procedure can require significant computing time. In general, automated variable selection methods should be seen as an aid rather than a directing force in model selection. A well-fitting model that doesn't make sense doesn't help you. Ultimately, it's your knowledge of the subject matter that should guide you.

8.7 Taking the analysis further

We'll end our discussion of regression by considering methods for assessing model generalizability and predictor relative importance.

8.7.1 Cross-validation

In the previous section, we examined methods for selecting the variables to include in a regression equation. When description is your primary goal, the selection and interpretation of a regression model signals the end of your labor. But when your goal is prediction, you can justifiably ask, "How well will this equation perform in the real world?"

By definition, regression techniques obtain model parameters that are optimal for a given set of data. In OLS regression, the model parameters are selected to minimize the sum of squared errors of prediction (residuals), and conversely, maximize the amount of variance accounted for in the response variable (R-squared). Because the equation has been optimized for the given set of data, it won't perform as well with a new set of data.

We began this chapter with an example involving a research physiologist who wanted to predict the number of calories an individual will burn from the duration and intensity of their exercise, age, gender, and BMI. If you fit an OLS regression equation to this data, you'll obtain model parameters that uniquely maximize the R-squared for this *particular* set of observations. But our researcher wants to use this equation to predict the calories burned by individuals in general, not only those in the original study. You know that the equation won't perform as well with a new sample of observations, but how much will you lose? Cross-validation is a useful method for evaluating the generalizability of a regression equation.

In cross-validation, a portion of the data is selected as the training sample and a portion is selected as the hold-out sample. A regression equation is developed on the training sample, and then applied to the hold-out sample. Because the hold-out sample wasn't involved in the selection of the model parameters, the performance on this sample is a more accurate estimate of the operating characteristics of the model with new data.

In k-fold cross-validation, the sample is divided into k subsamples. Each of the k subsamples serves as a hold-out group and the combined observations from the remaining k-1 subsamples serves as the training group. The performance for the k prediction equations applied to the k hold-out samples are recorded and then averaged. (When k equals n, the total number of observations, this approach is called jackknifing.)

k = n crazy unless n is small!

You can perform k-fold cross-validation using the `crossval()` function in the `bootstrap` package. The following listing provides a function (called `shrinkage()`) for cross-validating a model's R-square statistic using k-fold cross-validation.

Listing 8.15   Function for k-fold cross-validated R-square

```
shrinkage <- function(fit, k=10){
  require(bootstrap)

  theta.fit <- function(x,y){lsfit(x,y)}
  theta.predict <- function(fit,x){cbind(1,x)%*%fit$coef}

  x <- fit$model[,2:ncol(fit$model)]
  y <- fit$model[,1]

  results <- crossval(x, y, theta.fit, theta.predict, ngroup=k)
  r2 <- cor(y, fit$fitted.values)^2
  r2cv <- cor(y, results$cv.fit)^2
  cat("Original R-square =", r2, "\n")
  cat(k, "Fold Cross-Validated R-square =", r2cv, "\n")
  cat("Change =", r2-r2cv, "\n")
  }
```

Using this listing you define your functions, create a matrix of predictor and predicted values, get the raw R-squared, and get the cross-validated R-squared. (Chapter 12 covers bootstrapping in detail.)

The `shrinkage()` function is then used to perform a 10-fold cross-validation with the `states` data, using a model with all four predictor variables:

```
> fit <- lm(Murder ~ Population + Income + Illiteracy + Frost, data=states)
> shrinkage(fit)

Original R-square=0.567
10 Fold Cross-Validated R-square=0.4481
Change=0.1188
```

You can see that the R-square based on our sample (0.567) is overly optimistic. A better estimate of the amount of variance in murder rates our model will account for with new data is the cross-validated R-square (0.448). (Note that observations are assigned to the k groups randomly, so you will get a slightly different result each time you execute the `shrinkage()` function.)

You could use cross-validation in variable selection by choosing a model that demonstrates better generalizability. For example, a model with two predictors (Population and Illiteracy) shows less R-square shrinkage (.03 versus .12) than the full model:

```
> fit2 <- lm(Murder~Population+Illiteracy,data=states)
> shrinkage(fit2)

Original R-square=0.5668327
10 Fold Cross-Validated R-square=0.5346871
Change=0.03214554
```

This may make the two-predictor model a more attractive alternative.

All other things being equal, a regression equation that's based on a larger training sample and one that's more representative of the population of interest will cross-validate better. You'll get less R-squared shrinkage and make more accurate predictions.

8.7.2 Relative importance

Up to this point in the chapter, we've been asking, "Which variables are useful for predicting the outcome?" But often your real interest is in the question, "Which variables are *most important* in predicting the outcome?" You implicitly want to rank-order the predictors in terms of relative importance. There may be practical grounds for asking the second question. For example, if you could rank-order leadership practices by their relative importance for organizational success, you could help managers focus on the behaviors they most need to develop.

If predictor variables were uncorrelated, this would be a simple task. You would rank-order the predictor variables by their correlation with the response variable. In most cases, though, the predictors are correlated with each other, and this complicates the task significantly.

There have been many attempts to develop a means for assessing the relative importance of predictors. The simplest has been to compare standardized regression coefficients. Standardized regression coefficients describe the expected change in the response variable (expressed in standard deviation units) for a standard deviation change in a predictor variable, holding the other predictor variables constant. You can obtain the standardized regression coefficients in R by standardizing each of the variables in your dataset to a mean of 0 and standard deviation of 1 using the `scale()` function, before submitting the dataset to a regression analysis. (Note that because the `scale()` function returns a matrix and the `lm()` function requires a data frame, you convert between the two in an intermediate step.) The code and results for our multiple regression problem are shown here:

```
> zstates <- as.data.frame(scale(states))
> zfit <- lm(Murder~Population + Income + Illiteracy + Frost, data=zstates)
> coef(zfit)
```

```
(Intercept)   Population       Income   Illiteracy        Frost
 -9.406e-17    2.705e-01    1.072e-02    6.840e-01    8.185e-03
```

Here you see that a one standard deviation increase in illiteracy rate yields a 0.68 standard deviation increase in murder rate, when controlling for population, income, and temperature. Using standardized regression coefficients as our guide, Illiteracy is the most important predictor and Frost is the least.

There have been many other attempts at quantifying relative importance. Relative importance can be thought of as the contribution each predictor makes to R-square, both alone and in combination with other predictors. Several possible approaches to relative importance are captured in the `relaimpo` package written by Ulrike Grömping (http://prof.beuth-hochschule.de/groemping/relaimpo/).

A new method called *relative weights* shows significant promise. The method closely approximates the average increase in R-square obtained by adding a predictor variable across all possible submodels (Johnson, 2004; Johnson and Lebreton, 2004; LeBreton and Tonidandel, 2008). A function for generating relative weights is provided in the next listing.

Listing 8.16 `relweights()` function for calculating relative importance of predictors

```
relweights <- function(fit,...){
  R <- cor(fit$model)
  nvar <- ncol(R)
  rxx <- R[2:nvar, 2:nvar]
  rxy <- R[2:nvar, 1]
  svd <- eigen(rxx)
  evec <- svd$vectors
  ev <- svd$values
  delta <- diag(sqrt(ev))
  lambda <- evec %*% delta %*% t(evec)
  lambdasq <- lambda ^ 2
  beta <- solve(lambda) %*% rxy
  rsquare <- colSums(beta ^ 2)
  rawwgt <- lambdasq %*% beta ^ 2
  import <- (rawwgt / rsquare) * 100
  lbls <- names(fit$model[2:nvar])
  rownames(import) <- lbls
  colnames(import) <- "Weights"
  barplot(t(import),names.arg=lbls,
      ylab="% of R-Square",
      xlab="Predictor Variables",
      main="Relative Importance of Predictor Variables",
      sub=paste("R-Square=", round(rsquare, digits=3)),
      ...)
return(import)
}
```

NOTE   The code in listing 8.16 is adapted from an SPSS program generously provided by Dr. Johnson. See Johnson (2000, *Multivariate Behavioral Research*, 35, 1–19) for an explanation of how the relative weights are derived.

In listing 8.17 the `relweights()` function is applied to the `states` data with murder rate predicted by the population, illiteracy, income, and temperature.

You can see from figure 8.19 that the total amount of variance accounted for by the model (R-square=0.567) has been divided among the predictor variables. Illiteracy accounts for 59 percent of the R-square, Frost accounts for 20.79 percent, and so forth. Based on the method of relative weights, Illiteracy has the greatest relative importance, followed by Frost, Population, and Income, in that order.

Listing 8.17 Applying the `relweights()` function

```
> fit <- lm(Murder ~ Population + Illiteracy + Income + Frost, data=states)
> relweights(fit, col="lightgrey")
```

```
              Weights
Population     14.72
Illiteracy     59.00
Income          5.49
Frost          20.79
```

relative weights

Relative importance measures (and in particular, the method of relative weights) have wide applicability. They come much closer to our intuitive conception of relative importance than standardized regression coefficients do, and I expect to see their use increase dramatically in coming years.

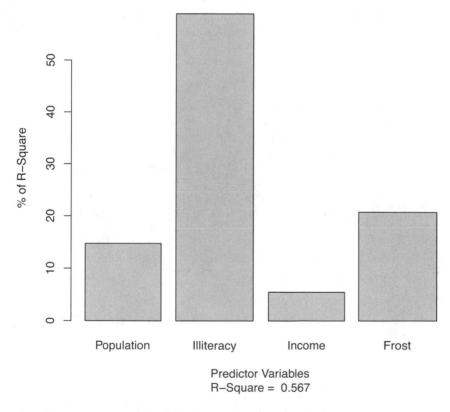

Figure 8.19   Bar plot of relative weights for the states multiple regression problem

8.8   *Summary*

Regression analysis is a term that covers a broad range of methodologies in statistics. You've seen that it's a highly interactive approach that involves fitting models, assessing their fit to statistical assumptions, modifying both the data and the models, and refitting to arrive at a final result. In many ways, this final result is based on art and skill as much as science.

This has been a long chapter, because regression analysis is a process with many parts. We've discussed fitting OLS regression models, using regression diagnostics to assess the data's fit to statistical assumptions, and methods for modifying the data to meet these assumptions more closely. We looked at ways of selecting a final regression model from many possible models, and you learned how to evaluate its likely performance on new samples of data. Finally, we tackled the thorny problem of variable importance: identifying which variables are the most important for predicting an outcome.

In each of the examples in this chapter, the predictor variables have been quantitative. However, there are no restrictions against using categorical variables as predictors as well. Using categorical predictors such as gender, treatment type, or manufacturing process allows you to examine group differences on a response or outcome variable. This is the focus of our next chapter.

y	x	method
quant	quant	OLS regression
quant	categorical	ANOVA
categorical		logistic regression

Analysis of variance

This chapter covers
- Using R to model basic experimental designs
- Fitting and interpreting ANOVA type models
- Evaluating model assumptions

In chapter 7, we looked at regression models for predicting a quantitative response variable from quantitative predictor variables. But there's no reason that we couldn't have included nominal or ordinal factors as predictors as well. When factors are included as explanatory variables, our focus usually shifts from prediction to understanding group differences, and the methodology is referred to as *analysis of variance (ANOVA)*. ANOVA methodology is used to analyze a wide variety of experimental and quasi-experimental designs. This chapter provides an overview of R functions for analyzing common research designs.

First we'll look at design terminology, followed by a general discussion of R's approach to fitting ANOVA models. Then we'll explore several examples that illustrate the analysis of common designs. Along the way, we'll treat anxiety disorders, lower blood cholesterol levels, help pregnant mice have fat babies, assure that pigs grow long in the tooth, facilitate breathing in plants, and learn which grocery shelves to avoid.

In addition to the base installation, we'll be using the car, gplots, HH, rrcov, and mvoutlier packages in our examples. Be sure to install them before trying out the sample code.

9.1   *A crash course on terminology*

Experimental design in general, and analysis of variance in particular, has its own language. Before discussing the analysis of these designs, we'll quickly review some important terms. We'll use a series of increasingly complex study designs to introduce the most significant concepts.

Say you're interested in studying the treatment of anxiety. Two popular therapies for anxiety are cognitive behavior therapy (CBT) and eye movement desensitization and reprocessing (EMDR). You recruit 10 anxious individuals and randomly assign half of them to receive five weeks of CBT and half to receive five weeks of EMDR. At the conclusion of therapy, each patient is asked to complete the State-Trait Anxiety Inventory (STAI), a self-report measure of anxiety. The design is outlined in table 9.1.

In this design, Treatment is a *between-groups factor with two levels* (CBT, EMDR). It's called a between-groups factor because patients are assigned to one and only one group. No patient receives both CBT and EMDR. The s characters represent the subjects (patients). STAI is the *dependent variable*, and Treatment is the *independent variable*. Because there are an equal number of observations in each treatment condition, you have a *balanced design.* When the sample sizes are unequal across the cells of a design, you have an *unbalanced design.*

The statistical design in table 9.1 is called a *one-way ANOVA* because there's a single classification variable. Specifically, it's a one-way between-groups ANOVA. Effects in ANOVA designs are primarily evaluated through F tests. If the F test for Treatment is significant, you can conclude that the mean STAI scores for two therapies differed after five weeks of treatment.

If you were interested in the effect of CBT on anxiety over time, you could place all 10 patients in the CBT group and assess them at the conclusion of therapy and again six months later. This design is displayed in table 9.2.

Time is a *within-groups factor* with two levels (five weeks, six months). It's called a within-groups factor because each patient is measured under both levels. The statistical

Table 9.1   One-way between-groups ANOVA

Treatment	
CBT	**EMDR**
s1	s6
s2	s7
s3	s8
s4	s9
s5	s10

Table 9.2   One-way within-groups ANOVA

	Time	
Patient	**5 weeks**	**6 months**
s1		
s2		
s3		
s4		
s5		
s6		
s7		
s8		
s9		
s10		

design is a *one-way within-groups ANOVA*. Because each subject is measured more than once, the design is also called *repeated measures ANOVA*. If the F test for Time is significant, you can conclude that patients' mean STAI scores changed between five weeks and six months.

If you were interested in both treatment differences *and* change over time, you could combine the first two study designs, and randomly assign five patients to CBT and five patients to EMDR, and assess their STAI results at the end of therapy (five weeks) and at six months (see table 9.3).

By including both Therapy and Time as factors, you're able to examine the impact of Therapy (averaged across time), Time (averaged across therapy type), and the interaction of Therapy and Time. The first two are called the *main effects*, whereas the interaction is (not surprisingly) called an *interaction effect*.

When you cross two or more factors, as you've done here, you have a *factorial ANOVA* design. Crossing two factors produces a two-way ANOVA, crossing three factors produces a three-way ANOVA, and so forth. When a factorial design includes both between-groups and within-groups factors, it's also called a *mixed-model ANOVA*. The current design is a two-way mixed-model factorial ANOVA (phew!).

In this case you'll have three F tests: one for Therapy, one for Time, and one for the Therapy x Time interaction. A significant result for Therapy indicates that CBT and EMDR differ in their impact on anxiety. A significant result for Time indicates that

Table 9.3   Two-way factorial ANOVA with one between-groups and one within-groups factor

			Time	
		Patient	5 weeks	6 months
Therapy	CBT	s1		
		s2		
		s3		
		s4		
		s5		
	EMDR	s6		
		s7		
		s8		
		s9		
		s10		

anxiety changed from week five to the six month follow-up. A significant Therapy x Time interaction indicates that the two treatments for anxiety had a differential impact over time (that is, the change in anxiety from five weeks to six months was different for the two treatments).

Now let's extend the design a bit. It's known that depression can have an impact on therapy, and that depression and anxiety often co-occur. Even though subjects were randomly assigned to treatment conditions, it's possible that the two therapy groups differed in patient depression levels at the initiation of the study. Any post-therapy differences might then be due to the preexisting depression differences and not to your experimental manipulation. Because depression could also explain the group differences on the dependent variable, it's a *confounding* factor. And because you're not interested in depression, it's called a *nuisance* variable.

If you recorded depression levels using a self-report depression measure such as the Beck Depression Inventory (BDI) when patients were recruited, you could statistically adjust for any treatment group differences in depression before assessing the impact of therapy type. In this case, BDI would be called a *covariate*, and the design would be called an *analysis of covariance (ANCOVA)*.

Finally, you've recorded a single dependent variable in this study (the STAI). You could increase the validity of this study by including additional measures of anxiety (such as family ratings, therapist ratings, and a measure assessing the impact of anxiety on their daily functioning). When there's more than one dependent variable, the design is called a *multivariate analysis of variance (MANOVA)*. If there are covariates present, it's called a *multivariate analysis of covariance (MANCOVA)*.

Now that you have the basic terminology under your belt, you're ready to amaze your friends, dazzle new acquaintances, and discuss how to fit ANOVA/ANCOVA/MANOVA models with R.

9.2   *Fitting ANOVA models*

Although ANOVA and regression methodologies developed separately, functionally they're both special cases of the general linear model. We could analyze ANOVA models using the same `lm()` function used for regression in chapter 8. However, we'll primarily use the `aov()` function in this chapter. The results of `lm()` and `aov()` are equivalent, but the `aov()` function presents these results in a format that's more familiar to ANOVA methodologists. For completeness, I'll provide an example using `lm()` at the end of this chapter.

9.2.1   *The aov() function*

The syntax of the `aov()` function is `aov(formula, data=dataframe)`. Table 9.4 describes special symbols that can be used in the formulas. In this table, `y` is the dependent variable and the letters A, B, and C represent factors.

Table 9.4 Special symbols used in R formulas

Symbol	Usage
~	Separates response variables on the left from the explanatory variables on the right. For example, a prediction of y from A, B, and C would be coded `y ~ A + B + C`.
+	Separates explanatory variables.
:	Denotes an interaction between variables. A prediction of y from A, B, and the interaction between A and B would be coded `y ~ A + B + A:B`.
*	Denotes the complete crossing variables. The code `y ~ A*B*C` expands to `y ~ A + B + C + A:B + A:C + B:C + A:B:C`.
^	Denotes crossing to a specified degree. The code `y ~ (A+B+C)^2` expands to `y ~ A + B + C + A:B + A:C + A:B`.
.	A place holder for all other variables in the data frame except the dependent variable. For example, if a data frame contained the variables y, A, B, and C, then the code `y ~ .` would expand to `y ~ A + B + C`.

Table 9.5 provides formulas for several common research designs. In this table, low-ercase letters are quantitative variables, uppercase letters are grouping factors, and Subject is a unique identifier variable for subjects.

Table 9.5 Formulas for common research designs

Design	Formula
One-way ANOVA	`y ~ A`
One-way ANCOVA with one covariate	`y ~ x + A`
Two-way Factorial ANOVA	`y ~ A * B`
Two-way Factorial ANCOVA with two covariates	`y ~ x1 + x2 + A * B`
Randomized Block	`y ~ B + A` (where B is a blocking factor)
One-way within-groups ANOVA	`y ~ A + Error(Subject/A)`
Repeated measures ANOVA with one within-groups factor (W) and one between-groups factor (B)	`y ~ B * W + Error(Subject/W)`

We'll explore in-depth examples of several of these designs later in this chapter.

9.2.2 The order of formula terms

The order in which the effects appear in a formula matters when (a) there's more than one factor and the design is unbalanced, or (b) covariates are present. When either of these two conditions is present, the variables on the right side of the equation will be correlated with each other. In this case, there's no unambiguous way to divide up their impact on the dependent variable.

For example, in a two-way ANOVA with unequal numbers of observations in the treatment combinations, the model `y ~ A*B` *will not* produce the same results as the model `y ~ B*A`.

By default, R employs the Type I (sequential) approach to calculating ANOVA effects (see the sidebar "Order counts!"). The first model can be written out as `y ~ A + B + A:B`. The resulting R ANOVA table will assess

- The impact of `A` on `y`
- The impact of `B` on `y`, controlling for `A`
- The interaction of `A` and `B`, controlling for the `A` and `B` main effects

Order counts!

When independent variables are correlated with each other or with covariates, there's no unambiguous method for assessing the independent contributions of these variables to the dependent variable. Consider an unbalanced two-way factorial design with factors `A` and `B` and dependent variable `y`. There are three effects in this design: the `A` and `B` main effects and the `A` x `B` interaction. Assuming that you're modeling the data using the formula

$$Y ~ A + B + A:B$$

there are three typical approaches for partitioning the variance in `y` among the effects on the right side of this equation.

Type I (sequential)
Effects are adjusted for those that appear earlier in the formula. `A` is unadjusted. `B` is adjusted for the `A`. The `A:B` interaction is adjusted for `A` and `B`.

Type II (hierarchical)
Effects are adjusted for other effects at the same or lower level. `A` is adjusted for `B`. `B` is adjusted for `A`. The `A:B` interaction is adjusted for both `A` and `B`.

Type III (marginal)
Each effect is adjusted for every other effect in the model. `A` is adjusted for `B` and `A:B`. `B` is adjusted for `A` and `A:B`. The `A:B` interaction is adjusted for `A` and `B`.
R employs the Type I approach by default. Other programs such as SAS and SPSS employ the Type III approach by default.

The greater the imbalance in sample sizes, the greater the impact that the order of the terms will have on the results. In general, more fundamental effects should be listed earlier in the formula. In particular, covariates should be listed first, followed by main effects, followed by two-way interactions, followed by three-way interactions, and so on. For main effects, more fundamental variables should be listed first. Thus gender would be listed before treatment. Here's the bottom line: When the research design isn't orthogonal (that is, when the factors and/or covariates are correlated), be careful when specifying the order of effects.

Before moving on to specific examples, note that the `Anova()` function in the `car` package (not to be confused with the standard `anova()` function) provides the option of using the Type II or Type III approach, rather than the Type I approach used by the `aov()` function. You may want to use the `Anova()` function if you're concerned about matching your results to those provided by other packages such as SAS and SPSS. See `help(Anova, package="car")` for details.

9.3 One-way ANOVA

In a one-way ANOVA, you're interested in comparing the dependent variable means of two or more groups defined by a categorical grouping factor. Our example comes from the `cholesterol` dataset in the `multcomp` package, and taken from Westfall, Tobia, Rom, & Hochberg (1999). Fifty patients received one of five cholesterol-reducing drug regiments (`trt`). Three of the treatment conditions involved the same drug administered as 20 mg once per day (1time), 10mg twice per day (2times), or 5 mg four times per day (4times). The two remaining conditions (drugD and drugE) represented competing drugs. Which drug regimen produced the greatest cholesterol reduction (`response`)? The analysis is provided in the following listing.

Listing 9.1 One-way ANOVA

```
> library(multcomp)
> attach(cholesterol)
> table(trt)                                        ←——❶ Group sample sizes
trt
 1time 2times 4times  drugD  drugE
    10     10     10     10     10        10 subjects for each treatment

> aggregate(response, by=list(trt), FUN=mean)       ←——❷ Group means
   Group.1     x
1   1time  5.78
2  2times  9.22              means                      cholesterol
3  4times 12.37                                          reduction
4   drugD 15.36                                          so big is
5   drugE 20.95                                          good

> aggregate(response, by=list(trt), FUN=sd)         ←
   Group.1     x                                       ❸ Group standard
1   1time 2.88                                            deviations
2  2times 3.48           std dev
3  4times 2.92
4   drugD 3.45
5   drugE 3.35

                                       ❹ Test for group
> fit <- aov(response ~ trt)             differences (ANOVA)
> summary(fit)
            Df Sum Sq Mean Sq  F value       Pr(>F)
trt          4   1351     338     32.4     9.8e-13  ***
Residuals   45    469      10
---
```

```
Signif. codes:  0 '***' 0.001 '**' 0.01 '*' 0.05 '.' 0.1 ' ' 1
```
⑤ Plot group means, confidence intervals

```
> library(gplots)
> plotmeans(response ~ trt, xlab="Treatment", ylab="Response",
      main="Mean Plot\nwith 95% CI")
> detach(cholesterol)
```

Looking at the output, you can see that 10 patients received each of the drug regiments **①**. From the means, it appears that drugE produced the greatest cholesterol reduction, whereas 1time produced the least **②**. Standard deviations were relatively constant across the five groups, ranging from 2.88 to 3.48 **③**. The ANOVA F test for treatment (trt) is significant (p < .0001), providing evidence that the five treatments aren't all equally effective **④**.

The plotmeans() function in the gplots package can be used to produce a graph of group means and their confidence intervals **⑤**. A plot of the treatment means, with 95 percent confidence limits, is provided in figure 9.1 and allows you to clearly see these treatment differences.

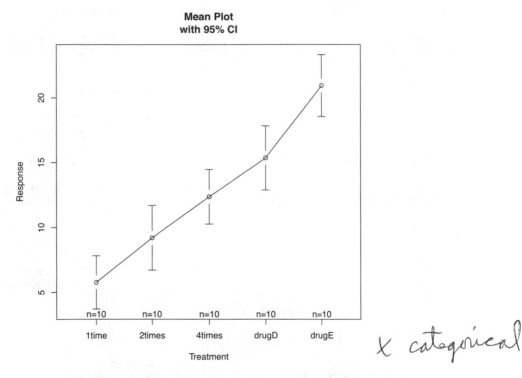

Figure 9.1   Treatment group means with 95 percent confidence intervals for five cholesterol-reducing drug regiments

9.3.1 Multiple comparisons

The ANOVA F test for treatment tells you that the five drug regiments aren't equally effective, but it doesn't tell you *which* treatments differ from one another. You can use a multiple comparison procedure to answer this question. For example, the TukeyHSD() function provides a test of all pairwise differences between group means (see listing 9.2). Note that the TukeyHSD() function has compatibility issues with package HH also used in this chapter; if HH is loaded, TukeyHSD() will fail. In that case, use detach("package:HH") to remove it from the search path and then call TukeyHSD().

Listing 9.2 Tukey HSD pairwise group comparisons

```
> TukeyHSD(fit)
  Tukey multiple comparisons of means
    95% family-wise confidence level

Fit: aov(formula = response ~ trt)

$trt
                 diff     lwr    upr p adj
2times-1time     3.44  -0.658   7.54 0.138
4times-1time     6.59   2.492  10.69 0.000
drugD-1time      9.58   5.478  13.68 0.000
drugE-1time     15.17  11.064  19.27 0.000
4times-2times    3.15  -0.951   7.25 0.205
drugD-2times     6.14   2.035  10.24 0.001
drugE-2times    11.72   7.621  15.82 0.000
drugD-4times     2.99  -1.115   7.09 0.251
drugE-4times     8.57   4.471  12.67 0.000
drugE-drugD      5.59   1.485   9.69 0.003

> par(las=2)
> par(mar=c(5,8,4,2))
> plot(TukeyHSD(fit))
```

For example, the mean cholesterol reductions for 1time and 2times aren't significantly different from each other (p = 0.138), whereas the difference between 1time and 4times is significantly different (p < .001).

The pairwise comparisons are plotted in figure 9.2. The first par statement rotates the axis labels, and the second one increases the left margin area so that the labels fit (par options are covered in chapter 3). In this graph, confidence intervals that include 0 indicate treatments that aren't significantly different (p > 0.5).

The glht() function in the multcomp package provides a much more comprehensive set of methods for multiple mean comparisons that you can use for both linear models (such as those described in this chapter) and generalized linear models (covered in chapter 13). The following code reproduces the Tukey HSD test, along with a different graphical representation of the results (figure 9.3):

```
> library(multcomp)
> par(mar=c(5,4,6,2))
> tuk <- glht(fit, linfct=mcp(trt="Tukey"))
> plot(cld(tuk, level=.05),col="lightgrey")
```

95% family-wise confidence level

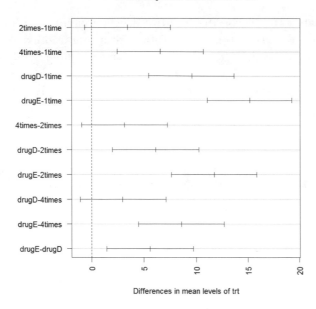

Figure 9.2   Plot of Tukey HSD pairwise mean comparisons

In this code, the `par` statement increased the top margin to fit the letter array. The `level` option in the `cld()` function provides the significance level to use (0.05, or 95 percent confidence in this case).

Groups (represented by box plots) that have the same letter don't have significantly different means. You can see that `1time` and `2times` aren't significantly different (they

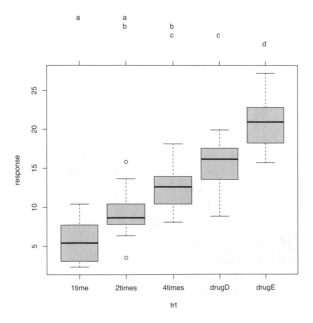

Figure 9.3   Tukey HSD tests provided by the `multcomp` package

both have the letter a) and that `2times` and `4times` aren't significantly different (they both have the letter b), but that `1time` and `4times` are different (they don't share a letter). Personally, I find figure 9.3 easier to read than figure 9.2. It also has the advantage of providing information on the distribution of scores within each group.

From these results, you can see that taking the cholesterol-lowering drug in 5 mg doses four times a day was better than taking a 20 mg dose once per day. The competitor drugD wasn't superior to this four-times-per-day regimen. But competitor drugE was superior to both drugD and all three dosage strategies for our focus drug.

Multiple comparisons methodology is a complex and rapidly changing area of study. To learn more, see Bretz, Hothorn, and Westfall (2010).

9.3.2 Assessing test assumptions

As we saw in the previous chapter, our confidence in results depends on the degree to which our data satisfies the assumptions underlying the statistical tests. In a one-way ANOVA, the dependent variable is assumed to be normally distributed, and have equal variance in each group. You can use a Q-Q plot to assess the normality assumption:

```
> library(car)
> qqPlot(lm(response ~ trt, data=cholesterol),
          simulate=TRUE, main="Q-Q Plot", labels=FALSE)
```

Note the `qqPlot()` requires an `lm()` fit. The graph is provided in figure 9.4.

The data fall within the 95 percent confidence envelope, suggesting that the normality assumption has been met fairly well.

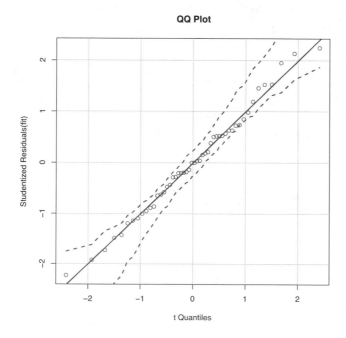

Figure 9.4   Test of normality

R provides several tests for the equality (homogeneity) of variances. For example, you can perform Bartlett's test with this code:

```
> bartlett.test(response ~ trt, data=cholesterol)

        Bartlett test of homogeneity of variances

data:  response by trt
Bartlett's K-squared = 0.5797, df = 4, p-value = 0.9653
```

Bartlett's test indicates that the variances in the five groups don't differ significantly ($p = 0.97$). Other possible tests include the Fligner–Killeen test (provided by the `fligner.test()` function), and the Brown–Forsythe test (provided by the `hov()` function in the HH package). Although not shown, the other two tests reach the same conclusion.

Finally, analysis of variance methodologies can be sensitive to the presence of outliers. You can test for outliers using the `outlierTest()` function in the car package:

```
> library(car)
> outlierTest(fit)

No Studentized residuals with Bonferonni p < 0.05
Largest |rstudent|:
   rstudent unadjusted p-value Bonferonni p
19 2.251149           0.029422           NA
```

From the output, you can see that there's no indication of outliers in the cholesterol data (NA occurs when $p > 1$). Taking the Q-Q plot, Bartlett's test, and outlier test together, the data appear to fit the ANOVA model quite well. This, in turn, adds to your confidence in the results.

9.4 *One-way ANCOVA*

A one-way analysis of covariance (ANCOVA) extends the one-way ANOVA to include one or more quantitative covariates. This example comes from the `litter` dataset in the `multcomp` package (see Westfall et al., 1999). Pregnant mice were divided into four treatment groups; each group received a different dose of a drug (0, 5, 50, or 500). The mean post-birth weight for each litter was the dependent variable and gestation time was included as a covariate. The analysis is given in the following listing.

Listing 9.3   One-way ANCOVA

```
> data(litter, package="multcomp")
> attach(litter)
> table(dose)
dose
  0   5  50 500
 20  19  18  17
> aggregate(weight, by=list(dose), FUN=mean)
  Group.1    x
1       0 32.3
2       5 29.3
```

```
3       50 29.9
4      500 29.6
> fit <- aov(weight ~ gesttime + dose)
> summary(fit)
            Df  Sum Sq Mean Sq F value   Pr(>F)
gesttime     1  134.30  134.30  8.0493 0.005971 **
dose         3  137.12   45.71  2.7394 0.049883 *
Residuals   69 1151.27   16.69
---
Signif. codes:  0 '***' 0.001 '**' 0.01 '*' 0.05 '.' 0.1 ' ' 1
```

From the `table()` function you can see that there are an unequal number of litters at each dosage level, with 20 litters at zero dosage (no drug) and 17 litters at dosage 500. Based on the group means provided by the `aggregate()` function, the *no-drug* group had the highest mean litter weight (32.3). The ANCOVA F tests indicate that (a) gestation time was related to birth weight, and (b) drug dosage was related to birth weight after controlling for gestation time. The mean birth weight isn't the same for each of the drug dosages, after controlling for gestation time.

Because you're using a covariate, you may want to obtain adjusted group means—that is, the group means obtained after partialing out the effects of the covariate. You can use the `effect()` function in the `effects` library to calculate adjusted means:

```
> library(effects)
> effect("dose", fit)

 dose effect
dose
   0    5   50  500
32.4 28.9 30.6 29.3
```

In this case, the adjusted means are similar to the unadjusted means produced by the `aggregate()` function, but this won't always be the case. The `effects` package provides a powerful method of obtaining adjusted means for complex research designs and presenting them visually. See the package documentation on CRAN for more details.

As with the one-way ANOVA example in the last section, the F test for dose indicates that the treatments don't have the same mean birth weight, but it doesn't tell you which means differ from one another. Again you can use the multiple comparison procedures provided by the `multcomp` package to compute all pairwise mean comparisons. Additionally, the `multcomp` package can be used to test specific user-defined hypotheses about the means.

Suppose you're interested in whether the no-drug condition differs from the three-drug condition. The code in the following listing can be used to test this hypothesis.

Listing 9.4   Multiple comparisons employing user-supplied contrasts

```
> library(multcomp)
> contrast <- rbind("no drug vs. drug" = c(3, -1, -1, -1))
> summary(glht(fit, linfct=mcp(dose=contrast)))

Multiple Comparisons of Means: User-defined Contrasts
```

```
Fit: aov(formula = weight ~ gesttime + dose)

Linear Hypotheses:
                     Estimate Std. Error t value Pr(>|t|)
no drug vs. drug == 0    8.284      3.209   2.581   0.0120 *
---
Signif. codes:  0 '***' 0.001 '**' 0.01 '*' 0.05 '.' 0.1 ' ' 1
```

The contrast c(3, -1, -1, -1) specifies a comparison of the first group with the average of the other three. The hypothesis is tested with a t statistic (2.581 in this case), which is significant at the $p < .05$ level. Therefore, you can conclude that the no-drug group has a higher birth weight than drug conditions. Other contrasts can be added to the rbind() function (see help(glht) for details).

9.4.1 *Assessing test assumptions*

ANCOVA designs make the same normality and homogeneity of variance assumptions described for ANOVA designs, and you can test these assumptions using the same procedures described in section 9.3.2. In addition, standard ANCOVA designs assumes homogeneity of regression slopes. In this case, it's assumed that the regression slope for predicting birth weight from gestation time is the same in each of the four treatment groups. A test for the homogeneity of regression slopes can be obtained by including a gestation*dose interaction term in your ANCOVA model. A significant interaction would imply that the relationship between gestation and birth weight depends on the level of the dose variable. The code and results are provided in the following listing.

Listing 9.5   Testing for homogeneity of regression slopes

```
> library(multcomp)
> fit2 <- aov(weight ~ gesttime*dose, data=litter)
> summary(fit2)
              Df Sum Sq Mean Sq F value Pr(>F)
gesttime       1    134     134    8.29 0.0054 **
dose           3    137      46    2.82 0.0456 *
gesttime:dose  3     82      27    1.68 0.1789
Residuals     66   1069      16
---
Signif. codes:  0 '***' 0.001 '**' 0.01 '*' 0.05 '.' 0.1 ' ' 1
```

The interaction is nonsignificant, supporting the assumption of equality of slopes. If the assumption is untenable, you could try transforming the covariate or dependent variable, using a model that accounts for separate slopes, or employing a nonparametric ANCOVA method that doesn't require homogeneity of regression slopes. See the sm.ancova() function in the sm package for an example of the latter.

9.4.2 *Visualizing the results*

The ancova() function in the HH package provides a plot of the relationship between the dependent variable, the covariate, and the factor. For example:

```
> library(HH)
> ancova(weight ~ gesttime + dose, data=litter)
```

produces the plot shown in the following figure 9.5. Note: the figure has been modified to display better in black and white and will look slightly different when you run the code yourself.

Here you can see that the regression lines for predicting birth weight from gestation time are parallel in each group but have different intercepts. As gestation time increases, birth weight increases. Additionally, you can see that the 0-dose group has the largest intercept and the 5-dose group has the lowest intercept. The lines are parallel because you've specified them to be. If you'd used the statement `ancova(weight ~ gesttime*dose)` instead, you'd generate a plot that allows both the slopes and intercepts to vary by group. This approach is useful for visualizing the case where the homogeneity of regression slopes doesn't hold.

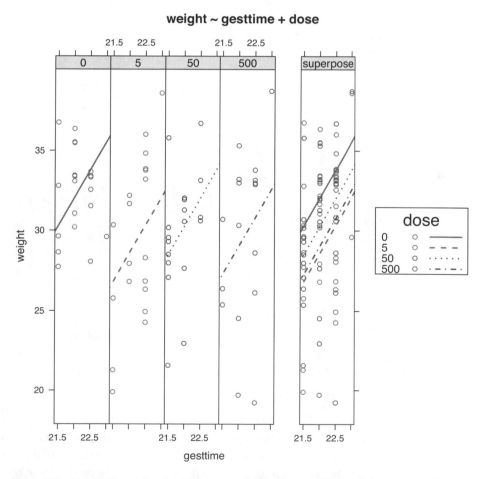

Figure 9.5 **Plot of the relationship between gestation time and birth weight for each of four drug treatment groups**

9.5   *Two-way factorial ANOVA*

In a two-way factorial ANOVA, subjects are assigned to groups that are formed from the cross-classification of two factors. This example uses the ToothGrowth dataset in the base installation to demonstrate a two-way between-groups ANOVA. Sixty guinea pigs are randomly assigned to receive one of three levels of ascorbic acid (0.5, 1, or 2mg), and one of two delivery methods (orange juice or Vitamin C), under the restriction that each treatment combination has 10 guinea pigs. The dependent variable is tooth length. The following listing shows the code for the analysis.

Listing 9.6   Two-way ANOVA

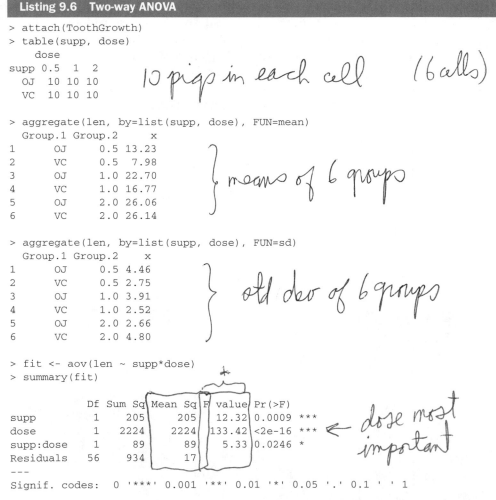

```
> attach(ToothGrowth)
> table(supp, dose)
    dose
supp 0.5  1   2
  OJ  10  10  10          10 pigs in each cell        (6 cells)
  VC  10  10  10

> aggregate(len, by=list(supp, dose), FUN=mean)
  Group.1 Group.2     x
1      OJ     0.5 13.23
2      VC     0.5  7.98        } means of 6 groups
3      OJ     1.0 22.70
4      VC     1.0 16.77
5      OJ     2.0 26.06
6      VC     2.0 26.14

> aggregate(len, by=list(supp, dose), FUN=sd)
  Group.1 Group.2    x
1      OJ     0.5 4.46
2      VC     0.5 2.75        } std dev of 6 groups
3      OJ     1.0 3.91
4      VC     1.0 2.52
5      OJ     2.0 2.66
6      VC     2.0 4.80

> fit <- aov(len ~ supp*dose)
> summary(fit)

            Df Sum Sq Mean Sq F value  Pr(>F)
supp         1    205     205   12.32  0.0009 ***    ← dose most
dose         1   2224    2224  133.42   <2e-16 ***        important
supp:dose    1     89      89    5.33  0.0246 *
Residuals   56    934      17
---
Signif. codes:  0 '***' 0.001 '**' 0.01 '*' 0.05 '.' 0.1 ' ' 1
```

The table statement indicates that you have a balanced design (equal sample sizes in each cell of the design), and the aggregate statements provide the cell means and standard deviations. The ANOVA table provided by the summary() function indicates that both main effects (supp and dose) and the interaction between these factors are significant.

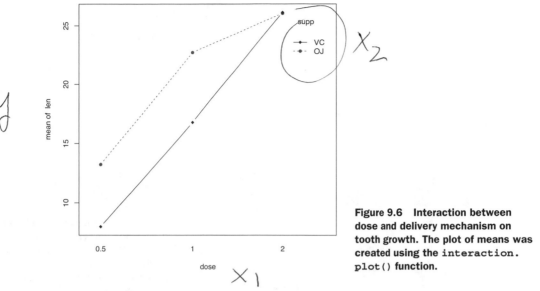

Figure 9.6 Interaction between dose and delivery mechanism on tooth growth. The plot of means was created using the `interaction.plot()` function.

You can visualize the results in several ways. You can use the `interaction.plot()` function to display the interaction in a two-way ANOVA. The code is

```
interaction.plot(dose, supp, len, type="b",
            col=c("red","blue"), pch=c(16, 18),
            main = "Interaction between Dose and Supplement Type")
```

and the resulting plot is presented in figure 9.6. The plot provides the mean tooth length for each supplement at each dosage.

With a little finesse, you can get an interaction plot out of the `plotmeans()` function in the `gplots` package. The following code produces the graph in figure 9.7:

```
library(gplots)
plotmeans(len ~ interaction(supp, dose, sep=" "),
        connect=list(c(1,3,5),c(2,4,6)),
        col=c("red", "darkgreen"),
        main = "Interaction Plot with 95% CIs",
        xlab="Treatment and Dose Combination")
```

The graph includes the means, as well as error bars (95 percent confidence intervals) and sample sizes.

Finally, you can use the `interaction2wt()` function in the `HH` package to produce a plot of both main effects and two-way interactions for any factorial design of any order (figure 9.8):

```
library(HH)
interaction2wt(len~supp*dose)
```

Again, this figure has been modified to display more clearly in black and white and will look slightly different when you run the code yourself.

All three graphs indicate that tooth growth increases with the dose of ascorbic acid for both orange juice and Vitamin C. For the 0.5 and 1mg doses, orange juice produced

Interaction Plot with 95% CIs

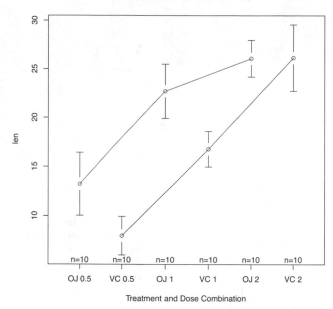

Figure 9.7　Interaction between dose and delivery mechanism on tooth growth. The mean plot with 95 percent confidence intervals was created by the `plotmeans()` function.

more tooth growth than Vitamin C. For 2mg of ascorbic acid, both delivery methods produced identical growth. Of the three plotting methods provided, I prefer the `interaction2wt()` function in the HH package. It displays both the main effects (the box plots) and the two-way interactions for designs of any complexity (two-way ANOVA, three-way ANOVA, etc.).

Although I don't cover the tests of model assumptions and mean comparison procedures, they're a natural extension of the methods you've seen so far. Additionally, the design is balanced, so you don't have to worry about the order of effects.

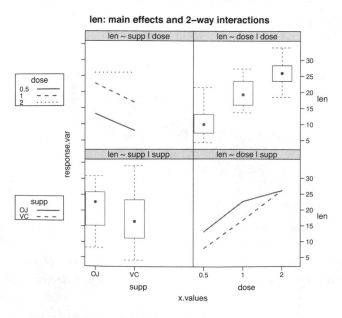

Figure 9.8　Main effects and two-way interaction for the `ToothGrowth` dataset. This plot was created by the `interaction2way()` function.

9.6 Repeated measures ANOVA

In repeated measures ANOVA, subjects are measured more than once. This section focuses on a repeated measures ANOVA with one within-groups and one between-groups factor (a common design). We'll take our example from the field of physiological ecology. Physiological ecologists study how the physiological and biochemical processes of living systems respond to variations in environmental factors (a crucial area of study given the realities of global warming). The CO2 dataset included in the base installation contains the results of a study of cold tolerance in Northern and Southern plants of the grass species *Echinochloa crus-galli* (Potvin, Lechowicz, & Tardif, 1990). The photosynthetic rates of chilled plants were compared with the photosynthetic rates of nonchilled plants at several ambient CO2 concentrations. Half the plants were from Quebec and half were from Mississippi.

In this example, we'll focus on chilled plants. The dependent variable is carbon dioxide uptake (uptake) in ml/L, and the independent variables are Type (Quebec versus Mississippi) and ambient CO2 concentration (conc) with seven levels (ranging from 95 to 1000 umol/m^2 sec). Type is a between-groups factor and conc is a within-groups factor. The analysis is presented in the next listing.

Listing 9.7 Repeated measures ANOVA with one between- and within-groups factor

```
> w1b1 <- subset(CO2, Treatment=='chilled')
> fit <- aov(uptake ~ conc*Type + Error(Plant/(conc)), w1b1)
> summary(fit)

Error: Plant
          Df   Sum Sq Mean Sq F value   Pr(>F)
Type       1 2667.24 2667.24  60.414 0.001477 **
Residuals  4  176.60   44.15
---
Signif. codes:  0 '***' 0.001 '**' 0.01 '*' 0.05 '.' 0.1 ' ' 1

Error: Plant:conc
          Df Sum Sq Mean Sq F value    Pr(>F)
conc       1 888.57  888.57  215.46 0.0001253 ***
conc:Type  1 239.24  239.24   58.01 0.0015952 **
Residuals  4  16.50    4.12
---
Signif. codes:  0 '***' 0.001 '**' 0.01 '*' 0.05 '.' 0.1 ' ' 1

Error: Within
           Df Sum Sq Mean Sq F value Pr(>F)
Residuals 30 869.05   28.97

> par(las=2)
> par(mar=c(10,4,4,2))
> with(w1b1, interaction.plot(conc,Type,uptake,
        type="b", col=c("red","blue"), pch=c(16,18),
        main="Interaction Plot for Plant Type and Concentration"))
> boxplot(uptake ~ Type*conc, data=w1b1, col=(c("gold", "green")),
          main="Chilled Quebec and Mississippi Plants",
          ylab="Carbon dioxide uptake rate (umol/m^2 sec)")
```

Interaction Plot for Plant Type and Concentration

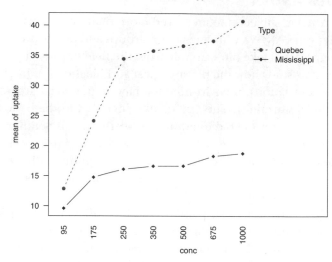

Figure 9.9   Interaction of ambient CO2 concentration and plant type on CO2 uptake. Graph produced by the `interaction.plot()` function.

The ANOVA table indicates that the Type and concentration main effects and the Type x concentration interaction are all significant at the 0.01 level. The interaction is plotted via the `interaction.plot()` function in figure 9.9.

In order to demonstrate a different presentation of the interaction, the `boxplot()` function is used to plot the same data. The results are provided in figure 9.10.

Chilled Quebec and Mississippi Plants

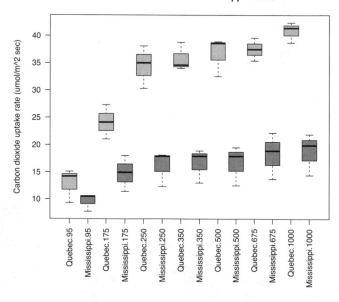

Figure 9.10   Interaction of ambient CO2 concentration and plant type on CO2 uptake. Graph produced by the `boxplot()` function.

From either graph, you can see that there's a greater carbon dioxide uptake in plants from Quebec compared to Mississippi. The difference is more pronounced at higher ambient CO2 concentrations.

NOTE The datasets that you work with are typically in *wide format*, where columns are variables and rows are observations, and there's a single row for each subject. The `litter` data frame from section 9.4 is a good example. When dealing with repeated measures designs, you typically need the data in *long format* before fitting your models. In long format, each measurement of the dependent variable is placed in its own row. The CO2 dataset follows this form. Luckily, the `reshape` package described in chapter 5 (section 5.6.3) can easily reorganize your data into the required format.

The many approaches to mixed-model designs

The CO2 example in this section was analyzed using a traditional repeated measures ANOVA. The approach assumes that the covariance matrix for any within-groups factor follows a specified form known as *sphericity*. Specifically, it assumes that the variances of the differences between any two levels of the within-groups factor are equal. In real-world data, it's unlikely that this assumption will be met. This has led to a number of alternative approaches, including the following:

- Using the `lmer()` function in the `lme4` package to fit linear mixed models (Bates, 2005)
- Using the `Anova()` function in the `car` package to adjust traditional test statistics to account for lack of sphericity (for example, Geisser–Greenhouse correction)
- Using the `gls()` function in the `nlme` package to fit generalized least squares models with specified variance-covariance structures (UCLA, 2009)
- Using multivariate analysis of variance to model repeated measured data (Hand, 1987)

Coverage of these approaches is beyond the scope of this text. If you're interested in learning more, check out Pinheiro and Bates (2000) and Zuur et al. (2009).

Up to this point, all the methods in this chapter have assumed that there's a single dependent variable. In the next section, we'll briefly consider designs that include more than one outcome variable.

9.7 *Multivariate analysis of variance (MANOVA)*

If there's more than one dependent (outcome) variable, you can test them simultaneously using a multivariate analysis of variance (MANOVA). The following example is based on the `UScereal` dataset in the `MASS` package. The dataset comes from Venables

& Ripley (1999). In this example, we're interested in whether the calories, fat, and sugar content of US cereals vary by store shelf, where 1 is the bottom shelf, 2 is the middle shelf, and 3 is the top shelf. Calories, fat, and sugars are the dependent variables, and shelf is the independent variable with three levels (1, 2, and 3). The analysis is presented in the following listing.

Listing 9.8   One-way MANOVA

```
> library(MASS)
> attach(UScereal)
> y <- cbind(calories, fat, sugars)
> aggregate(y, by=list(shelf), FUN=mean)
  Group.1 calories    fat sugars
1       1      119 0.662    6.3
2       2      130 1.341   12.5
3       3      180 1.945   10.9
> cov(y)
         calories    fat sugars
calories   3895.2  60.67 180.38
fat          60.7   2.71   4.00
sugars      180.4   4.00  34.05
> fit <- manova(y ~ shelf)
> summary(fit)
            Df Pillai approx F num Df den Df  Pr(>F)
shelf        1 0.1959   4.9550      3     61 0.00383 **
Residuals   63
---
Signif. codes:  0 '***' 0.001 '**' 0.01 '*' 0.05 '.' 0.1 ' ' 1

> summary.aov(fit)
 Response calories :
            Df Sum Sq Mean Sq F value        Pr(>F)
shelf        1  45313   45313  13.995 0.0003983  ***
Residuals   63 203982    3238
---
Signif. codes:  0 '***' 0.001 '**' 0.01 '*' 0.05 '.' 0.1 ' ' 1

 Response fat :
            Df  Sum Sq  Mean Sq F value       Pr(>F)
shelf        1  18.421   18.421   7.476 0.008108  **
Residuals   63 155.236    2.464
---
Signif. codes:  0 '***' 0.001 '**' 0.01 '*' 0.05 '.' 0.1 ' ' 1

 Response sugars :
            Df  Sum Sq  Mean Sq F value      Pr(>F)
shelf        1  183.34   183.34   5.787 0.01909  *
Residuals   63 1995.87    31.68
---
Signif. codes:  0 '***' 0.001 '**' 0.01 '*' 0.05 '.' 0.1 ' ' 1
```

Print univariate results ← (annotation pointing to `> summary.aov(fit)`)

This listing uses the `cbind()` function to form a matrix of the three dependent variables (calories, fat, and sugars). The `aggregate()` function provides the shelf means, and the `cov()` function provides the variance and the covariances across cereals.

The `manova()` function provides the multivariate test of group differences. The significant F value indicates that the three groups differ on the set of nutritional measures.

Because the multivariate test is significant, you can use the `summary.aov()` function to obtain the univariate one-way ANOVAs. Here, you see that the three groups differ on each nutritional measure considered separately. Finally, you can use a mean comparison procedure (such as `TukeyHSD`) to determine which shelves differ from each other for each of the three dependent variables (omitted here to save space).

9.7.1 Assessing test assumptions

The two assumptions underlying a one-way MANOVA are multivariate normality and homogeneity of variance-covariance matrices.

The first assumption states that the vector of dependent variables jointly follows a multivariate normal distribution. You can use a Q-Q plot to assess this assumption (see the sidebar "A Theory Interlude" for a statistical explanation of how this works).

A theory interlude

If you have p x 1 multivariate normal random vector x with mean μ and covariance matrix Σ, then the squared Mahalanobis distance between x and μ is chi-square distributed with p degrees of freedom. The Q-Q plot graphs the quantiles of the chi-square distribution for the sample against the Mahalanobis D-squared values. To the degree that the points fall along a line with slope 1 and intercept 0, there's evidence that the data is multivariate normal.

The code is provided in the following listing and the resulting graph is displayed in figure 9.11.

Listing 9.9 Assessing multivariate normality

```
> center <- colMeans(y)
> n <- nrow(y)
> p <- ncol(y)
> cov <- cov(y)
> d <- mahalanobis(y,center,cov)
> coord <- qqplot(qchisq(ppoints(n),df=p),
    d, main="Q-Q Plot Assessing Multivariate Normality",
    ylab="Mahalanobis D2")
> abline(a=0,b=1)
> identify(coord$x, coord$y, labels=row.names(UScereal))
```

If the data follow a multivariate normal distribution, then points will fall on the line. The `identify()` function allows you to interactively identify points in the graph. (The `identify()` function is covered in chapter 16, section 16.4.) Here, the dataset appears to violate multivariate normality, primarily due to the observations for *Wheaties Honey Gold* and *Wheaties*. You may want to delete these two cases and rerun the analyses.

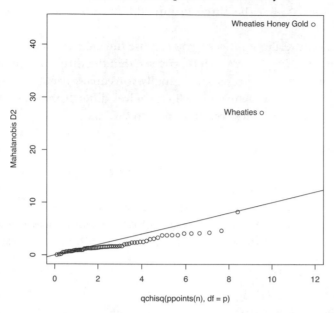

Figure 9.11   A Q-Q plot for assessing multivariate normality

The homogeneity of variance-covariance matrices assumption requires that the covariance matrix for each group are equal. The assumption is usually evaluated with a Box's M test. R doesn't include a function for Box's M, but an internet search will provide the appropriate code. Unfortunately, the test is sensitive to violations of normality, leading to rejection in most typical cases. This means that we don't yet have a good working method for evaluating this important assumption (but see Anderson [2006] and Silva et al. [2008] for interesting alternative approaches not yet available in R).

Finally, you can test for multivariate outliers using the `aq.plot()` function in the `mvoutlier` package. The code in this case looks like this:

```
library(mvoutlier)
outliers <- aq.plot(y)
outliers
```

Try it out and see what you get!

9.7.2   *Robust MANOVA*

If the assumptions of multivariate normality or homogeneity of variance-covariance matrices are untenable, or if you're concerned about multivariate outliers, you may want to consider using a robust or nonparametric version of the MANOVA test instead. A robust version of the one-way MANOVA is provided by the `Wilks.test()` function in the `rrcov` package. The `adonis()` function in the `vegan` package can provide the equivalent of a nonparametric MANOVA. Listing 9.10 applies `Wilks.test()` to our example.

Listing 9.10   Robust one-way MANOVA

```
library(rrcov)
> Wilks.test(y,shelf,method="mcd")

        Robust One-way MANOVA (Bartlett Chi2)

data:  x
Wilks' Lambda = 0.511, Chi2-Value = 23.71, DF = 4.85, p-value =
0.0002143
sample estimates:
  calories    fat sugars
1      120  0.701   5.66
2      128  1.185  12.54
3      161  1.652  10.35
```

From the results, you can see that using a robust test that's insensitive to both outliers and violations of MANOVA assumptions still indicates that the cereals on the top, middle, and bottom store shelves differ in their nutritional profiles.

9.8   *ANOVA as regression*

glm

In section 9.2, we noted that ANOVA and regression are both special cases of the same general linear model. As such, the designs in this chapter could have been analyzed using the lm() function. However, in order to understand the output, you need to understand how R deals with categorical variables when fitting models.

Consider the one-way ANOVA problem in section 9.3, which compares the impact of five cholesterol-reducing drug regiments (trt).

```
> library(multcomp)
> levels(cholesterol$trt)

[1] "1time"  "2times" "4times" "drugD"  "drugE"
```

First, let's fit the model using the aov() function:

```
> fit.aov <- aov(response ~ trt, data=cholesterol)
> summary(fit.aov)

            Df  Sum Sq Mean Sq  F value    Pr(>F)
trt          4 1351.37  337.84   32.433 9.819e-13 ***
Residuals   45  468.75   10.42
```

see p. 225

Now, let's fit the same model using lm(). In this case you get the results shown in the next listing.

Listing 9.11   A regression approach to the ANOVA problem in section 9.3

```
> fit.lm <- lm(response ~ trt, data=cholesterol)
> summary(fit.lm)

Coefficients:
            Estimate Std. Error t value Pr(>|t|)
(Intercept)    5.782      1.021   5.665 9.78e-07 ***
trt2times      3.443      1.443   2.385   0.0213 *
```

4 variables
= 5−1

```
trt4times        6.593      1.443    4.568 3.82e-05 ***
trtdrugD         9.579      1.443    6.637 3.53e-08 ***
trtdrugE        15.166      1.443   10.507 1.08e-13 ***

Residual standard error: 3.227 on 45 degrees of freedom
Multiple R-squared: 0.7425,      Adjusted R-squared: 0.7196
F-statistic: 32.43 on 4 and 45 DF,   p-value: 9.819e-13
```

What are we looking at? Because linear models require numeric predictors, when the `lm()` function encounters a factor, it replaces that factor with a set of numeric variables representing contrasts among the levels. If the factor has k levels, k-1 contrast variables will be created. R provides five built-in methods for creating these contrast variables (see table 9.6). You can also create your own (we won't cover that here). By default, treatment contrasts are used for unordered factors and orthogonal polynomials are used for ordered factors.

Table 9.6   Built-in contrasts

Contrast	Description
contr.helmert	Contrasts the second level with the first, the third level with the average of the first two, the fourth level with the average of the first three, and so on.
contr.poly	Contrasts used for trend analysis (linear, quadratic, cubic, and so on.) based on orthogonal polynomials. Use for ordered factors with equally spaced levels.
contr.sum	Contrasts are constrained to sum to zero. Also called deviation contrasts, they compare the mean of each level to the overall mean across levels.
contr.treatment	Contrasts each level with the baseline level (first level by default). Also called dummy coding.
contr.SAS	Similar to contr.treatment but the baseline level is the last level. This produces coefficients similar to contrasts used in most SAS procedures.

With treatment contrasts, the first level of the factor becomes the reference group and each subsequent level is compared with it. You can see the coding scheme via the `contrasts()` function:

```
> contrasts(cholesterol$trt)
        2times 4times drugD drugE
1time        0      0     0     0
2times       1      0     0     0
4times       0      1     0     0
drugD        0      0     1     0
drugE        0      0     0     1
```

If a patient is in the drugD condition, then the variable `drugD` equals 1, and the variables `2times`, `4times`, and `drugE` will each equal zero. You don't need a variable for the first group, because a zero on each of the four indicator variables uniquely determines that the patient is in the `1times` condition.

In listing 9.11, the variable `trt2times` represents a contrast between the levels `1time` and `2time`. Similarly, `trt4times` is a contrast between `1time` and `4times`, and so on. You can see from the probability values in the output that each drug condition is significantly different from the first (`1time`).

You can change the default contrasts used in `lm()` by specifying a `contrasts` option. For example, you can specify Helmert contrasts by using

```
fit.lm <- lm(response ~ trt, data=cholesterol, contrasts="contr.helmert")
```

You can change the default contrasts used during an R session via the `options()` function. For example,

```
options(contrasts = c("contr.SAS", "contr.helmert"))
```

would set the default contrast for unordered factors to `contr.SAS` and for ordered factors to `contr.helmert`. Although we've limited our discussion to the use of contrasts in linear models, note that they're applicable to other modeling functions in R. This includes the generalized linear models covered in chapter 13.

9.9 Summary

In this chapter, we reviewed the analysis of basic experimental and quasi-experimental designs using ANOVA/ANCOVA/MANOVA methodology. We reviewed the basic terminology used, and looked at examples of between and within-groups designs, including the one-way ANOVA, one-way ANCOVA, two-way factorial ANOVA, repeated measures ANOVA, and one-way MANOVA.

In addition to the basic analyses, we reviewed methods of assessing model assumptions and applying multiple comparison procedures following significant omnibus tests. Finally, we explored a wide variety of methods for displaying the results visually. If you're interested in learning more about the design of experiments (DOE) using R, be sure to see the CRAN View provided by Groemping (2009).

Chapters 8 and 9 have covered the statistical methods most often used by researchers in a wide variety of fields. In the next chapter, we'll address issues of power analysis. Power analysis helps us to determine the sample sizes needed to detect an effect of a given size with a given degree of confidence, and is a crucial component of research design.

Power analysis

10

As a statistical consultant, I am often asked the question, "How many subjects do I need for my study?" Sometimes the question is phrased this way: "I have *x* number of people available for this study. Is the study worth doing?" Questions like these can be answered through *power analysis*, an important set of techniques in experimental design.

Power analysis allows you to determine the sample size required to detect an effect of a given size with a given degree of confidence. Conversely, it allows you to determine the probability of detecting an effect of a given size with a given level of confidence, under sample size constraints. If the probability is unacceptably low, you'd be wise to alter or abandon the experiment.

In this chapter, you'll learn how to conduct power analyses for a variety of statistical tests, including tests of proportions, t-tests, chi-square tests, balanced one-way ANOVA, tests of correlations, and linear models. Because power analysis applies to hypothesis testing situations, we'll start with a brief review of null hypothesis significance testing (NHST). Then we'll review conducting power analyses within R, focusing primarily on the `pwr` package. Finally, we'll consider other approaches to power analysis available with R.

10.1 *A quick review of hypothesis testing*

To help you understand the steps in a power analysis, we'll briefly review statistical hypothesis testing in general. If you have a statistical background, feel free to skip to section 10.2.

In statistical hypothesis testing, you specify a hypothesis about a population parameter (your null hypothesis, or H_0). You then draw a sample from this population and calculate a statistic that's used to make inferences about the population parameter. Assuming that the null hypothesis is true, you calculate the probability of obtaining the observed sample statistic or one more extreme. If the probability is sufficiently small, you reject the null hypothesis in favor of its opposite (referred to as the alternative or research hypothesis, H_1).

An example will clarify the process. Say you're interested in evaluating the impact of cell phone use on driver reaction time. Your null hypothesis is Ho: $\mu_1 - \mu_2 = 0$, where μ_1 is the mean response time for drivers using a cell phone and μ_2 is the mean response time for drivers that are cell phone free (here, $\mu_1 - \mu_2$ is the population parameter of interest). If you reject this null hypothesis, you're left with the alternate or research hypothesis, namely H_1: $\mu_1 - \mu_2 \neq 0$. This is equivalent to $\mu_1 \neq \mu_2$, that the mean reaction times for the two conditions are not equal.

A sample of individuals is selected and randomly assigned to one of two conditions. In the first condition, participants react to a series of driving challenges in a simulator while talking on a cell phone. In the second condition, participants complete the same series of challenges but without a cell phone. Overall reaction time is assessed for each individual.

Based on the sample data, you can calculate the statistic

$$\left(\bar{X}_1 - \bar{X}_2\right) / \left(\frac{s}{\sqrt{n}}\right)$$

where $\bar{X}_1$ and $\bar{X}_2$ are the sample reaction time means in the two conditions, s is the pooled sample standard deviation, and n is the number of participants in each condition. If the null hypothesis is true and you can assume that reaction times are normally distributed, this sample statistic will follow a t distribution with 2n-2 degrees of freedom. Using this fact, you can calculate the probability of obtaining a sample statistic this large or larger. If the probability (p) is smaller than some predetermined cutoff (say p < .05), you reject the null hypothesis in favor of the alternate hypothesis. This predetermined cutoff (0.05) is called the *significance level* of the test.

Note that you use *sample* data to make an inference about the *population* it's drawn from. Your null hypothesis is that the mean reaction time of *all* drivers talking on cell phones isn't different from the mean reaction time of *all* drivers who aren't talking on cell phones, not just those drivers in your sample. The four possible outcomes from your decision are as follows:

- If the null hypothesis is false and the statistical test leads us to reject it, you've made a correct decision. You've correctly determined that reaction time is affected by cell phone use.

- If the null hypothesis is true and you don't reject it, again you've made a correct decision. Reaction time isn't affected by cell phone use.
- If the null hypothesis is true but you reject it, you've committed a Type I error. You've concluded that cell phone use affects reaction time when it doesn't.
- If the null hypothesis is false and you fail to reject it, you've committed a Type II error. Cell phone use affects reaction time, but you've failed to discern this.

Each of these outcomes is illustrated in the table below.

		Decision	
		Reject H_0	**Fail to Reject H_0**
Actual	**H_0 true**	Type I error	correct
	H_0 false	correct	Type II error

Controversy surrounding null hypothesis significance testing

Null hypothesis significance testing is not without controversy and detractors have raised numerous concerns about the approach, particularly as practiced in the field of psychology. They point to a widespread misunderstanding of p values, reliance on statistical significance over practical significance, the fact that the null hypothesis is never exactly true and will always be rejected for sufficient sample sizes, and a number of logical inconsistencies in NHST practices.

An in-depth discussion of this topic is beyond the scope of this book. Interested readers are referred to Harlow, Mulaik, and Steiger (1997).

In planning research, the researcher typically pays special attention to four quantities: sample size, significance level, power, and effect size (see figure 10.1).

Specifically:

- *Sample size* refers to the number of observations in each condition/group of the experimental design.
- The *significance level* (also referred to as alpha) is defined as the probability of making a Type I error. The significance level can also be thought of as the probability of finding an effect that is *not* there.
- *Power* is defined as one minus the probability of making a Type II error. Power can be thought of as the probability of finding an effect that *is* there.
- *Effect size* is the magnitude of the effect under the alternate or research hypothesis. The formula for effect size depends on the statistical methodology employed in the hypothesis testing.

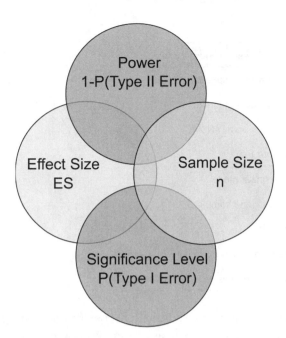

Figure 10.1 Four primary quantities considered in a study design power analysis. Given any three, you can calculate the fourth.

Although the sample size and significance level are under the direct control of the researcher, power and effect size are affected more indirectly. For example, as you relax the significance level (in other words, make it easier to reject the null hypothesis), power increases. Similarly, increasing the sample size increases power.

Your research goal is typically to maximize the power of your statistical tests while maintaining an acceptable significance level and employing as small a sample size as possible. That is, you want to maximize the chances of finding a real effect and minimize the chances of finding an effect that isn't really there, while keeping study costs within reason.

The four quantities (sample size, significance level, power, and effect size) have an intimate relationship. *Given any three, you can determine the fourth.* We'll use this fact to carry out various power analyses throughout the remainder of the chapter. In the next section, we'll look at ways of implementing power analyses using the R package `pwr`. Later, we'll briefly look at some highly specialized power functions that are used in biology and genetics.

10.2 *Implementing power analysis with the pwr package*

The `pwr` package, developed by Stéphane Champely, implements power analysis as outlined by Cohen (1988). Some of the more important functions are listed in table 10.1. For each function, the user can specify three of the four quantities (sample size, significance level, power, effect size) and the fourth will be calculated.

Table 10.1 pwr package functions

Function	Power calculations for
pwr.2p.test()	Two proportions (equal n)
pwr.2p2n.test()	Two proportions (unequal n)
pwr.anova.test()	Balanced one-way ANOVA
pwr.chisq.test()	Chi-square test
pwr.f2.test()	General linear model
pwr.p.test()	Proportion (one sample)
pwr.r.test()	Correlation
pwr.t.test()	t-tests (one sample, two sample, paired)
pwr.t2n.test()	t-test (two samples with unequal n)

Of the four quantities, effect size is often the most difficult to specify. Calculating effect size typically requires some experience with the measures involved and knowledge of past research. But what can you do if you have no clue what effect size to expect in a given study? You'll look at this difficult question in section 10.2.7. In the remainder of this section, you'll look at the application of pwr functions to common statistical tests. Before invoking these functions, be sure to install and load the pwr package.

10.2.1 *t-tests*

When the statistical test to be used is a t-test, the pwr.t.test() function provides a number of useful power analysis options. The format is

```
pwr.t.test(n=, d=, sig.level=, power=, alternative=)
```

where

- n is the sample size.
- d is the effect size defined as the standardized mean difference.

$$d = \frac{\mu_1 - \mu_2}{\sigma} \qquad \text{where} \quad \begin{aligned} \mu_1 &= \text{mean of group 1} \\ \mu_2 &= \text{mean of group 2} \\ \sigma^2 &= \text{common error variance} \end{aligned}$$

- sig.level is the significance level (0.05 is the default).
- power is the power level.
- type is two-sample t-test ("two.sample"), a one-sample t-test ("one.sample"), or a dependent sample t-test ("paired"). A two-sample test is the default.
- alternative indicates whether the statistical test is two-sided ("two.sided") or one-sided ("less" or "greater"). A two-sided test is the default.

Let's work through an example. Continuing the cell phone use and driving reaction time experiment from section 10.1, assume that you'll be using a two-tailed independent sample t-test to compare the mean reaction time for participants in the cell phone condition with the mean reaction time for participants driving unencumbered.

Let's assume that you know from past experience that reaction time has a standard deviation of 1.25 seconds. Also suppose that a 1-second difference in reaction time is considered an important difference. You'd therefore like to conduct a study in which you're able to detect an effect size of d = 1/1.25 = 0.8 or larger. Additionally, you want to be 90 percent sure to detect such a difference if it exists, and 95 percent sure that you won't declare a difference to be significant when it's actually due to random variability. How many participants will you need in your study?

Entering this information in the `pwr.t.test()` function, you have the following:

```
> library(pwr)
> pwr.t.test(d=.8, sig.level=.05, power=.9, type="two.sample",
  alternative="two.sided")

     Two-sample t test power calculation

            n = 34
            d = 0.8
    sig.level = 0.05
        power = 0.9
  alternative = two.sided

NOTE: n is number in *each* group
```

The results suggest that you need 34 participants in each group (for a total of 68 participants) in order to detect an effect size of 0.8 with 90 percent certainty and no more than a 5 percent chance of erroneously concluding that a difference exists when, in fact, it doesn't.

Let's alter the question. Assume that in comparing the two conditions you want to be able to detect a 0.5 standard deviation difference in population means. You want to limit the chances of falsely declaring the population means to be different to 1 out of 100. Additionally, you can only afford to include 40 participants in the study. What's the probability that you'll be able to detect a difference between the population means that's this large, given the constraints outlined?

Assuming that an equal number of participants will be placed in each condition, you have

```
> pwr.t.test(n=20, d=.5, sig.level=.01, type="two.sample",
  alternative="two.sided")

     Two-sample t test power calculation

            n = 20
            d = 0.5
    sig.level = 0.01
        power = 0.14
```

```
alternative = two.sided
```

```
NOTE: n is number in *each* group
```

With 20 participants in each group, an a priori significance level of 0.01, and a dependent variable standard deviation of 1.25 seconds, you have less than a 14 percent chance of declaring a difference of 0.625 seconds or less significant ($d = 0.5 = 0.625/1.25$). Conversely, there's a 86 percent chance that you'll miss the effect that you're looking for. You may want to seriously rethink putting the time and effort into the study as it stands.

The previous examples assumed that there are equal sample sizes in the two groups. If the sample sizes for the two groups are unequal, the function

```
pwr.t2n.test(n1=, n2=, d=, sig.level=, power=, alternative=)
```

can be used. Here, n1 and n2 are the sample sizes and the other parameters are the same as for pwr.t.test. Try varying the values input to the pwr.t2n.test function and see the effect on the output.

10.2.2 ANOVA

The pwr.anova.test() function provides power analysis options for a balanced one-way analysis of variance. The format is

```
pwr.anova.test(k=, n=, f=, sig.level=, power=)
```

where k is the number of groups and n is the common sample size in each group.

For a one-way ANOVA, effect size is measured by f, where

$$f = \sqrt{\frac{\sum_{i-1}^{k} p_i \times (\mu_i - \mu)^2}{\sigma^2}}$$

where $p_i = n_i/N$,

n_i = number of observations in group i

N = total number of observations

μ_i = mean of group i

μ = grand mean

σ^2 = error variance within groups

Let's try an example. For a one-way ANOVA comparing five groups, calculate the sample size needed in each group to obtain a power of 0.80, when the effect size is 0.25 and a significance level of 0.05 is employed. The code looks like this:

```
> pwr.anova.test(k=5, f=.25, sig.level=.05, power=.8)

     Balanced one-way analysis of variance power calculation

              k = 5
              n = 39
              f = 0.25
      sig.level = 0.05
          power = 0.8

NOTE: n is number in each group
```

The total sample size is therefore 5 × 39, or 195. Note that this example requires you to estimate what the means of the five groups will be, along with the common variance. When you have no idea what to expect, the approaches described in section 10.2.7 may help.

10.2.3 Correlations

The `pwr.r.test()` function provides a power analysis for tests of correlation coefficients. The format is as follows:

```
pwr.r.test(n=, r=, sig.level=, power=, alternative=)
```

where n is the number of observations, r is the effect size (as measured by a linear correlation coefficient), `sig.level` is the significance level, `power` is the power level, and `alternative` specifies a two-sided (`"two.sided"`) or a one-sided (`"less"` or `"greater"`) significance test.

For example, let's assume that you're studying the relationship between depression and loneliness. Your null and research hypotheses are

$$H_0: \rho \le 0.25 \text{ versus } H_1: \rho > 0.25$$

where ρ is the population correlation between these two psychological variables. You've set your significance level to 0.05 and you want to be 90 percent confident that you'll reject H_0 if it's false. How many observations will you need? This code provides the answer:

```
> pwr.r.test(r=.25, sig.level=.05, power=.90, alternative="greater")

     approximate correlation power calculation (arctangh transformation)

              n = 134
              r = 0.25
      sig.level = 0.05
          power = 0.9
    alternative = greater
```

Thus, you need to assess depression and loneliness in 134 participants in order to be 90 percent confident that you'll reject the null hypothesis if it's false.

10.2.4 Linear models

For linear models (such as multiple regression), the `pwr.f2.test()` function can be used to carry out a power analysis. The format is

```
pwr.f2.test(u=, v=, f2=, sig.level=, power=)
```

where u and v are the numerator and denominator degrees of freedom and f2 is the effect size.

$$f^2 = \frac{R^2}{1-R^2} \quad \text{where} \quad R^2 = \text{population squared multiple correlation}$$

$$f^2 = \frac{R_{AB}^2 - R_A^2}{1 - R_{AB}^2}$$

where R_A^2 = variance accounted for in the population by variable set A

R_{AB}^2 = variance accounted for in the population by variable set A and B together

The first formula for f2 is appropriate when you're evaluating the impact of a set of predictors on an outcome. The second formula is appropriate when you're evaluating the impact of one set of predictors above and beyond a second set of predictors (or covariates).

Let's say you're interested in whether a boss's leadership style impacts workers' satisfaction above and beyond the salary and perks associated with the job. Leadership style is assessed by four variables, and salary and perks are associated with three variables. Past experience suggests that salary and perks account for roughly 30 percent of the variance in worker satisfaction. From a practical standpoint, it would be interesting if leadership style accounted for at least 5 percent above this figure. Assuming a significance level of 0.05, how many subjects would be needed to identify such a contribution with 90 percent confidence?

Here, sig.level=0.05, power=0.90, u=3 (total number of predictors minus the number of predictors in set B), and the effect size is f2 = (.35-.30)/(1-.35) = 0.0769. Entering this into the function yields the following:

```
> pwr.f2.test(u=3, f2=0.0769, sig.level=0.05, power=0.90)

     Multiple regression power calculation

            u = 3
            v = 184.2426
           f2 = 0.0769
    sig.level = 0.05
        power = 0.9
```

In multiple regression, the denominator degrees of freedom equals N-k-1, where N is the number of observations and k is the number of predictors. In this case, N-7-1=185, which means the required sample size is N = 185 + 7 + 1 = 193.

10.2.5 *Tests of proportions*

The pwr.2p.test() function can be used to perform a power analysis when comparing two proportions. The format is

```
pwr.2p.test(h=, n=, sig.level=, power=)
```

where h is the effect size and n is the common sample size in each group. The effect size h is defined as

$$h = 2 \arcsin\left(\sqrt{p_1}\right) - 2 \arcsin\left(\sqrt{p_2}\right)$$

and can be calculated with the function ES.h(p1, p2).

For unequal ns the desired function is

```
pwr.2p2n.test(h =, n1 =, n2 =, sig.level=, power=).
```

The `alternative=` option can be used to specify a two-tailed (`"two.sided"`) or one-tailed (`"less"` or `"greater"`) test. A two-tailed test is the default.

Let's say that you suspect that a popular medication relieves symptoms in 60 percent of users. A new (and more expensive) medication will be marketed if it improves symptoms in 65 percent of users. How many participants will you need to include in a study comparing these two medications if you want to detect a difference this large?

Assume that you want to be 90 percent confident in a conclusion that the new drug is better and 95 percent confident that you won't reach this conclusion erroneously. You'll use a one-tailed test because you're only interested in assessing whether the new drug is better than the standard. The code looks like this:

```
> pwr.2p.test(h=ES.h(.65, .6), sig.level=.05, power=.9,
            alternative="greater")

    Difference of proportion power calculation for binomial
    distribution (arcsine transformation)

              h = 0.1033347
              n = 1604.007
      sig.level = 0.05
          power = 0.9
    alternative = greater

NOTE: same sample sizes
```

Based on these results, you'll need to conduct a study with 1,605 individuals receiving the new drug and 1,605 receiving the existing drug in order to meet the criteria.

10.2.6 Chi-square tests

Chi-square tests are often used to assess the relationship between two categorical variables. The null hypothesis is typically that the variables are independent versus a research hypothesis that they aren't. The `pwr.chisq.test()` function can be used to evaluate the power, effect size, or requisite sample size when employing a chi-square test. The format is

```
pwr.chisq.test(w =, N = , df = , sig.level =, power = )
```

where w is the effect size, N is the total sample size, and df is the degrees of freedom. Here, effect size w is defined as

$$w = \sqrt{\sum_{i=1}^{m} \frac{(p0_i - p1_i)^2}{p0_i}}$$
where $p0_i$ = cell probability in ith cell under H_0
       $p1_i$ = cell probability in ith cell under H_1

The summation goes from 1 to m, where m is the number of cells in the contingency table. The function `ES.w2(P)` can be used to calculate the effect size corresponding the alternative hypothesis in a two-way contingency table. Here, P is a hypothesized two-way probability table.

As a simple example, let's assume that you're looking the relationship between ethnicity and promotion. You anticipate that 70 percent of your sample will be Caucasian, 10 percent will be African American, and 20 percent will be Hispanic. Further, you believe that 60 percent of Caucasians tend to be promoted, compared with 30 percent for African Americans, and 50 percent for Hispanics. Your research hypothesis is that the probability of promotion follows the values in table 10.2.

Table 10.2   Proportion of individuals expected to be promoted based on the research hypothesis

Ethnicity	Promoted	Not promoted
Caucasian	0.42	0.28
African American	0.03	0.07
Hispanic	0.10	0.10

For example, you expect that 42 percent of the population will be promoted Caucasians (.42 = .70 × .60) and 7 percent of the population will be nonpromoted African Americans (.07 = .10 × .70). Let's assume a significance level of 0.05 and the desired power level is 0.90. The degrees of freedom in a two-way contingency table are (r-1)*(c-1), where r is the number of rows and c is the number of columns. You can calculate the hypothesized effect size with the following code:

```
> prob <- matrix(c(.42, .28, .03, .07, .10, .10), byrow=TRUE, nrow=3)
> ES.w2(prob)

[1] 0.1853198
```

Using this information, you can calculate the necessary sample size like this:

```
> pwr.chisq.test(w=.1853, df=2, sig.level=.05, power=.9)

     Chi squared power calculation

           w = 0.1853
           N = 368.5317
          df = 2
   sig.level = 0.05
       power = 0.9

NOTE: N is the number of observations
```

The results suggest that a study with 369 participants will be adequate to detect a relationship between ethnicity and promotion given the effect size, power, and significance level specified.

10.2.7 *Choosing an appropriate effect size in novel situations*

In power analysis, the expected effect size is the most difficult parameter to determine. It typically requires that you have experience with the subject matter and the measures employed. For example, the data from past studies can be used to calculate effect sizes, which can then be used to plan future studies.

But what can you do when the research situation is completely novel and you have no past experience to call upon? In the area of behavioral sciences, Cohen (1988) attempted to provide benchmarks for "small," "medium," and "large" effect sizes for various statistical tests. These guidelines are provided in table 10.3.

Table 10.3   Cohen's effect size benchmarks

Statistical method	Effect size measures	Suggested guidelines for effect size		
		Small	**Medium**	**Large**
t-test	d	0.20	0.50	0.80
ANOVA	f	0.10	0.25	0.40
Linear models	f2	0.02	0.15	0.35
Test of proportions	h	0.20	0.50	0.80
Chi-square	w	0.10	0.30	0.50

When you have no idea what effect size may be present, this table may provide some guidance. For example, what's the probability of rejecting a false null hypothesis (that is, finding a real effect), if you're using a one-way ANOVA with 5 groups, 25 subjects per group, and a significance level of 0.05?

Using the pwr.anova.test() function and the suggestions in f row of table 10.3, the power would be 0.118 for detecting a small effect, 0.574 for detecting a moderate effect, and 0.957 for detecting a large effect. Given the sample size limitations, you're only likely to find an effect if it's large.

It's important to keep in mind that Cohen's benchmarks are just general suggestions derived from a range of social research studies and may not apply to your particular field of research. An alternative is to vary the study parameters and note the impact on such things as sample size and power. For example, again assume that you want to compare five groups using a one-way ANOVA and a 0.05 significance level. The following listing computes the sample sizes needed to detect a range of effect sizes and plots the results in figure 10.2.

One Way ANOVA with Power=.90 and Alpha=.05

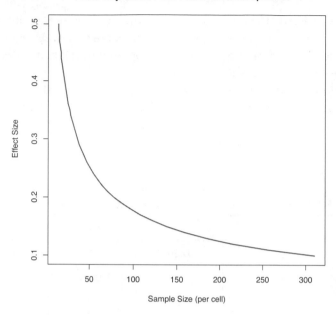

Figure 10.2   Sample size
needed to detect various
effect sizes in a one-way
ANOVA with five groups
(assuming a power of 0.90
and significance level of 0.05)

Listing 10.1   Sample sizes for detecting significant effects in a one-way ANOVA

```
library(pwr)
es <- seq(.1, .5, .01)
nes <- length(es)

samsize <- NULL
for (i in 1:nes){
    result <- pwr.anova.test(k=5, f=es[i], sig.level=.05, power=.9)
    samsize[i] <- ceiling(result$n)
}

plot(samsize,es, type="l", lwd=2, col="red",
     ylab="Effect Size",
     xlab="Sample Size (per cell)",
     main="One Way ANOVA with Power=.90 and Alpha=.05")
```

Graphs such as these can help you estimate the impact of various conditions on your experimental design. For example, there appears to be little bang for the buck increasing the sample size above 200 observations per group. We'll look at another plotting example in the next section.

10.3 *Creating power analysis plots*

Before leaving the `pwr` package, let's look at a more involved graphing example. Suppose you'd like to see the sample size necessary to declare a correlation coefficient statistically significant for a range of effect sizes and power levels. You can use the `pwr.r.test()` function and `for` loops to accomplish this task, as shown in the following listing.

Listing 10.2 Sample size curves for detecting correlations of various sizes

```
library(pwr)
r <- seq(.1,.5,.01)                                ◁──┐   Set range of
nr <- length(r)                                       │   correlations &
                                                    ❶  power values
p <- seq(.4,.9,.1)
np <- length(p)

samsize <- array(numeric(nr*np), dim=c(nr,np))     ◁──❷  Obtain sample sizes
for (i in 1:np){
  for (j in 1:nr){
    result <- pwr.r.test(n = NULL, r = r[j],
    sig.level = .05, power = p[i],
    alternative = "two.sided")
    samsize[j,i] <- ceiling(result$n)
  }
}

xrange <- range(r)                         ◁──❸  Set up graph
yrange <- round(range(samsize))
colors <- rainbow(length(p))
plot(xrange, yrange, type="n",
     xlab="Correlation Coefficient (r)",
     ylab="Sample Size (n)" )

for (i in 1:np){                                ◁──❹  Add power curves
  lines(r, samsize[,i], type="l", lwd=2, col=colors[i])
}

abline(v=0, h=seq(0,yrange[2],50), lty=2, col="grey89") ◁──❺  Add annotations
abline(h=0, v=seq(xrange[1],xrange[2],.02), lty=2,
       col="gray89")
title("Sample Size Estimation for Correlation Studies\n
      Sig=0.05 (Two-tailed)")
legend("topright", title="Power", as.character(p),
       fill=colors)
```

Listing 10.2 uses the seq function to generate a range of effect sizes r (correlation coefficients under H₁) and power levels p ❶. It then uses two for loops to cycle through these effect sizes and power levels, calculating the corresponding sample sizes required and saving them in the array samsize ❷. The graph is set up with the appropriate horizontal and vertical axes and labels ❸. Power curves are added using lines rather than points ❹. Finally, a grid and legend are added to aid in reading the graph ❺. The resulting graph is displayed in figure 10.3.

As you can see from the graph, you'd need a sample size of approximately 75 to detect a correlation of 0.20 with 40 percent confidence. You'd need approximately 185 additional observations (n=260) to detect the same correlation with 90 percent confidence. With simple modifications, the same approach can be used to create sample size and power curve graphs for a wide range of statistical tests.

We'll close this chapter by briefly looking at other R functions that are useful for power analysis.

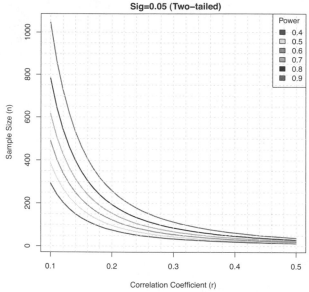

Figure 10.3   Sample size curves for detecting a significant correlation at various power levels

10.4 *Other packages*

There are several other packages in R that can be useful in the planning stages of studies. Some contain general tools, whereas some are highly specialized.

The `piface` package (see figure 10.4) provides a Java GUI for sample-size methods that interfaces with R. The GUI allows the user to vary study parameters interactively and see their impact on other parameters.

Although the package is described as Pre-Alpha, it's definitely worth checking out. You can download the package source and binaries for Windows and Mac OS X from http://r-forge.r-project.org/projects/piface/. In R, enter the code

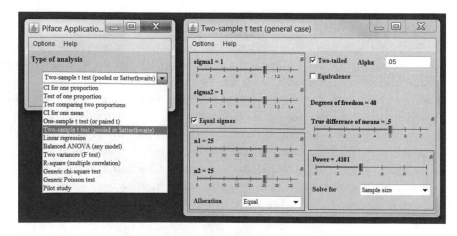

Figure 10.4   Sample dialog boxes from the piface program

```
install.packages("piface", repos="http://R-Forge.R-project.org")
library(piface)
piface()
```

The package is particularly useful for exploring the impact of changes in sample size, effect size, significance levels, and desired power on the other parameters.

Other packages related to power analysis are described in table 10.4. The last five are particularly focused on power analysis in genetic studies. Genome-wide association studies (GWAS) are studies used to identify genetic associations with observable traits. For example, these studies would focus on why some people get a specific type of heart disease.

Table 10.4 Specialized power analysis packages

Package	Purpose
asypow	Power calculations via asymptotic likelihood ratio methods
PwrGSD	Power analysis for group sequential designs
pamm	Power analysis for random effects in mixed models
powerSurvEpi	Power and sample size calculations for survival analysis in epidemiological studies
powerpkg	Power analyses for the affected sib pair and the TDT (transmission disequilibrium test) design
powerGWASinteraction	Power calculations for interactions for GWAS
pedantics	Functions to facilitate power analyses for genetic studies of natural populations
gap	Functions for power and sample size calculations in case-cohort designs
ssize.fdr	Sample size calculations for microarray experiments

Finally, the MBESS package contains a wide range of functions that can be used for various forms of power analysis. The functions are particularly relevant for researchers in the behavioral, educational, and social sciences.

10.5 Summary

In chapters 7, 8, and 9, we explored a wide range of R functions for statistical hypothesis testing. In this chapter, we focused on the planning stages of such research. Power analysis helps you to determine the sample sizes needed to discern an effect of a given size with a given degree of confidence. It can also tell you the probability of detecting such an effect for a given sample size. You can directly see the tradeoff between limiting the likelihood of wrongly declaring an effect significant (a Type I error) with the likelihood of rightly identifying a real effect (power).

The bulk of this chapter has focused on the use of functions provided by the pwr package. These functions can be used to carry out power and sample size determinations for common statistical methods (including t-tests, chi-square tests, and tests of proportions, ANOVA, and regression). Pointers to more specialized methods were provided in the final section.

Power analysis is typically an interactive process. The investigator varies the parameters of sample size, effect size, desired significance level, and desired power to observe their impact on each other. The results are used to plan studies that are more likely to yield meaningful results. Information from past research (particularly regarding effect sizes) can be used to design more effective and efficient future research.

An important side benefit of power analysis is the shift that it encourages, away from a singular focus on binary hypothesis testing (that is, does an effect exists or not), toward an appreciation of the *size* of the effect under consideration. Journal editors are increasingly requiring authors to include effect sizes as well as p values when reporting research results. This helps you to determine both the practical implications of the research and provides you with information that can be used to plan future studies.

In the next chapter, we'll look at additional and novel ways to visualize multivariate relationships. These graphic methods can complement and enhance the analytic methods that we've discussed so far and prepare you for the advanced methods covered in part 3.

Intermediate graphs

In chapter 6 (basic graphs), we considered a wide range of graph types for displaying the distribution of single categorical or continuous variables. Chapter 8 (regression) reviewed graphical methods that are useful when predicting a continuous outcome variable from a set of predictor variables. In chapter 9 (analysis of variance), we considered techniques that are particularly useful for visualizing how groups differ on a continuous outcome variable. In many ways, the current chapter is a continuation and extension of the topics covered so far.

In this chapter, we'll focus on graphical methods for displaying relationships between two variables (bivariate relationships) and between many variables (multivariate relationships). For example:

- What's the relationship between automobile mileage and car weight? Does it vary by the number of cylinders the car has?
- How can you picture the relationships among an automobile's mileage, weight, displacement, and rear axle ratio in a single graph?

- When plotting the relationship between two variables drawn from a large dataset (say 10,000 observations), how can you deal with the massive overlap of data points you're likely to see? In other words, what do you do when your graph is one big smudge?

- How can you visualize the multivariate relationships among three variables at once (given a 2D computer screen or sheet of paper, and a budget slightly less than that for *Avatar*)?

- How can you display the growth of several trees over time?

- How can you visualize the correlations among a dozen variables in a single graph? How does it help you to understand the structure of your data?

- How can you visualize the relationship of class, gender, and age with passenger survival on the *Titanic*? What can you learn from such a graph?

These are the types of questions that can be answered with the methods described in this chapter. The datasets that we'll use are examples of what's possible. It's the general techniques that are most important. If the topic of automobile characteristics or tree growth isn't interesting to you, plug in your own data!

We'll start with scatter plots and scatter plot matrices. Then, we'll explore line charts of various types. These approaches are well known and widely used in research. Next, we'll review the use of correlograms for visualizing correlations and mosaic plots for visualizing multivariate relationships among categorical variables. These approaches are also useful but much less well known among researchers and data analysts. You'll see examples of how you can use each of these approaches to gain a better understanding of your data and communicate these findings to others.

11.1   *Scatter plots*

As you've seen in previous chapters, scatter plots describe the relationship between two continuous variables. In this section, we'll start with a depiction of a single bivariate relationship (x versus y). We'll then explore ways to enhance this plot by superimposing additional information. Next, we'll learn how to combine several scatter plots into a scatter plot matrix so that you can view many bivariate relationships at once. We'll also review the special case where many data points overlap, limiting our ability to picture the data, and we'll discuss a number of ways around this difficulty. Finally, we'll extend the two-dimensional graph to three dimensions, with the addition of a third continuous variable. This will include 3D scatter plots and bubble plots. Each can help you understand the multivariate relationship among three variables at once.

The basic function for creating a scatter plot in R is `plot(x, y)`, where *x* and *y* are numeric vectors denoting the (*x*, *y*) points to plot. Listing 11.1 presents an example.

Listing 11.1 A scatter plot with best fit lines

```
attach(mtcars)
plot(wt, mpg,
     main="Basic Scatter plot of MPG vs. Weight",
     xlab="Car Weight (lbs/1000)",
     ylab="Miles Per Gallon ", pch=19)

abline(lm(mpg~wt), col="red", lwd=2, lty=1)

lines(lowess(wt,mpg), col="blue", lwd=2, lty=2)
```

The resulting graph is provided in figure 11.1.

The code in listing 11.1 attaches the `mtcars` data frame and creates a basic scatter plot using filled circles for the plotting symbol. As expected, as car weight increases, miles per gallon decreases, though the relationship isn't perfectly linear. The `abline()` function is used to add a linear line of best fit, while the `lowess()` function is used to add a smoothed line. This smoothed line is a nonparametric fit line based on locally weighted polynomial regression. See Cleveland (1981) for details on the algorithm.

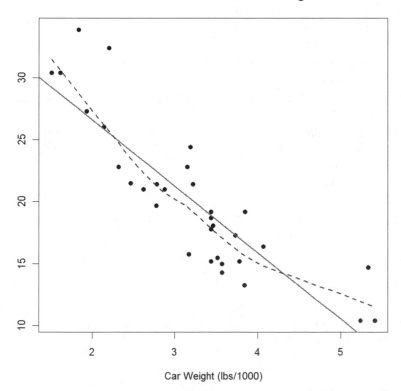

Basic Scatter Plot of MPG vs. Weight

Figure 11.1 Scatter plot of car mileage versus weight, with superimposed linear and lowess fit lines.

NOTE R has two functions for producing lowess fits: `lowess()` and `loess()`. The `loess()` function is a newer, formula-based version of `lowess()` and is more powerful. The two functions have different defaults, so be careful not to confuse them.

The `scatterplot()` function in the `car` package offers many enhanced features and convenience functions for producing scatter plots, including fit lines, marginal box plots, confidence ellipses, plotting by subgroups, and interactive point identification. For example, a more complex version of the previous plot is produced by the following code:

```
library(car)
scatterplot(mpg ~ wt | cyl, data=mtcars, lwd=2,
            main="Scatter Plot of MPG vs. Weight by # Cylinders",
            xlab="Weight of Car (lbs/1000)",
            ylab="Miles Per Gallon",
            legend.plot=TRUE,
            id.method="identify",
            labels=row.names(mtcars),
            boxplots="xy"
)
```

Here, the `scatterplot()` function is used to plot miles per gallon versus weight for automobiles that have four, six, or eight cylinders. The formula `mpg ~ wt | cyl` indicates conditioning (that is, separate plots between `mpg` and `wt` for each level of `cyl`). The graph is provided in figure 11.2.

By default, subgroups are differentiated by color and plotting symbol, and separate linear and loess lines are fit. By default, the loess fit requires five unique data points, so no smoothed fit is plotted for six-cylinder cars. The `id.method` option indicates that points will be identified interactively by mouse clicks, until the user selects Stop (via the Graphics or context-sensitive menu) or the Esc key. The `labels` option indicates that points will be identified with their row names. Here you see that the Toyota Corolla and Fiat 128 have unusually good gas mileage, given their weights. The `legend.plot` option adds a legend to the upper-left margin and marginal box plots

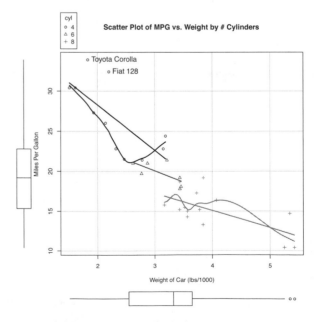

Figure 11.2 Scatter plot with subgroups and separately estimated fit lines

for `mpg` and `weight` are requested with the `boxplots` option. The `scatterplot()` function has many features worth investigating, including robust options and data concentration ellipses not covered here. See `help(scatterplot)` for more details.

Scatter plots help you visualize relationships between quantitative variables, two at a time. But what if you wanted to look at the bivariate relationships between automobile mileage, weight, displacement (cubic inch), and rear axle ratio? One way is to arrange these six scatter plots in a matrix. When there are several quantitative variables, you can represent their relationships in a scatter plot matrix, which is covered next.

11.1.1 Scatter plot matrices

There are at least four useful functions for creating scatter plot matrices in R. Analysts must love scatter plot matrices! A basic scatter plot matrix can be created with the `pairs()` function. The following code produces a scatter plot matrix for the variables `mpg`, `disp`, `drat`, and `wt`:

```
pairs(~mpg+disp+drat+wt, data=mtcars,
     main="Basic Scatter Plot Matrix")
```

All the variables on the right of the ~ are included in the plot. The graph is provided in figure 11.3.

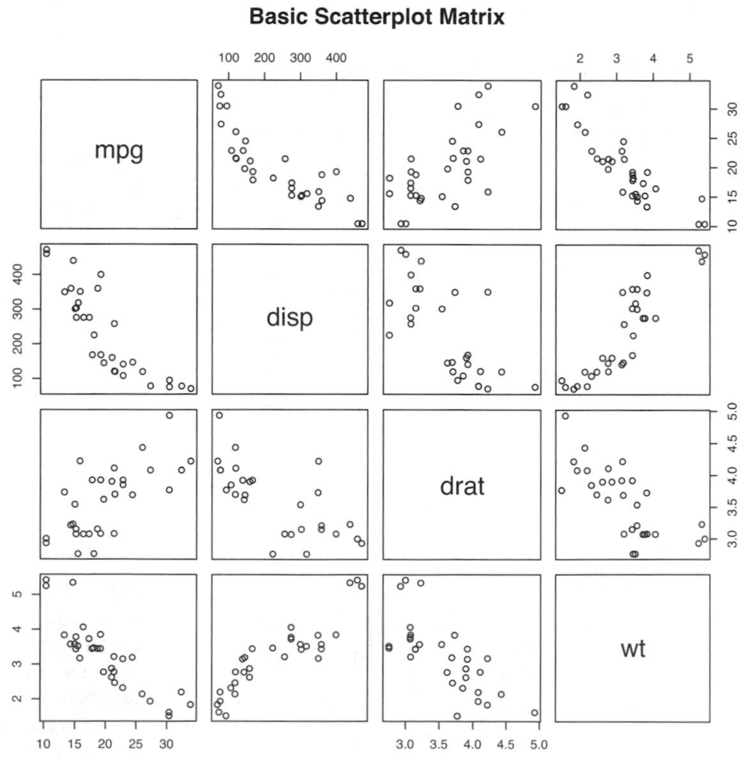

Basic Scatterplot Matrix

Figure 11.3   Scatter plot matrix created by the `pairs()` function

Here you can see the bivariate relationship among all the variables specified. For example, the scatter plot between mpg and disp is found at the row and column intersection of those two variables. Note that the six scatter plots below the principal diagonal are the same as those above the diagonal. This arrangement is a matter of convenience. By adjusting the options, you could display just the lower or upper triangle of plots. For example, the option upper.panel=NULL would produce a graph with just the lower triangle of plots.

The scatterplotMatrix() function in the car package can also produce scatter plot matrices and can optionally do the following:

- Condition the scatter plot matrix on a factor
- Include linear and loess fit lines
- Place box plots, densities, or histograms in the principal diagonal
- Add rug plots in the margins of the cells

Here's an example:

```
library(car)
scatterplotMatrix(~ mpg + disp + drat + wt, data=mtcars, spread=FALSE,
                  lty.smooth=2, main="Scatter Plot Matrix via car Package")
```

The graph is provided in figure 11.4. Here you can see that linear and smoothed (loess) fit lines are added by default and that kernel density and rug plots are

Scatterplot Matrix via car package

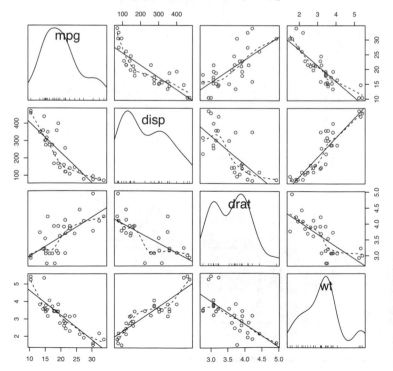

Figure 11.4
Scatter plot matrix created with the scatterplotMatrix() function. The graph includes kernel density and rug plots in the principal diagonal and linear and loess fit lines.

added to the principal diagonal. The `spread=FALSE` option suppresses lines showing spread and asymmetry, and the `lty.smooth=2` option displays the loess fit lines using dashed rather than solid lines.

As a second example of the `scatterplotMatrix()` function, consider the following code:

```
library(car)
scatterplotMatrix(~ mpg + disp + drat + wt | cyl, data=mtcars,
                  spread=FALSE, diagonal="histogram",
                  main="Scatter Plot Matrix via car Package")
```

Here, you change the kernel density plots to histograms and condition the results on the number of cylinders for each car. The results are displayed in figure 11.5.

By default, the regression lines are fit for the entire sample. Including the option `by.groups = TRUE` would have produced separate fit lines by subgroup.

An interesting variation on the scatter plot matrix is provided by the `cpairs()` function in the `gclus` package. The `cpairs()` function provides options to rearrange

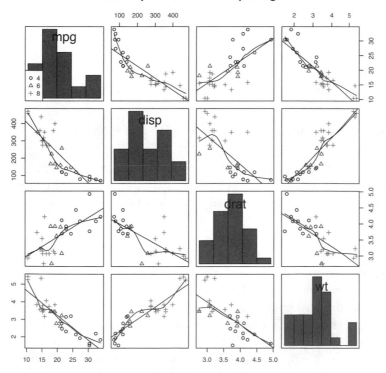

Figure 11.5 Scatter plot matrix produced by the `scatterplot.Matrix()` function. The graph includes histograms in the principal diagonal and linear and loess fit lines. Additionally, subgroups (defined by number of cylinders) are indicated by symbol type and color.

variables in the matrix so that variable pairs with higher correlations are closer to the principal diagonal. The function can also color-code the cells to reflect the size of these correlations. Consider the correlations among mpg, wt, disp, and drat:

```
> cor(mtcars[c("mpg", "wt", "disp", "drat")])
```

```
        mpg     wt   disp   drat
mpg    1.000 -0.868 -0.848  0.681
wt    -0.868  1.000  0.888 -0.712
disp  -0.848  0.888  1.000 -0.710
drat   0.681 -0.712 -0.710  1.000
```

You can see that the highest correlations are between weight and displacement (0.89) and between weight and miles per gallon (–0.87). The lowest correlation is between miles per gallon and rear axle ratio (0.68). You can reorder and color the scatter plot matrix among these variables using the code in the following listing.

Listing 11.2 Scatter plot matrix produced with the gclus package

```
library(gclus)
mydata <- mtcars[c(1, 3, 5, 6)]
mydata.corr <- abs(cor(mydata))

mycolors <- dmat.color(mydata.corr)

myorder <- order.single(mydata.corr)

cpairs(mydata,
       myorder,
       panel.colors=mycolors,
       gap=.5,
       main="Variables Ordered and Colored by Correlation"
)
```

The code in listing 11.2 uses the dmat.color(), order.single(), and cpairs() functions from the gclus package. First, you select the desired variables from the mtcars data frame and calculate the absolute values of the correlations among them. Next, you obtain the colors to plot using the dmat.color() function. Given a symmetric matrix (a correlation matrix in this case), dmat.color() returns a matrix of colors. You also sort the variables for plotting. The order.single() function sorts objects so that similar object pairs are adjacent. In this case, the variable ordering is based on the similarity of the correlations. Finally, the scatter plot matrix is plotted and colored using the new ordering (myorder) and the color list (mycolors). The gap option adds a small space between cells of the matrix. The resulting graph is provided in figure 11.6.

You can see from the figure that the highest correlations are between weight and displacement and weight and miles per gallon (red and closest to the principal diagonal). The lowest correlation is between rear axle ratio and miles per gallon

Variables Ordered and Colored by Correlation

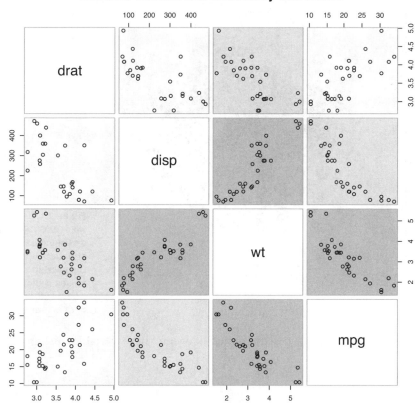

Figure 11.6 Scatter plot matrix produced with the `cpairs()` function in the `gclus` package. Variables closer to the principal diagonal are more highly correlated.

(yellow and far from the principal diagonal). This method is particularly useful when many variables, with widely varying inter-correlations, are considered. You'll see other examples of scatter plot matrices in chapter 16.

11.1.2 High-density scatter plots

When there's a significant overlap among data points, scatter plots become less useful for observing relationships. Consider the following contrived example with 10,000 observations falling into two overlapping clusters of data:

```
set.seed(1234)

n <- 10000
c1 <- matrix(rnorm(n, mean=0, sd=.5), ncol=2)
c2 <- matrix(rnorm(n, mean=3, sd=2), ncol=2)
mydata <- rbind(c1, c2)
mydata <- as.data.frame(mydata)
names(mydata) <- c("x", "y")
```

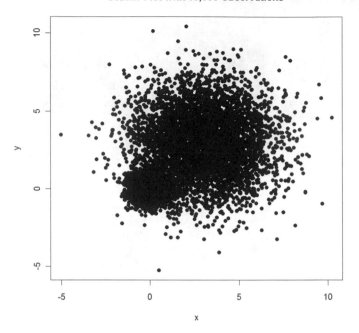

Figure 11.7   Scatter plot with 10,000 observations and significant overlap of data points. Note that the overlap of data points makes it difficult to discern where the concentration of data is greatest.

If you generate a standard scatter plot between these variables using the following code

```
with(mydata,
     plot(x, y, pch=19, main="Scatter Plot with 10,000 Observations"))
```

you'll obtain a graph like the one in figure 11.7.

The overlap of data points in figure 11.7 makes it difficult to discern the relationship between x and y. R provides several graphical approaches that can be used when this occurs. They include the use of binning, color, and transparency to indicate the number of overprinted data points at any point on the graph.

The smoothScatter() function uses a kernel density estimate to produce smoothed color density representations of the scatterplot. The following code

```
with(mydata,
     smoothScatter(x, y, main="Scatterplot Colored by Smoothed Densities"))
```

produces the graph in figure 11.8.

Using a different approach, the hexbin() function in the hexbin package provides bivariate binning into hexagonal cells (it looks better than it sounds). Applying this function to the dataset

```
library(hexbin)
with(mydata, {
    bin <- hexbin(x, y, xbins=50)
    plot(bin, main="Hexagonal Binning with 10,000 Observations")
    })
```

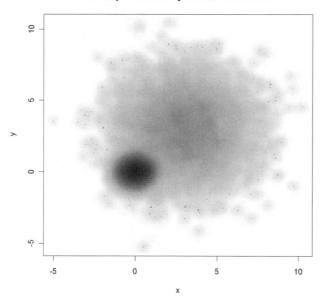

Figure 11.8 Scatterplot using `smoothScatter()` to plot smoothed density estimates. Densities are easy to read from the graph.

you get the scatter plot in figure 11.9.

Finally, the `iplot()` function in the `IDPmisc` package can be used to display density (the number of data points at a specific spot) using color. The code

```
library(IDPmisc)
with(mydata,
    iplot(x, y, main="Image Scatter Plot with Color Indicating Density"))
```

produces the graph in figure 11.10.

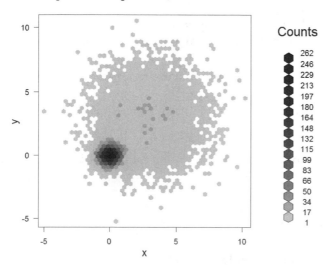

Figure 11.9 Scatter plot using hexagonal binning to display the number of observations at each point. Data concentrations are easy to see and counts can be read from the legend.

Image Scatter Plot with Color Indicating Density

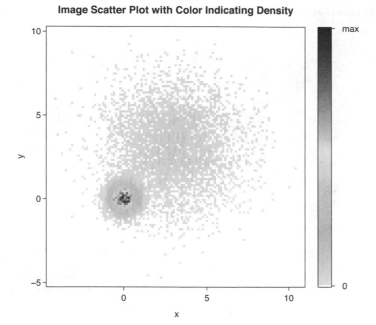

Figure 11.10   **Scatter plot of 10,000 observations, where density is indicated by color. The data concentrations are easily discernable.**

It's useful to note that the smoothScatter() function in the base package, along with the ipairs() function in the IDPmisc package, can be used to create readable scatter plot matrices for large datasets as well. See ?smoothScatter and ?ipairs for examples.

11.1.3 *3D scatter plots*

Scatter plots and scatter plot matrices display bivariate relationships. What if you want to visualize the interaction of three quantitative variables at once? In this case, you can use a 3D scatter plot.

For example, say that you're interested in the relationship between automobile mileage, weight, and displacement. You can use the scatterplot3d() function in the scatterplot3d package to picture their relationship. The format is

```
scatterplot3d(x, y, z)
```

where x is plotted on the horizontal axis, y is plotted on the vertical axis, and z is plotted in perspective. Continuing our example

```
library(scatterplot3d)
attach(mtcars)
scatterplot3d(wt, disp, mpg,
    main="Basic 3D Scatter Plot")
```

produces the 3D scatter plot in figure 11.11.

Basic 3D Scatterplot

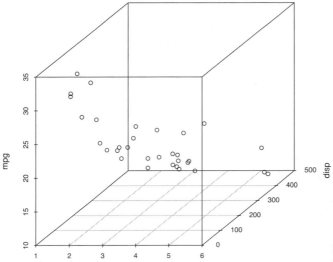

Figure 11.11   3D scatter plot of miles per gallon, auto weight, and displacement

The `scatterplot3d()` function offers many options, including the ability to specify symbols, axes, colors, lines, grids, highlighting, and angles. For example, the code

```
library(scatterplot3d)
attach(mtcars)
scatterplot3d(wt, disp, mpg,
            pch=16,
            highlight.3d=TRUE,
            type="h",
            main="3D Scatter Plot with Vertical Lines")
```

produces a 3D scatter plot with highlighting to enhance the impression of depth, and vertical lines connecting points to the horizontal plane (see figure 11.12).

As a final example, let's take the previous graph and add a regression plane. The necessary code is:

```
library(scatterplot3d)
attach(mtcars)
s3d <-scatterplot3d(wt, disp, mpg,
        pch=16,
        highlight.3d=TRUE,
        type="h",
        main="3D Scatter Plot with Vertical Lines and Regression Plane")
fit <- lm(mpg ~ wt+disp)
s3d$plane3d(fit)
```

The resulting graph is provided in figure 11.13.

3D Scatterplot with Vertical Lines

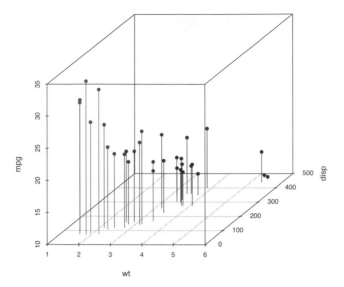

Figure 11.12   3D scatter plot with vertical lines and shading

The graph allows you to visualize the prediction of miles per gallon from automobile weight and displacement using a multiple regression equation. The plane represents the predicted values, and the points are the actual values. The vertical distances from the plane to the points are the residuals. Points that lie above the plane are under-predicted, while points that lie below the line are over-predicted. Multiple regression is covered in chapter 8.

3D Scatter Plot with Verical Lines and Regression Plane

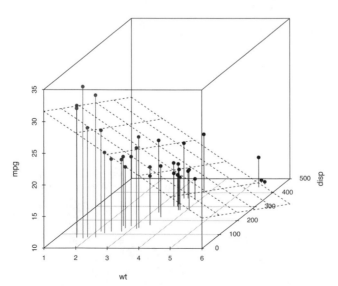

Figure 11.13   3D scatter plot with vertical lines, shading, and overlaid regression plane

SPINNING 3D SCATTER PLOTS

Three-dimensional scatter plots are much easier to interpret if you can interact with them. R provides several mechanisms for rotating graphs so that you can see the plotted points from more than one angle.

For example, you can create an interactive 3D scatter plot using the `plot3d()` function in the `rgl` package. It creates a spinning 3D scatter plot that can be rotated with the mouse. The format is

```
plot3d(x, y, z)
```

where *x*, *y*, and *z* are numeric vectors representing points. You can also add options like `col` and `size` to control the color and size of the points, respectively. Continuing our example, try the code

```
library(rgl)
attach(mtcars)
plot3d(wt, disp, mpg, col="red", size=5)
```

You should get a graph like the one depicted in figure 11.14. Use the mouse to rotate the axes. I think that you'll find that being able to rotate the scatter plot in three dimensions makes the graph much easier to understand.

You can perform a similar function with the `scatter3d()` in the `Rcmdr` package:

```
library(Rcmdr)
attach(mtcars)
scatter3d(wt, disp, mpg)
```

The results are displayed in figure 11.15.

The `scatter3d()` function can include a variety of regression surfaces, such as linear, quadratic, smooth, and additive. The linear surface depicted is the default. Additionally, there are options for interactively identifying points. See `help(scatter3d)` for more details. I'll have more to say about the `Rcmdr` package in appendix A.

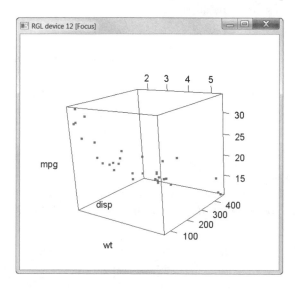

Figure 11.14 Rotating 3D scatter plot produced by the `plot3d()` function in the `rgl` package

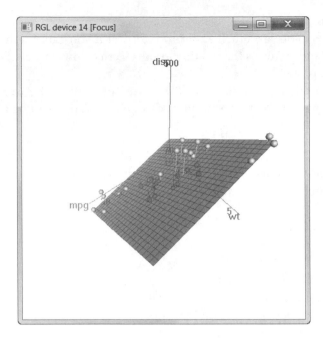

Figure 11.15 Spinning 3D scatter plot produced by the `scatter3d()` function in the `Rcmdr` package

11.1.4 *Bubble plots*

In the previous section, you displayed the relationship between three quantitative variables using a 3D scatter plot. Another approach is to create a 2D scatter plot and use the size of the plotted point to represent the value of the third variable. This approach is referred to as a *bubble plot*.

You can create a bubble plot using the `symbols()` function. This function can be used to draw circles, squares, stars, thermometers, and box plots at a specified set of (*x*, *y*) coordinates. For plotting circles, the format is

```
symbols(x, y, circle=radius)
```

where *x* and *y* and *radius* are vectors specifying the x and y coordinates and circle radiuses, respectively.

You want the areas, rather than the radiuses of the circles, to be proportional to the values of a third variable. Given the formula for the radius of a circle $(r = \sqrt{\frac{A}{\pi}})$ the proper call is

```
symbols(x, y, circle=sqrt(z/pi))
```

where *z* is the third variable to be plotted.

Let's apply this to the `mtcars` data, plotting car weight on the x-axis, miles per gallon on the y-axis, and engine displacement as the bubble size. The following code

```
attach(mtcars)
r <- sqrt(disp/pi)
symbols(wt, mpg, circle=r, inches=0.30,
        fg="white", bg="lightblue",
```

```
     main="Bubble Plot with point size proportional to displacement",
     ylab="Miles Per Gallon",
     xlab="Weight of Car (lbs/1000)")
text(wt, mpg, rownames(mtcars), cex=0.6)
detach(mtcars)
```

produces the graph in figure 11.16. The option `inches` is a scaling factor that can be used to control the size of the circles (the default is to make the largest circle 1 inch). The `text()` function is optional. Here it is used to add the names of the cars to the plot. From the figure, you can see that increased gas mileage is associated with both decreased car weight and engine displacement.

In general, statisticians involved in the R project tend to avoid bubble plots for the same reason they avoid pie charts. Humans typically have a harder time making judgments about volume than distance. But bubble charts are certainly popular in the business world, so I'm including them here for completeness.

I've certainly had a lot to say about scatter plots. This attention to detail is due, in part, to the central place that scatter plots hold in data analysis. While simple, they can help you visualize your data in an immediate and straightforward manner, uncovering relationships that might otherwise be missed.

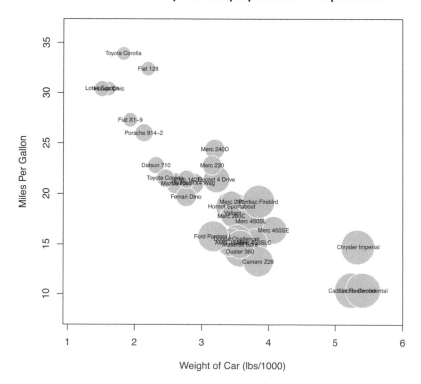

Bubble Plot with point size proportional to displacement

Figure 11.16   Bubble plot of car weight versus `mpg` where point size is proportional to engine displacement

11.2　Line charts

If you connect the points in a scatter plot moving from left to right, you have a line plot. The dataset `Orange` that come with the base installation contains age and circumference data for five orange trees. Consider the growth of the first orange tree, depicted in figure 11.17. The plot on the left is a scatter plot, and the plot on the right is a line chart. As you can see, line charts are particularly good vehicles for conveying change.

The graphs in figure 11.17 were created with the code in the following listing.

Listing 11.3　Creating side-by-side scatter and line plots

```
opar <- par(no.readonly=TRUE)
par(mfrow=c(1,2))
t1 <- subset(Orange, Tree==1)
plot(t1$age, t1$circumference,
     xlab="Age (days)",
     ylab="Circumference (mm)",
     main="Orange Tree 1 Growth")
plot(t1$age, t1$circumference,
     xlab="Age (days)",
     ylab="Circumference (mm)",
     main="Orange Tree 1 Growth",
     type="b")
par(opar)
```

You've seen the elements that make up this code in chapter 3, so I won't go into details here. The main difference between the two plots in figure 11.17 is produced by the option `type="b"`. In general, line charts are created with one of the following two functions

```
plot(x, y, type=)
lines(x, y, type=)
```

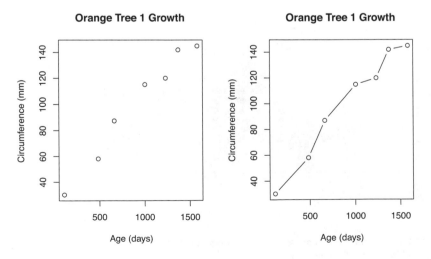

Figure 11.17　Comparison of a scatter plot and a line plot

where *x* and *y* are numeric vectors of (*x,y*) points to connect. The option `type=` can take the values described in table 11.1.

Table 11.1   Line chart options

Type	What is plotted
p	Points only
l	Lines only
o	Over-plotted points (that is, lines overlaid on top of points)
b, c	Points (empty if c) joined by lines
s, S	Stair steps
h	Histogram-line vertical lines
n	Doesn't produce any points or lines (used to set up the axes for later commands)

Examples of each type are given in figure 11.18. As you can see, `type="p"` produces the typical scatter plot. The option `type="b"` is the most common for line charts. The difference between b and c is whether the points appear or gaps are left instead. Both `type="s"` and `type="S"` produce stair steps (step functions). The first runs, then rises, whereas the second rises, then runs.

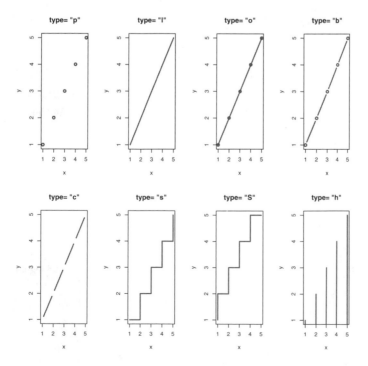

Figure 11.18   `type=` options in the `plot()` and `lines()` functions

There's an important difference between the plot() and lines() functions. The plot() function will create a new graph when invoked. The lines() function *adds* information to an existing graph but *can't* produce a graph on its own.

Because of this, the lines() function is typically used after a plot() command has produced a graph. If desired, you can use the type="n" option in the plot() function to set up the axes, titles, and other graph features, and then use the lines() function to add various lines to the plot.

To demonstrate the creation of a more complex line chart, let's plot the growth of all five orange trees over time. Each tree will have its own distinctive line. The code is shown in the next listing and the results in figure 11.19.

Listing 11.4   Line chart displaying the growth of five orange trees over time

```
Orange$Tree <- as.numeric(Orange$Tree)        Convert factor
ntrees <- max(Orange$Tree)                     to numeric for
                                               convenience
xrange <- range(Orange$age)
yrange <- range(Orange$circumference)

plot(xrange, yrange,
     type="n",
     xlab="Age (days)",                        Set up plot
     ylab="Circumference (mm)"
  )

colors <- rainbow(ntrees)
linetype <- c(1:ntrees)
plotchar <- seq(18, 18+ntrees, 1)

for (i in 1:ntrees) {
    tree <- subset(Orange, Tree==i)
    lines(tree$age, tree$circumference,
          type="b",
          lwd=2,
          lty=linetype[i],                     Add lines
          col=colors[i],
          pch=plotchar[i]
      )
}

title("Tree Growth", "example of line plot")

legend(xrange[1], yrange[2],
       1:ntrees,
       cex=0.8,
       col=colors,
       pch=plotchar,                           Add legend
       lty=linetype,
       title="Tree"
  )
```

Tree Growth

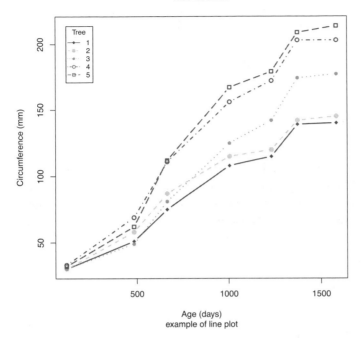

Figure 11.19 Line chart displaying the growth of five orange trees

In listing 11.4, the `plot()` function is used to set up the graph and specify the axis labels and ranges but plots no actual data. The `lines()` function is then used to add a separate line and set of points for each orange tree. You can see that tree 4 and tree 5 demonstrated the greatest growth across the range of days measured, and that tree 5 overtakes tree 4 at around 664 days.

Many of the programming conventions in R that I discussed in chapters 2, 3, and 4 are used in listing 11.4. You may want to test your understanding by working through each line of code and visualizing what it's doing. If you can, you are on your way to becoming a serious R programmer (and fame and fortune is near at hand)! In the next section, you'll explore ways of examining a number of correlation coefficients at once.

11.3 Correlograms

Correlation matrices are a fundamental aspect of multivariate statistics. Which variables under consideration are strongly related to each other and which aren't? Are there clusters of variables that relate in specific ways? As the number of variables grow, such questions can be harder to answer. Correlograms are a relatively recent tool for visualizing the data in correlation matrices.

It's easier to explain a correlogram once you've seen one. Consider the correlations among the variables in the `mtcars` data frame. Here you have 11 variables, each measuring some aspect of 32 automobiles. You can get the correlations using the following code:

```
> options(digits=2)
> cor(mtcars)
```

	mpg	cyl	disp	hp	drat	wt	qsec	vs	am	gear	carb
mpg	1.00	-0.85	-0.85	-0.78	0.681	-0.87	0.419	0.66	0.600	0.48	-0.551
cyl	-0.85	1.00	0.90	0.83	-0.700	0.78	-0.591	-0.81	-0.523	-0.49	0.527
disp	-0.85	0.90	1.00	0.79	-0.710	0.89	-0.434	-0.71	-0.591	-0.56	0.395
hp	-0.78	0.83	0.79	1.00	-0.449	0.66	-0.708	-0.72	-0.243	-0.13	0.750
drat	0.68	-0.70	-0.71	-0.45	1.000	-0.71	0.091	0.44	0.713	0.70	-0.091
wt	-0.87	0.78	0.89	0.66	-0.712	1.00	-0.175	-0.55	-0.692	-0.58	0.428
qsec	0.42	-0.59	-0.43	-0.71	0.091	-0.17	1.000	0.74	-0.230	-0.21	-0.656
vs	0.66	-0.81	-0.71	-0.72	0.440	-0.55	0.745	1.00	0.168	0.21	-0.570
am	0.60	-0.52	-0.59	-0.24	0.713	-0.69	-0.230	0.17	1.000	0.79	0.058
gear	0.48	-0.49	-0.56	-0.13	0.700	-0.58	-0.213	0.21	0.794	1.00	0.274
carb	-0.55	0.53	0.39	0.75	-0.091	0.43	-0.656	-0.57	0.058	0.27	1.000

Which variables are most related? Which variables are relatively independent? Are there any patterns? It isn't that easy to tell from the correlation matrix without significant time and effort (and probably a set of colored pens to make notations).

You can display that same correlation matrix using the `corrgram()` function in the `corrgram` package (see figure 11.20). The code is:

```
library(corrgram)
corrgram(mtcars, order=TRUE, lower.panel=panel.shade,
         upper.panel=panel.pie, text.panel=panel.txt,
         main="Correlogram of mtcars intercorrelations")
```

To interpret this graph, start with the lower triangle of cells (the cells below the principal diagonal). By default, a blue color and hashing that goes from lower left to upper right represents a positive correlation between the two variables that meet at that cell. Conversely, a red color and hashing that goes from the upper left to the lower right represents a negative correlation. The darker and more saturated the color, the greater the magnitude of the correlation. Weak correlations, near zero, will appear washed out. In the current graph, the rows and columns have been reordered (using principal components analysis) to cluster variables together that have similar correlation patterns.

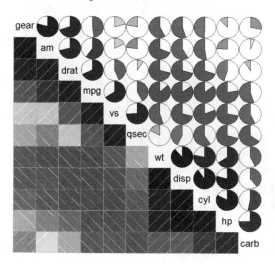

Correlogram of mtcars intercorrelations

Figure 11.20   Correlogram of the correlations among the variables in the `mtcars` data frame. Rows and columns have been reordered using principal components analysis.

You can see from shaded cells that gear, am, drat, and mpg are positively correlated with one another. You can also see that wt, disp, cyl, hp, and carb are positively correlated with one another. But the first group of variables is negatively correlated with the second group of variables. You can also see that the correlation between carb and am is weak, as is the correlation between vs and gear, vs and am, and drat and qsec.

The upper triangle of cells displays the same information using pies. Here, color plays the same role, but the strength of the correlation is displayed by the size of the filled pie slice. Positive correlations fill the pie starting at 12 o'clock and moving in a clockwise direction. Negative correlations fill the pie by moving in a counterclockwise direction. The format of the corrgram() function is

```
corrgram(x, order=, panel=, text.panel=, diag.panel=)
```

where *x* is a data frame with one observation per row. When order=TRUE, the variables are reordered using a principal component analysis of the correlation matrix. Reordering can help make patterns of bivariate relationships more obvious.

The option panel specifies the type of off-diagonal panels to use. Alternatively, you can use the options lower.panel and upper.panel to choose different options below and above the main diagonal. The text.panel and diag.panel options refer to the main diagonal. Allowable values for panel are described in table 11.2.

Table 11.2 Panel options for the corrgram() function

Placement	Panel Option	Description
Off diagonal	panel.pie	The filled portion of the pie indicates the magnitude of the correlation.
	panel.shade	The depth of the shading indicates the magnitude of the correlation.
	panel.ellipse	A confidence ellipse and smoothed line are plotted.
	panel.pts	A scatter plot is plotted.
Main diagonal	panel.minmax	The minimum and maximum values of the variable are printed.
	panel.txt	The variable name is printed.

Let's try a second example. The code

```
library(corrgram)
corrgram(mtcars, order=TRUE, lower.panel=panel.ellipse,
        upper.panel=panel.pts, text.panel=panel.txt,
        diag.panel=panel.minmax,
        main="Correlogram of mtcars data using scatter plots and ellipses")
```

produces the graph in figure 11.21. Here you're using smoothed fit lines and confidence ellipses in the lower triangle and scatter plots in the upper triangle.

Correlogram of mtcars data using scatter plots and ellipses

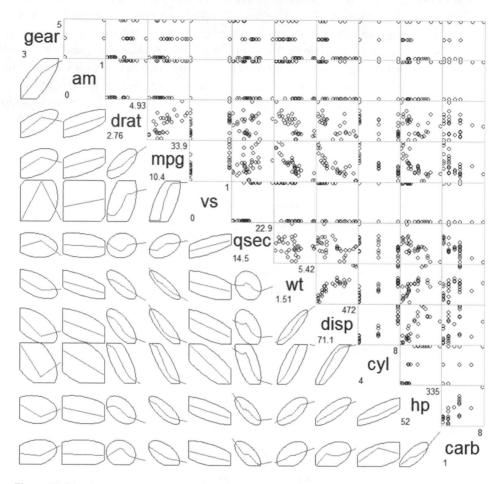

Figure 11.21 Correlogram of the correlations among the variables in the mtcars data frame. The lower triangle contains smoothed best fit lines and confidence ellipses, and the upper triangle contains scatter plots. The diagonal panel contains minimum and maximum values. Rows and columns have been reordered using principal components analysis.

Why do the scatter plots look odd?

Several of the variables that are plotted in figure 11.21 have limited allowable values. For example, the number of gears is 3, 4, or 5. The number of cylinders is 4, 6, or 8. Both am (transmission type) and vs (V/S) are dichotomous. This explains the odd-looking scatter plots in the upper diagonal.

Always be careful that the statistical methods you choose are appropriate to the form of the data. Specifying these variables as ordered or unordered factors can serve as a useful check. When R knows that a variable is categorical or ordinal, it attempts to apply statistical methods that are appropriate to that level of measurement.

We'll finish with one more example. The code

```
library(corrgram)
corrgram(mtcars, lower.panel=panel.shade,
        upper.panel=NULL, text.panel=panel.txt,
        main="Car Mileage Data (unsorted)")
```

produces the graph in figure 11.22. Here we're using shading in the lower triangle, keeping the original variable order, and leaving the upper triangle blank.

Before moving on, I should point out that you can control the colors used by the `corrgram()` function. To do so, specify four colors in the `colorRampPalette()` function within the `col.corrgram()` function. Here's an example:

```
library(corrgram)
col.corrgram <- function(ncol){
            colorRampPalette(c("darkgoldenrod4", "burlywood1",
                            "darkkhaki", "darkgreen"))(ncol)}
corrgram(mtcars, order=TRUE, lower.panel=panel.shade,
        upper.panel=panel.pie, text.panel=panel.txt,
        main="A Corrgram (or Horse) of a Different Color")
```

Try it and see what you get.

Correlograms can be a useful way to examine large numbers of bivariate relationships among quantitative variables. Because they're relatively new, the greatest challenge is to educate the recipient on how to interpret them.

To learn more, see Michael Friendly's article "*Corrgrams: Exploratory Displays for Correlation Matrices,*" available at http://www.math.yorku.ca/SCS/Papers/corrgram.pdf.

Car Mileage Data (unsorted)

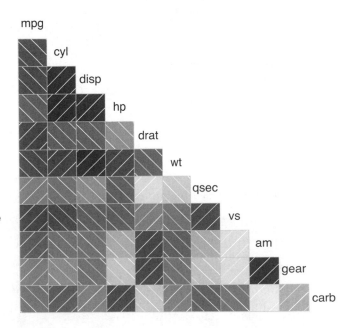

Figure 11.22 Correlogram of the correlations among the variables in the `mtcars` data frame. The lower triangle is shaded to represent the magnitude and direction of the correlations. The variables are plotted in their original order.

11.4 Mosaic plots

Up to this point, we've been exploring methods of visualizing relationships among quantitative/continuous variables. But what if your variables are categorical? When you're looking at a single categorical variable, you can use a bar or pie chart. If there are two categorical variables, you can look at a 3D bar chart (which, by the way, is not so easy to do in R). But what do you do if there are more than two categorical variables?

One approach is to use mosaic plots. In a mosaic plot, the frequencies in a multidimensional contingency table are represented by nested rectangular regions that are proportional to their cell frequency. Color and or shading can be used to represent residuals from a fitted model. For details, see Meyer, Zeileis and Hornick (2006), or Michael Friendly's Statistical Graphics page (http://datavis.ca). Steve Simon has created a good conceptual tutorial on how mosaic plots are created, available at http://www.childrensmercy.org/stats/definitions/mosaic.htm.

Mosaic plots can be created with the `mosaic()` function from the `vcd` library (there's a `mosaicplot()` function in the basic installation of R, but I recommend you use the `vcd` package for its more extensive features). As an example, consider the Titanic dataset available in the base installation. It describes the number of passengers who survived or died, cross-classified by their class (1st, 2nd, 3rd, Crew), sex (Male, Female), and age (Child, Adult). This is a well-studied dataset. You can see the cross-classification using the following code:

```
> ftable(Titanic)
                    Survived  No Yes
Class Sex    Age
1st   Male   Child            0   5
             Adult          118  57
      Female Child            0   1
             Adult            4 140
2nd   Male   Child            0  11
             Adult          154  14
      Female Child            0  13
             Adult           13  80
3rd   Male   Child           35  13
             Adult          387  75
      Female Child           17  14
             Adult           89  76
Crew  Male   Child            0   0
             Adult          670 192
      Female Child            0   0
             Adult            3  20
```

The `mosaic()` function can be invoked as

```
mosaic(table)
```

where *table* is a contingency table in array form, or

```
mosaic(formula, data=)
```

where *formula* is a standard R formula, and data specifies either a data frame or table. Adding the option `shade=TRUE` will color the figure based on Pearson residuals from a fitted model (independence by default) and the option `legend=TRUE` will display a legend for these residuals.

For example, both

```
library(vcd)
mosaic(Titanic, shade=TRUE, legend=TRUE)
```

and

```
library(vcd)
mosaic(~Class+Sex+Age+Survived, data=Titanic, shade=TRUE, legend=TRUE)
```

will produce the graph shown in figure 11.23. The formula version gives you greater control over the selection and placement of variables in the graph.

There's a great deal of information packed into this one picture. For example, as one moves from crew to first class, the survival rate increases precipitously. Most children were in third and second class. Most females in first class survived, whereas only about half the females in third class survived. There were few females in the crew, causing the Survived labels (No, Yes at the bottom of the chart) to overlap for this group. Keep looking and you'll see many more interesting facts. Remember to look at the relative widths and heights of the rectangles. What else can you learn about that night?

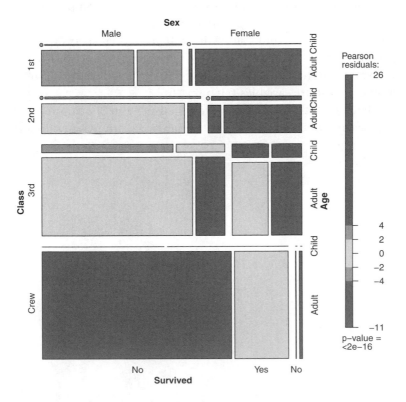

Figure 11.23   Mosaic plot describing Titanic survivors by class, sex, and age

Extended mosaic plots add color and shading to represent the residuals from a fitted model. In this example, the blue shading indicates cross-classifications that occur more often than expected, assuming that survival is unrelated to class, gender, and age. Red shading indicates cross-classifications that occur less often than expected under the independence model. Be sure to run the example so that you can see the results in color. The graph indicates that more first-class women survived and more male crew members died than would be expected under an independence model. Fewer third-class men survived than would be expected if survival was independent of class, gender, and age. If you would like to explore mosaic plots in greater detail, try running `example(mosaic)`.

11.5 *Summary*

In this chapter, we considered a wide range of techniques for displaying relationships among two or more variables. This included the use of 2D and 3D scatter plots, scatter plot matrices, bubble plots, line plots, correlograms, and mosaic plots. Some of these methods are standard techniques, while some are relatively new.

Taken together with methods that allow you to customize graphs (chapter 3), display univariate distributions (chapter 6), explore regression models (chapter 8), and visualize group differences (chapter 9), you now have a comprehensive toolbox for visualizing and extracting meaning from your data.

In later chapters, you'll expand your skills with additional specialized techniques, including graphics for latent variable models (chapter 14), methods for visualizing missing data patterns (chapter 15), and techniques for creating graphs that are conditioned on one or more variables (chapter 16).

In the next chapter, we'll explore resampling statistics and bootstrapping. These are computer intensive methods that allow you to analyze data in new and unique ways.

12
Resampling statistics and bootstrapping

This chapter covers

- Understanding the logic of permutation tests
- Applying permutation tests to linear models
- Using bootstrapping to obtain confidence intervals

In chapters 7, 8, and 9, we reviewed statistical methods that test hypotheses and estimate confidence intervals for population parameters by assuming that the observed data is sampled from a normal distribution or some other well-known theoretical distribution. But there will be many cases in which this assumption is unwarranted. Statistical approaches based on randomization and resampling can be used in cases where the data is sampled from unknown or mixed distributions, where sample sizes are small, where outliers are a problem, or where devising an appropriate test based on a theoretical distribution is too complex and mathematically intractable.

In this chapter, we'll explore two broad statistical approaches that use randomization: permutation tests and bootstrapping. Historically, these methods were only available to experienced programmers and expert statisticians. Contributed packages in R now make them readily available to a wider audience of data analysts.

We'll also revisit problems that were initially analyzed using traditional methods (for example, t-tests, chi-square tests, ANOVA, regression) and see how they can be approached using these robust, computer-intensive methods. To get the most out of section 12.2, be sure to read chapter 7 first. Chapters 8 and 9 serve as prerequisites for section 12.3. Other sections can be read on their own.

12.1 *Permutation tests*

Permutation tests, also called randomization or re-randomization tests, have been around for decades, but it took the advent of high-speed computers to make them practically available.

To understand the logic of a permutation test, consider the following hypothetical problem. Ten subjects have been randomly assigned to one of two treatment conditions (A or B) and an outcome variable (`score`) has been recorded. The results of the experiment are presented in table 12.1.

The data are also displayed in the strip chart in figure 12.1. Is there enough evidence to conclude that the treatments differ in their impact?

Table 12.1   Hypothetical two-group problem

Treatment A	Treatment B
40	57
57	64
45	55
55	62
58	65

In a parametric approach, you might assume that the data are sampled from normal populations with equal variances and apply a two-tailed independent groups t-test. The null hypothesis is that the population mean for treatment A is equal to the population mean for treatment B. You'd calculate a t-statistic from the data and compare it to the theoretical distribution. If the observed t-statistic is sufficiently extreme, say outside the middle 95 percent of values in the theoretical distribution, you'd reject the null hypothesis and declare that the population means for the two groups are unequal at the 0.05 level of significance.

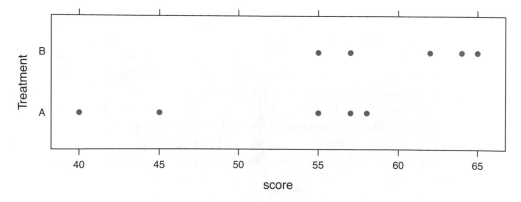

Figure 12.1   Strip chart of the hypothetical treatment data in table 12.1

A permutation test takes a different approach. If the two treatments are truly equivalent, the label (Treatment A or Treatment B) assigned to an observed score is arbitrary. To test for differences between the two treatments, we could follow these steps:

1. Calculate the observed t-statistic, as in the parametric approach; call this t0.
2. Place all 10 scores in a single group.
3. Randomly assign five scores to Treatment A and five scores to Treatment B.
4. Calculate and record the new observed t-statistic.
5. Repeat steps 3–4 for every possible way of assigning five scores to Treatment A and five scores to Treatment B. There are 252 such possible arrangements.
6. Arrange the 252 t-statistics in ascending order. This is the empirical distribution, based on (or conditioned on) the sample data.
7. If t0 falls outside the middle 95 percent of the empirical distribution, reject the null hypothesis that the population means for the two treatment groups are equal at the 0.05 level of significance.

Notice that the same t-statistic is calculated in both the permutation and parametric approaches. But instead of comparing the statistic to a theoretical distribution in order to determine if it was extreme enough to reject the null hypothesis, it's compared to an empirical distribution created from permutations of the observed data. This logic can be extended to most classical statistical tests and linear models.

In the previous example, the empirical distribution was based on all possible permutations of the data. In such cases, the permutation test is called an "exact" test. As the sample sizes increase, the time required to form all possible permutations can become prohibitive. In such cases, you can use Monte Carlo simulation to sample from all possible permutations. Doing so provides an approximate test.

If you're uncomfortable assuming that the data is normally distributed, concerned about the impact of outliers, or feel that the dataset is too small for standard parametric approaches, a permutation test provides an excellent alternative.

R has some of the most comprehensive and sophisticated packages for performing permutation tests currently available. The remainder of this section focuses on two contributed packages: the `coin` package and the `lmPerm` package. Be sure to install them before first use:

```
install.packages(c("coin","lmPerm"))
```

The `coin` package provides a comprehensive framework for permutation tests applied to independence problems, whereas the `lmPerm` package provides permutation tests for ANOVA and regression designs. We'll consider each in turn, and end the section with a quick review of other permutation packages available in R.

Before moving on, it's important to remember that permutation tests use pseudo-random numbers to sample from all possible permutations (when performing an approximate test). Therefore, the results will change each time the test is performed. Setting the random number seed in R allows you to fix the random numbers generated.

This is particularly useful when you want to share your examples with others, because results will always be the same if the calls are made with the same seed. Setting the random number seed to 1234 (that is, `set.seed(1234)`) will allow you to replicate the results presented in this chapter.

12.2 *Permutation test with the coin package*

The `coin` package provides a general framework for applying permutation tests to independence problems. With this package, we can answer such questions as

- Are responses independent of group assignment?
- Are two numeric variables independent?
- Are two categorical variables independent?

Using convenience functions provided in the package (see table 12.2), we can perform permutation test equivalents for most of the traditional statistical tests covered in chapter 7.

Table 12.2   `coin` functions providing permutation test alternatives to traditional tests

Test	coin function
Two- and K-sample permutation test	`oneway_test(y ~ A)`
Two- and K-sample permutation test with a stratification (blocking) factor	`oneway_test(y ~ A | C)`
Wilcoxon–Mann–Whitney rank sum test	`wilcox_test(y ~ A )`
Kruskal–Wallis test	`kruskal_test(y ~ A)`
Person's chi-square test	`chisq_test(A ~ B)`
Cochran–Mantel–Haenszel test	`cmh_test(A ~ B | C)`
Linear-by-linear association test	`lbl_test(D ~ E)`
Spearman's test	`spearman_test(y ~ x)`
Friedman test	`friedman_test(y ~ A | C)`
Wilcoxon–Signed–Rank test	`wilcoxsign_test(y1 ~ y2)`

In the `coin` function column, y and x are numeric variables, A and B are categorical factors, C is a categorical blocking variable, D and E are ordered factors, and y1 and y2 are matched numeric variables.

Each of the functions listed in table 12.2 take the form

```
function_name( formula, data, distribution= )
```

where

- `formula` describes the relationship among variables to be tested. Examples are given in the table.
- `data` identifies a data frame.
- `distribution` specifies how the empirical distribution under the null hypothesis should be derived. Possible values are `exact`, `asymptotic`, and `approximate`.

If `distribution="exact"`, the distribution under the null hypothesis is computed exactly (that is, from all possible permutations). The distribution can also be approximated by its asymptotic distribution (`distribution="asymptotic"`) or via Monte Carlo resampling (`distribution="approximate(B=#)"`), where # indicates the number of replications used to approximate the exact distribution. At present, `distribution="exact"` is only available for two-sample problems.

NOTE In the `coin` package, categorical variables and ordinal variables must be coded as factors and ordered factors, respectively. Additionally, the data must be stored in a data frame.

In the remainder of this section, we'll apply several of the permutation tests described in table 12.2 to problems from previous chapters. This will allow you to compare the results with more traditional parametric and nonparametric approaches. We'll end this discussion of the `coin` package by considering advanced extensions.

12.2.1 Independent two-sample and k-sample tests

To begin, compare an independent samples t-test with a one-way exact test applied to the hypothetical data in table 12.2. The results are given in the following listing.

Listing 12.1 t-test versus one-way permutation test for the hypothetical data

```
> library(coin)
> score <- c(40, 57, 45, 55, 58, 57, 64, 55, 62, 65)
> treatment <- factor(c(rep("A",5), rep("B",5)))
> mydata <- data.frame(treatment, score)
> t.test(score~treatment, data=mydata, var.equal=TRUE)

        Two Sample t-test

data:  score by treatment
t = -2.3, df = 8, p-value = 0.04705
alternative hypothesis: true difference in means is not equal to 0
95 percent confidence interval:
 -19.04  -0.16
sample estimates:
mean in group A mean in group B
            51              61

> oneway_test(score~treatment, data=mydata, distribution="exact")

        Exact 2-Sample Permutation Test

data:  score by treatment (A, B)
Z = -1.9, p-value = 0.07143
alternative hypothesis: true mu is not equal to 0
```

The traditional t-test indicates a significant group difference ($p < .05$), whereas the exact test doesn't ($p > 0.072$). With only 10 observations, I'd be more inclined to trust the results of the permutation test and attempt to collect more data before reaching a final conclusion.

Next, consider the Wilcoxon–Mann–Whitney U test. In chapter 7, we examined the difference in the probability of imprisonment in Southern versus non-Southern US states using the `wilcox.test()` function. Using an exact Wilcoxon rank sum test, we'd get

```
> library(MASS)
> UScrime <- transform(UScrime, So = factor(So))
> wilcox_test(Prob ~ So, data=UScrime, distribution="exact")

        Exact Wilcoxon Mann-Whitney Rank Sum Test

data:  Prob by So (0, 1)
Z = -3.7, p-value = 8.488e-05
alternative hypothesis: true mu is not equal to 0
```

suggesting that incarceration is more likely in Southern states. Note that in the previous code, the numeric variable `So` was transformed into a factor. This is because the `coin` package requires that all categorical variables be coded as factors. Additionally, the astute reader may have noted that these results agree exactly with the results of the `wilcox.test()` in chapter 7. This is because the `wilcox.test()` also computes an exact distribution by default.

Finally, consider a k-sample test. In chapter 9, we used a one-way ANOVA to evaluate the impact of five drug regimens on cholesterol reduction in a sample of 50 patients. An approximate k-sample permutation test can be performed instead, using this code:

```
> library(multcomp)
> set.seed(1234)
> oneway_test(response~trt, data=cholesterol,
  distribution=approximate(B=9999))

        Approximative K-Sample Permutation Test

data:  response by
        trt (1time, 2times, 4times, drugD, drugE)
maxT = 4.7623, p-value < 2.2e-16
```

Here, the reference distribution is based on 9,999 permutations of the data. The random number seed was set so that your results would be the same as mine. There's clearly a difference in response among patients in the various groups.

12.2.2 Independence in contingency tables

We can use permutation tests to assess the independence of two categorical variables using either the `chisq_test()` or the `cmh_test()` function. The latter function is used when the data is stratified on a third categorical variable. If both variables are ordinal, we can use the `lbl_test()` function to test for a linear trend.

In chapter 7, we applied a chi-square test to assess the relationship between Arthritis treatment and improvement. Treatment had two levels (Placebo, Treated), and Improved had three levels (None, Some, Marked). The `Improved` variable was encoded as an ordered factor.

If you want to perform a permutation version of the chi-square test, you could use the following code:

```
> library(coin)
> library(vcd)
> Arthritis <- transform(Arthritis,
  Improved=as.factor(as.numeric(Improved)))
> set.seed(1234)
> chisq_test(Treatment~Improved, data=Arthritis,
            distribution=approximate(B=9999))

          Approximative Pearson's Chi-Squared Test

data:  Treatment by Improved (1, 2, 3)
chi-squared = 13.055, p-value = 0.0018
```

This gives you an approximate chi-square test based on 9,999 replications. You might ask why you transformed the variable `Improved` from an ordered factor to a categorical factor. (Good question!) If you'd left it an ordered factor, `coin()` would have generated a linear x linear trend test instead of a chi-square test. Although a trend test would be a good choice in this situation, keeping it a chi-square test allows you to compare the results with those reported in chapter 7.

12.2.3 *Independence between numeric variables*

The `spearman_test()` function provides a permutation test of the independence of two numeric variables. In chapter 7, we examined the correlation between illiteracy rates and murder rates for US states. You can test the association via permutation, using the following code:

```
> states <- as.data.frame(state.x77)
> set.seed(1234)
> spearman_test(Illiteracy~Murder, data=states,
                distribution=approximate(B=9999))

         Approximative Spearman Correlation Test

data:  Illiteracy by Murder
Z = 4.7065, p-value < 2.2e-16
alternative hypothesis: true mu is not equal to 0
```

Based on an approximate permutation test with 9,999 replications, the hypothesis of independence can be rejected. Note that state.x77 is a matrix. It had to be converted into a data frame for use in the `coin` package.

12.2.4 *Dependent two-sample and k-sample tests*

Dependent sample tests are used when observations in different groups have been matched, or when repeated measures are used. For permutation tests with two paired groups, the `wilcoxsign_test()` function can be used. For more than two groups, use the `friedman_test()` function.

In chapter 7, we compared the unemployment rate for urban males age 14–24 (U1) with urban males age 35–39 (U2). Because the two variables are reported for each of the 50 US states, you have a two-dependent groups design (state is the matching variable). We can use an exact Wilcoxon Signed Rank Test to see if unemployment rates for the two age groups are equal:

```
> library(coin)
> library(MASS)
> wilcoxsign_test(U1~U2, data=UScrime, distribution="exact")

        Exact Wilcoxon-Signed-Rank Test

data:  y by x (neg, pos)
        stratified by block
Z = 5.9691, p-value = 1.421e-14
alternative hypothesis: true mu is not equal to 0
```

Based on the results, you'd conclude that the unemployment rates differ.

12.2.5 Going further

The coin package provides a general framework for testing that one group of variables is independent of a second group of variables (with optional stratification on a blocking variable) against arbitrary alternatives, via approximate permutation tests. In particular, the independence_test() function allows the user to approach most traditional tests from a permutation perspective, and to create new and novel statistical tests for situations not covered by traditional methods. This flexibility comes at a price: a high level of statistical knowledge is required to use the function appropriately. See the vignettes that accompany the package (accessed via vignette("coin")) for further details.

In the next section, you'll learn about the lmPerm package. This package provides a permutation approach to linear models, including regression and analysis of variance.

12.3 Permutation tests with the lmPerm package

The lmPerm package provides support for a permutation approach to linear models. In particular, the lmp() and aovp() functions are the lm() and aov() functions modified to perform permutation tests rather than normal theory tests.

The parameters within the lmp() and aovp() functions are similar to those in the lm() and aov() functions, with the addition of a perm= parameter. The perm= option can take on the values "Exact", "Prob", or "SPR". Exact produces an exact test, based on all possible permutations. Prob samples from all possible permutations. Sampling continues until the estimated standard deviation falls below 0.1 of the estimated p-value. The stopping rule is controlled by an optional Ca parameter. Finally, SPR uses a sequential probability ratio test to decide when to stop sampling. Note that if the number of observations is greater than 10, perm="Exact" will automatically default to perm="Prob"; exact tests are only available for small problems.

To see how this works, we'll apply a permutation approach to simple regression, polynomial regression, multiple regression, one-way analysis of variance, one-way analysis of covariance, and a two-way factorial design.

12.3.1 *Simple and polynomial regression*

In chapter 8, we used linear regression to study the relationship between weight and height for a group of 15 women. Using `lmp()` instead of `lm()` generates the permutation test results shown in the following listing.

Listing 12.2   Permutation tests for simple linear regression

```
> library(lmPerm)
> set.seed(1234)
> fit <- lmp(weight~height, data=women, perm="Prob")
[1] "Settings:  unique SS : numeric variables centered"
> summary(fit)

Call:
lmp(formula = weight ~ height, data = women, perm = "Prob")

Residuals:
   Min    1Q Median    3Q    Max
-1.733 -1.133 -0.383  0.742  3.117

Coefficients:
       Estimate Iter Pr(Prob)
height     3.45 5000   <2e-16 ***
---
Signif. codes:  0 '***' 0.001 '**' 0.01 '*' 0.05 '.' 0.1 ' ' 1

Residual standard error: 1.5 on 13 degrees of freedom
Multiple R-Squared: 0.991,       Adjusted R-squared: 0.99
F-statistic: 1.43e+03 on 1 and 13 DF,  p-value: 1.09e-14
```

To fit a quadratic equation, you could use the code in this next listing.

Listing 12.3   Permutation tests for polynomial regression

```
> library(lmPerm)
> set.seed(1234)
> fit <- lmp(weight~height + I(height^2), data=women, perm="Prob")
[1] "Settings:  unique SS : numeric variables centered"
> summary(fit)

Call:
lmp(formula = weight ~ height + I(height^2), data = women, perm = "Prob")

Residuals:
    Min     1Q  Median     3Q    Max
-0.5094 -0.2961 -0.0094  0.2862  0.5971

Coefficients:
           Estimate Iter Pr(Prob)
```

```
height        -7.3483 5000    <2e-16 ***
I(height^2)    0.0831 5000    <2e-16 ***
---
Signif. codes:  0 '***' 0.001 '**' 0.01 '*' 0.05 '.' 0.1 ' ' 1

Residual standard error: 0.38 on 12 degrees of freedom
Multiple R-Squared: 0.999,      Adjusted R-squared: 0.999
F-statistic: 1.14e+04 on 2 and 12 DF,  p-value: <2e-16
```

As you can see, it's a simple matter to test these regressions using permutation tests and requires little change in the underlying code. The output is also similar to that produced by the `lm()` function. Note that an `Iter` column is added indicating how many iterations were required to reach the stopping rule.

12.3.2 Multiple regression

In chapter 8, multiple regression was used to predict the murder rate from population, illiteracy, income, and frost for 50 US states. Applying the `lmp()` function to this problem, results in the following output.

Listing 12.4   Permutation tests for multiple regression

```
> library(lmPerm)
> set.seed(1234)
> states <- as.data.frame(state.x77)
> fit <- lmp(Murder~Population + Illiteracy+Income+Frost,
            data=states, perm="Prob")
[1] "Settings:  unique SS : numeric variables centered"
> summary(fit)

Call:
lmp(formula = Murder ~ Population + Illiteracy + Income + Frost,
    data = states, perm = "Prob")

Residuals:
    Min       1Q   Median       3Q      Max
-4.79597 -1.64946 -0.08112  1.48150  7.62104

Coefficients:
            Estimate Iter Pr(Prob)
Population 2.237e-04   51   1.0000
Illiteracy 4.143e+00 5000   0.0004 ***
Income     6.442e-05   51   1.0000
Frost      5.813e-04   51   0.8627
---
Signif. codes:  0 '***' 0.001 '**' 0.01 '*' 0.05 '. ' 0.1 ' ' 1

Residual standard error: 2.535 on 45 degrees of freedom
Multiple R-Squared: 0.567,      Adjusted R-squared: 0.5285
F-statistic: 14.73 on 4 and 45 DF,  p-value: 9.133e-08
```

Looking back to chapter 8, both `Population` and `Illiteracy` are significant ($p < 0.05$) when normal theory is used. Based on the permutation tests, the `Population` variable is no longer significant. When the two approaches don't agree, you should look at your data more carefully. It may be that the assumption of normality is untenable or that outliers are present.

12.3.3 One-way ANOVA and ANCOVA

Each of the analysis of variance designs discussed in chapter 9 can be performed via permutation tests. First, let's look at the one-way ANOVA problem considered in sections 9.1 on the impact of treatment regimens on cholesterol reduction. The code and results are given in the next listing.

Listing 12.5   Permutation test for One-Way ANOVA

```
> library(lmPerm)
> library(multcomp)
> set.seed(1234)
> fit <- aovp(response~trt, data=cholesterol, perm="Prob")
[1] "Settings:  unique SS "
> summary(fit)
Component 1 :
           Df R Sum Sq R Mean Sq Iter  Pr(Prob)
trt         4  1351.37    337.84 5000 < 2.2e-16 ***
Residuals  45   468.75     10.42
---
Signif. codes:  0 '***' 0.001 '**' 0.01 '*' 0.05 '. ' 0.1 ' ' 1
```

The results suggest that the treatment effects are not all equal.

This second example in this section applies a permutation test to a one-way analysis of covariance. The problem is from chapter 9, where you investigated the impact of four drug doses on the litter weights of rats, controlling for gestation times. The next listing shows the permutation test and results.

Listing 12.6   Permutation test for one-way ANCOVA

```
> library(lmPerm)
> set.seed(1234)
> fit <- aovp(weight ~ gesttime + dose, data=litter, perm="Prob")
[1] "Settings:  unique SS : numeric variables centered"
> summary(fit)
Component 1 :
           Df R Sum Sq R Mean Sq Iter  Pr(Prob)
gesttime    1   161.49   161.493 5000    0.0006 ***
dose        3   137.12    45.708 5000    0.0392 *
Residuals  69  1151.27    16.685
---
Signif. codes:  0 '***' 0.001 '**' 0.01 '*' 0.05 '.' 0.1 ' ' 1
```

Based on the p-values, the four drug doses do not equally impact litter weights, controlling for gestation time.

12.3.4 Two-way ANOVA

We'll end this section by applying permutation tests to a factorial design. In chapter 9, we examined the impact of vitamin C on the tooth growth in guinea pigs. The two manipulated factors were dose (three levels) and delivery method (two levels). Ten guinea pigs were placed in each treatment combination, resulting in a balanced 3 x 2 factorial design. The permutation tests are provided in the next listing.

Listing 12.7   Permutation test for two-way ANOVA

```
> library(lmPerm)
> set.seed(1234)
> fit <- aovp(len~supp*dose, data=ToothGrowth, perm="Prob")
[1] "Settings:  unique SS : numeric variables centered"
> summary(fit)
Component 1 :
            Df R Sum Sq R Mean Sq Iter Pr(Prob)
supp         1   205.35    205.35 5000  < 2e-16 ***
dose         1  2224.30   2224.30 5000  < 2e-16 ***
supp:dose    1    88.92     88.92 2032  0.04724 *
Residuals   56   933.63     16.67
---
Signif. codes:  0 '***' 0.001 '**' 0.01 '*' 0.05 '.' 0.1 ' ' 1
```

At the .05 level of significance, all three effects are statistically different from zero. At the .01 level, only the main effects are significant.

It's important to note that when `aovp()` is applied to ANOVA designs, it defaults to unique sums of squares (also called SAS Type III sums of squares). Each effect is adjusted for every other effect. The default for parametric ANOVA designs in R is sequential sums of squares (SAS Type I sums of squares). Each effect is adjusted for those that appear *earlier* in the model. For balanced designs, the two approaches will agree, but for unbalanced designs with unequal numbers of observations per cell, they won't. The greater the imbalance, the greater the disagreement. If desired, specifying `seqs=TRUE` in the `aovp()` function will produce sequential sums of squares. For more on Type I and Type III sums of squares, see chapter 9, section 9.2.

12.4   Additional comments on permutation tests

R offers other permutation packages besides `coin` and `lmPerm`. The `perm` package provides some of the same functionality provided by the `coin` package and can act as an independent validation of that package. The `corrperm` package provides permutation tests of correlations with repeated measures. The `logregperm` package offers a permutation test for logistic regression. Perhaps most importantly, the `glmperm` package extends permutation tests to generalized linear models. Generalized linear models are described in the next chapter.

Permutation tests provide a powerful alternative to tests that rely on a knowledge of the underlying sampling distribution. In each of the permutation tests described, we were able to test statistical hypotheses without recourse to the normal, t, F, or chi-square distributions.

You may have noticed how closely the results of the tests based on normal theory agreed with the results of the permutation approach in previous sections. The data in these problems were well behaved and the agreement between methods is a testament to how well normal theory methods work in such cases.

Where permutation tests really shine are in cases where the data is clearly non-normal (for example, highly skewed), outliers are present, samples sizes are small, or no parametric tests exist. However, if the original sample is a poor representation of the population of interest, no test, including permutation tests, will improve the inferences generated.

Permutation tests are primarily useful for generating p-values that can be used to test null hypotheses. They can help answer the question, "Does an effect exist?" It's more difficult to use permutation methods to obtain confidence intervals and estimates of measurement precision. Fortunately, this is an area in which bootstrapping excels.

12.5 Bootstrapping

Bootstrapping generates an empirical distribution of a test statistic or set of test statistics, by repeated random sampling with replacement, from the original sample. It allows you to generate confidence intervals and test statistical hypotheses without having to assume a specific underlying theoretical distribution.

It's easiest to demonstrate the logic of bootstrapping with an example. Say that you want to calculate the 95 percent confidence interval for a sample mean. Your sample has 10 observations, a sample mean of 40, and a sample standard deviation of 5. If you're willing to assume that the sampling distribution of the mean is normally distributed, the $(1-\alpha/2)\%$ confidence interval can be calculated using

$$\overline{X} - t\frac{s}{\sqrt{n}} < \mu < \overline{X} + t\frac{s}{\sqrt{n}}$$

where t is the upper $1-\alpha/2$ critical value for a t distribution with n-1 degrees of freedom. For a 95 percent confidence interval, you have $40 - 2.262(5/3.163) < \mu < 40 + 2.262(5/3.162)$ or $36.424 < \mu < 43.577$. You'd expect 95 percent of confidence intervals created in this way to surround the true population mean.

But what if you aren't willing to assume that the sampling distribution of the mean is normally distributed? You could use a bootstrapping approach instead:

1 Randomly select 10 observations from the sample, with replacement after each selection. Some observations may be selected more than once, and some may not be selected at all.
2 Calculate and record the sample mean.
3 Repeat steps 1 and 2 a thousand times.
4 Order the 1,000 sample means from smallest to largest.
5 Find the sample means representing the 2.5th and 97.5th percentiles. In this case, it's the 25th number from the bottom and top. These are your 95 percent confidence limits.

In the present case, where the sample mean is likely to be normally distributed, you gain little from the bootstrap approach. Yet there are many cases where the bootstrap approach is advantageous. What if you wanted confidence intervals for the sample median, or the difference between two sample medians? There are no simple normal theory formulas here, and bootstrapping is the approach of choice. If the underlying distributions are unknown, if outliers are a problem, if sample sizes are small, or if parametric approaches don't exist, bootstrapping can often provide a useful method of generating confidence intervals and testing hypotheses.

12.6 *Bootstrapping with the boot package*

The `boot` package provides extensive facilities for bootstrapping and related resampling methods. You can bootstrap a single statistic (for example, a median), or a vector of statistics (for example, a set of regression coefficients). Be sure to download and install the `boot` package before first use:

```
install.packages("boot")
```

The bootstrapping process will seem complicated, but once you review the examples it should make sense.

In general, bootstrapping involves three main steps:

1 Write a function that returns the statistic or statistics of interest. If there is a single statistic (for example, a median), the function should return a number. If there is a set of statistics (for example, a set of regression coefficients), the function should return a vector.

2 Process this function through the `boot()` function in order to generate R bootstrap replications of the statistic(s).

3 Use the `boot.ci()` function to obtain confidence intervals for the statistic(s) generated in step 2.

Now to the specifics.

The main bootstrapping function is `boot()`. The `boot()` function has the format

```
bootobject <- boot(data=, statistic=, R=, ...)
```

The parameters are described in table 12.3.

Table 12.3 Parameters of the `boot()` function

Parameter	Description
`data`	A vector, matrix, or data frame.
`statistic`	A function that produces the `k` statistics to be bootstrapped (`k=1` if bootstrapping a single statistic).
	The function should include an `indices` parameter that the `boot()` function can use to select cases for each replication (see examples in the text).
`R`	Number of bootstrap replicates.
`...`	Additional parameters to be passed to the function that is used to produce statistic(s) of interest.

The `boot()` function calls the statistic function R times. Each time, it generates a set of random indices, with replacement, from the integers `1:nrow(data)`. These indices are used within the statistic function to select a sample. The statistics are calculated on the sample and the results are accumulated in the *bootobject*. The *bootobject* structure is described in table 12.4.

Table 12.4   Elements of the object returned by the `boot()` function

Element	Description
t0	The observed values of k statistics applied to the original data
t	An R x k matrix where each row is a bootstrap replicate of the k statistics

You can access these elements as *bootobject$t0* and *bootobject$t*.

Once you generate the bootstrap samples, you can use `print()` and `plot()` to examine the results. If the results look reasonable, you can use the `boot.ci()` function to obtain confidence intervals for the statistic(s). The format is

```
boot.ci(bootobject, conf=, type= )
```

The parameters are given in table 12.5.

Table 12.5   Parameters of the `boot.ci()` function

Parameter	Description
bootobject	The object returned by the `boot()` function.
conf	The desired confidence interval (default: conf=0.95).
type	The type of confidence interval returned. Possible values are "norm", "basic", "stud", "perc", "bca", and "all" (default: type="all").

The `type` parameter specifies the method for obtaining the confidence limits. The perc method (percentile) was demonstrated in the sample mean example. The bca provides an interval that makes simple adjustments for bias. I find bca preferable in most circumstances. See Mooney and Duval (1993) for an introduction to these methods.

In the remaining sections, we'll look at bootstrapping a single statistic and a vector of statistics.

12.6.1 Bootstrapping a single statistic

The `mtcars` dataset contains information on 32 automobiles reported in the 1974 *Motor Trend* magazine. Suppose you're using multiple regression to predict miles per gallon from a car's weight (lb/1,000) and engine displacement (cu. in.). In addition to the standard regression statistics, you'd like to obtain a 95 percent confidence interval for the R-squared value (the percent of variance in the response variable explained by the predictors). The confidence interval can be obtained using nonparametric bootstrapping.

The first task is to write a function for obtaining the R-squared value:

```
rsq <- function(formula, data, indices) {
        d <- data[indices,]
        fit <- lm(formula, data=d)
        return(summary(fit)$r.square)

}
```

The function returns the R-square value from a regression. The `d <- data[indices,]` statement is required for `boot()` to be able to select samples.

You can then draw a large number of bootstrap replications (say, 1,000) with the following code:

```
library(boot)
set.seed(1234)
results <- boot(data=mtcars, statistic=rsq,
                R=1000, formula=mpg~wt+disp)
```

The boot object can be printed using

```
> print(results)

ORDINARY NONPARAMETRIC BOOTSTRAP


Call:
boot(data = mtcars, statistic = rsq, R = 1000, formula = mpg ~
    wt + disp)


Bootstrap Statistics :
     original      bias      std. error
t1* 0.7809306 0.01333670   0.05068926
```

and plotted using `plot(results)`. The resulting graph is shown in figure 12.2.

In figure 12.2, you can see that the distribution of bootstrapped R-squared values isn't normally distributed. A 95 percent confidence interval for the R-squared values can be obtained using

```
> boot.ci(results, type=c("perc", "bca"))
BOOTSTRAP CONFIDENCE INTERVAL CALCULATIONS
Based on 1000 bootstrap replicates

CALL :
boot.ci(boot.out = results, type = c("perc", "bca"))

Intervals :
Level      Percentile             BCa
95%    ( 0.6838,  0.8833 )    ( 0.6344,  0.8549 )
Calculations and Intervals on Original Scale
Some BCa intervals may be unstable
```

You can see from this example that different approaches to generating the confidence intervals can lead to different intervals. In this case the bias adjusted interval is

Histogram of t

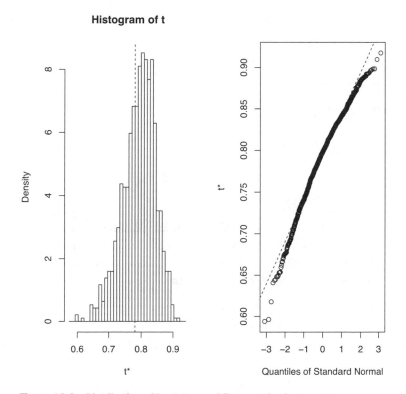

Figure 12.2   Distribution of bootstrapped R-squared values

moderately different from the percentile method. In either case, the null hypothesis H_0: R-square = 0, would be rejected, because zero is outside the confidence limits.

In this section, we estimated the confidence limits of a single statistic. In the next section, we'll estimate confidence intervals for several statistics.

12.6.2 *Bootstrapping several statistics*

In the previous example, bootstrapping was used to estimate the confidence interval for a single statistic (R-squared). Continuing the example, let's obtain the 95 percent confidence intervals for a vector of statistics. Specifically, let's get confidence intervals for the three model regression coefficients (intercept, car weight, and engine displacement).

First, create a function that returns the vector of regression coefficients:

```
bs <- function(formula, data, indices) {
        d <- data[indices,]
        fit <- lm(formula, data=d)
        return(coef(fit))
}
```

Then use this function to bootstrap 1,000 replications:

```
library(boot)
set.seed(1234)
results <- boot(data=mtcars, statistic=bs,
                R=1000, formula=mpg~wt+disp)
> print(results)
ORDINARY NONPARAMETRIC BOOTSTRAP
Call:
boot(data = mtcars, statistic = bs, R = 1000, formula = mpg ~
    wt + disp)

Bootstrap Statistics :
    original    bias    std. error
t1*  34.9606  0.137873     2.48576
t2*  -3.3508 -0.053904     1.17043
t3*  -0.0177 -0.000121     0.00879
```

When bootstrapping multiple statistics, add an index parameter to the `plot()` and `boot.ci()` functions to indicate which column of `bootobject$t` to analyze. In this example, index 1 refers to the intercept, index 2 is car weight, and index 3 is the engine displacement. To plot the results for car weight, use

```
plot(results, index=2)
```

The graph is given in figure 12.3.

To get the 95 percent confidence intervals for car weight and engine displacement, use

```
> boot.ci(results, type="bca", index=2)
BOOTSTRAP CONFIDENCE INTERVAL CALCULATIONS
Based on 1000 bootstrap replicates

CALL :
boot.ci(boot.out = results, type = "bca", index = 2)
```

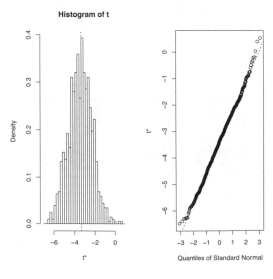

Figure 12.3 Distribution of bootstrapping regression coefficients for car weight

```
Intervals :
Level        BCa
95%    (-5.66, -1.19 )
Calculations and Intervals on Original Scale

> boot.ci(results, type="bca", index=3)

BOOTSTRAP CONFIDENCE INTERVAL CALCULATIONS
Based on 1000 bootstrap replicates

CALL :
boot.ci(boot.out = results, type = "bca", index = 3)

Intervals :
Level        BCa
95%    (-0.0331,  0.0010 )
Calculations and Intervals on Original Scale
```

NOTE   In the previous example, we resampled the entire sample of data each time. If we assume that the predictor variables have fixed levels (typical in planned experiments), we'd do better to only resample residual terms. See Mooney and Duval (1993, pp. 16–17) for a simple explanation and algorithm.

Before we leave bootstrapping, it's worth addressing two questions that come up often:

- How large does the original sample need to be?
- How many replications are needed?

There's no simple answer to the first question. Some say that an original sample size of 20–30 is sufficient for good results, as long as the sample is representative of the population. Random sampling from the population of interest is the most trusted method for assuring the original sample's representativeness. With regard to the second question, I find that 1,000 replications are more than adequate in most cases. Computer power is cheap and you can always increase the number of replications if desired.

There are many helpful sources of information on permutation tests and bootstrapping. An excellent starting place is an online article by Yu (2003). Good (2006) provides a comprehensive overview of resampling in general and includes R code. A good, accessible introduction to the bootstrap is provided by Mooney and Duval (1993). The definitive source on bootstrapping is Efron and Tibshirani (1998). Finally, there are a number of great online resources, including Simon (1997), Canty (2002), Shah (2005), and Fox (2002).

12.7 *Summary*

In this chapter, we introduced a set of computer-intensive methods based on randomization and resampling that allow you to test hypotheses and form confidence intervals without reference to a known theoretical distribution. They're particularly valuable when your data comes from unknown population distributions, when there are serious outliers, when your sample sizes are small, and when there are no existing parametric methods to answer the hypotheses of interest.

The methods in this chapter are particularly exciting because they provide an avenue for answering questions when your standard data assumptions are clearly untenable, or when you have no other idea how to approach the problem. Permutation tests and bootstrapping aren't panaceas, though. They can't turn bad data into good data. If your original samples aren't representative of the population of interest, or are too small to accurately reflect it, then these techniques won't help.

In the next chapter, we'll consider data models for variables that follow known, but not necessarily normal, distributions.

Part 4

Advanced methods

In this final section, we consider advanced methods of statistical and graphical analysis to round out your data analysis toolkit. Chapter 13 expands on the regression methods in chapter 8 to cover parametric approaches to data that aren't normally distributed. The chapter starts with a discussion of the generalized linear model, and then focuses on cases where we're trying to predict an outcome variable that's either categorical (logistic regression) or a count (poisson regression).

Dealing with a large number of variables can be challenging, due to the complexity inherent in multivariate data. Chapter 14 describes two popular methods for exploring and simplifying multivariate data. Principal components analysis can be used to transform a large number of correlated variables into a smaller set of composite variables. Factor analysis consists of a set of techniques for uncovering the latent structure underlying a given set of variables. Chapter 14 provides step-by-step instructions for carrying out each.

More often than not, researchers must deal with incomplete datasets. Chapter 15 considers modern approaches to the ubiquitous problem of missing data values. R supports a number of elegant approaches for analyzing datasets that are incomplete for various reasons. Several of the best approaches are described here, along with guidance around which ones to use, and which ones to avoid.

Chapter 16 completes our discussion of graphics with presentations of some of R's most advanced and useful approaches to visualizing data. This includes visual representations of complex data using the lattice package, and an introduction to the new, and increasingly popular, ggplot2 package. The chapter ends with a review of packages that provide functions for interacting with graphs in real-time.

After completing part 4, you will have the tools to manage a wide range of complex data analysis problems. This includes modeling non-normal outcome variables, dealing with large numbers of correlated variables, and handling messy and incomplete data. Additionally, you will have the tools to visualize complex data in useful, innovative and creative ways.

Generalized linear models

This chapter covers
- Formulating a generalized linear model
- Predicting categorical outcomes
- Modeling count data

In chapters 8 (regression) and 9 (ANOVA), we explored linear models that can be used to predict a normally distributed response variable from a set of continuous and/or categorical predictor variables. But there are many situations in which it's unreasonable to assume that the dependent variable is normally distributed (or even continuous). For example:

- The outcome variable may be categorical. Binary variables (for example, yes/no, passed/failed, lived/died) and polytomous variables (for example, poor/good/excellent, republican/democrat/independent) are clearly not normally distributed.
- The outcome variable may be a count (for example, number of traffic accidents in a week, number of drinks per day). Such variables take on a limited number of values and are never negative. Additionally, their mean and variance are often related (which isn't true for normally distributed variables).

Generalized linear models extend the linear model framework to include dependent variables that are decidedly non-normal.

In this chapter, we'll start with a brief overview of generalized linear models and the `glm()` function used to estimate them. Then we'll focus on two popular models within this framework: logistic regression (where the dependent variable is categorical) and Poisson regression (where the dependent variable is a count variable).

To motivate the discussion, we'll apply generalized linear models to two research questions that aren't easily addressed with standard linear models:

- What personal, demographic, and relationship variables predict marital infidelity? In this case, the outcome variable is binary (affair/no affair).
- What impact does a drug treatment for seizures have on the number of seizures experienced over an eight-week period? In this case, the outcome variable is a count (number of seizures).

We'll apply logistic regression to address the first question and Poisson regression to address the second. Along the way, we'll consider extensions of each technique.

13.1 *Generalized linear models and the glm() function*

A wide range of popular data analytic methods are subsumed within the framework of the generalized linear model. In this section we'll briefly explore some of the theory behind this approach. You can safely skip over this section if you like and come back to it later.

Let's say that you want to model the relationship between a response variable Y and a set of p predictor variables $X_1 ... X_p$. In the standard linear model, you assume that Y is normally distributed and that the form of the relationship is

$$\mu_Y = \beta_0 + \sum\nolimits_{j=1}^{p} \beta_j X_j$$

This equation states that the conditional mean of the response variable is a linear combination of the predictor variables. The β_j are the parameters specifying the expected change in Y for a unit change in X_j and β_0 is the expected value of Y when all the predictor variables are 0. You're saying that you can predict the mean of the Y distribution for observations with a given set of X values by applying the proper weights to the X variables and adding them up.

Note that you've made no distributional assumptions about the predictor variables, X_j. Unlike Y, there's no requirement that they be normally distributed. In fact, they're often categorical (for example, ANOVA designs). Additionally, nonlinear functions of the predictors are allowed. You often include such predictors as X^2 or $X_1 \times X_2$. What is important is that the equation is linear in the parameters (β_0, β_1,... β_p).

In generalized linear models, you fit models of the form

$$g(\mu_Y) = \beta_0 + \sum\nolimits_{j=1}^{p} \beta_j X_j$$

where $g(\mu_Y)$ is a function of the conditional mean (called the link function). Additionally, you relax the assumption that Y is normally distributed. Instead, you assume that

Y follows a distribution that's a member of the exponential family. You specify the link function and the probability distribution, and the parameters are derived through an iterative maximum likelihood estimation procedure.

13.1.1 The glm() function

Generalized linear models are typically fit in R through the `glm()` function (although other specialized functions are available). The form of the function is similar to `lm()` but includes additional parameters. The basic format of the function is

```
glm(formula, family=family(link=function), data=)
```

where the probability distribution (*family*) and corresponding default link function (*function*) are given in table 13.1.

Table 13.1   glm() parameters

Family	Default link function
binomial	(link = "logit")
gaussian	(link = "identity")
gamma	(link = "inverse")
inverse.gaussian	(link = "1/mu^2")
poisson	(link = "log")
quasi	(link = "identity", variance = "constant")
quasibinomial	(link = "logit")
quasipoisson	(link = "log")

$$\pi = \frac{1}{1 + e^y}$$

The `glm()` function allows you to fit a number of popular models, including logistic regression, Poisson regression, and survival analysis (not considered here). You can demonstrate this for the first two models as follows. Assume that you have a single response variable (`Y`), three predictor variables (`X1, X2, X3`), and a data frame (`mydata`) containing the data.

Logistic regression is applied to situations in which the response variable is dichotomous (0,1). The model assumes that Y follows a binomial distribution, and that you can fit a linear model of the form

$$\log_e\left(\frac{\pi}{1-\pi}\right) = \beta_0 + \sum_{j=1}^{p} \beta_j X_j$$

where $\pi = \mu_Y$ is the conditional mean of Y (that is, the probability that Y = 1 given a set of X values), $(\pi/1 - \pi)$ is the odds that Y = 1, and $\log(\pi/1 - \pi)$ is the log odds, or *logit*. In this case, $\log(\pi/1 - \pi)$ is the link function, the probability distribution is binomial, and the logistic regression model can be fit using

```
glm(Y~X1+X2+X3, family=binomial(link="logit"), data=mydata)
```

Logistic regression is described more fully in section 13.2.

$$y = \ln\left(\frac{\pi}{1-\pi}\right) \quad \text{so} \quad e^y = \frac{\pi}{1-\pi}. \quad \text{If } \frac{\pi}{1-\pi} = \gamma, \text{ then } \pi = \frac{1}{1+\gamma}.$$

Poisson regression is applied to situations in which the response variable is the number of events to occur in a given period of time. The Poisson regression model assumes that Y follows a Poisson distribution, and that you can fit a linear model of the form

$$\log_e(\lambda) = \beta_0 + \sum_{j=1}^{p} \beta_j X_j$$

where λ is the mean (and variance) of Y. In this case, the link function is $\log(\lambda)$, the probability distribution is Poisson, and the Poisson regression model can be fit using

```
glm(Y~X1+X2+X3, family=poisson(link="log"), data=mydata)
```

Poisson regression is described in section 13.3.

It is worth noting that the standard linear model is also a special case of the generalized linear model. If you let the link function $g(\mu_Y) = \mu_Y$ or the identity function and specify that the probability distribution is normal (Gaussian), then

```
glm(Y~X1+X2+X3, family=gaussian(link="identity"), data=mydata)
```

would produce the same results as

```
lm(Y~X1+X2+X3, data=mydata)
```

To summarize, generalized linear models extend the standard linear model by fitting a *function* of the conditional mean response (rather than the conditional mean response), and assuming that the response variable follows a member of the *exponential* family of distributions (rather than being limited to the normal distribution). The parameter estimates are derived via maximum likelihood rather than least squares.

13.1.2 *Supporting functions*

Many of the functions that you used in conjunction with `lm()` when analyzing standard linear models have corresponding versions for `glm()`. Some commonly used functions are given in table 13.2.

We'll explore examples of these functions in later sections. In the next section, we'll briefly consider the assessment of model adequacy.

Table 13.2 Functions that support `glm()`

Function	Description
`summary()`	Displays detailed results for the fitted model
`coefficients()`, `coef()`	Lists the model parameters (intercept and slopes) for the fitted model
`confint()`	Provides confidence intervals for the model parameters (95 percent by default)
`residuals()`	Lists the residual values for a fitted model
`anova()`	Generates an ANOVA table comparing two fitted models
`plot()`	Generates diagnostic plots for evaluating the fit of a model
`predict()`	Uses a fitted model to predict response values for a new dataset

13.1.3 Model fit and regression diagnostics

The assessment of model adequacy is as important for generalized linear models as it is for standard (OLS) linear models. Unfortunately, there's less agreement in the statistical community regarding appropriate assessment procedures. In general, you can use the techniques described in chapter 8, with the following caveats.

When assessing model adequacy, you'll typically want to plot predicted values expressed in the metric of the original response variable against residuals of the deviance type. For example, a common diagnostic plot would be

```
plot(predict(model, type="response"),
    residuals(model, type= "deviance"))
```

where *model* is the object returned by the glm() function.

The hat values, studentized residuals, and Cook's D statistics that R provides will be approximate values. Additionally, there's no general consensus on cutoff values for identifying problematic observations. Values have to be judged relative to each other. One approach is to create index plots for each statistic and look for unusually large values. For example, you could use the following code to create three diagnostic plots:

```
plot(hatvalues(model))
plot(rstudent(model))
plot(cooks.distance(model))
```

Alternatively, you could use the code

```
library(car)
influencePlot(model)
```

to create one omnibus plot. In the latter graph, the horizontal axis is the leverage, the vertical axis is the studentized residual, and the plotted symbol is proportional to the Cook's distance.

Diagnostic plots tend to be most helpful when the response variable takes on many values. When the response variable can only take on a limited number of values (for example, logistic regression), their utility is decreased.

For more on regression diagnostics for generalized linear models, see Fox (2008) and Faraway (2006). In the remaining portion of this chapter, we'll consider two of the most popular forms of the generalized linear model in detail: logistic regression and Poisson regression.

13.2 Logistic regression

Logistic regression is useful when predicting a binary outcome from a set of continuous and/or categorical predictor variables. To demonstrate this, we'll explore the data on infidelity contained in the data frame Affairs, provided with the AER package. Be sure to download and install the package (using install.packages("AER")) before first use.

The infidelity data, known as Fair's Affairs, is based on a cross-sectional survey conducted by *Psychology Today* in 1969, and is described in Greene (2003) and Fair

(1978). It contains nine variables collected on 601 participants and includes how often the respondent engaged in extramarital sexual intercourse during the past year, as well as their gender, age, years married, whether or not they had children, their religiousness (on a 5-point scale from 1=anti to 5=very), education, occupation (Hollingshead 7-point classification with reverse numbering), and a numeric self-rating of their marriage (from 1=very unhappy to 5=very happy).

Let's look at some descriptive statistics:

```
> data(Affairs, package="AER")
> summary(Affairs)
     affairs            gender          age          yearsmarried     children
 Min.   : 0.000    female:315    Min.   :17.50    Min.   : 0.125    no :171
 1st Qu.: 0.000    male  :286    1st Qu.:27.00    1st Qu.: 4.000    yes:430
 Median : 0.000                  Median :32.00    Median : 7.000
 Mean   : 1.456                  Mean   :32.49    Mean   : 8.178
 3rd Qu.: 0.000                  3rd Qu.:37.00    3rd Qu.:15.000
 Max.   :12.000                  Max.   :57.00    Max.   :15.000
  religiousness        education        occupation         rating
 Min.   :1.000    Min.   : 9.00    Min.   :1.000    Min.   :1.000
 1st Qu.:2.000    1st Qu.:14.00    1st Qu.:3.000    1st Qu.:3.000
 Median :3.000    Median :16.00    Median :5.000    Median :4.000
 Mean   :3.116    Mean   :16.17    Mean   :4.195    Mean   :3.932
 3rd Qu.:4.000    3rd Qu.:18.00    3rd Qu.:6.000    3rd Qu.:5.000
 Max.   :5.000    Max.   :20.00    Max.   :7.000    Max.   :5.000

> table(Affairs$affairs)
  0   1   2   3   7  12
451  34  17  19  42  38
```

From these statistics, you can see that that 52 percent of respondents were female, that 72 percent had children, and that the median age for the sample was 32 years. With regard to the response variable, 75 percent of respondents reported not engaging in an infidelity in the past year (451/601). The largest number of encounters reported was 12 (6 percent).

Although the *number* of indiscretions was recorded, our interest here is in the binary outcome (had an affair/didn't have an affair). You can transform affairs into a dichotomous factor called ynaffair with the following code.

```
> Affairs$ynaffair[Affairs$affairs  > 0] <- 1
> Affairs$ynaffair[Affairs$affairs == 0] <- 0
> Affairs$ynaffair <- factor(Affairs$ynaffair,
                             levels=c(0,1),
                             labels=c("No","Yes"))
> table(Affairs$ynaffair)
No Yes
451 150
```

create new variable

This dichotomous factor can now be used as the outcome variable in a logistic regression model:

```
> fit.full <- glm(ynaffair ~ gender + age + yearsmarried + children +
                  religiousness + education + occupation +rating,
                  data=Affairs,family=binomial())
```

```
> summary(fit.full)

Call:
glm(formula = ynaffair ~ gender + age + yearsmarried + children +
    religiousness + education + occupation + rating, family = binomial(),
    data = Affairs)

Deviance Residuals:
   Min      1Q  Median      3Q     Max
-1.571  -0.750  -0.569  -0.254   2.519

Coefficients:
                Estimate Std  Error  z value  Pr(>|z|)
(Intercept)       1.3773      0.8878    1.55   0.12081
gendermale        0.2803      0.2391    1.17   0.24108
age              -0.0443      0.0182   -2.43   0.01530 *
yearsmarried      0.0948      0.0322    2.94   0.00326 **
childrenyes       0.3977      0.2915    1.36   0.17251
religiousness    -0.3247      0.0898   -3.62   0.00030 ***
education         0.0211      0.0505    0.42   0.67685
occupation        0.0309      0.0718    0.43   0.66663
rating           -0.4685      0.0909   -5.15   2.6e-07 ***
---
Signif. codes:  0 '***' 0.001 '**' 0.01 '*' 0.05 '.' 0.1 ' ' 1

(Dispersion parameter for binomial family taken to be 1)

    Null deviance: 675.38  on 600  degrees of freedom
Residual deviance: 609.51  on 592  degrees of freedom
AIC: 627.5

Number of Fisher Scoring iterations: 4
```

From the p-values for the regression coefficients (last column), you can see that gender, presence of children, education, and occupation may not make a significant contribution to the equation (you can't reject the hypothesis that the parameters are 0). Let's fit a second equation without them, and test whether this reduced model fits the data as well:

```
> fit.reduced <- glm(ynaffair ~ age + yearsmarried + religiousness +
                     rating, data=Affairs, family=binomial())
> summary(fit.reduced)

Call:
glm(formula = ynaffair ~ age + yearsmarried + religiousness + rating,
    family = binomial(), data = Affairs)

Deviance Residuals:
   Min      1Q  Median      3Q     Max
-1.628  -0.755  -0.570  -0.262   2.400

Coefficients:
                Estimate Std. Error  z value  Pr(>|z|)
(Intercept)       1.9308      0.6103    3.16   0.00156 **
age              -0.0353      0.0174   -2.03   0.04213 *
```

```
yearsmarried    0.1006    0.0292    3.44   0.00057 ***
religiousness  -0.3290    0.0895   -3.68   0.00023 ***
rating         -0.4614    0.0888   -5.19   2.1e-07 ***
---
Signif. codes:   0 '***' 0.001 '**' 0.01 '*' 0.05 '.' 0.1 ' ' 1

(Dispersion parameter for binomial family taken to be 1)

    Null deviance: 675.38  on 600  degrees of freedom
Residual deviance: 615.36  on 596  degrees of freedom
AIC: 625.4

Number of Fisher Scoring iterations: 4
```

Each regression coefficient in the reduced model is statistically significant ($p < .05$). Because the two models are nested (fit.reduced is a subset of fit.full), you can use the anova() function to compare them. For generalized linear models, you'll want a chi-square version of this test.

```
> anova(fit.reduced, fit.full, test="Chisq")
Analysis of Deviance Table

Model 1: ynaffair ~ age + yearsmarried + religiousness + rating
Model 2: ynaffair ~ gender + age + yearsmarried + children +
    religiousness + education + occupation + rating
  Resid. Df Resid. Dev Df Deviance P(>|Chi|)
1       596        615
2       592        610  4     5.85      0.21
```

The nonsignificant chi-square value ($p = 0.21$) suggests that the reduced model with four predictors fits as well as the full model with nine predictors, reinforcing your belief that gender, children, education, and occupation don't add significantly to the prediction above and beyond the other variables in the equation. Therefore, you can base your interpretations on the simpler model.

13.2.1 *Interpreting the model parameters*

Let's take a look at the regression coefficients:

```
> coef(fit.reduced)
(Intercept)          age  yearsmarried religiousness        rating
      1.931       -0.035         0.101        -0.329        -0.461
```

In a logistic regression, the response being modeled is the log(odds) that $Y = 1$. The regression coefficients give the change in log(odds) in the response for a unit change in the predictor variable, holding all other predictor variables constant.

Because log(odds) are difficult to interpret, you can exponentiate them to put the results on an odds scale:

```
> exp(coef(fit.reduced))
(Intercept)          age  yearsmarried religiousness        rating
      6.895        0.965         1.106         0.720         0.630
```

Now you can see that the odds of an extramarital encounter are increased by a factor of 1.106 for a one-year increase in years married (holding age, religiousness, and marital rating constant). Conversely, the odds of an extramarital affair are multiplied by a factor of 0.965 for every year increase in age. The odds of an extramarital affair increase with years married, and decrease with age, religiousness, and marital rating. Because the predictor variables can't equal 0, the intercept isn't meaningful in this case.

If desired, you can use the confint() function to obtain confidence intervals for the coefficients. For example, exp(confint(fit.reduced)) would print 95 percent confidence intervals for each of the coefficients on an odds scale.

Finally, a one-unit change in a predictor variable may not be inherently interesting. For binary logistic regression, the change in the odds of the higher value on the response variable for an *n* unit change in a predictor variable is $\exp(\beta_j)^n$. If a one-year increase in years married multiplies the odds of an affair by 1.106, a 10-year increase would increase the odds by a factor of 1.106^10, or 2.7, holding the other predictor variables constant.

13.2.2 Assessing the impact of predictors on the probability of an outcome

For many of us, it's easier to think in terms of probabilities than odds. You can use the predict() function to observe the impact of varying the levels of a predictor variable on the probability of the outcome. The first step is to create an artificial dataset containing the values of the predictor variables that you're interested in. Then you can use this artificial dataset with the predict() function to predict the probabilities of the outcome event occurring for these values.

Let's apply this strategy to assess the impact of marital ratings on the probability of having an extramarital affair. First, create an artificial dataset, where age, years married, and religiousness are set to their means, and marital rating varies from 1 to 5.

```
> testdata <- data.frame(rating=c(1, 2, 3, 4, 5), age=mean(Affairs$age),
                yearsmarried=mean(Affairs$yearsmarried),
                religiousness=mean(Affairs$religiousness))
> testdata
  rating  age yearsmarried religiousness
1      1 32.5         8.18          3.12
2      2 32.5         8.18          3.12
3      3 32.5         8.18          3.12
4      4 32.5         8.18          3.12
5      5 32.5         8.18          3.12
```

Next, use the test dataset and prediction equation to obtain probabilities:

```
> testdata$prob <- predict(fit.reduced, newdata=testdata, type="response")
  testdata
  rating  age yearsmarried religiousness  prob
1      1 32.5         8.18          3.12 0.530
2      2 32.5         8.18          3.12 0.416
3      3 32.5         8.18          3.12 0.310
4      4 32.5         8.18          3.12 0.220
5      5 32.5         8.18          3.12 0.151
```

From these results you see that the probability of an extramarital affair decreases from 0.53 when the marriage is rated 1=very unhappy to 0.15 when the marriage is rated 5=very happy (holding age, years married, and religiousness constant). Now look at the impact of age:

```
> testdata <- data.frame(rating=mean(Affairs$rating),
                         age=seq(17, 57, 10),
                         yearsmarried=mean(Affairs$yearsmarried),
                         religiousness=mean(Affairs$religiousness))
> testdata
  rating age yearsmarried religiousness
1   3.93  17         8.18          3.12
2   3.93  27         8.18          3.12
3   3.93  37         8.18          3.12
4   3.93  47         8.18          3.12
5   3.93  57         8.18          3.12

> testdata$prob <- predict(fit.reduced, newdata=testdata, type="response")
> testdata
  rating age yearsmarried religiousness    prob
1   3.93  17         8.18          3.12   0.335
2   3.93  27         8.18          3.12   0.262
3   3.93  37         8.18          3.12   0.199
4   3.93  47         8.18          3.12   0.149
5   3.93  57         8.18          3.12   0.109
```

Here, you see that as age increases from 17 to 57, the probability of an extramarital encounter decreases from 0.34 to 0.11, holding the other variables constant. Using this approach, you can explore the impact of each predictor variable on the outcome.

13.2.3 Overdispersion

The expected variance for data drawn from a binomial distribution is $\sigma^2 = n\pi(1 - \pi)$, where n is the number of observations and π is the probability of belonging to the Y=1 group. Overdispersion occurs when the observed variance of the response variable is larger than what would be expected from a binomial distribution. Overdispersion can lead to distorted test standard errors and inaccurate tests of significance.

When overdispersion is present, you can still fit a logistic regression using the `glm()` function, but in this case, you should use the quasibinomial distribution rather than the binomial distribution.

One way to detect overdispersion is to compare the residual deviance with the residual degrees of freedom in your binomial model. If the ratio

$$\phi = \frac{Residual\ deviance}{Residual\ df}$$

is considerably larger than 1, you have evidence of overdispersion. Applying this to the Affairs example, you have

$$\phi = \frac{Residual\ deviance}{Residual\ df} = \frac{615.36}{596} = 1.03$$

which is close to 1, suggesting no overdispersion.

You can also test for overdispersion. To do this, you fit the model twice, but in the first instance you use `family="binomial"` and in the second instance you use `family="quasibinomial"`. If the `glm()` object returned in the first case is called `fit` and the object returned in the second case is called `fit.od`, then

```
pchisq(summary(fit.od)$dispersion * fit$df.residual,
       fit$df.residual, lower = F)
```

provides the p-value for testing the null hypothesis H_0: $\phi = 1$ versus the alternative hypothesis H_1: $\phi \neq 1$. If p is small (say, less than 0.05), you'd reject the null hypothesis.

Applying this to the Affairs dataset, you have

```
> fit <- glm(ynaffair ~ age + yearsmarried + religiousness +
             rating, family = binomial(), data = Affairs)
> fit.od <- glm(ynaffair ~ age + yearsmarried + religiousness +
               rating, family = quasibinomial(), data = Affairs)
> pchisq(summary(fit.od)$dispersion * fit$df.residual,
         fit$df.residual, lower = F)
```

```
[1] 0.34
```

The resulting p-value (0.34) is clearly not significant (p > 0.05), strengthening our belief that overdispersion isn't a problem. We'll return to the issue of overdispersion when we discuss Poisson regression.

13.2.4 Extensions

Several logistic regression extensions and variations are available in R:

- *Robust logistic regression*—The `glmRob()` function in the `robust` package can be used to fit a robust generalized linear model, including robust logistic regression. Robust logistic regression can be helpful when fitting logistic regression models to data containing outliers and influential observations.
- *Multinomial logistic regression*—If the response variable has more than two unordered categories (for example, married/widowed/divorced), you can fit a polytomous logistic regression using the `mlogit()` function in the `mlogit` package.
- *Ordinal logistic regression*—If the response variable is a set of ordered categories (for example, credit risk as poor/good/excellent), you can fit an ordinal logistic regression using the `lrm()` function in the `rms` package.

The ability to model a response variable with multiple categories (both ordered and unordered) is an important extension, but it comes at the expense of greater interpretive complexity. Assessing model fit and regression diagnostics in these cases will also be more complex.

In the Affairs example, the number of extramarital contacts was dichotomized into a yes/no response variable because our interest centered on whether respondents had an affair in the past year. If our interest had been centered on magnitude—the number of encounters in the past year—we would have analyzed the count data directly. One popular approach to analyzing count data is Poisson regression, the next topic we'll address.

13.3 *Poisson regression*

Poisson regression is useful when you're predicting an outcome variable representing counts from a set of continuous and/or categorical predictor variables. A comprehensive yet accessible introduction to Poisson regression is provided by Coxe, West, and Aiken (2009).

To illustrate the fitting of a Poisson regression model, along with some issues that can come up in the analysis, we'll use the Breslow seizure data (Breslow, 1993) provided in the `robust` package. Specifically, we'll consider the impact of an antiepileptic drug treatment on the number of seizures occurring over an eight-week period following the initiation of therapy. Be sure to install the `robust` package before continuing.

Data were collected on the age and number of seizures reported by patients suffering from simple or complex partial seizures during an eight-week period before, and eight-week period after, randomization into a drug or placebo condition. `sumY` (the number of seizures in the eight-week period post-randomization) is the response variable. Treatment condition (`Trt`), age in years (`Age`), and number of seizures reported in the baseline eight-week period (`Base`) are the predictor variables. The baseline number of seizures and age are included because of their potential effect on the response variable. We are interested in whether or not evidence exists that the drug treatment decreases the number of seizures after accounting for these covariates.

First, let's look at summary statistics for the dataset:

```
> data(breslow.dat, package="robust")
> names(breslow.dat)
 [1] "ID"    "Y1"    "Y2"    "Y3"    "Y4"    "Base"  "Age"   "Trt"   "Ysum"
[10] "sumY"  "Age10" "Base4"

> summary(breslow.dat[c(6,7,8,10)])
     Base             Age              Trt          sumY
 Min.   :  6.0   Min.   :18.0   placebo  :28   Min.   :  0.0
 1st Qu.: 12.0   1st Qu.:23.0   progabide:31   1st Qu.: 11.5
 Median : 22.0   Median :28.0                  Median : 16.0
 Mean   : 31.2   Mean   :28.3                  Mean   : 33.1
 3rd Qu.: 41.0   3rd Qu.:32.0                  3rd Qu.: 36.0
 Max.   :151.0   Max.   :42.0                  Max.   :302.0
```

Note that although there are 12 variables in the dataset, we're limiting our attention to the four described earlier. Both the baseline and post-randomization number of seizures is highly skewed. Let's look at the response variable in more detail. The following code produces the graphs in figure 13.1.

```
opar <- par(no.readonly=TRUE)
par(mfrow=c(1,2))
attach(breslow.dat)
hist(sumY, breaks=20, xlab="Seizure Count",
     main="Distribution of Seizures")
boxplot(sumY ~ Trt, xlab="Treatment", main="Group Comparisons")
par(opar)
```

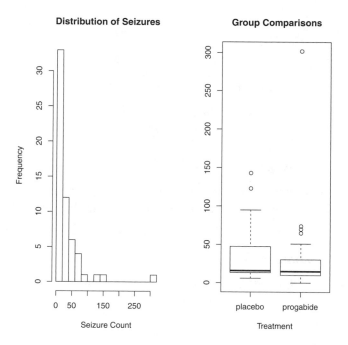

Figure 13.1 Distribution of post-treatment seizure counts (Source: Breslow seizure data)

You can clearly see the skewed nature of the dependent variable and the possible presence of outliers. At first glance, the number of seizures in the drug condition appears to be smaller and have a smaller variance. (You'd expect a smaller variance to accompany a smaller mean with Poisson distributed data.) Unlike standard OLS regression, this heterogeneity of variance isn't a problem in Poisson regression.

The next step is to fit the Poisson regression:

```
> fit <- glm(sumY ~ Base + Age + Trt, data=breslow.dat, family=poisson())
> summary(fit)

Call:
glm(formula = sumY ~ Base + Age + Trt, family = poisson(), data = breslow.
    dat)

Deviance Residuals:
   Min      1Q   Median      3Q      Max
-6.057  -2.043   -0.940   0.793   11.006

Coefficients:
             Estimate Std. Error z value Pr(>|z|)
(Intercept)  1.948826   0.135619   14.37  < 2e-16 ***
```

```
Base           0.022652   0.000509   44.48  < 2e-16 ***
Age            0.022740   0.004024    5.65  1.6e-08 ***
Trtprogabide  -0.152701   0.047805   -3.19   0.0014 **
---
Signif. codes:   0 '***' 0.001 '**' 0.01 '*' 0.05 '.' 0.1 ' ' 1

(Dispersion parameter for poisson family taken to be 1)

    Null deviance: 2122.73  on 58  degrees of freedom
Residual deviance:  559.44  on 55  degrees of freedom
AIC: 850.7

Number of Fisher Scoring iterations: 5
```

The output provides the deviances, regression parameters, standard errors, and tests that these parameters are 0. Note that each of the predictor variables is significant at the $p < 0.05$ level.

13.3.1 *Interpreting the model parameters*

The model coefficients are obtained using the `coef()` function, or by examining the `Coefficients` table in the `summary()` function output:

```
> coef(fit)
 (Intercept)        Base         Age Trtprogabide
      1.9488      0.0227      0.0227      -0.1527
```

In a Poisson regression, the dependent variable being modeled is the log of the conditional mean $\log_e(\lambda)$. The regression parameter 0.0227 for Age indicates that a one-year increase in age is associated with a 0.03 increase in the log mean number of seizures, holding baseline seizures and treatment condition constant. The intercept is the log mean number of seizures when each of the predictors equals 0. Because you can't have a zero age and none of the participants had a zero number of baseline seizures, the intercept isn't meaningful in this case.

It's usually much easier to interpret the regression coefficients in the original scale of the dependent variable (number of seizures, rather than log number of seizures). To accomplish this, exponentiate the coefficients:

```
> exp(coef(fit))
 (Intercept)        Base         Age Trtprogabide
       7.020       1.023       1.023        0.858
```

Now you see that a one-year increase in age *multiplies* the expected number of seizures by 1.023, holding the other variables constant. This means that increased age is associated with higher numbers of seizures. More importantly, a one-unit change in Trt (that is, moving from placebo to progabide) multiplies the expected number of seizures by 0.86. You'd expect a 20 percent decrease in the number of seizures for the drug group compared with the placebo group, holding baseline number of seizures and age constant.

It's important to remember that, like the exponeniated parameters in logistic regression, the exponeniated parameters in the Poisson model have a multiplicative rather than an additive effect on the response variable. Also, as with logistic regression, you must evaluate your model for overdispersion.

13.3.2 Overdispersion

In a Poisson distribution, the variance and mean are equal. Overdispersion occurs in Poisson regression when the observed variance of the response variable is larger than would be predicted by the Poisson distribution. Because overdispersion is often encountered when dealing with count data, and can have a negative impact on the interpretation of the results, we'll spend some time discussing it.

There are several reasons why overdispersion may occur (Coxe et al., 2009):

- The omission of an important predictor variable can lead to overdispersion.
- Overdispersion can also be caused by a phenomenon known as state dependence. Within observations, each event in a count is assumed to be independent. For the seizure data, this would imply that for any patient, the probability of a seizure is independent of each other seizure. But this assumption is often untenable. For a given individual, the probability of having a first seizure is unlikely to be the same as the probability of having a 40th seizure, given that they've already had 39.
- In longitudinal studies, overdispersion can be caused by the clustering inherent in repeated measures data. We won't discuss longitudinal Poisson models here.

If overdispersion is present and you don't account for it in your model, you'll get standard errors and confidence intervals that are too small, and significance tests that are too liberal (that is, you'll find effects that aren't really there).

As with logistic regression, overdispersion is suggested if the ratio of the residual deviance to the residual degrees of freedom is much larger than 1. For your seizure data, the ratio is

$$\frac{Residual\ deviance}{Residual\ df} = \frac{559.44}{55} = 10.17$$

which is clearly much larger than 1.

The qcc package provides a test for overdispersion in the Poisson case. (Be sure to download and install this package before first use.) You can test for overdispersion in the seizure data using the following code:

```
> library(qcc)
> qcc.overdispersion.test(breslow.dat$sumY, type="poisson")

Overdispersion test Obs.Var/Theor.Var Statistic p-value
        poisson data              62.9      3646       0
```

Not surprisingly, the significance test has a p-value less than 0.05, strongly suggesting the presence of overdispersion.

You can still fit a model to your data using the `glm()` function, by replacing `family="poisson"` with `family="quasipoisson"`. Doing so is analogous to our approach to logistic regression when overdispersion is present.

```
> fit.od <- glm(sumY ~ Base + Age + Trt, data=breslow.dat,
                family=quasipoisson())
> summary(fit.od)

Call:
glm(formula = sumY ~ Base + Age + Trt, family = quasipoisson(),
    data = breslow.dat)

Deviance Residuals:
   Min      1Q  Median      3Q     Max
-6.057  -2.043  -0.940   0.793  11.006

Coefficients:
             Estimate Std. Error t value Pr(>|t|)
(Intercept)   1.94883    0.46509    4.19  0.00010 ***
Base          0.02265    0.00175   12.97  < 2e-16 ***
Age           0.02274    0.01380    1.65  0.10509
Trtprogabide -0.15270    0.16394   -0.93  0.35570
---
Signif. codes:  0 '***' 0.001 '**' 0.01 '*' 0.05 '.' 0.1 ' ' 1

(Dispersion parameter for quasipoisson family taken to be 11.8)

    Null deviance: 2122.73  on 58  degrees of freedom
Residual deviance:  559.44  on 55  degrees of freedom
AIC: NA

Number of Fisher Scoring iterations: 5
```

Notice that the parameter estimates in the quasi-Poisson approach are identical to those produced by the Poisson approach. The standard errors are much larger, though. In this case, the larger standard errors have led to p-values for `Trt` (and `Age`) that are greater than 0.05. When you take overdispersion into account, there's insufficient evidence to declare that the drug regimen reduces seizure counts more than receiving a placebo, after controlling for baseline seizure rate and age.

Please remember that this example is used for demonstration purposes only. The results shouldn't be taken to imply anything about the efficacy of progabide in the real world. I'm not a doctor—at least not a medical doctor—and I don't even play one on TV.

We'll finish this exploration of Poisson regression with a discussion of some important variants and extensions.

13.3.3 *Extensions*

R provides several useful extensions to the basic Poisson regression model, including models that allow varying time periods, models that correct for too many zeros, and robust models that are useful when data includes outliers and influential observations. I'll describe each separately.

POISSON REGRESSION WITH VARYING TIME PERIODS

Our discussion of Poisson regression has been limited to response variables that measure a count over a fixed length of time (for example, number of seizures in an eight-week period, number of traffic accidents in the past year, number of pro-social behaviors in a day). The length of time is constant across observations. But you can fit Poisson regression models that allow the time period to vary for each observation. In this case, the outcome variable is a rate.

To analyze rates, you must include a variable (for example, `time`) that records the length of time over which the count occurs for each observation. You then change your model from

$$\log_e(\lambda) = \beta_0 + \sum_{j=1}^{p} \beta_j X_j$$

to

$$\log_e\left(\frac{\lambda}{time}\right) = \beta_0 + \sum_{j=1}^{p} \beta_j X_j$$

or equivalently to

$$\log_e(\lambda) = \log_e(time) + \beta_0 + \sum_{j=1}^{p} \beta_j X_j$$

To fit this new model, you use the `offset` option in the `glm()` function. For example, assume that the length of time that patients participated post-randomization in the Breslow study varied from 14 days to 60 days. You could use the rate of seizures as the dependent variable (assuming you had recorded time for each patient in days), and fit the model

```
fit <- glm(sumY ~ Base + Age + Trt, data=breslow.dat,
           offset= log(time), family=poisson())
```

where `sumY` is the number of seizures that occurred post-randomization for a patient during the time the patient was studied. In this case you're assuming that rate doesn't vary over time (for example, 2 seizures in 4 days is equivalent to 10 seizures in 20 days).

ZERO-INFLATED POISSON REGRESSION

There are times when the number of zero counts in a dataset is larger than would be predicted by the Poisson model. This can occur when there's a subgroup of the population that would never engage in the behavior being counted. For example, in the Affairs dataset described in the section on logistic regression, the original outcome variable (`affairs`) counted the number of extramarital sexual intercourse experience participants had in the past year. It's likely that there's a subgroup of faithful marital partners who would never have an affair, no matter how long the period of time studied. These are called *structural zeros* (primarily by the swingers in the group).

In such cases, you can analyze the data using an approach called *zero-inflated Poisson regression*. The approach fits two models simultaneously—one that predicts who would or would not have an affair, and the second that predicts how many affairs a participant would have if you excluded the permanently faithful. Think of this as a model that combines a logistic regression (for predicting structural zeros) and a Poisson regression model (that predicts counts for observations that aren't structural zeros). Zero-inflated Poisson regression can be fit using the `zeroinfl()` function in the `pscl` package.

ROBUST POISSON REGRESSION

Finally, the `glmRob()` function in the robust package can be used to fit a robust generalized linear model, including robust Poisson regression. As mentioned previously, this can be helpful in the presence of outliers and influential observations.

Going further

Generalized linear models are a complex and mathematically sophisticated subject, but many fine resources are available for learning about them. A good, short introduction to the topic is Dunteman and Ho (2006). The classic (and advanced) text on generalized linear models is provided by McCullagh and Nelder (1989). Comprehensive and accessible presentations are provided by Dobson and Barnett (2008) and Fox (2008). Faraway (2006) and Fox (2002) provide excellent introductions within the context of R.

13.4 Summary

In this chapter, we used generalized linear models to expand the range of approaches available for helping you to understand your data. In particular, the framework allows you to analyze response variables that are decidedly non-normal, including categorical outcomes and discrete counts. After briefly describing the general approach, we focused on logistic regression (for analyzing a dichotomous outcome) and Poisson regression (for analyzing outcomes measured as counts or rates).

We also discussed the important topic of overdispersion, including how to detect it and how to adjust for it. Finally, we looked at some of the extensions and variations that are available in R.

Each of the statistical approaches covered so far has dealt with directly observed and recorded variables. In the next chapter, we'll look at statistical models that deal with latent variables—unobserved, theoretical variables that you believe underlie and account for the behavior of the variables you do observe. In particular, you'll see how you can use factor analytic methods to detect and test hypotheses about these unobserved variables.

Principal components and factor analysis 14

One of the most challenging aspects of multivariate data is the sheer complexity of the information. If you have a dataset with 100 variables, how do you make sense of all the interrelationships present? Even with 20 variables, there are 190 pairwise correlations to consider when you're trying to understand how the individual variables relate to one another. Two related but distinct methodologies for exploring and simplifying complex multivariate data are principal components and exploratory factor analysis.

Principal components analysis (PCA) is a data reduction technique that transforms a larger number of correlated variables into a much smaller set of uncorrelated variables called principal components. For example, you might use PCA to transform 30 correlated (and possibly redundant) environmental variables into five uncorrelated composite variables that retain as much information from the original set of variables as possible.

In contrast, exploratory factor analysis (EFA) is a collection of methods designed to uncover the latent structure in a given set of variables. It looks for a smaller set of underlying or latent constructs that can explain the relationships among the observed or manifest variables. For example, the dataset `Harman74.cor` contains the correlations among 24 psychological tests given to 145 seventh- and eighth-grade children. If you apply EFA to this data, the results suggest that the 276 test intercorrelations can be explained by the children's abilities on four underlying factors (verbal ability, processing speed, deduction, and memory).

The differences between the PCA and EFA models can be seen in figure 14.1. Principal components (PC1 and PC2) are linear combinations of the observed variables (X1 to X5). The weights used to form the linear composites are chosen to maximize the variance each principal component accounts for, while keeping the components uncorrelated.

In contrast, factors (F1 and F2) are assumed to underlie or "cause" the observed variables, rather than being linear combinations of them. The errors (e1 to e5) represent the variance in the observed variables unexplained by the factors. The circles indicate that the factors and errors aren't directly observable but are inferred from the correlations among the variables. In this example, the curved arrow between the factors indicates that they're correlated. Correlated factors are common, but not required, in the EFA model.

The methods described in this chapter require large samples to derive stable solutions. What constitutes an adequate sample size is somewhat complicated. Until recently, analysts used rules of thumb like "factor analysis requires 5–10 times as many subjects as variables." Recent studies suggest that the required sample size depends on the number of factors, the number of variables associated with each factor, and how well the set of factors explains the variance in the variables (Bandalos and Boehm-Kaufman, 2009). I'll go out on a limb and say that if you have several hundred observations, you're probably safe. In this chapter, we'll look at artificially small problems in order to keep the output (and page count) manageable.

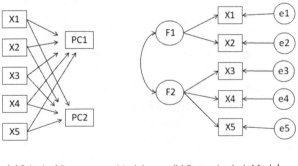

(a) Principal Components Model   (b) Factor Analysis Model

Figure 14.1   Comparing principal components and factor analysis models. The diagrams show the observed variables (X1 to X5), the principal components (PC1, PC2), factors (F1, F2), and errors (e1 to e5).

We'll start by reviewing the functions in R that can be used to perform PCA or EFA and give a brief overview of the steps involved. Then we'll work carefully through two PCA examples, followed by an extended EFA example. A brief overview of other packages in R that can be used for fitting latent variable models is provided at the end of the chapter. This discussion includes packages for confirmatory factor analysis, structural equation modeling, correspondence analysis, and latent class analysis.

14.1 Principal components and factor analysis in R

In the base installation of R, the functions for PCA and EFA are `princomp()` and `factanal()`, respectively. In this chapter, we'll focus on functions provided in the `psych` package. They offer many more useful options than their base counterparts. Additionally, the results are reported in a metric that will be more familiar to social scientists and more likely to match the output provided by corresponding programs in other statistical packages such as SAS and SPSS.

The `psych` package functions that are most relevant here are listed in table 14.1. Be sure to install the package before trying the examples in this chapter.

Table 14.1   Useful factor analytic functions in the `psych` package

Function	Description
`principal()`	Principal components analysis with optional rotation
`fa()`	Factor analysis by principal axis, minimum residual, weighted least squares, or maximum likelihood
`fa.parallel()`	Scree plots with parallel analyses
`factor.plot()`	Plot the results of a factor or principal components analysis
`fa.diagram()`	Graph factor or principal components loading matrices
`scree()`	Scree plot for factor and principal components analysis

EFA (and to a lesser degree PCA) are often confusing to new users. The reason is that they describe a wide range of approaches, and each approach requires several steps (and decisions) to achieve a final result. The most common steps are as follows:

1   *Prepare the data.* Both PCA and EFA derive their solutions from the correlations among the observed variables. Users can input either the raw data matrix or the correlation matrix to the `principal()` and `fa()` functions. If raw data is input, the correlation matrix will automatically be calculated. Be sure to screen the data for missing values before proceeding.

2   *Select a factor model.* Decide whether PCA (data reduction) or EFA (uncovering latent structure) is a better fit for your research goals. If you select an EFA approach, you'll also need to choose a specific factoring method (for example, maximum likelihood).

3 *Decide how many components/factors to extract.*
4 *Extract the components/factors.*
5 *Rotate the components/factors.*
6 *Interpret the results.*
7 *Compute component or factor scores.*

In the remainder of this chapter, we'll carefully consider each of the steps, starting with PCA. At the end of the chapter, you'll find a detailed flow chart of the possible steps in PCA/EFA (figure 14.7). The chart will make more sense once you've read through the intervening material.

14.2 Principal components

The goal of PCA is to replace a large number of correlated variables with a smaller number of uncorrelated variables while capturing as much information in the original variables as possible. These derived variables, called principal components, are linear combinations of the observed variables. Specifically, the first principal component

$$PC_1 = a_1 X_1 + a_2 X_2 + \ldots + a_k X_k$$

is the weighted combination of the k observed variables that accounts for the most variance in the original set of variables. The second principal component is the linear combination that accounts for the most variance in the original variables, under the constraint that it's *orthogonal* (uncorrelated) to the first principal component. Each subsequent component maximizes the variance accounted for, while at the same time remaining uncorrelated with all previous components. Theoretically, you can extract as many principal components as there are variables. But from a practical viewpoint, you hope that you can approximate the full set of variables with a much smaller set of components. Let's look at a simple example.

The dataset USJudgeRatings contains lawyers' ratings of state judges in the US Superior Court. The data frame contains 43 observations on 12 numeric variables. The variables are listed in table 14.2.

Table 14.2 Variables in the `USJudgeRatings` dataset

Variable	Description	Variable	Description
CONT	Number of contacts of lawyer with judge	PREP	Preparation for trial
INTG	Judicial integrity	FAMI	Familiarity with law
DMNR	Demeanor	ORAL	Sound oral rulings
DILG	Diligence	WRIT	Sound written rulings
CFMG	Case flow managing	PHYS	Physical ability
DECI	Prompt decisions	RTEN	Worthy of retention

From a practical point of view, can you summarize the 11 evaluative ratings (INTG to RTEN) with a smaller number of composite variables? If so, how many will you need and how will they be defined? Because our goal is to simplify the data, we'll approach this problem using PCA. The data are in raw score format and there are no missing values. Therefore, your next decision is deciding how many principal components you'll need.

14.2.1 *Selecting the number of components to extract*

Several criteria are available for deciding how many components to retain in a PCA. They include:

- Basing the number of components on prior experience and theory
- Selecting the number of components needed to account for some threshold cumulative amount of variance in the variables (for example, 80 percent)
- Selecting the number of components to retain by examining the eigenvalues of the k x k correlation matrix among the variables

The most common approach is based on the eigenvalues. Each component is associated with an eigenvalue of the correlation matrix. The first PC is associated with the largest eigenvalue, the second PC with the second-largest eigenvalue, and so on. The Kaiser–Harris criterion suggests retaining components with eigenvalues greater than 1. Components with eigenvalues less than 1 explain less variance than contained in a single variable. In the Cattell Scree test, the eigenvalues are plotted against their component numbers. Such plots will typically demonstrate a bend or elbow, and the components above this sharp break are retained. Finally, you can run simulations, extracting eigenvalues from random data matrices of the same size as the original matrix. If an eigenvalue based on real data is larger than the average corresponding eigenvalues from a set of random data matrices, that component is retained. The approach is called *parallel analysis* (see Hayton, Allen, and Scarpello, 2004 for more details).

You can assess all three eigenvalue criteria at the same time via the `fa.parallel()` function. For the 11 ratings (dropping the CONT variable), the necessary code is as follows:

```
library(psych)
fa.parallel(USJudgeRatings[,-1], fa="PC", n.iter=100,
         show.legend=FALSE, main="Scree plot with parallel analysis")
```

This code produces the graph shown in figure 14.2. The plot displays the scree test based on the observed eigenvalues (as straight-line segments and x's), the mean eigenvalues derived from 100 random data matrices (as dashed lines), and the eigenvalues greater than 1 criteria (as a horizontal line at y=1).

All three criteria suggest that a single component is appropriate for summarizing this dataset. Your next step is to extract the principal component using the `principal()` function.

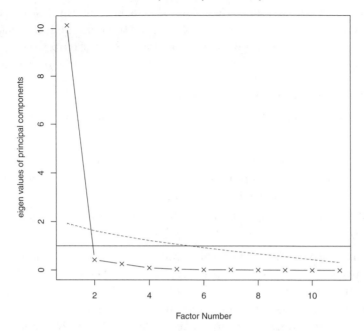

Scree plot with parallel analysis

Figure 14.2   **Assessing the number of principal components to retain for the US Judge Rating example. A scree plot (the line with x's), eigenvalues greater than 1 criteria (horizontal line), and parallel analysis with 100 simulations (dashed line) suggest retaining a single component.**

14.2.2 *Extracting principal components*

As indicated earlier, the `principal()` function will perform a principal components analysis starting with either a raw data matrix or a correlation matrix. The format is

```
principal(r, nfactors=, rotate=, scores=)
```

where

- *r* is a correlation matrix or a raw data matrix
- `nfactors` specifies the number of principal components to extract (1 by default)
- `rotate` indicates the rotation to be applied (varimax by default; see section 14.2.3)
- `scores` specifies whether or not to calculate principal component scores (false by default)

To extract the first principal component, you can use the code in the following listing.

Listing 14.1   Principal components analysis of US Judge Ratings

```
> library(psych)
> pc <- principal(USJudgeRatings[,-1], nfactors=1)
> pc
```

```
Principal Components Analysis
Call: principal(r = USJudgeRatings[, -1], nfactors=1)
Standardized loadings based upon correlation matrix
       PC1   h2    u2
INTG 0.92 0.84 0.157
DMNR 0.91 0.83 0.166
DILG 0.97 0.94 0.061
CFMG 0.96 0.93 0.072
DECI 0.96 0.92 0.076
PREP 0.98 0.97 0.030
FAMI 0.98 0.95 0.047
ORAL 1.00 0.99 0.009
WRIT 0.99 0.98 0.020
PHYS 0.89 0.80 0.201
RTEN 0.99 0.97 0.028


                     PC1
SS loadings        10.13
Proportion Var      0.92
[… additional output omitted …]
```

Here, you're inputting the raw data without the CONT variable and specifying that one unrotated component should be extracted. (Rotation will be explained in section 14.3.3.) Because PCA is performed on a correlation matrix, the raw data is automatically converted to a correlation matrix before extracting the components.

The column labeled PC1 contains the component *loadings,* which are the correlations of the observed variables with the principal component(s). If you had extracted more than one principal component, there would be columns for PC2, PC3, and so on. Component loadings are used to interpret the meaning of components. You can see that each variable correlates highly with the first component (PC1). It therefore appears to be a general evaluative dimension.

The column labeled h2 contains the component *communalities*—the amount of variance in each variable explained by the components. The u2 column contains the component *uniquenesses,* the amount of variance not accounted for by the components (or 1–h2). For example, 80 percent of the variance in physical ability (PHYS) ratings is accounted for by the first PC, and 20 percent is not. PHYS is the variable least well represented by a one-component solution.

The row labeled SS loadings contains the eigenvalues associated with the components. The eigenvalues are the standardized variance associated with a particular component (in this case, the value for the first component is 10.). Finally, the row labeled Proportion Var represents the amount of variance accounted for by each component. Here you see that the first principal component accounts for 92 percent of the variance in the 11 variables.

Let's consider a second example, one that results in a solution with more than one principal component. The dataset Harman23.cor contains data on 8 body measurements for 305 girls. In this case, the dataset consists of the correlations among the variables rather than the original data (see table 14.3).

Table 14.3   Correlations among body measurements for 305 girls (`Harman23.cor`)

	height	arm span	forearm	lower leg	weight	bitro diameter	chest girth	chest width
height	1.00	0.85	0.80	0.86	0.47	0.40	0.30	0.38
arm span	0.85	1.00	0.88	0.83	0.38	0.33	0.28	0.41
forearm	0.80	0.88	1.00	0.80	0.38	0.32	0.24	0.34
lower.leg	0.86	0.83	0.8	1.00	0.44	0.33	0.33	0.36
weight	0.47	0.38	0.38	0.44	1.00	0.76	0.73	0.63
bitro diameter	0.40	0.33	0.32	0.33	0.76	1.00	0.58	0.58
chest girth	0.30	0.28	0.24	0.33	0.73	0.58	1.00	0.54
chest width	0.38	0.41	0.34	0.36	0.63	0.58	0.54	1.00

Source: Harman, H. H. (1976) *Modern Factor Analysis, Third Edition Revised*, University of Chicago Press, Table 2.3.

Again, you wish to replace the original physical measurements with a smaller number of derived variables. You can determine the number of components to extract using the following code. In this case, you need to identify the correlation matrix (the `cov` component of the `Harman23.cor` object) and specify the sample size (`n.obs`):

```
library(psych)
fa.parallel(Harman23.cor$cov, n.obs=302, fa="pc", n.iter=100,
            show.legend=FALSE, main="Scree plot with parallel analysis")
```

The resulting graph is displayed in figure 14.3.

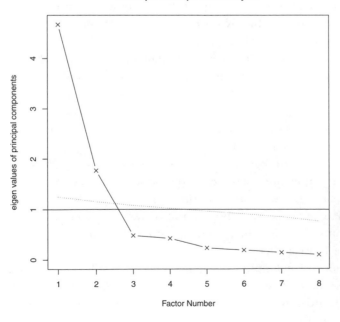

Scree plot with parallel analysis

Figure 14.3   Assessing the number of principal components to retain for the Body Measurements example. The scree plot (line with x's), eigenvalues greater than 1 criteria (horizontal line), and parallel analysis with 100 simulations (dashed line) suggest retaining two components.

You can see from the plot that a two-component solution is suggested. As in the first example, the Kaiser–Harris criteria, scree test, and parallel analysis agree. This won't always be the case, and you may need to extract different numbers of components and select the solution that appears most useful. The next listing extracts the first two principal components from the correlation matrix.

Listing 14.2   Principal components analysis of body measurements

```
> library(psych)
> PC <- principal(Harman23.cor$cov, nfactors=2, rotate="none")
> PC

Principal Components Analysis
Call: principal(r = Harman23.cor$cov, nfactors = 2, rotate = "none")
Standardized loadings based upon correlation matrix
                 PC1   PC2   h2    u2
height          0.86 -0.37 0.88 0.123
arm.span        0.84 -0.44 0.90 0.097
forearm         0.81 -0.46 0.87 0.128
lower.leg       0.84 -0.40 0.86 0.139
weight          0.76  0.52 0.85 0.150
bitro.diameter  0.67  0.53 0.74 0.261
chest.girth     0.62  0.58 0.72 0.283
chest.width     0.67  0.42 0.62 0.375


                 PC1   PC2
SS loadings     4.67  1.77
Proportion Var  0.58  0.22
Cumulative Var  0.58  0.81
```

`[… additional output omitted …]`

If you examine the `PC1` and `PC2` columns in listing 14.2, you see that the first component accounts for 58 percent of the variance in the physical measurements, while the second component accounts for 22 percent. Together, the two components account for 81 percent of the variance. The two components together account for 88 percent of the variance in the height variable.

Components and factors are interpreted by examining their loadings. The first component correlates positively with each physical measure and appears to be a general size factor. The second component contrasts the first four variables (`height`, `arm.span`, `forearm`, and `lower.leg`), with the second four variables (`weight`, `bitro.diameter`, `chest.girth`, and `chest.width`). It therefore appears to be a length-versus-volume factor. Conceptually, this isn't an easy construct to work with. Whenever two or more components have been extracted, you can rotate the solution to make it more interpretable. This is the topic we'll turn to next.

14.2.3 *Rotating principal components*

Rotations are a set of mathematical techniques for transforming the component loading matrix into one that's more interpretable. They do this by "purifying" the components as much as possible. Rotation methods differ with regard to whether the resulting components remain uncorrelated (*orthogonal rotation*) or are allowed to correlate (*oblique rotation*). They also differ in their definition of purifying. The most popular orthogonal rotation is the *varimax* rotation, which attempts to purify the columns of the loading matrix, so that each component is defined by a limited set of variables (that is, each column has a few large loadings and many very small loadings). Applying a varimax rotation to the body measurement data, you get the results provided in the next listing. You'll see an example of an oblique rotation in section 14.4.

Listing 14.3   Principal components analysis with varimax rotation

```
> rc <- principal(Harman23.cor$cov, nfactors=2, rotate="varimax")
> rc

Principal Components Analysis
Call: principal(r = Harman23.cor$cov, nfactors = 2, rotate = "varimax")
Standardized loadings based upon correlation matrix
               RC1   RC2   h2    u2
height         0.90 0.25 0.88 0.123
arm.span       0.93 0.19 0.90 0.097
forearm        0.92 0.16 0.87 0.128
lower.leg      0.90 0.22 0.86 0.139
weight         0.26 0.88 0.85 0.150
bitro.diameter 0.19 0.84 0.74 0.261
chest.girth    0.11 0.84 0.72 0.283
chest.width    0.26 0.75 0.62 0.375

               RC1   RC2
SS loadings    3.52 2.92
Proportion Var 0.44 0.37
Cumulative Var 0.44 0.81

[… additional output omitted …]
```

The column names change from PC to RC to denote rotated components. Looking at the loadings in column RC1, you see that the first component is primarily defined by the first four variables (length variables). The loadings in the column RC2 indicate that the second component is primarily defined by variables 5 through 8 (volume variables). Note that the two components are still uncorrelated and that together, they still explain the variables equally well. You can see that the rotated solution explains the variables equally well because the variable communalities haven't changed. Additionally, the cumulative variance accounted for by the two-component rotated solution (81 percent) hasn't changed. But the proportion of variance accounted for by each individual component has changed (from 58 percent to 44 percent for component 1 and from 22 percent to 37 percent for component 2). This spreading out of the variance across components is common, and technically you should now call them components rather than principal components (because the variance maximizing properties of individual components has not been retained).

Our ultimate goal is to replace a larger set of correlated variables with a smaller set of derived variables. To do this, you need to obtain scores for each observation on the components.

14.2.4 Obtaining principal components scores

In the US Judge Rating example, you extracted a single principal component from the raw data describing lawyers' ratings on 11 variables. The `principal()` function makes it easy to obtain scores for each participant on this derived variable (see the next listing).

Listing 14.4 Obtaining component scores from raw data

```
> library(psych)
> pc <- principal(USJudgeRatings[,-1], nfactors=1, score=TRUE)
> head(pc$scores)
                      PC1
AARONSON,L.H.   -0.1857981
ALEXANDER,J.M.   0.7469865
ARMENTANO,A.J.   0.0704772
BERDON,R.I.      1.1358765
BRACKEN,J.J.    -2.1586211
BURNS,E.B.       0.7669406
```

The principal component scores are saved in the `scores` element of the object returned by the `principal()` function when the option `scores=TRUE`. If you wanted, you could now get the correlation between the number of contacts occurring between a lawyer and a judge and their evaluation of the judge using

```
> cor(USJudgeRatings$CONT, PC$score)
             PC1
[1,] -0.008815895
```

Apparently, there's no relationship between the lawyer's familiarity and his or her opinions!

When the principal components analysis is based on a correlation matrix and the raw data aren't available, getting principal component scores for each observation is clearly not possible. But you can get the coefficients used to calculate the principal components.

In the body measurement data, you have correlations among body measurements, but you don't have the individual measurements for these 305 girls. You can get the scoring coefficients using the code in the following listing.

Listing 14.5 Obtaining principal component scoring coefficients

```
> library(psych)
> rc <- principal(Harman23.cor$cov, nfactors=2, rotate="varimax")
> round(unclass(rc$weights), 2)
             RC1   RC2
height      0.28 -0.05
arm.span    0.30 -0.08
```

```
forearm             0.30 -0.09
lower.leg           0.28 -0.06
weight             -0.06  0.33
bitro.diameter     -0.08  0.32
chest.girth        -0.10  0.34
chest.width        -0.04  0.27
```

The component scores are obtained using the formulas

```
PC1 = 0.28*height + 0.30*arm.span + 0.30*forearm + 0.29*lower.leg -
      0.06*weight - 0.08*bitro.diameter - 0.10*chest.girth -
      0.04*chest.width
```

and

```
PC2 = -0.05*height - 0.08*arm.span - 0.09*forearm - 0.06*lower.leg +
      0.33*weight + 0.32*bitro.diameter + 0.34*chest.girth +
      0.27*chest.width
```

These equations assume that the physical measurements have been standardized (mean=0, sd=1). Note that the weights for PC1 tend to be around 0.3 or 0. The same is true for PC2. As a practical matter, you could simplify your approach further by taking the first composite variable as the mean of the standardized scores for the first four variables. Similarly, you could define the second composite variable as the mean of the standardized scores for the second four variables. This is typically what I'd do in practice.

Little Jiffy conquers the world

There's quite a bit of confusion among data analysts regarding PCA and EFA. One reason for this is historical and can be traced back to a program called Little Jiffy (no kidding). Little Jiffy was one of the most popular early programs for factor analysis, and defaulted to a principal components analysis, extracting components with eigenvalues greater than 1 and rotating them to a varimax solution. The program was so widely used that many social scientists came to think of this defaults as synonymous with EFA. Many later statistical packages also incorporated these defaults in their EFA programs.

As I hope you'll see in the next section, there are important and fundamental differences between PCA and EFA. To learn more about the PCA/EFA confusion, see Hayton, Allen, and Scarpello, 2004.

If your goal is to look for latent underlying variables that explain your observed variables, you can turn to factor analysis. This is the topic of the next section.

14.3 *Exploratory factor analysis*

The goal of EFA is to explain the correlations among a set of observed variables by uncovering a smaller set of more fundamental unobserved variables underlying the data. These hypothetical, unobserved variables are called *factors*. (Each factor is assumed to explain the variance shared among two or more observed variables, so technically, they are called *common factors*.)

The model can be represented as

$$X_i = a_1 F_1 + a_2 F_2 + \ldots + a_p F_p + U_i$$

where X_i is the ith observed variable (i = 1...k), F_j are the common factors (j=1...p), and p<k. U_i is the portion of variable X_i unique to that variable (not explained by the common factors). The a_i can be thought of as the degree to which each factor contributes to the composition of an observed variable. If we go back to the `Harman74.cor` example at the beginning of this chapter, we'd say that an individual's scores on each of the 24 observed psychological tests is due to a weighted combination of their ability on four underlying psychological constructs.

Although the PCA and EFA models differ, many of the steps will appear similar. To illustrate the process, we'll apply EFA to the correlations among six psychological tests. One hundred twelve individuals were given six tests, including a nonverbal measure of general intelligence (`general`), a picture-completion test (`picture`), a block design test (`blocks`), a maze test (`maze`), a reading comprehension test (`reading`), and a vocabulary test (`vocab`). Can we explain the participants' scores on these tests with a smaller number of underlying or latent psychological constructs?

The covariance matrix among the variables is provided in the dataset `ability.cov`. You can transform this into a correlation matrix using the `cov2cor()` function. There are no missing data present.

```
> options(digits=2)
> covariances <- ability.cov$cov
> correlations <- cov2cor(covariances)
> correlations
        general picture blocks maze reading vocab
general    1.00    0.47   0.55 0.34    0.58  0.51
picture    0.47    1.00   0.57 0.19    0.26  0.24
blocks     0.55    0.57   1.00 0.45    0.35  0.36
maze       0.34    0.19   0.45 1.00    0.18  0.22
reading    0.58    0.26   0.35 0.18    1.00  0.79
vocab      0.51    0.24   0.36 0.22    0.79  1.00
```

Because you're looking for hypothetical constructs that explain the data, you'll use an EFA approach. As in PCA, the next task is to decide how many factors to extract.

14.3.1 Deciding how many common factors to extract

To decide on the number of factors to extract, turn to the `fa.parallel()` function:

```
> library(psych)
> covariances <- ability.cov$cov
> correlations <- cov2cor(covariances)
> fa.parallel(correlations, n.obs=112, fa="both", n.iter=100,
              main="Scree plots with parallel analysis")
```

The resulting plot is shown in figure 14.4. Notice you've requested that the function display results for both a principal components and common factor approach, so that you can compare them (`fa="both"`).

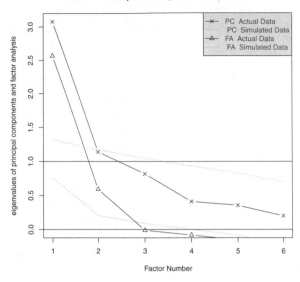

Figure 14.4   **Assessing the number of factors to retain for the psychological tests example. Results for both PCA and EFA are present. The PCA results suggest one or two components. The EFA results suggest two factors.**

There are several things to notice in this graph. If you'd taken a PCA approach, you might have chosen one component (scree test, parallel analysis) or two components (eigenvalues greater than 1). When in doubt, it's usually a better idea to overfactor than to underfactor. Overfactoring tends to lead to less distortion of the "true" solution.

Looking at the EFA results, a two-factor solution is clearly indicated. The first two eigenvalues (triangles) are above the bend in the scree test and also above the mean eigenvalues based on 100 simulated data matrices. For EFA, the Kaiser–Harris criterion is number of eigenvalues above 0, rather than 1. (Most people don't realize this, so it's a good way to win bets at parties.) In the present case the Kaiser–Harris criteria also suggest two factors.

14.3.2 *Extracting common factors*

Now that you've decided to extract two factors, you can use the `fa()` function to obtain your solution. The format of the `fa()` function is

```
fa(r, nfactors=, n.obs=, rotate=, scores=, fm=)
```

where

- `r` is a correlation matrix or a raw data matrix
- `nfactors` specifies the number of factors to extract (1 by default)
- `n.obs` is the number of observations (if a correlation matrix is input)
- `rotate` indicates the rotation to be applied (oblimin by default)
- `scores` specifies whether or not to calculate factor scores (false by default)
- `fm` specifies the factoring method (minres by default)

Unlike PCA, there are many methods of extracting common factors. They include maximum likelihood (`ml`), iterated principal axis (`pa`), weighted least square (`wls`), generalized weighted least squares (`gls`), and minimum residual (`minres`). Statisticians tend to prefer the maximum likelihood approach because of its well-defined statistical model. Sometimes, this approach fails to converge, in which case the iterated principal axis option often works well. To learn more about the different approaches, see Mulaik (2009) and Gorsuch (1983).

For this example, you'll extract the unrotated factors using the iterated principal axis (`fm="pa"`) approach. The results are given in the next listing.

Listing 14.6 Principal axis factoring without rotation

```
> fa <- fa(correlations, nfactors=2, rotate="none", fm="pa")
> fa
Factor Analysis using method =  pa
Call: fa(r = correlations, nfactors = 2, rotate = "none", fm = "pa")
Standardized loadings based upon correlation matrix
          PA1    PA2   h2   u2
general 0.75   0.07 0.57 0.43
picture 0.52   0.32 0.38 0.62
blocks  0.75   0.52 0.83 0.17
maze    0.39   0.22 0.20 0.80
reading 0.81 -0.51 0.91 0.09
vocab   0.73 -0.39 0.69 0.31


                PA1   PA2
SS loadings     2.75  0.83
Proportion Var  0.46  0.14
Cumulative Var  0.46  0.60
[… additional output deleted …]
```

You can see that the two factors account for 60 percent of the variance in the six psychological tests. When you examine the loadings, though, they aren't easy to interpret. Rotating them should help.

14.3.3 Rotating factors

You can rotate the two-factor solution from section 14.3.4 using either an orthogonal rotation or an oblique rotation. Let's try both so you can see how they differ. First try an orthogonal rotation (in the next listing).

Listing 14.7 Factor extraction with orthogonal rotation

```
> fa.varimax <- fa(correlations, nfactors=2, rotate="varimax", fm="pa")
> fa.varimax
Factor Analysis using method =  pa
Call: fa(r = correlations, nfactors = 2, rotate = "varimax", fm = "pa")
Standardized loadings based upon correlation matrix
          PA1  PA2   h2   u2
general 0.49 0.57 0.57 0.43
picture 0.16 0.59 0.38 0.62
blocks  0.18 0.89 0.83 0.17
maze    0.13 0.43 0.20 0.80
reading 0.93 0.20 0.91 0.09
```

```
vocab    0.80 0.23 0.69 0.31

                    PA1  PA2
SS loadings     1.83 1.75
Proportion Var 0.30 0.29
Cumulative Var 0.30 0.60
```

[... additional output omitted ...]

Looking at the factor loadings, the factors are certainly easier to interpret. Reading and vocabulary load on the first factor, and picture completion, block design, and mazes loads on the second factor. The general nonverbal intelligence measure loads on both factors. This may indicate a verbal intelligence factor and a nonverbal intelligence factor.

By using an orthogonal rotation, you've artificially forced the two factors to be uncorrelated. What would you find if you allowed the two factors to correlate? You can try an oblique rotation such as *promax* (see the next listing).

Listing 14.8   Factor extraction with oblique rotation

```
> fa.promax <- fa(correlations, nfactors=2, rotate="promax", fm="pa")
> fa.promax
Factor Analysis using method =  pa
Call: fa(r = correlations, nfactors = 2, rotate = "promax", fm = "pa")
Standardized loadings based upon correlation matrix
          PA1   PA2   h2   u2
general  0.36  0.49 0.57 0.43
picture -0.04  0.64 0.38 0.62
blocks  -0.12  0.98 0.83 0.17
maze    -0.01  0.45 0.20 0.80
reading  1.01 -0.11 0.91 0.09
vocab    0.84 -0.02 0.69 0.31

                    PA1  PA2
SS loadings     1.82 1.76
Proportion Var 0.30 0.29
Cumulative Var 0.30 0.60

 With factor correlations of
      PA1   PA2
PA1 1.00 0.57
PA2 0.57 1.00
[... additional output omitted ...]
```

Several differences exist between the orthogonal and oblique solutions. In an orthogonal solution, attention focuses on the *factor structure matrix* (the correlations of the variables with the factors). In an oblique solution, there are three matrices to consider: the factor structure matrix, the factor pattern matrix, and the factor intercorrelation matrix.

The *factor pattern matrix* is a matrix of standardized regression coefficients. They give the weights for predicting the variables from the factors. The *factor intercorrelation matrix* gives the correlations among the factors.

In listing 14.8, the values in the PA1 and PA2 columns constitute the factor pattern matrix. They're standardized regression coefficients rather than correlations. Examination of the columns of this matrix is still used to name the factors (although there's some controversy here). Again you'd find a verbal and nonverbal factor.

The factor intercorrelation matrix indicates that the correlation between the two factors is 0.57. This is a hefty correlation. If the factor intercorrelations had been low, you might have gone back to an orthogonal solution to keep things simple.

The factor structure matrix (or factor loading matrix) isn't provided. But you can easily calculate it using the formula F = P*Phi, where F is the factor loading matrix, P is the factor pattern matrix, and Phi is the factor intercorrelation matrix. A simple function for carrying out the multiplication is as follows:

```
fsm <- function(oblique) {
    if (class(oblique)[2]=="fa" & is.null(oblique$Phi)) {
        warning("Object doesn't look like oblique EFA")
    } else {
        P <- unclass(oblique$loading)
        F <- P %*% oblique$Phi
        colnames(F) <- c("PA1", "PA2")
        return(F)
    }
}
```

Applying this to the example, you get

```
> fsm(fa.promax)
          PA1  PA2
general 0.64 0.69
picture 0.33 0.61
blocks  0.44 0.91
maze    0.25 0.45
reading 0.95 0.47
vocab   0.83 0.46
```

Now you can review the correlations between the variables and the factors. Comparing them to the factor loading matrix in the orthogonal solution, you see that these columns aren't as pure. This is because you've allowed the underlying factors to be correlated. Although the oblique approach is more complicated, it's often a more realistic model of the data.

You can graph an orthogonal or oblique solution using the factor.plot() or fa.diagram() function. The code

```
 factor.plot(fa.promax, labels=rownames(fa.promax$loadings))
```

produces the graph in figure 14.5.

The code

```
fa.diagram(fa.promax, simple=FALSE)
```

produces the diagram in figure 14.6. If you let simple=TRUE, only the largest loading per item would be displayed. It shows the largest loadings for each factor, as well as the correlations between the factors. This type of diagram is helpful when there are several factors.

Factor Analysis

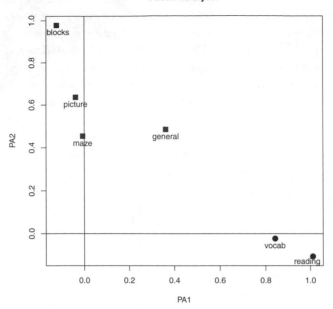

Figure 14.5   Two factor plot for the psychological tests in ability.cov. Vocab and reading load on the first factor (PA1). while blocks, picture, and maze load on the second factor (PA2). The general intelligence test loads on both.

When you're dealing with data in real life, it's unlikely that you'd apply factor analysis to a dataset with so few variables. You've done it here to keep things manageable. If you'd like to test your skills, try factor-analyzing the 24 psychological tests contained in Harman74.cor. The code

```
library(psych)
fa.24tests <- fa(Harman74.cor$cov, nfactors=4, rotate="promax")
```

should get you started!

Factor Analysis

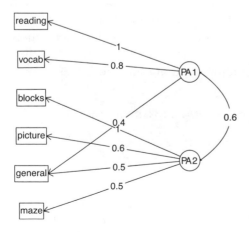

Figure 14.6   Diagram of the oblique two factor solution for the psychological test data in ability.cov

14.3.4 Factor scores

Compared with PCA, the goal of EFA is much less likely to be the calculation of factor scores. But these scores are easily obtained from the `fa()` function by including the `score=TRUE` option (when raw data is available). Additionally, the scoring coefficients (standardized regression weights) are available in the `weights` element of the object returned.

For the `ability.cov` dataset, you can obtain the beta weights for calculating the factor score estimates for the two-factor oblique solution using

```
> fa.promax$weights
          [,1]  [,2]
general 0.080 0.210
picture 0.021 0.090
blocks  0.044 0.695
maze    0.027 0.035
reading 0.739 0.044
vocab   0.176 0.039
```

Unlike component scores, which are calculated exactly, factor scores can only be estimated. Several methods exist. The fa() function uses the regression approach. To learn more about factor scores, see DiStefano, Zhu, and Mîndrilă, (2009).

Before moving on, let's briefly review other R packages that are useful for exploratory factor analysis.

14.3.5 Other EFA-related packages

R contains a number of other contributed packages that are useful for conducting factor analyses. The `FactoMineR` package provides methods for PCA and EFA, as well as other latent variable models. It provides many options that we haven't considered here, including the use of both numeric and categorical variables. The `FAiR` package estimates factor analysis models using a genetic algorithm that permits the ability to impose inequality restrictions on model parameters. The `GPArotation` package offers many additional factor rotation methods. Finally, the `nFactors` package offers sophisticated techniques for determining the number of factors underlying data.

14.4 Other latent variable models

EFA is only one of a wide range of latent variable models used in statistics. We'll end this chapter with a brief description of other models that can be fit within R. These include models that test a priori theories, that can handle mixed data types (numeric and categorical), or that are based solely on categorical multiway tables.

In EFA, you allow the data to determine the number of factors to be extracted and their meaning. But you could start with a theory about how many factors underlie a set of variables, how the variables load on those factors, and how the factors correlate with one another. You could then test this theory against a set of collected data. The approach is called confirmatory factor analysis (CFA).

CFA is a subset of a methodology called structural equation modeling (SEM). SEM not only allows you to posit the number and composition of underlying factors but how these factors impact one another as well. You can think of SEM as a combination of confirmatory factor analyses (for the variables) and regression analyses (for the factors). The resulting output includes statistical tests and fit indices. There are several excellent packages for CFA and SEM in R. They include `sem`, `openMx`, and `lavaan`.

The `ltm` package can be used to fit latent models to the items contained in tests and questionnaires. The methodology is often used to create large scale standardized tests. Examples include the Scholastic Aptitude Test (SAT) and the Graduate Record Exam (GRE).

Latent class models (where the underlying factors are assumed to be categorical rather than continuous) can be fit with the `FlexMix`, `lcmm`, `randomLCA`, and `poLC` packages. The `lcda` package performs latent class discriminant analysis, and the `lsa` package performs latent semantic analysis, a methodology used in natural language processing.

The `ca` package provides functions for simple and multiple correspondence analysis. These methods allow you to explore the structure of categorical variables in two-way and multiway tables, respectively.

Finally, R contains numerous methods for multidimensional scaling (MDS). MDS is designed to detect underlying dimensions that explain the similarities and distances between a set of measured objects (for example, countries). The `cmdscale()` function in the base installation performs a classical MDS, while the `isoMDS()` function in the MASS package performs a nonmetric MDS. The `vegan` package also contains functions for classical and nonmetric MDS.

14.5 *Summary*

In this chapter, we reviewed methods for principal components (PCA) analysis and exploratory factor analysis (EFA). PCA is a useful data reduction method that can replace a large number of correlated variables with a smaller number of uncorrelated variables, simplifying the analyses. EFA contains a broad range of methods for identifying latent or unobserved constructs (factors) that may underlie a set of observed or manifest variables.

Whereas the goal of PCA is typically to summarize the data and reduce its dimensionality, EFA can be used as a hypothesis generating tool, useful when you're trying to understand the relationships between a large number of variables. It's often used in the social sciences for theory development.

Although there are many superficial similarities between the two approaches, important differences exist as well. In this chapter, we considered the models underlying each, methods for selecting the number of components/factors to extract, methods for extracting components/factors and rotating (transforming) them to enhance interpretability, and techniques for obtaining component or factor scores. The steps in a PCA or EFA are summarized in figure 14.7. We ended the chapter with a brief discussion of other latent variable methods available in R.

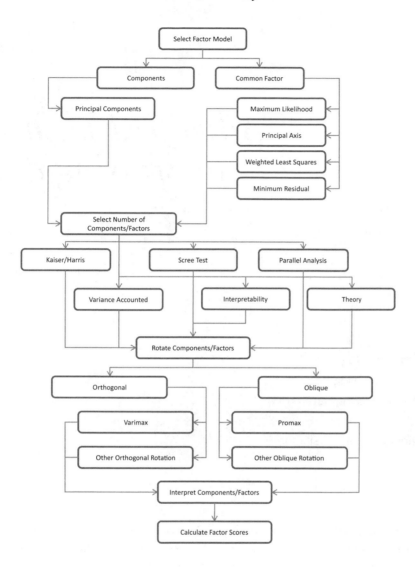

Figure 14.7   A principal components/exploratory factor analysis decision chart

Because PCA and EFA are based on correlation matrices, it's important that any missing data be eliminated before proceeding with the analyses. Section 4.5 briefly mentioned simple methods for dealing with missing data. In the next chapter, we'll consider more sophisticated methods for both understanding and handling missing values.

Advanced methods for missing data

15

This chapter covers

- Identification of missing data
- Visualization of missing data patterns
- Complete-case analysis
- Multiple imputation of missing data

In previous chapters, we focused on the analysis of complete datasets (that is, datasets without missing values). Although doing so has helped simplify the presentation of statistical and graphical methods, in the real world, missing data are ubiquitous.

In some ways, the impact of missing data is a subject that most of us want to avoid. Statistics books may not mention it or may limit discussion to a few paragraphs. Statistical packages offer automatic handling of missing data using methods that may not be optimal. Even though most data analyses (at least in social sciences) involve missing data, this topic is rarely mentioned in the methods and results sections of journal articles. Given how often missing values occur, and the degree to which their presence can invalidate study results, it's fair to say that the subject has received insufficient attention outside of specialized books and courses.

Data can be missing for many reasons. Survey participants may forget to answer one or more questions, refuse to answer sensitive questions, or grow fatigued and fail to complete a long questionnaire. Study participants may miss appointments or drop out of a study prematurely. Recording equipment may fail, internet connections may be lost, and data may be miscoded. The presence of missing data may even be planned. For example, to increase study efficiency or reduce costs, you may choose not to collect all data from all participants. Finally, data may be lost for reasons that you're never able to ascertain.

Unfortunately, most statistical methods assume that you're working with complete matrices, vectors, and data frames. In most cases, you have to eliminate missing data before you address the substantive questions that led you to collect the data. You can eliminate missing data by (1) removing cases with missing data, or (2) replacing missing data with reasonable substitute values. In either case, the end result is a dataset without missing values.

In this chapter, we'll look at both traditional and modern approaches for dealing with missing data. We'll primarily use the VIM and mice packages. The command `install.packages(c("VIM", "mice"))` will download and install both.

To motivate the discussion, we'll look at the mammal sleep dataset (sleep) provided in the VIM package (not to be confused with the sleep dataset describing the impact of drugs on sleep provided in the base installation). The data come from a study by Allison and Chichetti (1976) that examined the relationship between sleep, ecological, and constitutional variables for 62 mammal species. The authors were interested in why animals' sleep requirements vary from species to species. The sleep variables served as the dependent variables, whereas the ecological and constitutional variables served as the independent or predictor variables.

Sleep variables included length of dreaming sleep (Dream), nondreaming sleep (NonD), and their sum (Sleep). The constitutional variables included body weight in kilograms (BodyWgt), brain weight in grams (BrainWgt), life span in years (Span), and gestation time in days (Gest). The ecological variables included degree to which species were preyed upon (Pred), degree of their exposure while sleeping (Exp), and overall danger (Danger) faced. The ecological variables were measured on 5-point rating scales that ranged from 1 (low) to 5 (high).

In their original article, Allison and Chichetti limited their analyses to the species that had complete data. We'll go further, analyzing all 62 cases using a multiple imputation approach.

15.1 Steps in dealing with missing data

Readers new to the study of missing data will find a bewildering array of approaches, critiques, and methodologies. The classic text in this area is Little and Rubin (2002). Excellent, accessible reviews can be found in Allison (2001), Schafer and Graham (2002) and Schlomer, Bauman, and Card (2010). A comprehensive approach will usually include the following steps:

1　Identify the missing data.
2　Examine the causes of the missing data.
3　Delete the cases containing missing data or replace (impute) the missing values with reasonable alternative data values.

Unfortunately, identifying missing data is usually the only unambiguous step. Learning why data are missing depends on your understanding of the processes that generated the data. Deciding how to treat missing values will depend on your estimation of which procedures will produce the most reliable and accurate results.

A classification system for missing data

Statisticians typically classify missing data into one of three types. These types are usually described in probabilistic terms, but the underlying ideas are straightforward. We'll use the measurement of dreaming in the `sleep` study (where 12 animals have missing values) to illustrate each type in turn.

(1) *Missing completely at random*—If the presence of missing data on a variable is unrelated to any other observed or unobserved variable, then the data are missing completely at random (MCAR). If there's no systematic reason why dream sleep is missing for these 12 animals, the data is said to be MCAR. Note that if every variable with missing data is MCAR, you can consider the complete cases to be a simple random sample from the larger dataset.

(2) *Missing at random*—If the presence of missing data on a variable is related to other observed variables but *not* to its own unobserved value, the data is missing at random (MAR). For example, if animals with smaller body weights are more likely to have missing values for dream sleep (perhaps because it's harder to observe smaller animals), and the "missingness" is unrelated to an animal's time spent dreaming, the data would be considered MAR. In this case, the presence or absence of dream sleep data would be random, once you controlled for body weight.

(3) *Not missing at random*—If the missing data for a variable is neither MCAR nor MAR, it is not missing at random (NMAR). For example, if animals that spend less time dreaming are also more likely to have a missing dream value (perhaps because it's harder to measure shorter events), the data would be considered NMAR.

Most approaches to missing data assume that the data is either MCAR or MAR. In this case, you can ignore the mechanism producing the missing data and (after replacing or deleting the missing data) model the relationships of interest directly. Data that's NMAR can be difficult to analyze properly. When data is NMAR, you have to model the mechanisms that produced the missing values, as well as the relationships of interest. (Current approaches to analyzing NMAR data include the use of selection models and pattern mixtures. The analysis of NMAR data can be quite complex and is beyond the scope of this book.)

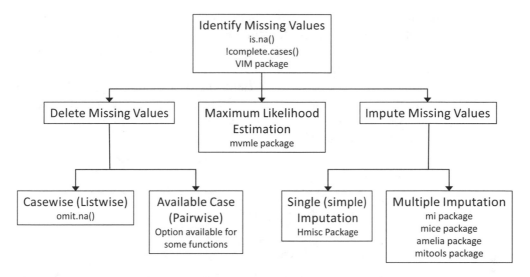

Figure 15.1 Methods for handling incomplete data, along with the R packages that support them

There are *many* methods for dealing with missing data—and no guarantee that they'll produce the same results. Figure 15.1 describes an array of methods used for handling incomplete data and the R packages that support them.

A complete review of missing data methodologies would require a book in itself. In this chapter, we'll review methods for exploring missing values patterns and focus on the three most popular methods for dealing with incomplete data (a rational approach, listwise deletion, and multiple imputation). We'll end the chapter with a brief discussion of other methods, including those that are useful in special circumstances.

15.2 Identifying missing values

To begin, let's review the material introduced in chapter 4, section 4.5, and expand on it. R represents missing values using the symbol NA (not available) and impossible values by the symbol NaN (not a number). In addition, the symbols Inf and -Inf represent positive infinity and negative infinity, respectively. The functions is.na(), is.nan(), and is.infinite() can be used to identify missing, impossible, and infinite values respectively. Each returns either TRUE or FALSE. Examples are given in table 15.1.

Table 15.1 Examples of return values for the is.na(), is.nan(), and is.infinite() functions

x	is.na(x)	is.nan(x)	is.infinite(x)
x <- NA	TRUE	FALSE	FALSE
x <- 0 / 0	TRUE	TRUE	FALSE
x <- 1 / 0	FALSE	FALSE	TRUE

These functions return an object that's the same size as its argument, with each element replaced by TRUE if the element is of the type being tested, and FALSE otherwise. For example, let y <- c(1, 2, 3, NA). Then is.na(y) will return the vector c(FALSE, FALSE, FALSE, TRUE).

The function complete.cases() can be used to identify the rows in a matrix or data frame that don't contain missing data. It returns a logical vector with TRUE for every row that contains complete cases and FALSE for every row that has one or more missing values.

Let's apply this to the sleep dataset:

```
# load the dataset
data(sleep, package="VIM")

# list the rows that do not have missing values
sleep[complete.cases(sleep),]

# list the rows that have one or more missing values
sleep[!complete.cases(sleep),]
```

Examining the output reveals that 42 cases have complete data and 20 cases have one or more missing values.

Because the logical values TRUE and FALSE are equivalent to the numeric values 1 and 0, the sum() and mean() functions can be used to obtain useful information about missing data. Consider the following:

```
> sum(is.na(sleep$Dream))
[1] 12
> mean(is.na(sleep$Dream))
[1] 0.19
> mean(!complete.cases(sleep))
[1] 0.32
```

The results indicate that there are 12 missing values for the variable Dream. Nineteen percent of the cases have a missing value on this variable. In addition, 32 percent of the cases in the dataset contain one or more missing values.

There are two things to keep in mind when identifying missing values. First, the complete.cases() function only identifies NA and NaN as missing. Infinite values (Inf and –Inf) are treated as valid values. Second, you must use missing values functions, like those in this section, to identify the missing values in R data objects. Logical comparisons such as myvar == NA are never true.

Now that you know how to identify missing values programmatically, let's look at tools that help you explore possible *patterns* in the occurrence of missing data.

15.3 *Exploring missing values patterns*

Before deciding how to deal with missing data, you'll find it useful to determine which variables have missing values, in what amounts, and in what combinations. In this section, we'll review tabular, graphical, and correlational methods for exploring missing values patterns. Ultimately, you want to understand *why* the data is missing. The answer will have implications for how you proceed with further analyses.

15.3.1 Tabulating missing values

You've already seen a rudimentary approach to identifying missing values. You can use the `complete.cases()` function from section 15.2 to list cases that are complete, or conversely, list cases that have one or more missing values. As the size of a dataset grows, though, it becomes a less attractive approach. In this case, you can turn to other R functions.

The `md.pattern()` function in the `mice` package will produce a tabulation of the missing data patterns in a matrix or data frame. Applying this function to the sleep dataset, you get the following:

```
> library(mice)
> data(sleep, package="VIM")
> md.pattern(sleep)
   BodyWgt BrainWgt Pred Exp Danger Sleep Span Gest Dream NonD
42       1        1    1   1      1     1    1    1     1    1  0
2        1        1    1   1      1     1    0    1     1    1  1
3        1        1    1   1      1     1    1    0     1    1  1
9        1        1    1   1      1     1    1    1     0    0  2
2        1        1    1   1      1     0    1    1     1    0  2
1        1        1    1   1      1     1    0    0     1    1  2
2        1        1    1   1      1     0    1    1     0    0  3
1        1        1    1   1      1     1    0    1     0    0  3
         0        0    0   0      0     4    4    4    12   14 38
```

The 1's and 0's in the body of the table indicate the missing values patterns, with a 0 indicating a missing value for a given column variable and a 1 indicating a nonmissing value. The first row describes the pattern of "no missing values" (all elements are 1). The second row describes the pattern "no missing values except for `Span`." The first column indicates the number of cases in each missing data pattern, and the last column indicates the number of variables with missing values present in each pattern. Here you can see that there are 42 cases without missing data and 2 cases that are missing `Span` alone. Nine cases are missing both `NonD` and `Dream` values. The dataset contains a total of (42 x 0) + (2 x 1) + ... + (1 x 3) = 38 missing values. The last row gives the total number of missing values present on each variable.

15.3.2 Exploring missing data visually

Although the tabular output from the `md.pattern()` function is compact, I often find it easier to discern patterns visually. Luckily, the `VIM` package provides numerous functions for visualizing missing values patterns in datasets. In this section, we'll review several, including `aggr()`, `matrixplot()`, and `scattMiss()`.

The `aggr()` function plots the number of missing values for each variable alone and for each combination of variables. For example, the code

```
library("VIM")
aggr(sleep, prop=FALSE, numbers=TRUE)
```

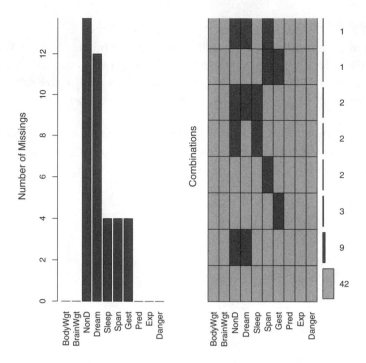

Figure 15.2 `aggr()` produced plot of missing values patterns for the sleep dataset.

produces the graph in figure 15.2. (The `VIM` package opens up a GUI interface. You can close it; we'll be using code to accomplish the tasks in this chapter.)

You can see that the variable `NonD` has the largest number of missing values (14), and that 2 mammals are missing `NonD`, `Dream`, and `Sleep` scores. Forty-two mammals have no missing data.

The statement `aggr(sleep, prop=TRUE, numbers=TRUE)` produces the same plot, but proportions are displayed instead of counts. The option `numbers=FALSE` (the default) suppresses the numeric labels.

The `matrixplot()` function produces a plot displaying the data for each case. A graph created using `matrixplot(sleep)` is displayed in figure 15.3. Here, the numeric data is rescaled to the interval [0, 1] and represented by grayscale colors, with lighter colors representing lower values and darker colors representing larger values. By default, missing values are represented in red. Note that in figure 15.3, red has been replaced with crosshatching by hand, so that the missing values are viewable in grayscale. It will look different when you create the graph yourself.

The graph is interactive: clicking on a column will re-sort the matrix by that variable. The rows in figure 15.3 are sorted in descending order by `BodyWgt`. A matrix plot allows you to see if the presence of missing values on one or more variables is related to the actual values of other variables. Here, you can see that there are no missing values on sleep variables (`Dream`, `NonD`, `Sleep`) for low values of body or brain weight (`BodyWgt`, `BrainWgt`).

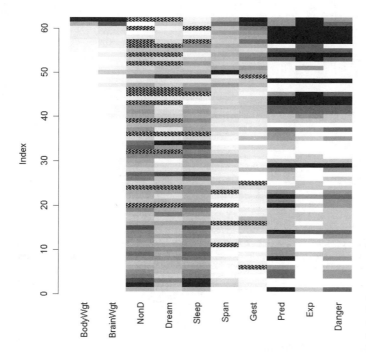

Figure 15.3 Matrix plot of actual and missing values by case (row) for the sleep dataset. The matrix is sorted by BodyWgt.

The `marginplot()` function produces a scatter plot between two variables with information about missing values shown in the plot's margins. Consider the relationship between amount of dream sleep and the length of a mammal's gestation. The statement

```
marginplot(sleep[c("Gest","Dream")], pch=c(20),
          col=c("darkgray", "red", "blue"))
```

produces the graph in figure 15.4. The `pch` and `col` parameters are optional and provide control over the plotting symbols and colors used.

The body of the graph displays the scatter plot between `Gest` and `Dream` (based on complete cases for the two variables). In the left margin, box plots display the distribution of `Dream` for mammals with (dark gray) and without (red) `Gest` values. Note that in grayscale, red is the darker shade. Four red dots represent the values of `Dream` for mammals missing `Gest` scores. In the bottom margin, the roles of `Gest` and `Dream` are reversed. You can see that a negative relationship exists between length of gestation and dream sleep and that dream sleep tends to be higher for mammals that are missing a gestation score. The number of observations with missing values on both variables at the same time is printed in blue at the intersection of both margins (bottom left).

The `VIM` package has many graphs that can help you understand the role of missing data in a dataset and is well worth exploring. There are functions to produce scatter plots, box plots, histograms, scatter plot matrices, parallel plots, rug plots, and bubble plots that incorporate information about missing values.

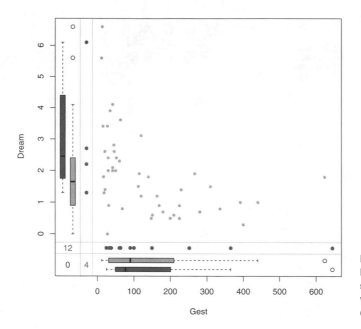

Figure 15.4 Scatter plot between amount of dream sleep and length of gestation, with information about missing data in the margins

15.3.3 *Using correlations to explore missing values*

Before moving on, there's one more approach worth noting. You can replace the data in a dataset with indicator variables, coded 1 for missing and 0 for present. The resulting matrix is sometimes called a *shadow matrix*. Correlating these indicator variables with each other and with the original (observed) variables can help you to see which variables tend to be missing together, as well as relationships between a variable's "missingness" and the values of the other variables.

Consider the following code:

```
x <- as.data.frame(abs(is.na(sleep)))
```

The elements of data frame x are 1 if the corresponding element of sleep is missing and 0 otherwise. You can see this by viewing the first few rows of each:

```
> head(sleep, n=5)
   BodyWgt BrainWgt NonD Dream Sleep Span Gest Pred Exp Danger
1 6654.000   5712.0  NA    NA   3.3 38.6  645    3   5      3
2    1.000      6.6 6.3   2.0   8.3  4.5   42    3   1      3
3    3.385     44.5  NA    NA  12.5 14.0   60    1   1      1
4    0.920      5.7  NA    NA  16.5   NA   25    5   2      3
5 2547.000   4603.0 2.1   1.8   3.9 69.0  624    3   5      4

> head(x, n=5)
  BodyWgt BrainWgt NonD Dream Sleep Span Gest Pred Exp Danger
1       0        0    1     1     0    0    0    0   0      0
2       0        0    0     0     0    0    0    0   0      0
3       0        0    1     1     0    0    0    0   0      0
4       0        0    1     1     0    1    0    0   0      0
5       0        0    0     0     0    0    0    0   0      0
```

The statement

```
y <- x[which(sd(x) > 0)]
```

extracts the variables that have some (but not all) missing values, and

```
cor(y)
```

gives you the correlations among these indicator variables:

```
        NonD   Dream  Sleep   Span    Gest
NonD    1.000  0.907  0.486   0.015  -0.142
Dream   0.907  1.000  0.204   0.038  -0.129
Sleep   0.486  0.204  1.000  -0.069  -0.069
Span    0.015  0.038 -0.069   1.000   0.198
Gest   -0.142 -0.129 -0.069   0.198   1.000
```

Here, you can see that Dream and NonD tend to be missing together (r=0.91). To a lesser extent, Sleep and NonD tend to be missing together (r=0.49) and Sleep and Dream tend to be missing together (r=0.20).

Finally, you can look at the relationship between the presence of missing values in a variable and the observed values on other variables:

```
> cor(sleep, y, use="pairwise.complete.obs")
           NonD   Dream   Sleep    Span    Gest
BodyWgt    0.227   0.223   0.0017 -0.058 -0.054
BrainWgt   0.179   0.163   0.0079 -0.079 -0.073
NonD         NA      NA       NA  -0.043 -0.046
Dream     -0.189      NA  -0.1890  0.117  0.228
Sleep     -0.080  -0.080      NA   0.096  0.040
Span       0.083   0.060   0.0052     NA -0.065
Gest       0.202   0.051   0.1597 -0.175     NA
Pred       0.048  -0.068   0.2025  0.023 -0.201
Exp        0.245   0.127   0.2608 -0.193 -0.193
Danger     0.065  -0.067   0.2089 -0.067 -0.204
Warning message:
In cor(sleep, y, use = "pairwise.complete.obs") :
  the standard deviation is zero
```

In this correlation matrix, the rows are observed variables, and the columns are indicator variables representing missingness. You can ignore the warning message and NA values in the correlation matrix; they're artifacts of our approach.

From the first column of the correlation matrix, you can see that nondreaming sleep scores are more likely to be missing for mammals with higher body weight (r=0.227), gestation period (r=0.202), and sleeping exposure (0.245). Other columns are read in a similar fashion. None of the correlations in this table are particularly large or striking, which suggests that the data deviates minimally from MCAR and may be MAR.

Note that you can never rule out the possibility that the data are NMAR because you don't know what the actual values would have been for data that are missing. For example, you don't know if there's a relationship between the amount of dreaming a mammal engages in and the probability of obtaining a missing value on this variable. In the absence of strong external evidence to the contrary, we typically assume that data is either MCAR or MAR.

15.4 *Understanding the sources and impact of missing data*

We identify the amount, distribution, and pattern of missing data in order to evaluate (1) the potential mechanisms producing the missing data and (2) the impact of the missing data on our ability to answer substantive questions. In particular, we want to answer the following questions:

- What percentage of the data is missing?
- Is it concentrated in a few variables, or widely distributed?
- Does it appear to be random?
- Does the covariation of missing data with each other or with observed data suggest a possible mechanism that's producing the missing values?

Answers to these questions will help determine which statistical methods are most appropriate for analyzing your data. For example, if the missing data are concentrated in a few relatively unimportant variables, you may be able to delete these variables and continue your analyses normally. If there's a small amount of data (say less than 10 percent) that's randomly distributed throughout the dataset (MCAR), you may be able to limit your analyses to cases with complete data and still get reliable and valid results. If you can assume that the data are either MCAR or MAR, you may be able to apply multiple imputation methods to arrive at valid conclusions. If the data are NMAR, you can turn to specialized methods, collect new data, or go into an easier and more rewarding profession.

Here are some examples:

- In a recent survey employing paper questionnaires, I found that several items tended to be missing together. It became apparent that these items clustered together because participants didn't realize that the third page of the questionnaire had a reverse side containing them. In this case, the data could be considered MCAR.
- In another study, an education variable was frequently missing in a global survey of leadership styles. Investigation revealed that European participants were more likely to leave this item blank. It turned out that the categories didn't make sense for participants in certain countries. In this case, the data was most likely MAR.
- Finally, I was involved in a study of depression in which older patients were more likely to omit items describing depressed mood when compared with younger patients. Interviews revealed that older patients were loath to admit to such symptoms because doing so violated their values about keeping a "stiff upper lip." Unfortunately, it was also determined that severely depressed patients were more likely to omit these items due to a sense of hopelessness and difficulties with concentration. In this case, the data had to be considered NMAR.

As you can see, the identification of patterns is only the first step. You need to bring your understanding of the research subject matter and the data collection process to bear in order to determine the source of the missing values.

Now that we've considered the source and impact of missing data, let's see how standard statistical approaches can be altered to accommodate them. We'll focus on three approaches that are very popular: a rational approach for recovering data, a traditional approach that involves deleting missing data, and a modern approach that involves the use of simulation. Along the way, we'll briefly look at methods for specialized situations, and methods that have become obsolete and should be retired. Our goal will remain constant: to answer, as accurately as possible, the substantive questions that led us to collect the data, given the absence of complete information.

15.5 *Rational approaches for dealing with incomplete data*

In a rational approach, you use mathematical or logical relationships among variables to attempt to fill in or recover the missing values. A few examples will help clarify this approach.

In the `sleep` dataset, the variable `Sleep` is the sum of the `Dream` and `NonD` variables. If you know a mammal's scores on any two, you can derive the third. Thus, if there were some observations that were missing only one of the three variables, you could recover the missing information through addition or subtraction.

As a second example, consider research that focuses on work/life balance differences between generational cohorts (for example, Silents, Early Boomers, Late Boomers, Xers, Millennials), where cohorts are defined by their birth year. Participants are asked both their date of birth and their age. If date of birth is missing, you can recover their birth year (and therefore their generational cohort) by knowing their age and the date they completed the survey.

An example that uses logical relationships to recover missing data comes from a set of leadership studies in which participants were asked if they were a manager (yes/no) and the number of their direct reports (integer). If they left the manager question blank but indicated that they had one or more direct reports, it would be reasonable to infer that they were a manager.

As a final example, I frequently engage in gender research that compares the leadership styles and effectiveness of men and women. Participants complete surveys that include their name (first and last), gender, and a detailed assessment of their leadership approach and impact. If participants leave the gender question blank, I have to impute the value in order to include them in the research. In one recent study of 66,000 managers, 11,000 (17 percent) had a missing value for gender.

To remedy the situation, I employed the following rational process. First, I cross-tabulated first name with gender. Some first names were associated with males, some with females, and some with both. For example, "William" appeared 417 times and was always a male. Conversely, the name "Chris" appeared 237 times but was sometimes a male (86 percent) and sometimes a female (14 percent). If a first name appeared more than 20 times in the dataset and was always associated with males or with females (but never both), I assumed that the name represented a single gender. I used this assumption to create a gender lookup table for gender-specific first names. Using this lookup table for participants with missing gender values, I was able to recover 7,000 cases (63 percent of the missing responses).

A rational approach typically requires creativity and thoughtfulness, along with a degree of data management skill. Data recovery may be exact (as in the sleep example) or approximate (as in the gender example). In the next section, we'll explore an approach that creates complete datasets by removing observations.

15.6 *Complete-case analysis (listwise deletion)*

In complete-case analysis, only observations containing valid data values on every variable are retained for further analysis. Practically, this involves deleting any row containing one or more missing values, and is also known as listwise, or case-wise, deletion. Most popular statistical packages employ listwise deletion as the default approach for handling missing data. In fact, it's so common that many analysts carrying out analyses like regression or ANOVA may not even realize that there's a "missing values problem" to be dealt with!

The function `complete.cases()` can be used to save the cases (rows) of a matrix or data frame without missing data:

```
newdata <- mydata[complete.cases(mydata),]
```

The same result can be accomplished with the `na.omit` function:

```
newdata <- na.omit(mydata)
```

In both statements, any rows containing missing data are deleted from `mydata` before the results are saved to `newdata`.

Suppose you're interested in the correlations among the variables in the sleep study. Applying listwise deletion, you'd delete all mammals with missing data prior to calculating the correlations:

```
> options(digits=1)
> cor(na.omit(sleep))
          BodyWgt BrainWgt NonD Dream Sleep  Span  Gest  Pred  Exp Danger
BodyWgt    1.00     0.96  -0.4 -0.07  -0.3  0.47  0.71  0.10  0.4   0.26
BrainWgt   0.96     1.00  -0.4 -0.07  -0.3  0.63  0.73 -0.02  0.3   0.15
NonD      -0.39    -0.39   1.0  0.52   1.0 -0.37 -0.61 -0.35 -0.6  -0.53
Dream     -0.07    -0.07   0.5  1.00   0.7 -0.27 -0.41 -0.40 -0.5  -0.57
Sleep     -0.34    -0.34   1.0  0.72   1.0 -0.38 -0.61 -0.40 -0.6  -0.60
Span       0.47     0.63  -0.4 -0.27  -0.4  1.00  0.65 -0.17  0.3   0.01
Gest       0.71     0.73  -0.6 -0.41  -0.6  0.65  1.00  0.09  0.6   0.31
Pred       0.10    -0.02  -0.4 -0.40  -0.4 -0.17  0.09  1.00  0.6   0.93
Exp        0.41     0.32  -0.6 -0.50  -0.6  0.32  0.57  0.63  1.0   0.79
Danger     0.26     0.15  -0.5 -0.57  -0.6  0.01  0.31  0.93  0.8   1.00
```

The correlations in this table are based solely on the 42 mammals that have complete data on all variables. (Note that the statement `cor(sleep, use="complete.obs")` would have produced the same results.)

If you wanted to study the impact of life span and length of gestation on the amount of dream sleep, you could employ linear regression with listwise deletion:

```
> fit <- lm(Dream ~ Span + Gest, data=na.omit(sleep))
> summary(fit)
```

```
Call:
lm(formula = Dream ~ Span + Gest, data = na.omit(sleep))

Residuals:
   Min     1Q Median     3Q    Max
-2.333 -0.915 -0.221  0.382  4.183

Coefficients:
             Estimate Std. Error t value Pr(>|t|)
(Intercept)  2.480122   0.298476    8.31  3.7e-10 ***
Span        -0.000472   0.013130   -0.04    0.971
Gest        -0.004394   0.002081   -2.11    0.041 *
---
Signif. codes:  0 '***' 0.001 '**' 0.01 '*' 0.05 '.' 0.1 ' ' 1

Residual standard error: 1 on 39 degrees of freedom
Multiple R-squared: 0.167,      Adjusted R-squared: 0.125
F-statistic: 3.92 on 2 and 39 DF,  p-value: 0.0282
```

Here you see that mammals with shorter gestation periods have more dream sleep (controlling for life span) and that life span is unrelated to dream sleep when controlling for gestation period. The analysis is based on 42 cases with complete data.

In the previous example, what would have happened if data=na.omit(sleep) had been replaced with data=sleep? Like many R function, lm() uses a limited definition of listwise deletion. Cases with any missing data on the variables fitted by the function (Dream, Span, and Gest in this case) would have been deleted. The analysis would have been based on 44 cases.

Listwise deletion assumes that the data are MCAR (that is, the complete observations are a random subsample of the full dataset). In the current example, we've assumed that the 42 mammals used are a random subsample of the 62 mammals collected. To the degree that the MCAR assumption is violated, the resulting regression parameters will be biased. Deleting all observations with missing data can also reduce statistical power by reducing the available sample size. In the current example, listwise deletion reduced the sample size by 32 percent. Next, we'll consider an approach that employs the entire dataset (including cases with missing data).

15.7 *Multiple imputation*

Multiple imputation (MI) provides an approach to missing values that's based on repeated simulations. MI is frequently the method of choice for complex missing values problems. In MI, a set of complete datasets (typically 3 to 10) is generated from an existing dataset containing missing values. Monte Carlo methods are used to fill in the missing data in each of the simulated datasets. Standard statistical methods are applied to each of the simulated datasets, and the outcomes are combined to provide estimated results and confidence intervals that take into account the uncertainty introduced by the missing values. Good implementations are available in R through the Amelia, mice, and mi packages. In this section we'll focus on the approach provided by the mice (multivariate imputation by chained equations) package.

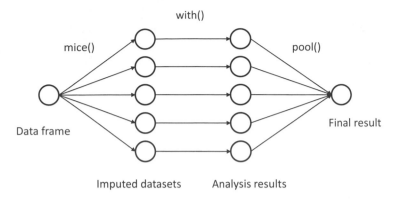

Figure 15.5   Steps in applying multiple imputation to missing data via the
`mice` **approach.**

To understand how the `mice` package operates, consider the diagram in figure 15.5.

The function `mice()` starts with a data frame containing missing data and returns an object containing several complete datasets (the default is 5). Each complete dataset is created by imputing values for the missing data in the original data frame. There's a random component to the imputations, so each complete dataset is slightly different. The `with()` function is then used to apply a statistical model (for example, linear or generalized linear model) to each complete dataset in turn. Finally, the `pool()` function combines the results of these separate analyses into a single set of results. The standard errors and p-values in this final model correctly reflect the uncertainty produced by both the missing values and the multiple imputations.

How does the `mice()` function impute missing values?

Missing values are imputed by Gibbs sampling. By default, each variable containing missing values is predicted from all other variables in the dataset. These prediction equations are used to impute plausible values for the missing data. The process iterates until convergence over the missing values is achieved. For each variable, the user can choose the form of the prediction model (called an elementary imputation method), and the variables entered into it.

By default, predictive mean matching is used to replace missing data on continuous variables, while logistic or polytomous logistic regression is used for target variables that are dichotomous (factors with two levels) or polytomous (factors with more than two levels) respectively. Other elementary imputation methods include Bayesian linear regression, discriminant function analysis, two-level normal imputation, and random sampling from observed values. Users can supply their own methods as well.

An analysis based on the `mice` package will typically conform to the following structure:

```
library(mice)
imp <- mice(mydata, m)
fit <- with(imp, analysis)
pooled <- pool(fit)
summary(pooled)
```

where

- `mydata` is a matrix or data frame containing missing values.
- `imp` is a list object containing the *m* imputed datasets, along with information on how the imputations were accomplished. By default, *m* = 5.
- `analysis` is a formula object specifying the statistical analysis to be applied to each of the *m* imputed datasets. Examples include `lm()` for linear regression models, `glm()` for generalized linear models, `gam()` for generalized additive models, and `nbrm()` for negative binomial models. Formulas within the parentheses give the response variables on the left of the ~ and the predictor variables (separated by + signs) on the right.
- `fit` is a list object containing the results of the *m* separate statistical analyses.
- `pooled` is a list object containing the averaged results of these *m* statistical analyses.

Let's apply multiple imputation to our sleep dataset. We'll repeat the analysis from section 15.6, but this time, use all 62 mammals. Set the seed value for the random number generator to 1234 so that your results will match mine.

```
> library(mice)
> data(sleep, package="VIM")
> imp <- mice(sleep, seed=1234)

 [...output deleted to save space...]

> fit <- with(imp, lm(Dream ~ Span + Gest))
> pooled <- pool(fit)
> summary(pooled)
                est      se      t   df Pr(>|t|)      lo 95
(Intercept)  2.58858 0.27552  9.395 52.1 8.34e-13  2.03576
Span        -0.00276 0.01295 -0.213 52.9 8.32e-01 -0.02874
Gest        -0.00421 0.00157 -2.671 55.6 9.91e-03 -0.00736
               hi 95 nmis   fmi
(Intercept)  3.14141   NA 0.0870
Span         0.02322    4 0.0806
Gest        -0.00105    4 0.0537
```

Here, you see that the regression coefficient for `Span` isn't significant (p ≈ 0.08), and the coefficient for `Gest` is significant at the p < 0.01 level. If you compare these results with those produced by a complete case analysis (section 15.6), you see that you'd come to the same conclusions in this instance. Length of gestation has a (statistically) significant, negative relationship with amount of dream sleep, controlling for life span. Although the complete-case analysis was based on the 42 mammals with complete data, the current analysis is based on information gathered from the full set of 62 mammals. By the way, the `fmi` column reports the fraction of missing information (that is, the proportion of variability that is attributable to the uncertainty introduced by the missing data).

You can access more information about the imputation by examining the objects created in the analysis. For example, let's view a summary of the `imp` object:

```
> imp

Multiply imputed data set
Call:
mice(data = sleep, seed = 1234)
Number of multiple imputations:  5
Missing cells per column:
  BodyWgt BrainWgt     NonD    Dream    Sleep     Span     Gest     Pred
        0        0       14       12        4        4        4        0
      Exp   Danger
        0        0
Imputation methods:
  BodyWgt BrainWgt     NonD    Dream    Sleep     Span     Gest     Pred
       ""       ""    "pmm"    "pmm"    "pmm"    "pmm"    "pmm"       ""
      Exp   Danger
       ""       ""

VisitSequence:
 NonD Dream Sleep  Span  Gest
    3     4     5     6     7
PredictorMatrix:
         BodyWgt BrainWgt NonD Dream Sleep Span Gest Pred Exp Danger
BodyWgt        0        0    0     0     0    0    0    0   0      0
BrainWgt       0        0    0     0     0    0    0    0   0      0
NonD           1        1    0     1     1    1    1    1   1      1
Dream          1        1    1     0     1    1    1    1   1      1
Sleep          1        1    1     1     0    1    1    1   1      1
Span           1        1    1     1     1    0    1    1   1      1
Gest           1        1    1     1     1    1    0    1   1      1
Pred           0        0    0     0     0    0    0    0   0      0
Exp            0        0    0     0     0    0    0    0   0      0
Danger         0        0    0     0     0    0    0    0   0      0
Random generator seed value:  1234
```

From the resulting output, you can see that five synthetic datasets were created, and that the predictive mean matching (`pmm`) method was used for each variable with missing data. No imputation (`""`) was needed for `BodyWgt`, `BrainWgt`, `Pred`, `Exp`, or `Danger`, because they had no missing values. The Visit Sequence tells you that variables were imputed from right to left, starting with `NonD` and ending with `Gest`. Finally, the Predictor Matrix indicates that each variable with missing data was imputed using all the other variables in the dataset. (In this matrix, the rows represent the variables being imputed, the columns represent the variables used for the imputation, and 1's/0's indicate used/not used).

You can view the actual imputations by looking at subcomponents of the `imp` object. For example,

```
> imp$imp$Dream
      1   2   3   4   5
1   0.5 0.5 0.5 0.5 0.0
3   2.3 2.4 1.9 1.5 2.4
4   1.2 1.3 5.6 2.3 1.3
14  0.6 1.0 0.0 0.3 0.5
24  1.2 1.0 5.6 1.0 6.6
26  1.9 6.6 0.9 2.2 2.0
30  1.0 1.2 2.6 2.3 1.4
31  5.6 0.5 1.2 0.5 1.4
47  0.7 0.6 1.4 1.8 3.6
53  0.7 0.5 0.7 0.5 0.5
55  0.5 2.4 0.7 2.6 2.6
62  1.9 1.4 3.6 5.6 6.6
```

displays the five imputed values for each of the 12 mammals with missing data on the `Dream` variable. A review of these matrices helps you determine if the imputed values are reasonable. A negative value for length of sleep might give you pause (or nightmares).

You can view each of the *m* imputed datasets via the `complete()` function. The format is

```
complete(imp, action=#)
```

where *#* specifies one of the *m* synthetically complete datasets. For example,

```
> dataset3 <- complete(imp, action=3)
> dataset3
  BodyWgt BrainWgt NonD Dream Sleep Span Gest Pred Exp Danger
1 6654.00   5712.0  2.1   0.5   3.3 38.6  645    3   5      3
2    1.00      6.6  6.3   2.0   8.3  4.5   42    3   1      3
3    3.38     44.5 10.6   1.9  12.5 14.0   60    1   1      1
4    0.92      5.7 11.0   5.6  16.5  4.7   25    5   2      3
5 2547.00   4603.0  2.1   1.8   3.9 69.0  624    3   5      4
6   10.55    179.5  9.1   0.7   9.8 27.0  180    4   4      4
[...output deleted to save space...]
```

displays the third (out of five) complete datasets created by the multiple imputation process.

Due to space limitations, we've only briefly considered the MI implementation provided in the `mice` package. The `mi` and `Amelia` packages also contain valuable approaches. If you are interested in the multiple imputation approach to missing data, I recommend the following resources:

- The multiple imputation FAQ page (www.stat.psu.edu/~jls/mifaq.html)
- Articles by Van Buuren and Groothuis-Oudshoorn (2010) and Yu-Sung, Gelman, Hill, and Yajima (2010)
- Amelia II: A Program for Missing Data (http://gking.harvard.edu/amelia/)

Each can help to reinforce and extend your understanding of this important, but underutilized, methodology.

15.8 *Other approaches to missing data*

R supports several other approaches for dealing with missing data. Although not as broadly applicable as the methods described thus far, the packages described in table 15.2 offer functions that can be quite useful in specialized circumstances.

Table 15.2 **Specialized methods for dealing with missing data**

Package	Description
Hmisc	Contains numerous functions supporting simple imputation, multiple imputation, and imputation using canonical variates
mvnmle	Maximum likelihood estimation for multivariate normal data with missing values
cat	Multiple imputation of multivariate categorical data under log-linear models
arrayImpute, arrayMissPattern, SeqKnn	Useful functions for dealing with missing microarray data
longitudinalData	Contains utility functions, including interpolation routines for imputing missing time series values
kmi	Kaplan–Meier multiple imputation for survival analysis with missing data
mix	Multiple imputation for mixed categorical and continuous data under the general location model
pan	Multiple imputation for multivariate panel or clustered data

Finally, there are two methods for dealing with missing data that are still in use, but should now be considered obsolete. They are pairwise deletion and simple imputation.

15.8.1 *Pairwise deletion*

Pairwise deletion is often considered an alternative to listwise deletion when working with datasets containing missing values. In pairwise deletion, observations are only deleted if they're missing data for the variables involved in a specific analysis. Consider the following code:

```
> cor(sleep, use="pairwise.complete.obs")
         BodyWgt BrainWgt NonD Dream Sleep  Span Gest   Pred   Exp Danger
BodyWgt     1.00     0.93 -0.4  -0.1  -0.3  0.30  0.7   0.06   0.3   0.13
BrainWgt    0.93     1.00 -0.4  -0.1  -0.4  0.51  0.7   0.03   0.4   0.15
NonD       -0.38    -0.37  1.0   0.5   1.0 -0.38 -0.6  -0.32  -0.5  -0.48
Dream      -0.11    -0.11  0.5   1.0   0.7 -0.30 -0.5  -0.45  -0.5  -0.58
Sleep      -0.31    -0.36  1.0   0.7   1.0 -0.41 -0.6  -0.40  -0.6  -0.59
Span        0.30     0.51 -0.4  -0.3  -0.4  1.00  0.6  -0.10   0.4   0.06
Gest        0.65     0.75 -0.6  -0.5  -0.6  0.61  1.0   0.20   0.6   0.38
Pred        0.06     0.03 -0.3  -0.4  -0.4 -0.10  0.2   1.00   0.6   0.92
Exp         0.34     0.37 -0.5  -0.5  -0.6  0.36  0.6   0.62   1.0   0.79
Danger      0.13     0.15 -0.5  -0.6  -0.6  0.06  0.4   0.92   0.8   1.00
```

In this example, correlations between any two variables use all available observations for those two variables (ignoring the other variables). The correlation between `Body-Wgt` and `BrainWgt` is based on all 62 mammals (the number of mammals with data on both variables). The correlation between `BodyWgt` and `NonD` is based on the 42 mammals, and the correlation between `Dream` and `NonDream` is based on 46 mammals.

Although pairwise deletion appears to use all available data, in fact each calculation is based on a different subset of the data. This can lead to distorted and difficult-to-interpret results. I recommend staying away from this approach.

15.8.2 Simple (nonstochastic) imputation

In simple imputation, the missing values in a variable are replaced with a single value (for example, mean, median, or mode). Using *mean substitution* you could replace missing values on `Dream` with the value 1.97 and missing values on `NonD` with the value 8.67 (the means on `Dream` and `NonD`, respectively). Note that the substitution is nonstochastic, meaning that random error isn't introduced (unlike multiple imputation).

An advantage to simple imputation is that it solves the "missing values problem" without reducing the sample size available for the analyses. Simple imputation is, well, simple, but it produces biased results for data that aren't MCAR. If there are moderate to large amounts of missing data, simple imputation is likely to underestimate standard errors, distort correlations among variables, and produce incorrect p-values in statistical tests. Like pairwise deletion, I recommend avoiding this approach for most missing data problems.

15.9 Summary

Most statistical methods assume that the input data is complete and doesn't include missing values (for example, `NA`, `NaN`, `Inf`). But most datasets in real-world settings contain missing values. Therefore, you must either delete the missing values or replace them with reasonable substitute values before continuing with the desired analyses. Often, statistical packages will provide default methods for handling missing data, but these approaches may not be optimal. Therefore, it's important that you understand the various approaches available, and the ramifications of using each.

In this chapter, we examined methods for identifying missing values and exploring patterns of missing data. Our goal was to understand the mechanisms that led to the missing data and their possible impact on subsequent analyses. We then reviewed three popular methods for dealing with missing data: a rational approach, listwise deletion, and the use of multiple imputation.

Rational approaches can be used to recover missing values when there are redundancies in the data, or external information that can be brought to bear on the problem. The listwise deletion of missing data is useful if the data are MCAR and the subsequent sample size reduction doesn't seriously impact the power of statistical tests. Multiple imputation is rapidly becoming the method of choice for complex missing data problems when you can assume that the data are MCAR or MAR. Although many analysts may be unfamiliar with multiple imputation strategies, user-contributed packages (`mice`, `mi`, `Amelia`) make them readily accessible. I believe that we'll see a rapid growth in their use over the next few years.

We ended the chapter by briefly mentioning R packages that provide specialized approaches for dealing with missing data, and singled out general approaches for handling missing data (pairwise deletion, simple imputation) that should be avoided.

In the next chapter, we'll explore advanced graphical methods, including the use of lattice graphs, the ggplot2 system, and interactive graphical methods.

Advanced graphics

16

This chapter covers
- Trellis graphs and the lattice package
- The grammar of graphs via ggplot2
- Interactive graphics

In previous chapters, we created a wide variety of both general and specialized graphs (and had lots of fun in the process). Most were produced using R's base graphics system. Given the diversity of methods available in R, it may not surprise you to learn that there are actually four separate and complete graphics systems currently available.

In addition to base graphics, we have graphics systems provided by the `grid`, `lattice`, and `ggplot2` packages. Each is designed to expand on the capabilities of, and correct for deficiencies in, R's base graphics system.

The `grid` graphics system provides low-level access to graphic primitives, giving programmers a great deal of flexibility in the creation of graphic output. The `lattice` package provides an intuitive approach for examining multivariate relationships through conditional 1-, 2-, or 3-dimensional graphs called *trellis graphs*. The `ggplot2` package provides a method of creating innovative graphs based on a comprehensive graphical "grammar."

In this chapter, we'll start with an overview of the four graphic systems. Then we'll focus on graphs that can be generated with the `lattice` and `ggplot2` packages. These packages greatly expand the range and quality of the graphs you can produce in R.

We'll end the chapter by considering interactive graphics. Interacting with graphs in real time can help you understand your data more thoroughly and develop greater insights into the relationships among variables. Here, we'll focus on the functionality offered by the `iplots`, `playwith`, `latticist`, and `rggobi` packages.

16.1 *The four graphic systems in R*

As stated earlier, four primary graphical systems are available in R. The base graphic system in R, written by Ross Ihaka, is included in every R installation. Most of the graphs produced in previous chapters rely on base graphics functions.

The grid graphics system, written by Paul Murrell (2006), is implemented through the `grid` package. Grid graphics offer a lower-level alternative to the standard graphics system. The user can create arbitrary rectangular regions on graphics devices, define coordinate systems for each region, and use a rich set of drawing primitives to control the arrangement and appearance of graphic elements.

This flexibility makes grid graphics a valuable tool for software developers. But the `grid` package doesn't provide functions for producing statistical graphics or complete plots. Because of this, the package is rarely used directly by data analysts.

The `lattice` package, written by Deepayan Sarkar (2008), implements trellis graphics as outlined by Cleveland (1985, 1993) and described on the Trellis website (http://netlib.bell-labs.com/cm/ms/departments/sia/project/trellis/). Built using the `grid` package, the `lattice` package has grown beyond Cleveland's original approach to visualizing multivariate data, and now provides a comprehensive alternative system for creating statistical graphics in R.

The `ggplot2` package, written by Hadley Wickham (2009a), provides a system for creating graphs based on the grammar of graphics described by Wilkinson (2005) and expanded by Wickham (2009b). The intention of the `ggplot2` package is to provide a comprehensive, grammar-based system for generating graphs in a unified and coherent manner, allowing users to create new and innovative data visualizations.

Access to the four systems differs, as outlined in table 16.1. Base graphic functions are automatically available. To access `grid` and `lattice` functions, you must load the package explicitly (for example, `library(lattice)`). To access `ggplot2` functions, you have to download and install the package (`install.packages("ggplot2")`) before first use, and then load it (`library(ggplot2)`).

Table 16.1 Access to graphic systems

System	Included in base installation?	Must be explicitly loaded?
base	Yes	No
grid	Yes	Yes
lattice	Yes	Yes
ggplot2	No	Yes

Because our attention is primarily focused on practical data analyses, we won't elaborate on the `grid` package in this chapter. (If you're interested, refer to Dr. Murrell's Grid website [www.stat.auckland.ac.nz/~paul/grid/grid.html] for details on this package.) Instead, we'll explore the `lattice` and `ggplot2` packages in some detail. Each allows you to create unique and useful graphs that aren't easily created in other ways.

16.2 *The lattice package*

The `lattice` package provides a comprehensive graphical system for visualizing univariate and multivariate data. In particular, many users turn to the `lattice` package because of its ability to easily generate trellis graphs.

A trellis graph displays the distribution of a variable or the relationship between variables, separately for each level of one or more other variables. Consider the following question: *How do the heights of singers in the New York Choral Society vary by their vocal parts?*

Data on the heights and voice parts of choral members is provided in the `singer` dataset contained in the `lattice` package. In the following code

```
library(lattice)
histogram(~height | voice.part, data = singer,
    main="Distribution of Heights by Voice Pitch",
    xlab="Height (inches)")
```

`height` is the dependent variable, `voice.part` is called the *conditioning variable*, and a histogram is created for each of the eight voice parts. The graph is shown in figure 16.1. It appears that tenors and basses tend to be taller than altos and sopranos.

In trellis graphs, a separate *panel* is created for each level of the conditioning variable. If more than one conditioning variable is specified, a panel is created for each combination of factor levels. The panels are arranged into an array to facilitate comparisons. A label is provided for each panel in an area called the *strip*. As you'll see, the user has control over the graph displayed in each panel, the format and placement of the strip, the arrangement of the panels, the placement and content of legends, and many other graphic features.

The `lattice` package provides a wide variety of functions for producing univariate (dot plots, kernel density plots, histograms, bar charts, box plots), bivariate (scatter plots, strip plots, parallel box plots), and multivariate (3D plots, scatter plot matrices) graphs.

Each high-level graphing function follows the format

```
graph_function(formula, data=, options)
```

where:

- *graph_function* is one of the functions listed in the second column of table 16.2.
- *formula* specifies the variable(s) to display and any conditioning variables.
- `data` specifies a data frame.
- *options* are comma-separated parameters used to modify the content, arrangement, and annotation of the graph. See table 16.3 for a description of common options.

Distribution of Heights by Voice Pitch

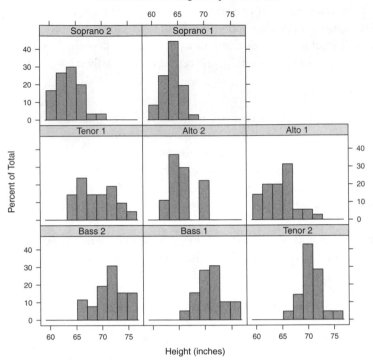

Figure 16.1   Trellis graph of singer heights by voice pitch

Let lowercase letters represent numeric variables and uppercase letters represent categorical variables (factors). The formula in a high-level graphing function typically takes the form

```
y ~ x | A * B
```

where variables on the left side of the vertical bar are called the *primary* variables and variables on the right are the *conditioning* variables. Primary variables map variables to the axes in each panel. Here, y~x describes the variables to place on the vertical and horizontal axes, respectively. For single-variable plots, replace y~x with ~x. For 3D plots, replace y~x with z~x*y. Finally, for multivariate plots (scatter plot matrix or parallel coordinates plot) replace y~x with a data frame. Note that conditioning variables are always optional.

Following this logic, ~x|A displays numeric variable x for each level of factor A. y~x|A*B displays the relationship between numeric variables y and x separately for every combination of factor A and B levels. A~x displays categorical variable A on the vertical axis and numeric variable x on the horizontal axis. ~x displays numeric variable x alone. Other examples are shown in table 16.2.

To gain a quick overview of lattice graphs, try running the code in listing 16.1. The graphs are based on the automotive data (mileage, weight, number of gears, number

Table 16.2 Graph types and corresponding functions in the `lattice` package

Graph type	Function	Formula examples
3D contour plot	`contourplot()`	z~x*y
3D level plot	`levelplot()`	z~y*x
3D scatter plot	`cloud()`	z~x*y|A
3D wireframe graph	`wireframe()`	z~y*x
Bar chart	`barchart()`	x~A or A~x
Box plot	`bwplot()`	x~A or A~x
Dot plot	`dotplot()`	~x|A
Histogram	`histogram()`	~x
Kernel density plot	`densityplot()`	~x|A*B
Parallel coordinates plot	`parallel()`	dataframe
Scatter plot	`xyplot()`	y~x|A
Scatter plot matrix	`splom()`	dataframe
Strip plots	`stripplot()`	A~x or x~A

Note: In these formulas, lowercase letters represent numeric variables and uppercase letters represent categorical variables.

of cylinders, and so on) included in the `mtcars` data frame. You may want to vary the formulas and view the results. (The resulting output has been omitted to save space.)

Listing 16.1 `lattice` plot examples

```
library(lattice)
attach(mtcars)

gear <- factor(gear, levels=c(3, 4, 5),              ◁─┐ Create factors
               labels=c("3 gears", "4 gears", "5 gears"))   with value labels
cyl <- factor(cyl, levels=c(4, 6, 8),
              labels=c("4 cylinders", "6 cylinders", "8 cylinders"))

densityplot(~mpg,
          main="Density Plot",
          xlab="Miles per Gallon")

densityplot(~mpg | cyl,
          main="Density Plot by Number of Cylinders",
          xlab="Miles per Gallon")

bwplot(cyl ~ mpg | gear,
```

```
            main="Box Plots by Cylinders and Gears",
            xlab="Miles per Gallon", ylab="Cylinders")

xyplot(mpg ~ wt | cyl * gear,
         main="Scatter Plots by Cylinders and Gears",
         xlab="Car Weight", ylab="Miles per Gallon")

cloud(mpg ~ wt * qsec | cyl,
        main="3D Scatter Plots by Cylinders")

dotplot(cyl ~ mpg | gear,
          main="Dot Plots by Number of Gears and Cylinders",
          xlab="Miles Per Gallon")

splom(mtcars[c(1, 3, 4, 5, 6)],
        main="Scatter Plot Matrix for mtcars Data")

detach(mtcars)
```

High-level plotting functions in the `lattice` package produce graphic objects that can be saved and manipulated. For example,

```
library(lattice)
mygraph <- densityplot(~height|voice.part, data=singer)
```

creates a trellis density plot and saves it as object `mygraph`. But no graph is displayed. Issuing the statement `plot(mygraph)` (or simply `mygraph`) will display the graph.

It's easy to modify lattice graphs through the use of options. Common options are given in table 16.3. You'll see examples of many of these later in the chapter.

Table 16.3 Common options for lattice high-level graphing functions

Options	Description
aspect	A number specifying the aspect ratio (height/width) for the graph in each panel.
col, pch, lty, lwd	Vectors specifying the colors, symbols, line types, and line widths to be used in plotting, respectively.
groups	Grouping variable (factor).
index.cond	List specifying the display order of the panels.
key (or auto.key)	Function used to supply legend(s) for grouping variable(s).
layout	Two-element numeric vector specifying the arrangement of the panels (number of columns, number of rows). If desired, a third element can be added to indicate the number of pages.
main, sub	Character vectors specifying the main title and subtitle.
panel	Function used to generate the graph in each panel.

Table 16.3 **Common options for lattice high-level graphing functions (*continued*)**

Options	Description
scales	List providing axis annotation information.
strip	Function used to customize panel strips.
split, position	Numeric vectors used to place more than one graph on a page.
type	Character vector specifying one or more plotting options for scatter plots (p=points, l=lines, r=regression line, smooth=loess fit, g=grid, and so on).
xlab, ylab	Character vectors specifying horizontal and vertical axis labels.
xlim, ylim	Two-element numeric vectors giving the minimum and maximum values for the horizontal and vertical axes, respectively.

You can issue these options in the high-level function calls or within the panel functions discussed in section 16.2.2.

You can also use the `update()` function to modify a lattice graphic object. Continuing the `singer` example, the following

```
update(mygraph, col="red", pch=16, cex=.8, jitter=.05, lwd=2)
```

would redraw the graph using red curves and symbols (`color="red"`), filled dots (`pch=16`), smaller (`cex=.8`) and more highly jittered points (`jitter=.05`), and curves of double thickness (`lwd=2`). Now that we've reviewed the general structure of a high-level lattice function, let's look at conditioning variables in more detail.

16.2.1 *Conditioning variables*

As you've seen, one of the most powerful features of lattice graphs is the ability to add conditioning variables. If one conditioning variable is present, a separate panel is created for each level. If two conditioning variables are present, a separate panel is created for each combination of levels for the two variables. It's rarely useful to include more than two conditioning variables.

Typically, conditioning variables are factors. But what if you want to condition on a continuous variable? One approach would be to transform the continuous variable into a discrete variable using R's `cut()` function. Alternatively, the `lattice` package provides functions for transforming a continuous variable into a data structure called a `shingle`. Specifically, the continuous variable is divided up into a series of (possibly) overlapping ranges. For example, the function

```
myshingle <- equal.count(x, number=#, overlap=proportion)
```

will take continuous variable *x* and divide it up into # intervals, with *proportion* overlap, and equal numbers of observations in each range, and return it as the variable `myshingle` (of class `shingle`). Printing or plotting this object (for example, `plot(myshingle)`) will display the shingle's intervals.

Once a continuous variable has been converted to a shingle, you can use it as a conditioning variable. For example, let's use the `mtcars` dataset to explore the relationship between miles per gallon and car weight conditioned on engine displacement. Because engine displacement is a continuous variable, first let's convert it to a shingle variable with three levels:

```
displacement <- equal.count(mtcars$disp, number=3, overlap=0)
```

Next, use this variable in the `xyplot()` function:

```
xyplot(mpg~wt|displacement, data=mtcars,
    main = "Miles per Gallon vs. Weight by Engine Displacement",
    xlab = "Weight", ylab = "Miles per Gallon",
    layout=c(3, 1), aspect=1.5)
```

The results are shown in figure 16.2. Note that we've also used options to modify the layout of the panels (three columns and one row) and the aspect ratio (height/width) in order to make comparisons among the three groups easier.

You can see that the labels in the panel strips of figure 16.1 and figure 16.2 differ. The representation in figure 16.2 indicates the continuous nature of the conditioning variable, with the darker color indicating the range of values for the conditioning variable in the given panel. In the next section, we'll use panel functions to customize the output further.

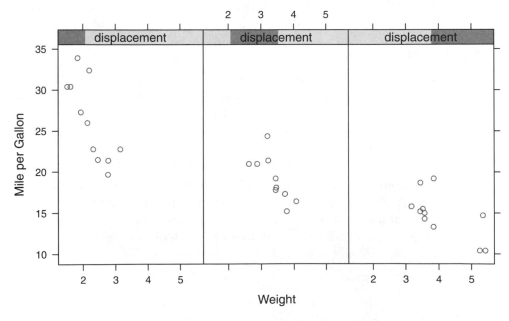

Figure 16.2 **Trellis plot of mpg versus car weight conditioned on engine displacement. Because engine displacement is a continuous variable, it has been converted to three nonoverlapping shingles with equal numbers of observations.**

16.2.2 Panel functions

Each of the high-level plotting functions in table 16.2 employs a default function to draw the panels. These default functions follow the naming convention `panel.graph_function,` where `graph_function` is the high-level function. For example,

```
xyplot(mpg~wt|displacement, data=mtcars)
```

could have also be written as

```
xyplot(mpg~wt|displacement, data=mtcars, panel=panel.xyplot)
```

This is a powerful feature because it allows you to replace the default panel function with a customized function of your own design. You can incorporate one or more of the 50+ default panel functions in the `lattice` package into your customized function as well. Customized panel functions give you a great deal of flexibility in designing an output that meets your needs. Let's look at some examples.

In the previous section, you plotted gas mileage by automobile weight, conditioned on engine displacement. What if you wanted to include regression lines, rug plots, and grid lines? You can do this by creating your own panel function (see the following listing). The resulting graph is provided in figure 16.3.

Listing 16.2 `xyplot` with custom panel function

```
displacement <- equal.count(mtcars$disp, number=3, overlap=0)

mypanel <- function(x, y) {
        panel.xyplot(x, y, pch=19)          ← ❶ Customized panel
        panel.rug(x, y)                          function
        panel.grid(h=-1, v=-1)
        panel.lmline(x, y, col="red", lwd=1, lty=2)
    }

xyplot(mpg~wt|displacement, data=mtcars,
      layout=c(3, 1),
      aspect=1.5,
      main = "Miles per Gallon vs. Weight by Engine Displacement",
      xlab = "Weight",
      ylab = "Miles per Gallon",
      panel = mypanel)
```

Here, we've wrapped four separate building block functions into our own `mypanel()` function and applied it within `xyplot()` through the `panel=` option ❶. The `panel.xyplot()` function generates the scatter plot using a filled circle (`pch=19`). The `panel.rug()` function adds rug plots to both the x and y axes of each panel. `panel.rug(x, FALSE)` or `panel.rug(FALSE, y)` would have added rugs to just the horizontal or vertical axis, respectively. The `panel.grid()` function adds horizontal and vertical grid lines (using negative numbers forces them to line up with the axis labels). Finally, the `panel.lmline()` function adds a regression line that's rendered as red (`col="red"`), dashed (`lty=2`) lines, of standard thickness (`lwd=1`). Each default panel function has its own structure and options. See the help page on each (for example, `help(panel.abline)`) for further details.

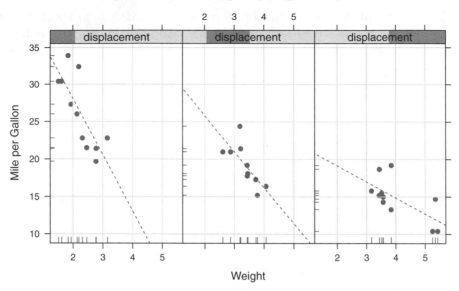

Figure 16.3   Trellis plot of mpg versus car weight conditioned on engine displacement. A custom panel function has been used to add regression lines, rug plots, and grid lines.

As a second example, we'll graph the relationship between gas mileage and engine displacement (considered as a continuous variable), conditioned on type of automobile transmission. In addition to creating separate panels for automatic and manual transmission engines, we'll add smoothed fit lines and horizontal mean lines. The code is given in the following listing.

Listing 16.3   `xyplot` with custom panel function and additional options

```
library(lattice)
mtcars$transmission <- factor(mtcars$am, levels=c(0,1),
                              labels=c("Automatic", "Manual"))

panel.smoother <- function(x, y) {
                    panel.grid(h=-1, v=-1)
                    panel.xyplot(x, y)
                    panel.loess(x, y)
                    panel.abline(h=mean(y), lwd=2, lty=2, col="green")
                  }

xyplot(mpg~disp|transmission,data=mtcars,
       scales=list(cex=.8, col="red"),
       panel=panel.smoother,
       xlab="Displacement", ylab="Miles per Gallon",
       main="MGP vs Displacement by Transmission Type",
       sub = "Dotted lines are Group Means", aspect=1)
```

The graph produced by this code is provided in figure 16.4.

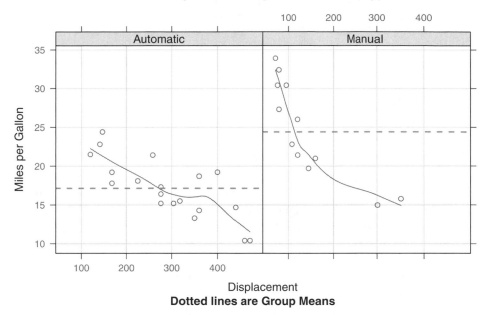

MGP vs Displacement by Transmission Type

Figure 16.4 Trellis graph of mpg versus engine displacement conditioned on transmission type. Smoothed lines (loess), grids, and group mean levels have been added.

There are several things to note in this new code. The `panel.xyplot()` function plots the individual points, and the `panel.loess()` function plots nonparametric fit lines in each panel. The `panel.abline()` function adds horizontal reference lines at the mean mpg value for each level of the conditioning variable. (If we had replaced `h=mean(y)` with `h=mean(mtcars$mpg)`, a single reference line would have been drawn at the mean mpg value for the entire sample.) The `scales=` option renders scale annotations in red and at 80 percent of their default size.

In the previous example, we could have used `scales=list(x=list(), y=list())` to specify separate options for the horizontal and vertical axes. See `help(xyplot)` for details on the many scale options available. In the next section, you'll learn how to superimpose data from groups of observations, rather than presenting them in separate panels.

16.2.3 Grouping variables

When you include a conditioning variable in a lattice graph formula, a separate panel is produced for each level of that variable. If you want to *superimpose* the results for each level instead, you can specify the variable as a group variable.

Let's say that you want to display the distribution of gas mileage for cars with manual and automatic transmissions using kernel density plots. You can superimpose these plots using this code:

```
library(lattice)
mtcars$transmission <- factor(mtcars$am, levels=c(0, 1),
                              labels=c("Automatic", "Manual"))
densityplot(~mpg, data=mtcars,
            group=transmission,
            main="MPG Distribution by Transmission Type",
            xlab="Miles per Gallon",
            auto.key=TRUE)
```

The resulting graph is presented in figure 16.5. By default, the group=option super-imposes the plots from each level of the grouping variable. Points are plotted as open circles, lines are solid, and level information is distinguished by color. As you can see, the colors are difficult to differentiate when printed in grayscale. Later you'll see how to change these defaults.

Note that legends or keys aren't produced by default. The option auto.key=TRUE will create a rudimentary legend and place it above the graph. You can make limited changes to this automated key by specifying options in a list. For example,

```
auto.key=list(space="right", columns=1, title="Transmission")
```

would move the legend to the right of the graph, present the key values in a single column, and add a legend title.

If you want to exert greater control over the legend, you can use the key= option. An example is given in listing 16.4. The resulting graph is provided in figure 16.6.

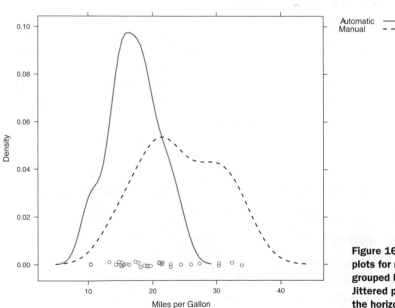

Figure 16.5   Kernel density plots for miles per gallon grouped by transmission type. Jittered points are provided on the horizontal axis.

Listing 16.4 Kernel density plot with a group variable and customized legend

```
library(lattice)
mtcars$transmission <- factor(mtcars$am, levels=c(0, 1),
                              labels=c("Automatic", "Manual"))

colors = c("red", "blue")                        Color, line, point
lines  = c(1,2)                                ❶ specifications
points = c(16,17)

key.trans <- list(title="Trasmission",           Legend
                  space="bottom", columns=2,    ❷ customization
                  text=list(levels(mtcars$transmission)),
                  points=list(pch=points, col=colors),
                  lines=list(col=colors, lty=lines),
                  cex.title=1, cex=.9)

densityplot(~mpg, data=mtcars,
            group=transmission,
            main="MPG Distribution by Transmission Type",
            xlab="Miles per Gallon",
            pch=points, lty=lines, col=colors,      Density plot
            lwd=2, jitter=.005,                    ❸ customization
            key=key.trans)
```

Here, the plotting symbols, line types, and colors are specified as vectors ❶. The first element of each vector will be applied to the first level of the group variable, the second element to the second level, and so forth. A list object is created to hold the legend options ❷. These options place the legend below the graph in two columns, and include the level names, point symbols, line types, and colors. The legend title is rendered slightly larger than the text for the symbols.

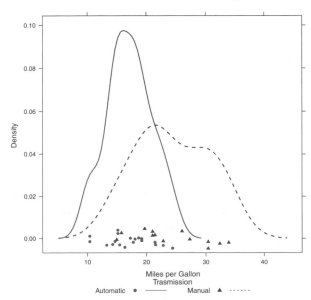

Figure 16.6 Kernel density plots for miles per gallon grouped by transmission type. Graphical parameters have been modified and a customized legend has been added. The custom legend specifies color, shape, line type, character size, and title.

The same plot symbols, line types, and colors are specified within the `densityplot()` function ❸. Additionally, the line width and jitter are increased to improve the appearance of the graph. Finally, the key is set to use the previously defined list. This approach to specifying a legend for the grouping variable allows a great deal of flexibility. In fact, you can create more than one legend and place them in different areas of the graph (not shown here).

Before completing this section, let's consider an example that includes group and conditioning variables in a single plot. The `CO2` data frame, included with the base R installation, describes a study of cold tolerance of the grass species *Echinocholoa crus-galli.*

The data describe carbon dioxide uptake rates (`uptake`) for 12 plants (`Plant`), at seven ambient carbon dioxide concentrations (`conc`). Six plants were from Quebec and six plants were from Mississippi. Three plants from each location were studied under chilled conditions and three plants were studied under nonchilled conditions. In this example, `Plant` is the group variable and both `Type` (Quebec/Mississippi) and `Treatment` (chilled/nonchilled) are conditioning variables. The following code produces the plot in figure 16.7.

Listing 16.5 `xyplot` with group and conditioning variables and customized legend

```
library(lattice)
colors <- "darkgreen"
symbols <- c(1:12)
linetype <- c(1:3)

key.species <- list(title="Plant",
                    space="right",
                    text=list(levels(CO2$Plant)),
                    points=list(pch=symbols, col=colors))

xyplot(uptake~conc|Type*Treatment, data=CO2,
       group=Plant,
       type="o",
       pch=symbols, col=colors, lty=linetype,
       main="Carbon Dioxide Uptake\nin Grass Plants",
       ylab=expression(paste("Uptake ",
             bgroup("(", italic(frac("umol","m"^2)), ")"))),
       xlab=expression(paste("Concentration ",
             bgroup("(", italic(frac(mL,L)), ")"))),
       sub = "Grass Species: Echinochloa crus-galli",
       key=key.species)
```

Note the use of `\n` to give you a two-line title and the use of the `expression()` function to add mathematical notation to the axis labels. Here, color is suppressed as a group differentiator by specifying a single color in the `col=` option. In this case, adding 12 different colors is overkill and distracts from the goal of easily visualizing the relationships in each panel. Clearly, there's something different about the Mississippi grasses in the chilled condition.

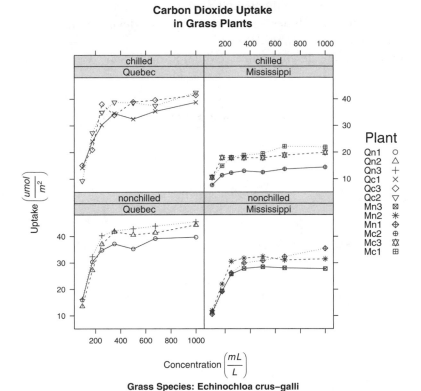

Figure 16.7 `xyplot` **showing the impact of ambient carbon dioxide concentrations on carbon dioxide uptake for 12 plants in two treatment conditions and two types.** `Plant` **is the group variable and** `Treatment` **and** `Type` **are the conditioning variables.**

Up to this point, you've been modifying graphic elements in your charts through options passed to either the high-level graph function (for example, `xyplot(pch=17)`) or within the panel functions that they use (for example, `panel.xyplot(pch=17)`). But such changes are in effect only for the duration of the function call. In the next section, we'll review a method for changing graphical parameters that persists for the duration of the interactive session or batch execution.

16.2.4 *Graphic parameters*

In chapter 3, you learned how to view and set default graphics parameters using the `par()` function. Although this works for graphs produced with R's native graphic system, lattice graphs are unaffected by these settings. Instead, the graphic defaults used by lattice functions are contained in a large list object that can be accessed with the `trellis.par.get()` function and modified through the `trellis.par.set()` function. The `show.settings()` function can be used to display the current graphic settings visually.

As an example, let's change the default symbol used for superimposed points (that is, points in a graph that includes a group variable). The default is an open circle. We'll give each group their own symbol instead.

First, view the current defaults and save them into a list called `mysettings`:

```
> show.settings()
> mysettings <- trellis.par.get()
```

Next, look at the defaults that are specific to superimposed symbols:

```
> mysettings$superpose.symbol
$alpha
[1] 1 1 1 1 1 1 1

$cex
[1] 0.8 0.8 0.8 0.8 0.8 0.8 0.8

$col
[1] "#0080ff"   "#ff00ff"   "darkgreen" "#ff0000"   "orange"    "#00ff00"
[7] "brown"

$fill
[1] "#CCFFFF" "#FFCCFF" "#CCFFCC" "#FFE5CC" "#CCE6FF" "#FFFFCC" "#FFCCCC"

$font
[1] 1 1 1 1 1 1 1

$pch
[1] 1 1 1 1 1 1 1
```

Here you see that the symbol used for each level of a group variable is an open circle (pch=1). Seven levels are defined, after which symbols recycle.

Finally, issue the following statements:

```
mysettings$superpose.symbol$pch <- c(1:10)
trellis.par.set(mysettings)
show.settings()
```

Lattice graphs now use symbol 1 (open circle) for the first level of a group variable, symbol 2 (open triangle) for the second, and so on. Additionally, symbols have been defined for 10 levels of a grouping variable, rather than 7. The changes will remain in effect until all graphic devices are closed. You can change any graphic setting in this manner.

16.2.5 *Page arrangement*

In chapter 3 you learned how to place more than one graph on a page using the `par()` function. Because lattice functions don't recognize `par()` settings, you'll need a different approach. The easiest method involves saving your lattice graphs as objects, and using the `plot()` function with either the `split=` or `position=` option specified.

The `split` option divides a page up into a specified number of rows and columns and places graphs into designated cells of the resulting matrix. The format for the `split` option is

```
split=c(placement row, placement column,
    total number of rows, total number of columns)
```

For example, the following code

```
library(lattice)
graph1 <- histogram(~height|voice.part, data=singer,
                    main="Heights of Choral Singers by Voice Part")
graph2 <- densityplot(~height, data=singer, group=voice.part,
                    plot.points=FALSE, auto.key=list(columns=4))
plot(graph1, split=c(1, 1, 1, 2))
    plot(graph2, split=c(1, 2, 1, 2), newpage=FALSE)
```

places the first graph directly above the second graph. Specifically, the first `plot()` statement divides the page up into one column and two rows and places the graph in the first column and first row (counting top-down and left-right). The second `plot()` statement divides the page up in the same way, but places the graph in the first column and second row. Because the `plot()` function starts a new page by default, you suppress this action by including the `newpage=FALSE` option. (I've omitted the graph to save space.)

You can gain more control of sizing and placement by using the `position=` option. Consider the following code:

```
library(lattice)
graph1 <- histogram(~height|voice.part, data=singer,
                    main="Heights of Choral Singers by Voice Part")
graph2 <- densityplot(~height, data=singer, group=voice.part,
                    plot.points=FALSE, auto.key=list(columns=4))
plot(graph1, position=c(0, .3, 1, 1))
plot(graph2, position=c(0, 0, 1, .3), newpage=FALSE)
```

Here, `position=c(xmin, ymin, xmax, ymax)`, where the x-y coordinate system for the page is a rectangle with dimensions ranging from 0 to 1 on both the x and y axes, and the origin (0,0) at the bottom left. (Again, the resulting graph is omitted to save space.)

You can also change the order of the panels in a lattice graph. The `index.cond=` option in a high-level lattice graph function specifies the order of the conditioning variable levels. For the `voice.part` factor, the levels are

```
> levels(singer$voice.part)
[1] "Bass 2"    "Bass 1"    "Tenor 2"    "Tenor 1"    "Alto 2"    "Alto 1"
[7] "Soprano 2" "Soprano 1"
```

Adding `index.cond=list(c(2, 4, 6, 8, 1, 3, 5, 7))` would place the "1" voice parts together, followed by "2" voice parts. When there are two conditioning variables, include two vectors in the list. In listing 16.5, adding `index.cond=list(c(1, 2), c(2, 1))` would reverse the order of treatments in figure 16.7.

To learn more about lattice graphs, take a look the excellent text by Sarkar (2008) and its supporting website at http://lmdvr.r-forge.r-project.org. The Trellis Graphics User's Manual (http://cm.bell-labs.com/cm/ms/departments/sia/doc/trellis.user. pdf) is also an excellent source of information.

In the next section, we'll explore a second comprehensive alternative to R's native graphic system. This one is based on the `ggplot2` package.

16.3 *The ggplot2 package*

The ggplot2 package implements a system for creating graphics in R based on a comprehensive and coherent grammar. This provides a consistency to graph creation often lacking in R, and allows the user to create graph types that are innovative and novel.

The simplest approach for creating graphs in ggplot2 is through the qplot() or quick plot function. The format is

```
qplot(x, y, data=, color=, shape=, size=, alpha=, geom=, method=, formula=,
    facets=, xlim=, ylim=, xlab=, ylab=, main=, sub=)
```

where the parameters/options are defined in table 16.4.

Table 16.4   qplot options

Option	Description
alpha	Alpha transparency for overlapping elements expressed as a fraction between 0 (complete transparency) and 1 (complete opacity).
color, shape, size, fill	Associates the levels of variable with symbol color, shape, or size. For line plots, color associates levels of a variable with line color. For density and box plots, fill associates fill colors with a variable. Legends are drawn automatically.
data	Specifies a data frame.
facets	Creates a trellis graph by specifying conditioning variables. Its value is expressed as rowvar ~ colvar (see the example in figure 16.10). To create trellis graphs based on a single conditioning variable, use rowvar~. or .~colvar.
geom	Specifies the geometric objects that define the graph type. The geom option is expressed as a character vector with one or more entries. geom values include "point", "smooth", "boxplot", "line", "histogram", "density", "bar", and "jitter".
main, sub	Character vectors specifying the title and subtitle.
method, formula	If geom="smooth", a loess fit line and confidence limits are added by default. When the number of observations is greater than 1,000, a more efficient smoothing algorithm is employed. Methods include "lm" for regression, "gam" for generalized additive models, and "rlm" for robust regression. The formula parameter gives the form of the fit.
	For example, to add simple linear regression lines, you'd specify geom="smooth", method="lm", formula=y~x. Changing the formula to y~poly(x,2) would produce a quadratic fit. Note that the formula uses the letters x and y, not the names of the variables.
	For method="gam", be sure to load the mgcv package. For method="rml", load the MASS package.
x, y	Specifies the variables placed on the horizontal and vertical axis. For univariate plots (for example, histograms), omit y.
xlab, ylab	Character vectors specifying horizontal and vertical axis labels.
xlim, ylim	Two-element numeric vectors giving the minimum and maximum values for the horizontal and vertical axes, respectively.

To see how `qplot()` works, let's review some examples. The following code creates box plots of gas mileage by number of cylinders. The actual data points are superimposed (and jittered to reduce overlap). Box plot colors vary by number of cylinders.

```
library(ggplot2)
mtcars$cylinder <- as.factor(mtcars$cyl)
qplot(cylinder, mpg, data=mtcars, geom=c("boxplot", "jitter"),
      fill=cylinder,
      main="Box plots with superimposed data points",
      xlab= "Number of Cylinders",
        ylab="Miles per Gallon")
```

The graph is displayed in figure 16.8.

As a second example, let's create a scatter plot matrix of gas mileage by car weight and use color and symbol shape to differentiate cars with automatic transmissions from those with manual transmissions. Additionally, we'll add separate regression lines and confidence bands for each transmission type.

```
library(ggplot2)
transmission <- factor(mtcars$am, levels=c(0, 1),
                       labels=c("Automatic",  "Manual"))
qplot(wt,mpg, data=mtcars,
      color=transmission, shape=transmission,
      geom=c("point", "smooth"),
      method="lm", formula=y~x,
      xlab="Weight", ylab="Miles Per Gallon",
      main="Regression Example")
```

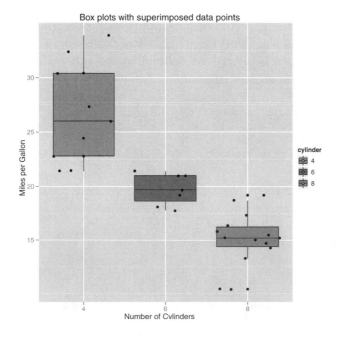

Figure 16.8   Box plots of auto mileage by number of cylinders. Data points are superimposed and jittered.

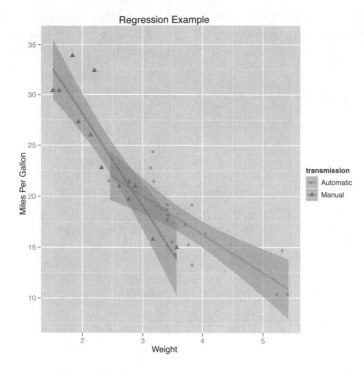

Figure 16.9 **Scatter plot between auto mileage and car weight, with separate regression lines and confidence bands by engine transmission type (manual, automatic)**

The resulting graph is provided in figure 16.9. This is a useful type of graph, not easily created using other packages.

As a third example, we'll create a faceted (trellis) graph. Each facet (panel) displays the scatter plot between gas mileage and car weight. Row facets are defined by the transmission type, whereas column facets are defined by the number of cylinders present. The size of each data point represents the car's horsepower rating.

```
library(ggplot2)
mtcars$cyl <- factor(mtcars$cyl, levels=c(4, 6, 8),
                     labels=c("4 cylinders", "6 cylinders", "8 cylinders"))
mtcars$am <- factor(mtcars$am, levels=c(0, 1),
                    labels=c("Automatic",  "Manual"))
qplot(wt,mpg, data=mtcars, facets=am~cyl, size=hp)
```

The graph is displayed in figure 16.10. Note how simple it is to create a complex graph (actually a bubble chart). You may want to try adding shape and color options to the function call and see how the resulting graph is affected.

We'll end this section by revisiting the `singer` data with which we began the chapter. This code produces the graph in figure 16.11:

```
library(ggplot2)
data(singer, package="lattice")
qplot(height, data=singer, geom=c("density"),
      facets=voice.part~., fill=voice.part)
```

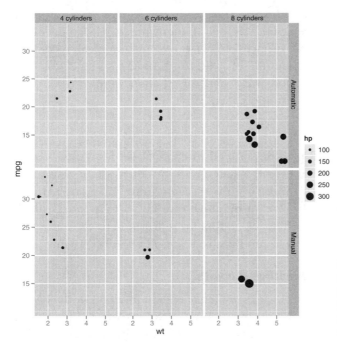

Figure 16.10   Scatter plot between auto mileage and car weight, faceted by transmission type (manual, automatic) and number of cylinders (4, 6, or 8). Symbol size represents horsepower.

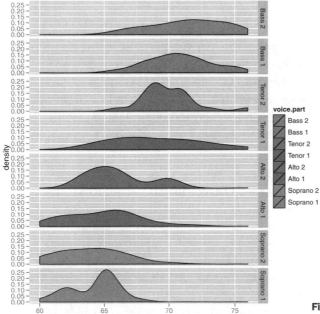

Figure 16.11   Faceted density plots for singer heights by voice part

Comparing the distribution of heights is easier in this format than in the format presented in figure 16.1. (Once again, this looks better when displayed in color.)

We've only scratched the surface of this powerful graphical system. Interested readers are referred to Wickham (2009), and the ggplot2 website (http://had.co.nz/ ggplot2/) for more information. We'll end this chapter with a review of interactive graphics and R functions that support them.

16.4   *Interactive graphs*

The base installation of R provides limited interactivity with graphs. You can modify graphs by issuing additional program statements, but there's little that you can do to modify them or gather new information from them using the mouse. However, there are contributed packages that greatly enhance your ability to interact with the graphs you create. In this section, we'll focus on functions provided by the `playwith`, `latti-cist`, `iplots`, and `rggobi` packages. Be sure to install them before first use.

16.4.1 *Interacting with graphs: identifying points*

Before getting to the specialize packages, let's review a function in the base R installation that allows you to identify and label points in scatter plots. Using the `identify()` function, you can label selected points in a scatter plot with their row number or row name using your mouse. Identification continues until you select Stop or right-click on the graph. For example, after issuing the following statements

```
plot(mtcars$wt, mtcars$mpg)
identify(mtcars$wt, mtcars$mpg, labels=row.names(mtcars))
```

the cursor will change from a pointer to a crosshair. Clicking on scatter plot points will label them until you select Stop from the Graphics Device menu or right-click on the graph and select Stop from the context menu.

Many graphic functions in contributed packages (including functions from the `car` package discussed in chapter 8) employ this method for labeling points. Unfortunately, the `identify()` function doesn't work with `lattice` or `ggplot2` graphs.

16.4.2 *playwith*

The `playwith` package provides a GTK+ graphical user interface that allows users to edit and interact with R plots. You can install the `playwith` package on any platform using `install.packages("playwith", depend=TRUE)`. On platforms running Mac OS X and Linux, it's best to also install the JGR graphic user interface (see appendix A), and run `playwith` from within this GUI.

The `playwith()` function allows users to identify and label points, view all variable values for an observation, zoom and pan, add annotations (text, arrows, lines, rectangles, titles, labels), change visual elements (colors, text sizes, and so on), apply previously saved styles, and output the resulting graph in a variety of formats. This is easily demonstrated with an example. After running the following code

```
library(playwith)
library(lattice)

playwith(
    xyplot(mpg~wt|factor(cyl)*factor(am),
           data=mtcars, subscripts=TRUE,
           type=c("r", "p"))
)
```

the window in figure 16.12 will appear on the screen. Try out the buttons on the left, as well as the menu items. The GUI is fairly self-explanatory. Unlike the `identify()` function, `playwith()` works with `lattice` and `ggplot2` graphs as well as base R graphs. Some options in the Theme menu only work properly with base graphics. Additionally, some features work with `ggplot2` graphs (such as annotating) and some don't (such as identifying points).

To learn more about the `playwith` package, visit the project website at http://code. google.com/p/playwith/.

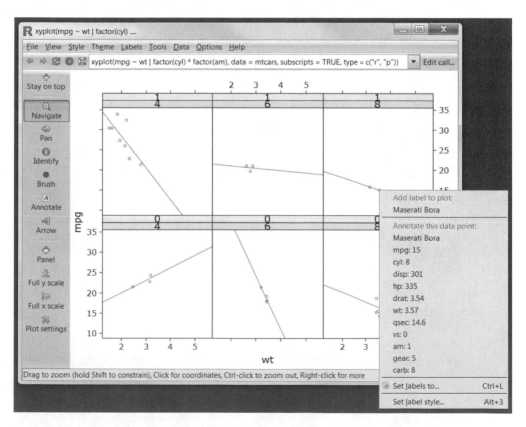

Figure 16.12   The `playwith` window. The user can edit the graph using the mouse with this GTK+ GUI.

16.4.3 *latticist*

The `latticist` package lets you explore a data set using lattice displays. It provides a graphic user interface to the graphs described in section 16.2, but it can also be used to create displays from the `vcd` package (see chapter 11, section 11.4). If desired, `latticist` and can also be integrated with `playwith`. For example, executing the following code

```
library(latticist)
mtcars$cyl <- factor(mtcars$cyl)
mtcars$gear <- factor(mtcars$gear)
latticist(mtcars, use.playwith=TRUE)
```

will bring up the interface in figure 16.13.

In addition to having the `playwith` functionality (point identification, annotation, zooming, panning, styles), the user can now create lattice graphs by selecting from drop-down menus and buttons. To learn more about the `latticist` package, see http://code.google.com/p/latticist/.

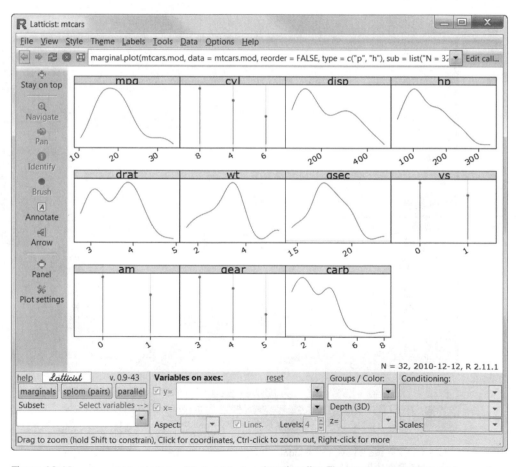

Figure 16.13 `playwith` window with `latticist` functionality. The user can create `lattice` and `vcd` graphs interactively.

A similar interface is available for ggplot2 graphs, through Plot Builder, a plug-in for Deducer, a popular GUI for R (see appendix A). Because it can't be run from the R console, we won't discuss it here. If you're interested, visit the Deducer website at www. deducer.org.

16.4.4 Interactive graphics with the iplots package

Whereas playwith and latticist allow you to interact with a single graph, the iplots package takes interaction in a different direction. This package provides interactive mosaic plots, bar plots, box plots, parallel plots, scatter plots, and histograms that can be linked together and color brushed. This means that you can select and identify observations using the mouse, and highlighting observations in one graph will automatically highlight the same observations in all other open graphs. You can also use the mouse to obtain information about graphic objects such as points, bars, lines, and box plots.

The iplots package is implemented through Java and the primary functions are listed in table 16.5.

To understand how iplots works, execute the code provided in listing 16.6.

Table 16.5 iplot functions

Function	Description
ibar()	Interactive bar chart
ibox()	Interactive box plot
ihist()	Interactive histogram
imap()	Interactive map
imosaic()	Interactive mosaic plot
ipcp()	Interactive parallel coordinates plot
iplot()	Interactive scatter plot

Listing 16.6 iplots demonstration

```
library(iplots)
attach(mtcars)
cylinders <- factor(cyl)
gears <- factor(gear)
transmission <- factor(am)
ihist(mpg)
ibar(gears)
iplot(mpg, wt)
ibox(mtcars[c("mpg", "wt", "qsec", "disp", "hp")])
ipcp(mtcars[c("mpg", "wt", "qsec", "disp", "hp")])
imosaic(transmission, cylinders)
detach(mtcars)
```

Six windows containing graphs will open. Rearrange them on the desktop so that each is visible (each can be resized if necessary). A portion of the display is provided in figure 16.14.

Now try the following:

- Click on the three-gear bar in the Barchart (gears) window. The bar will turn red. In addition, all cars with three-gear engines will be highlighted in the other graphic windows.

- Mouse down and drag to select a rectangular region of points in the Scatter plot (wt vs mpg) window. These points will be highlighted and the corresponding observations in every other graphics window will also turn red.

- Hold down the Ctrl key and move the mouse pointer over a point, bar, box plot, or line in one of the graphs. Details about that object will appear in a pop-up window.

- Right-click on any object and note the options that are offered in the context menu. For example, you can right-click on the Boxplot (mpg) window and change the graph to a parallel coordinates plot (PCP).

- You can drag to select more than one object (point, bar, and so on) or use Shift-click to select noncontiguous objects. Try selecting both the three- and five-gear bars in the Barchart (gears) window.

The functions in the `iplots` package allow you to explore the variable distributions and relationships among variables in subgroups of observations that you select interactively. This can provide insights that would be difficult and time-consuming to obtain in other ways. For more information on the `iplots` package, visit the project website at http://rosuda.org/iplots/.

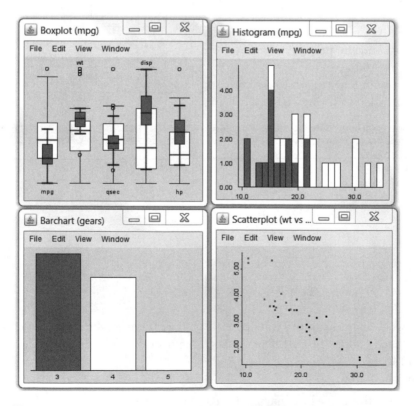

Figure 16.14   An `iplots` demonstration created by listing 16.6. Only four of the six windows are displayed to save room. In these graphs, the user has clicked on the three-gear bar in the bar chart window.

16.4.5 *rggobi*

For our final example of interactivity, we'll actually look beyond the R platform to the open source GGobi application (www.ggobi.org). GGobi is a comprehensive program for the visual and dynamic exploration of high-dimensional data and is freely available for Windows, Mac OS X, and Linux platforms. It offers a number of attractive features, including linked interactive scatter plots, bar charts, parallel coordinate plots, time series plots, scatter plot matrices, and 3D rotation; brushing and identification; multivariate transformation methods; and sophisticated exploratory support, including guided and manual 1D and 2D tours. Happily, the `rggobi` package provides a seamless interface between GGobi and R.

The first step in using GGobi is to download and install the appropriate software for your platform (www.ggobi.org/downloads/). Then install the `rggobi` package within R using `install.packages("rggobi", depend=TRUE)`.

Once you've installed both, you can use the `ggobi()` function to run GGobi from within R. This gives you sophisticated interactive graphics access to all of your R data. To see this in action, execute the following code:

```
library(rggobi)
g <- ggobi(mtcars)
```

The GGobi interface will open and allow you to explore the `mtcars` dataset in a highly interactive fashion. To learn more, review the introduction, tutorial, manual, and video guides available on the GGobi website. A comprehensive overview is also provided in Cook and Swayne (2008).

16.5   Summary

In this chapter, we reviewed several packages that provide access to advanced graphical methods. We started with the `lattice` package, designed to provide a system for creating trellis graphs, followed by the `ggplot2` package, based on a comprehensive grammar of graphics. Both packages are designed to provide you with a complete and comprehensive alternative to the native graphics provided with R. Each offers methods of creating attractive and meaningful visualizations of data that are difficult to generate in other ways.

We then explored several packages for dynamically interacting with graphs, including `playwith`, `latticist`, `iplots`, and `rggobi`. These packages allow you to interact directly with data in graphs, leading to a greater intimacy with your data and expanded opportunities for developing insights.

You should now have a firm grasp of the many ways that R allows you to create visual representations of data. If a picture is worth a thousand words, and R provides a thousand ways to create a picture, then R must be worth a million words (or something to that effect). These resources are a testament to the hard and selfless work of the initial R development team and the thousands of hours of work contributed by package authors.

afterword: Into the rabbit hole

We've covered a broad range of topics in the book, including major ones like the R development environment, data management, traditional statistical models, and statistical graphics. We've also covered hidden gems like resampling statistics, missing values imputation, and interactive graphics. The great (or perhaps infuriating) thing about R is that there's always more to learn.

R is a large, robust, and evolving statistical platform and programming language. With so many new packages, frequent updates, and new directions, how can a user stay current? Happily, many websites support this active community and provide coverage of platform and package changes, new methodologies, and a wealth of tutorials. I've listed some of my favorite sites below.

The R Project (http://www.r-project.org/)
The official R website and your first stop for all things R. The site includes extensive documentation, including *An Introduction to R*, *The R Language Definition*, *Writing R Extensions*, *R Data Import/Export*, *R Installation and Administration*, and *The R FAQ*.

The R Journal (http://journal.r-project.org/)
A freely accessible refereed journal containing articles on the R project and contributed packages.

R Bloggers (http://www.r-bloggers.com/)
A central hub (blog aggregator) collecting content from bloggers writing about R. Contains new articles daily. I'm addicted to it.

Planet R (http://planetr.stderr.org)
Another good site-aggregator, including information from a wide range of sources. Updated daily.

CRANberries (http://dirk.eddelbuettel.com/cranberries/)
A site that aggregates information about new and updated packages, and contains links to CRAN for each.

R Graph Gallery (http://addictedtor.free.fr/graphiques/)
A collection of innovative graphs, along with their source code.

R Graphics Manual (http://bm2.genes.nig.ac.jp/)
A collection of R graphics from all R packages, arranged by topic, package, and function. At last count, there were 35,000+ images!

Journal of Statistical Software (http://www.jstatsoft.org/)
A freely accessible refereed journal containing articles, book reviews, and code snippets on statistical computing. Contains frequent articles about R.

Revolutions (http://blog.revolution-computing.com/)
A popular, well-organized blog, dedicated to news and information about R.

CRAN Task Views (http://cran.r-project.org/web/views/)
Task views are guides to the use of R in different academic and research fields. They include a description of the packages and methods available for a given area. Currently there are 28 task views available (see table below).

CRAN Task Views	
Bayesian Inference	Machine Learning & Statistical Learning
Chemometrics and Computational Physics	Medical Image Analysis
Design, Monitoring, and Analysis of Clinical Trials	Multivariate Statistics
Clinical Trial Design, Monitoring, and Analysis	Natural Language Processing
Cluster Analysis & Finite Mixture Models	Official Statistics & Survey Methodology
Probability Distributions	Optimization and Mathematical Programming
Computational Econometrics	Analysis of Pharmacokinetic Data
Analysis of Ecological and Environmental Data	Phylogenetics, Especially Comparative Methods
Design of Experiments (DoE)	Psychometric Models and Methods
Empirical Finance	Robust Statistical Methods
Statistical Genetics	Statistics for the Social Sciences
Graphic Displays & Dynamic Graphics	Analysis of Spatial Data
gRaphical Models in R	Survival Analysis
High-Performance and Parallel Computing with R	Time Series Analysis

R-Help Main R Mailing List (https://stat.ethz.ch/mailman/listinfo/r-help)
This electronic mailing list is the best place to ask questions about R. The archives are also searchable. Be sure to read the FAQ before posting questions.

Quick-R (http://www.statmethods.net)
This is my R website. It's stocked with more than 80 brief tutorials on R topics. False modesty forbids me from saying more.

The R community is a helpful, vibrant, and exciting lot. Welcome to Wonderland.

appendix A
Graphic user interfaces

You turned here first, didn't you? By default, R provides a simple command-line interface (CLI). The user enters statements at a command-line prompt (> by default) and each command is executed one at a time. For many data analysts, the CLI is one of R's most significant limitations.

There have been a number of attempts to create more graphical interfaces, ranging from code editors that interact with R (such as RStudio), to GUIs for specific functions or packages (such as BiplotGUI), to full-blown GUIs that allow the user to construct analyses through interactions with menus and dialog boxes (such as R Commander).

Several of the more useful code editors are listed in table A.1.

Table A.1 Integrated development environments and syntax editors

Name	URL
Eclipse with StatET plug-in	http://www.eclipse.org and http://www.walware.de/goto/statet
ESS (Emacs Speaks Statistics)	http://ess.r-project.org/
Komodo Edit with SciViews-K plug-in	http://www.activestate.com/komodo_edit/ http://www.sciviews.org/SciViews-K/
JGR	http://www.rforge.net/JGR/

Table A.1   Integrated development environments and syntax editors (*continued*)

Name	URL
RStudio	http://www.rstudio.org
Tinn-R (Windows only)	http://www.sciviews.org/Tinn-R/
Notepad++ with NppToR (windows only)	http://notepad-plus-plus.org/ http://sourceforge.net/projects/npptor/

The code editors in table A.1 allow the user to edit and execute R code and include syntax highlighting, statement completion, object exploration, project organization, and online help. A screenshot of RStudio is provided in figure A.1.

    Several promising full-blown GUIs for R are listed in table A.2. The GUIs available for R are less comprehensive and mature than those offered by SAS or IBM SPSS, but they're developing rapidly.

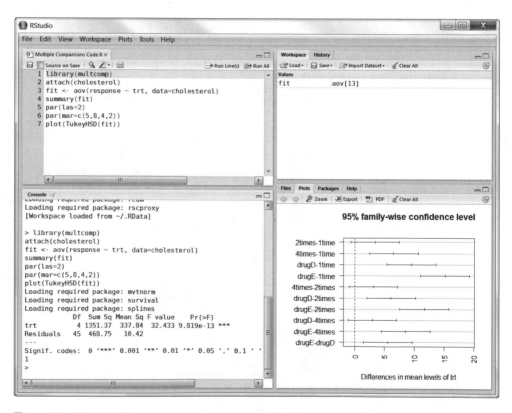

Figure A.1   RStudio IDE

Table A.2 Comprehensive GUIs for R

Name	URL
JGR/Deducer	http://ifellows.ucsd.edu/pmwiki/pmwiki.php?n=Main.DeducerManual
R AnalyticFlow	http://www.ef-prime.com/products/ranalyticflow_en/
Rattle (for data mining)	http://rattle.togaware.com/
R Commander	http://socserv.mcmaster.ca/jfox/Misc/Rcmdr/
Red R	http://www.red-r.org/
Rkward	http://rkward.sourceforge.net/

My favorite GUI for introductory statistics courses is R Commander (shown in figure A.2).

Finally, there are a number of applications that allow the user to create a GUI wrapper for any given R function (including user-written functions). These include the R GUI Generator (RGG) (http://rgg.r-forge.r-project.org/), and the `fgui` and `twiddler` packages available from CRAN.

GUI projects in R are undergoing rapid change and expansion. For more information, visit the R GUI Projects page at http://www.sciviews.org/_rgui/.

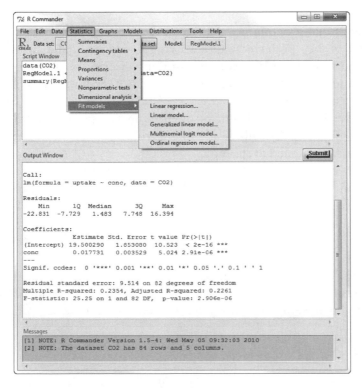

Figure A.2
R Commander GUI

appendix B
Customizing the startup environment

One of the first things that programmers like to do is customize their startup environment to conform to their preferred way of working. Customizing the startup environment allows you to set R options, specify a working directory, load commonly used packages, load user-written functions, set a default CRAN download site, and perform any number of housekeeping tasks.

You can customize the R environment through either a site initialization file (Rprofile.site) or a directory initialization file (.Rprofile). These are text files containing R code to be executed at startup.

At startup, R will source the file Rprofile.site from the *R_HOME*/etc directory, where *R_HOME* is an environment value. It will then look for an .Rprofile file to source in the current working directory. If R doesn't find this file, it will look for it in the user's home directory. You can use `Sys.getenv("R_HOME")`, `Sys.getenv("HOME")`, and `getwd()` to identify the location of the *R_HOME*, *HOME*, and current working directory, respectively.

You can place two special functions in these files. The `.First()` function is executed at the start of each R session, and the `.Last()` function is executed at the end of each session. An example of an Rprofile.site file is shown in listing B.1.

Listing B.1 Sample Rprofile.site file

```
options(papersize="a4")
options(editor="notepad")          ←┐ Set common options
options(pager="internal")
options(tab.width = 2)
options(width = 130)
options(graphics.record=TRUE)
options(show.signif.stars=FALSE)

options(prompt="> ")               ←┐ Set R interactive prompt
options(continue="+ ")

.libPaths("C:/my_R_library")       ←── Set path for local library

local({r <- getOption("repos")     ←┐ Set CRAN mirror
    r["CRAN"] <- "http://cran.case.edu/"   │ default
    options(repos=r)})

.First <- function(){              ←── Startup function
 library(lattice)
 library(Hmisc)
 source("C:/mydir/myfunctions.R")
 cat("\nWelcome at", date(), "\n")
}

.Last <- function(){               ←┐ Session end
 cat("\nGoodbye at ", date(), "\n")  │ function
}
```

There are several things you should note about this file:

- Setting a .libPaths value allows you to create a local library for packages outside of the R directory tree. This can be useful for retaining packages during an upgrade.
- Setting a default CRAN mirror site frees you from having to choose one each time you issue an install.packages() command.
- The .First() function is an excellent place to load libraries that you use often, as well as source text files containing user-written functions that you apply frequently.
- The .Last() function is an excellent place for any cleanup activities, including archiving command histories, program output, and data files.

There are other ways to customize the startup environment, including the use of command-line options and environment variables. See help(Startup) and appendix B in the *Introduction to R* manual (http://cran.r-project.org/doc/manuals/R-intro.pdf) for more details.

appendix C
Exporting data from R

In chapter 2, we reviewed a wide range of methods for importing data into R. But there are times that you'll want to go the other way—exporting data from R—so that data can be archived or imported into external applications. In this appendix, you'll learn how to output an R object to a delimited text file, an Excel spreadsheet, or a statistical application (such as SPSS, SAS, or Stata).

C.1 Delimited text file

You can use the `write.table()` function to output an R object to a delimited text file. The format is

```
write.table(x, outfile, sep=delimiter, quote=TRUE, na="NA")
```

where *x* is the object and *outfile* is the target file. For example, the statement

```
write.table(mydata, "mydata.txt", sep=",")
```

would save the dataset `mydata` to a comma-delimited file named mydata.txt in the current working directory. Include a path (for example, "c:/myprojects/mydata.txt") to save the output file elsewhere. Replacing `sep=","` with `sep="\t"` would save the data in a tab-delimited file. By default, strings are enclosed in quotes (" ") and missing values are written as NA.

C.2   *Excel spreadsheet*

The `write.xlsx()` function in the `xlsx` package can be used to save an R data frame to an Excel 2007 workbook. The format is

```
library(xlsx)
write.xlsx(x, outfile, col.Names=TRUE, row.names=TRUE,
           sheetName="Sheet 1", append=FALSE)
```

For example, the statements

```
library(xlsx)
write.xlsx(mydata, "mydata.xlsx")
```

export the data frame `mydata` to a worksheet (`Sheet 1` by default) in an Excel workbook named mydata.xlsx in the current working directory. By default, the variable names in the dataset are used to create column headings in the spreadsheet and row names are placed in the first column of the spreadsheet. If mydata.xlsx already exists, it is overwritten.

The `xlsx` package is a powerful tool for manipulating Excel 2007 workbooks. See the package documentation for more details.

C.3   *Statistical applications*

The `write.foreign()` function in the `foreign` package can be used to export a data frame to an external statistical application. Two files are created—a free-format text file containing the data, and a code file containing instructions for reading the data into the external statistical application. The format is

```
write.foreign(dataframe, datafile, codefile, package=package)
```

For example, the code

```
library(foreign)
write.foreign(mydata, "mydata.txt", "mycode.sps", package="SPSS")
```

would export the dataframe `mydata` into a free-format text file named mydata.txt in the current working directory and an SPSS program named mycode.sps that can be used to read the text file. Other values of `package` include `"SAS"` and `"Stata"`.

To learn more about exporting data from R, see the *R Data Import/Export* documentation, available from http://cran.r-project.org/doc/manuals/R-data.pdf.

appendix D
Creating publication-quality output

Research doesn't end when the last statistical analysis or graph is completed. We need to include the results in a report that effectively communicates these findings to a teacher, supervisor, client, government agency, or journal editor. Although R creates state-of-the-art graphics, its text output is woefully retro—tables of mono-spaced text with columns lined up using spaces.

There are two common approaches to creating publication quality reports in R: Sweave and odfWeave. The `Sweave` package allows you to embed R code and output in LaTeX documents, in order to produce high-end typeset reports in PDF, PostScript, and DVI formats. Sweave is an elegant, precise, and highly flexible system, but it requires the author to be conversant with LaTeX coding.

In a similar fashion, the `odfWeave` package provides a mechanism for embedding R code and output in documents that follow the Open Documents Format (ODF). These reports can be further edited via an ODF word processor, such as OpenOffice Writer, and saved in either ODF or Microsoft Word format. The process is not as flexible as the Sweave approach, but it eliminates the need to learn LaTeX. We'll look at each approach in turn.

D.1 High-quality typesetting with Sweave (R + LaTeX)

LaTeX is a document preparation system for high-quality typesetting (http://www.latex-project.org) that's freely available for Windows, Mac, and Linux platforms. An author creates a text document that includes markup code for formatting the content. The document is then processed through a LaTeX compiler, producing a finished document in PDF, PostScript, or DVI format.

The `Sweave` package allows you to embed R code and output (including graphs) within the LaTeX document. This is a multistep process:

1 A special document called a *noweb* file (typically with the extension .Rnw) is created using any text editor. The file contains the written content, LaTeX markup code, and R code chunks. Each R code chunk starts with the delimiter `<<>>=` and ends with the delimiter `@`.

2 The `Sweave()` function processes the noweb file and generates a LaTeX file. During this step, the R code chunks are processed, and depending on options, replaced with LaTeX-formatted R code and output. This step can be accomplished from within R or from the command line.

Within R, the format is

```
Sweave("infile.Rnw")
```

By default, `Sweave("example.Rnw")` would input the file example.Rnw from the current working directory and output the file example.tex to the same directory. Alternatively, use can use

```
Sweave("infile.Rnw", syntax="SweaveSyntaxNoweb")
```

Specifying this syntax option can help avoid some common parsing errors, as well as conflicts with the `R2HTML` package.

Execution from the command line will depend on the operating system. For example, on a Linux system, this might look like `$ R CMD Sweave infile.Rnw`

3 The LaTeX file is then run through a LaTeX compiler, creating a PDF, PostScript, or DVI file. Popular LaTeX compilers include TeX Live for Linux, MacTeX for Mac, and proTeXt for Windows.

The complete process is outlined in figure D.1.

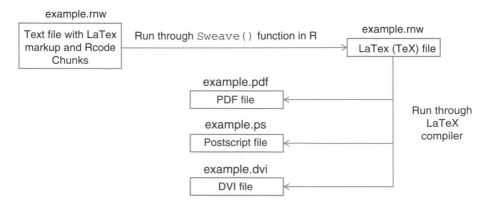

Figure D.1 Process for generating a publication-quality report using Sweave

As indicated earlier, each chunk of R code is surrounded by <<>>= and @. You can add options to each <<>>= delimiter in order to control the processing of the corresponding R code chunk. For example

```
<<echo=TRUE, results=HIDE>>=
summary(lm(Y~X, data=mydata))
@
```

would output the code, but not the results, whereas

```
<<echo=FALSE, fig=TRUE>>=
plot(A)
@
```

wouldn't print the code but would include the graph in the output. Common delimiter options are described in table D.1.

Table D.1   Common options for R code chunks

Option	Description
echo	Include the code in the output (echo=TRUE) or not (echo=FALSE). The default is TRUE.
eval	Use eval=FALSE to keep the code from being evaluated/executed. The default is TRUE.
fig	Use fig=TRUE when the output is a graph. The default is FALSE.
results	Include R code output (results=verbatim), suppress the output (results=hide), or include the output and assume that it contains LaTeX markup (results=tex). The default is verbatim. Use results=tex when the output is generated by the xtable() function in the xtable package or the latex() function in the Hmisc package.

By default, Sweave will add LaTeX markup code to attractively format data frames, matrices, and vectors. Additionally, R objects can be embedded inline using a \Sexpr{} statement. Note that lattice graphs must be embedded in a print() statement to be processed properly.

The xtable() function in the xtable package can be used to format data frames and matrices more precisely. In addition, it can be used to format other R objects, including those produced by lm(), glm(), aov(), table(), ts(), and coxph(). Use method(xtable) to view a comprehensive list. When formatting R output using xtable(), be sure to include the results=tex option in the code chunk delimiter.

It's easier to see how this all works with an example. Consider the noweb file in listing D.1. This is a reworking of the one-way ANOVA example in section 8.3. LaTeX markup code begins with a backslash (\). The exception is \Sexpr{}, which is a Sweave addition. R related code is presented in bold italics.

Listing D.1   A sample noweb file (example.nrw)

```
\documentclass[12pt]{article}
\title{Sample Report}
```

```
\author{Robert I. Kabacoff, Ph.D.}
\date{}
\begin{document}
\maketitle

<<echo=false, results=hide>>=
library(multcomp)
library(xtable)
attach(cholesterol)
@

\section{Results}

Cholesterol reduction was assessed in a study
that randomized \Sexpr{nrow(cholesterol)} patients
to one of \Sexpr{length(unique(trt))} treatments.
Summary statistics are provided in
Table \ref{table:descriptives}.

<<echo = false, results = tex>>=
descTable <- data.frame("Treatment" = sort(unique(trt)),
    "N"    = as.vector(table(trt)),
    "Mean" = tapply(response, list(trt), mean, na.rm=TRUE),
    "SD"   = tapply(response, list(trt), sd, na.rm=TRUE)
 )
print(xtable(descTable, caption = "Descriptive statistics
for each treatment group", label = "table:descriptives"),
caption.placement = "top", include.rownames = FALSE)
@

The analysis of variance is provided in Table \ref{table:anova}.

<<echo=false, results=tex>>=
fit <- aov(response ~ trt)
print(xtable(fit, caption = "Analysis of variance",
    label = "table:anova"), caption.placement = "top")
@

\noindent and group differences are plotted in Figure \ref{figure:tukey}.

\begin{figure}\label{figure:tukey}
\begin{center}

<<fig=TRUE,echo=FALSE>>=
par(mar=c(5,4,6,2))
tuk <- glht(fit, linfct=mcp(trt="Tukey"))
plot(cld(tuk, level=.05),col="lightgrey",xlab="Treatment", ylab="Response")
box("figure")
@

\caption{Distribution of response times and pairwise comparisons.}
\end{center}
\end{figure}
\end{document}
```

Sample Report

Robert I. Kabacoff, Ph.D.

1   Results

Cholesterol reduction was assessed in a study that randomized 50 patients to one of 5 treatments. Summary statistics are provided in Table 1.

Table 1: Descriptive statistics for each treatment group

Treatment	N	Mean	SD
1time	10	5.78	2.88
2times	10	9.22	3.48
4times	10	12.37	2.92
drugD	10	15.36	3.45
drugE	10	20.95	3.35

The analysis of variance is provided in Table 2.

Table 2: Analysis of variance

	Df	Sum Sq	Mean Sq	F value	Pr(>F)
trt	4	1351.37	337.84	32.43	0.0000
Residuals	45	468.75	10.42		

and group differences are plotted in Figure 1.

Figure D.2   Page 1 of the report created from the sample noweb file in listing D.1. The noweb file was processed through the `Sweave()` function in R and the resulting TeX file was processed through a LaTeX compiler to produce a PDF document.

After processing the noweb file through the Sweave() function in R and processing the resulting TeX file through a LaTeX compiler, the PDF document in figures D.2 and D.3 is generated.

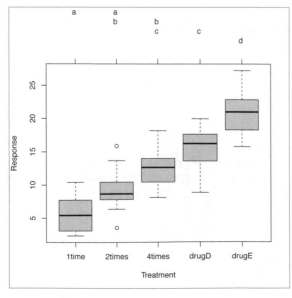

Figure 1: Distribution of response times and pairwise comparisons.

Figure D.3   Page 2 of the report created from the sample noweb file in listing D.1.

To learn more about Sweave, visit the Sweave home page (www.stat.uni-muenchen. de/~leisch/Sweave/). An excellent presentation is also provided by Theresa Scott (http://biostat.mc.vanderbilt.edu/TheresaScott). To learn more about LaTeX, check out the article "The Not So Short Introduction to LaTeX 2e," available on the LaTeX home page (www.latex-project.org).

D.2   *Joining forces with OpenOffice using odfWeave*

Sweave provides a means of embedding R code and output in a LaTeX document that's compiled into a PDF, PostScript, or DVI file. Although beautiful, the final document isn't editable. Additionally, many recipients require reports in a format such as Word.

odfWeave provides a mechanism for embedding R code and output in OpenOffice documents. Instead of placing R code chunks in a LaTeX document, the user places R code chunks in an OpenOffice ODT file (see figure D.3.). An advantage is that the ODT file can be created with a WYSIWYG editor such as OpenOffice Writer (www. OpenOffice.org); there's no need to learn a markup language.

Once the noweb document is created as an ODT file, you process it through the odfWeave() function in the odfWeave package. Unlike Sweave, odfWeave has to be downloaded, installed before first use (install.packages("odfWeave")), and loaded in each session in which it will be used. For example,

```
library(odfWeave)
infile <- "example.odt"
outfile <- "example-out.odt"
odfWeave(infile, outfile)
```

will take the example.odt file displayed in figure D.4 and produce the example-out. odt file displayed in figure D.5. Adding options(SweaveSyntax="SweaveSyntaxNo web") before the odfWeave() statement may help reduce parsing errors on some platforms.

There are several differences between Sweave and odfWeave:

- The xtable() function doesn't work with odfWeave. By default, odfWeave will render data frames, matrices, and vectors in an attractive format. Optionally, the odfTable() function can be used to format these objects with a high degree of control.
- ODF documents use XML markup rather than LaTeX. Therefore, the code chunk option result=tex should never be used. Use result=xml for code chunks that use odfTable().
- The infile and outfile names should be different. Unlike Sweave, odfWeave("example.odt") would overwrite the noweb document with the final report.

If you look at Figure D.4, you'll note that the ANOVA table isn't attractively formatted (as it was in Sweave). Rather, the table is in the standard monospaced font produced by R. This is because odfWeave doesn't have a formatting function for the objects

---

My Sample Report

Robert I. Kabacoff, Ph.D.

```
<<echo=false, results=hide>>=
library(multcomp)
library(xtable)
attach(cholesterol)
@
```

1 Results

Cholesterol reduction was assessed in a study that randomized \Sexpr{nrow(cholesterol)} patients to one of \Sexpr{length(unique(trt))} treatments. Summary statistics are provided in Table 1.

Table 1. Descriptive Statistics for each treatment group
```
<<echo = false, results = xml>>=
descTable <- data.frame("Treatment" = sort(unique(trt)),
  "N"    = as.vector(table(trt)),
  "Mean" = tapply(response, list(trt), mean, na.rm=TRUE),
  "SD"   = tapply(response, list(trt), sd, na.rm=TRUE)
 )
odfTable(descTable)
@
```

The analysis of variance is provided Table 2.

Table 2. Analysis of Variance
```
<<echo=false>>=
fit <- aov(response ~ trt)
summary(fit)
@
```

and group differences are plotted in Figure 1.

```
<<fig=TRUE,echo=FALSE>>=
par(mar=c(5,4,6,2))
tuk <- glht(fit, linfct=mcp(trt="Tukey"))
plot(cld(tuk, level=.05),col="lightgrey",xlab="Treatment", ylab="Response")
box("figure")
@
```
Figure1. Distribution of response times and pair-wise comparisons.

Figure D.4   Initial noweb file (example.odt) to be processed through odfWeave

My Sample Report

Robert I. Kabacoff, Ph.D.

1 Results

Cholesterol reduction was assessed in a study that randomized 50 patients to one of 5 treatments. Summary statistics are provided in Table 1.

Table 1. Descriptive Statistics for each treatment group

	Treatment	N	Mean	SD
1time	1time	10	5.782	2.878
2times	2times	10	9.225	3.483
4times	4times	10	12.375	2.923
drugD	drugD	10	15.361	3.455
drugE	drugE	10	20.948	3.345

The analysis of variance is provided Table 2.

Table 2. Analysis of Variance

```
          Df  Sum Sq Mean Sq F value    Pr(>F)
trt        4 1351.37  337.84  32.433 9.819e-13 ***
Residuals 45  468.75   10.42
---
Signif. codes: 0 '***' 0.001 '**' 0.01 '*' 0.05 '.' 0.1 ' ' 1
```

and group differences are plotted in Figure 1.

Figure D.5 Final report in ODF format (example-out.odt). Page 2 is similar to the second page of the Sweave output in figure D.2 and is omitted to save space

returned by `lm()`, `glm()`, and so forth. To properly format these results, we'd have to pull the components out of the object in question (`fit` in this case), and arrange them in a matrix or data frame.

Once you have your report in ODF format, you can continue to edit it, tighten up the formatting, and save the results to an ODT, HTML, DOC, or DOCX file format. To learn more, read the `odfWeave` manual and vignette.

D.3   *Comments*

There are several advantages to the Sweave and odfWeave approaches described here. By embedding the code needed to perform the statistical analyses directly into the final report, you document exactly how the results were calculated. Six months from now, you can easily see what was done. You can also modify the statistical analyses or add new data and immediately regenerate the report with minimum effort. Additionally, you avoid the need to cut and paste and reformat the results.

Unfortunately, you gain these advantages by putting in significantly more work at the front-end. There are other disadvantages as well. In the case of LaTeX, you need to learn a typesetting language. In the case of ODF, you need to use a program like OpenOffice that may not be standard in your work environment.

For good or ill, Microsoft Word and PowerPoint are the current report and presentation standards in the business world. The packages R2wd and R2PPT can be used to dynamically create Word and PowerPoint documents with inserted R output, but they are in their formative stages of development. I'm looking forward to seeing fully developed implementations.

appendix E
Matrix Algebra in R

Many of the functions described in this book operate on matrices. The manipulation of matrices is built deeply into the R language. Table E.1 describes operators and functions that are particularly important for solving linear algebra problems. In the following table, A and B are matrices, x and b are vectors, and k is a scalar.

Table E.1   R functions and operators for matrix algebra

Operator or Function	Description
+ - * / ^	Element-wise addition, subtraction, multiplication, division, and exponentiation, respectively.
A %*% B	Matrix multiplication.
A %o% B	Outer product. AB'.
cbind(A, B, …)	Combine matrices or vectors horizontally.
chol(A)	Choleski factorization of A. If R <- chol(A), then chol(A) contains the upper triangular factor, such that R'R = A.
colMeans(A)	Returns a vector containing the column means of A.
crossprod(A)	A'A.
crossprod(A,B)	A'B.

Table E.1   R functions and operators for matrix algebra (*continued*)

Operator or Function	Description
colSums(A)	Returns a vector containing the column sums of A.
diag(A)	Returns a vector containing the elements of the principal diagonal.
diag(x)	Creates a diagonal matrix with the elements of x in the principal diagonal.
diag(k)	If k is a scalar, this creates a k x k identity matrix.
eigen(A)	Eigenvalues and eigenvectors of A. If y <- eigen(A), then y$val are the eigenvalues of A and y$vec are the eigenvectors of A.
ginv(A)	Moore-Penrose Generalized Inverse of A. (Requires the MASS package).
qr(A)	QR decomposition of A. If y <- qr(A), then y$qr has an upper triangle containing the decomposition and a lower triangle that contains information on the decomposition, y$rank is the rank of A, y$qraux is a vector containing additional information on Q, and y$pivot contains information on the pivoting strategy used.
rbind(A, B, …)	Combines matrices or vectors vertically.
rowMeans(A)	Returns a vector containing the row means of A.
rowSums(A)	Returns a vector containing the row sums of A.
solve(A)	Inverse of A where A is a square matrix.
solve(A, b)	Solves for vector x in the equation b = Ax.
svd(A)	Single value decomposition of A. If y <- svd(A), then y$d is a vector containing the singular values of A, y$u is a matrix with columns containing the left singular vectors of A, and y$v is a matrix with columns containing the right singular vectors of A.
t(A)	Transpose of A.

There are several user-contributed packages that are particularly useful for matrix algebra. The matlab package contains wrapper functions and variables used to replicate MATLAB function calls as closely as possible. These functions can help port MATLAB applications and code to R. There's also a useful cheat sheet for converting MATLAB statements to R statements at http://mathesaurus.sourceforge.net/octave-r.html.

The Matrix package contains functions that extend R in order to support highly dense or sparse matrices. It provides efficient access to BLAS (Basic Linear Algebra Subroutines), Lapack (dense matrix), TAUCS (sparse matrix), and UMFPACK (sparse matrix) routines.

Finally, the matrixStats package provides methods for operating on the rows and columns of matrices, including functions that calculate counts, sums, products, central tendency, dispersion, and more. Each is optimized for speed and efficient memory use.

appendix F
Packages used in this book

R derives much of its breadth and power from the contributions of selfless authors. Table F.1 lists the user-contributed packages described in this book, along with the chapter(s) in which they appear.

Table F.1   Contributed packages used in this book

Package	Authors	Description	Chapters
AER	Christian Kleiber and Achim Zeileis	Functions, data sets, examples, demos, and vignettes from the book *Applied Econometrics with R* by Christian Kleiber and Achim Zeileis	13
Amelia	James Honaker, Gary King, and Matthew Blackwell	Amelia II: A program for missing data via multiple imputation	15
arrayImpute	Eun-kyung Lee, Dankyu Yoon, and Taesung Park	Missing imputation for microarray data	15
arrayMissPattern	Eun-kyung Lee and Taesung Park	Exploratory analysis of missing patterns for microarray data	15

Table F.1   Contributed packages used in this book (*continued*)

Package	Authors	Description	Chapters
boot	S original by Angelo Canty. R port by Brian Ripley.	Bootstrap functions	12
ca	Michael Greenacre and Oleg Nenadic	Simple, multiple and joint correspondence analysis	7
car	John Fox and Sanford Weisberg	Companion to Applied Regression	1, 8, 9, 10, 11
cat	Ported to R by Ted Harding and Fernando Tusell. Original by Joseph L. Schafer.	Analysis of categorical-variable datasets with missing values	15
coin	Torsten Hothorn, Kurt Hornik, Mark A. van de Wiel, and Achim Zeileis	Conditional inference procedures in a permutation test framework	12
corrgram	Kevin Wright	Plot a correlogram	11
corrperm	Douglas M. Potter	Permutation tests of correlation with repeated measurements	12
doBy	Søren Højsgaard with contributions from Kevin Wright and Alessandro A. Leidi.	Group-wise computations of summary statistics, general linear contrasts and other utilities	7
effects	John Fox and Jangman Hong	Effect displays for linear, generalized linear, multinomial-logit, and proportional-odds logit models	8, 9
FactoMineR	Francois Husson, Julie Josse, Sebastien Le, and Jeremy Mazet	Multivariate exploratory data analysis and data mining with R	14
FAiR	Ben Goodrich	Factor analysis using a genetic algorithm	14
fCalendar	Diethelm Wuertz and Yohan Chalabi	Functions for chronological and calendarical objects	4
foreign	R-core members, Saikat DebRoy, Roger Bivand, and others	Read data stored by Minitab, S, SAS, SPSS, Stata, Systat, dBase, and others	2
gclus	Catherine Hurley	Clustering graphics	1, 11
ggplot2	Hadley Wickam	An implementation of the Grammar of Graphics	16

Table F.1 Contributed packages used in this book (*continued*)

Package	Authors	Description	Chapters
glmPerm	Wiebke Werft and Douglas M. Potter	Permutation test for inference in generalized linear models	12
gmodels	Gregory R. Warnes. Includes R source code and/or documentation contributed by Ben Bolker, Thomas Lumley, and Randall C Johnson. Contributions from Randall C. Johnson are Copyright (2005) SAIC-Frederick, Inc.	Various R programming tools for model fitting	7
gplots	Gregory R. Warnes. Includes R source code and/or documentation contributed by Ben Bolker, Lodewijk Bonebakker, Robert Gentleman, Wolfgang Huber Andy Liaw, Thomas Lumley, Martin Maechler, Arni Magnusson, Steffen Moeller, Marc Schwartz, and Bill Venables	Various R programming tools for plotting data	6, 9
grid	Paul Murrell	A rewrite of the graphics layout capabilities, plus some support for interaction	16
gvlma	Edsel A. Pena and Elizabeth H. Slate	Global validation of linear models assumptions	8
hdf5	Marcus G. Daniels	Interface to the NCSA HDF5 library	2
hexbin	Dan Carr, ported by Nicholas Lewin-Koh and Martin Maechler	Hexagonal binning routines	11
HH	Richard M. Heiberger	Support software for *Statistical Analysis and Data Display* by Heiberger and Holland	9
Hmisc	Frank E Harrell Jr, with contributions from many other users	Harrell miscellaneous functions for data analysis, high-level graphics, utility operations, and more	2, 3, 7

Table F.1   Contributed packages used in this book (*continued*)

Package	Authors	Description	Chapters
kmi	Arthur Allignol	Kaplan-Meier multiple imputation for the analysis of cumulative incidence functions in the competing risks setting	15
lattice	Deepayan Sarkar	Lattice graphics	16
latticist	Felix Andrews	GUI for exploratory visualization	16
lavaan	Yves Rosseel	Functions for latent variable models, including confirmatory factor analysis, structural equation modeling, and latent growth curve models	14
lcda	Michael Buecker	Latent class discriminant analysis	14
leaps	Thomas Lumley using Fortran code by Alan Miller	Regression subset selection including exhaustive search	8
lmPerm	Bob Wheeler	Permutation tests for linear models	12
logregperm	Douglas M. Potter	Permutation test for inference in logistic regression	12
longitudinalData	Christophe Genolini	Tools for longitudinal data	15
lsa	Fridolin Wild	Latent semantic analysis	14
ltm	Dimitris Rizopoulos	Latent trait models under item response theory	14
lubridate	Garrett Grolemund and Hadley Wickham	Functions to identify and parse date-time data, extract and modify components of a date-time, perform accurate math on date-times, and handle time zones and Daylight Savings Time	4
MASS	S original by Venables and Ripley. R port by Brian Ripley, following earlier work by Kurt Hornik and Albrecht Gebhardt.	Functions and datasets to support Venables and Ripley's *Modern Applied Statistics with S* (4th edition)	4, 5, 7, 8, 9, 12

Table F.1 Contributed packages used in this book (*continued*)

Package	Authors	Description	Chapters
mlogit	Yves Croissant	Estimation of the multinomial logit model	13
multcomp	Torsten Hothorn, Frank Bretz Peter Westfall, Richard M. Heiberger, and Andre Schuetzenmeister	Simultaneous tests and confidence intervals for general linear hypotheses in parametric models, including linear, generalized linear, linear mixed effects, and survival models	9, 12
mvnmle	Kevin Gross, with help from Douglas Bates	ML estimation for multivariate normal data with missing values	15
mvoutlier	Moritz Gschwandtner and Peter Filzmoser	Multivariate outlier detection based on robust methods	9
ncdf, ncdf4	David Pierce	Interface to Unidata netCDF data files	2
nFactors	Gilles Raiche	Parallel analysis and non graphical solutions to the Cattell scree test	14
npmc	Joerg Helms and Ullrich Munzel	Nonparametric multiple comparisons	7
OpenMx	Steven Boker, Michael Neale, Hermine Maes, Michael Wilde, Michael Spiegel, Timothy R. Brick, Jeffrey Spies, Ryne Estabrook, Sarah Kenny, Timothy Bates, Paras Mehta, and John Fox	Advanced structural equation modeling.	14
pastecs	Frederic Ibanez, Philippe Grosjean, and Michele Etienne	Package for the analysis of space-time ecological series	7
piface	Russell Lenth, R package interface by Tobias Verbeke	Java applets for power and sample size assessment	10
playwith	Felix Andrews	A GTK+ graphical user interface for editing and interacting with R plots	16
poLCA	Drew Linzer and Jeffrey Lewis	Polytomous variable latent class analysis	14

Table F.1   Contributed packages used in this book (*continued*)

Package	Authors	Description	Chapters
psych	William Revelle	Procedures for psychological, psychometric, and personality research	7, 14
pwr	Stephane Champely	Basic functions for power analysis	10
qcc	Luca Scrucca	Quality control charts	13
randomLCA	Ken Beath	Random effects latent class analysis	14
Rcmdr	John Fox, with contributions from Liviu Andronic, Michael Ash, Theophilius Boye, Stefano Calza, Andy Chang, Philippe Grosjean, Richard Heiberger, G. Jay Kerns, Renaud Lancelot, Matthieu Lesnoff, Uwe Ligges, Samir Messad, Martin Maechler, Robert Muenchen, Duncan Murdoch, Erich Neuwirth, Dan Putler, Brian Ripley, Miroslav Ristic, and Peter Wolf.	R Commander, a platform-independent basic-statistics graphical user interface for R, based on the tcltk package	11
reshape	Hadley Wickham	Flexibly reshape data	4, 5, 7
rggobi	Duncan Temple Lang, Debby Swayne, Hadley Wickham, and Michael Lawrence	An interface between R and GGobi	16
rgl	Daniel Adler and Duncan Murdoch	3D visualization device system (OpenGL)	11
RJDBC	Simon Urbanek	Provides access to databases through the JDBC interface	2
rms	Frank E. Harrell, Jr.	Regression modeling strategies - about 225 function that assist with and streamline regression modeling, testing, estimations, validation, graphics, prediction, and typesetting	13

Table F.1 Contributed packages used in this book (*continued*)

Package	Authors	Description	Chapters
robust	Jiahui Wang, Ruben Zamar, Alfio Marazzi, Victor Yohai, Matias Salibian-Barrera, Ricardo Maronna, Eric Zivot, David Rocke, Doug Martin, Martin Maechler, and Kjell Konis	A package of robust methods	13
RODBC	Brian Ripley and Michael Lapsley	ODBC database access	2
ROracle	David A. James and Jake Luciani	Oracle database interface for R	2
rrcov	Valentin Todorov	Robust location and scatter estimation and robust multivariate analysis with high breakdown point	9
sampling	Yves Tillé and Alina Matei	Functions for drawing and calibrating samples	4
scatterplot3d	Uwe Ligges	Plots a three dimensional (3D) point cloud	11
sem	John Fox with contributions from Adam Kramer and Michael Friendly	Structural equation models	14
SeqKnn	Ki-Yeol Kim and Gwan-Su Yi, CSBio lab., Information and Communications University	Sequential KNN imputation method	15
sm	Adrian Bowman and Adelchi Azzalini. Ported to R by B. D. Ripley up to version 2.0, version 2.1 by Adrian Bowman and Adelchi Azzalini, version 2.2 by Adrian Bowman.	Smoothing methods for nonparametric regression and density estimation	6, 9
vcd	David Meyer, Achim Zeileis, and Kurt Hornik	Functions for visualizing categorical data	1, 6, 7, 11, 12
vegan	Jari Oksanen, F. Guillaume Blanchet, Roeland Kindt, Pierre Legendre, R. B. O'Hara, Gavin L. Simpson, Peter Solymos, M. Henry H. Stevens, and Helene Wagner	Ordination methods, diversity analysis, and other functions for community and vegetation ecologists	9

Table F.1   Contributed packages used in this book (*continued*)

Package	Authors	Description	Chapters
VIM	Matthias Templ, Andreas Alfons, and Alexander Kowarik	Visualization and imputation of missing values	15
xlsx	Adrian A. Dragulescu	Read, write, and format Excel 2007 (xlsx) files	2
XML	Duncan Temple Lang	Tools for parsing and generating XML within R and S-Plus	2

appendix G
Working with large datasets

R holds all of its objects in virtual memory. For most of us, this design decision has led to a zippy interactive experience, but for analysts working with large datasets, it can lead to slow program execution and memory-related errors.

Memory limits will depend primarily on the R build (32 versus 64-bit) and for 32-bit Windows, on the OS version involved. Error messages starting with cannot allocate vector of size typically indicate a failure to obtain sufficient contiguous memory, while error messages starting with cannot allocate vector of length indicate that an address limit has been exceeded. When working with large datasets, try to use a 64-bit build if at all possible. For all builds, the number of elements in a vector is limited to 2,147,483,647 (see ?Memory for more information).

There are three issues to consider when working with large datasets: (a) efficient programming to speed execution, (b) storing data externally to limit memory issues, and (c) using specialized statistical routines designed to efficiently analyze massive amounts of data. We will briefly consider each.

G.1   Efficient programming

There are a number of programming tips that improve performance when working with large datasets.

- Vectorize calculations when possible. Use R's built-in functions for manipulating vectors, matrices, and lists (for example, sapply, lappy, and mapply) and avoid loops (for and while) when feasible.

- Use matrices rather than data frames (they have less overhead).
- When using the `read.table()` family of functions to input external data into data frames, specify the `colClasses` and `nrows` options explicitly, set `comment.char = ""`, and specify `"NULL"` for columns that aren't needed. This will decrease memory usage and speed up processing considerably. When reading external data into a matrix, use the `scan()` function instead.
- Test programs on subsets of the data, in order to optimize code and remove bugs, before attempting a run on the full dataset.
- Delete temporary objects and objects that are no longer needed. The call `rm(list=ls())` will remove all objects from memory, providing a clean slate. Specific objects can be removed with `rm(`*object*`)`.
- Use the function `.ls.objects()` described in Jeromy Anglim's blog entry "Memory Management in R: A Few Tips and Tricks" (jeromyanglim.blogspot. com), to list all workspace objects sorted by size (MB). This function will help you find and deal with memory hogs.
- Profile your programs to see how much time is being spent in each function. You can accomplish this with the `Rprof()` and `summaryRprof()` functions. The `system.time()` function can also help. The `profr` and `prooftools` packages provide functions that can help in analyzing profiling output.
- The `Rcpp` package can be used to transfer R objects to C++ functions and back when more optimized subroutines are needed.

With large datasets, increasing code efficiency will only get you so far. When bumping up against memory limits, you can also store our data externally and use specialized analysis routines.

G.2   *Storing data outside of RAM*

There are several packages available for storing data outside of R's main memory. The strategy involves storing data in external databases or in binary flat files on disk, and then accessing portions as they are needed. Several useful packages are described in table G.1.

Table G.1   R packages for accessing large datasets

Package	Description
ff	Provides data structures that are stored on disk but behave as if they were in RAM.
bigmemory	Supports the creation, storage, access, and manipulation of massive matrices. Matrices are allocated to shared memory and memory-mapped files.
filehash	Implements a simple key-value database where character string keys are associated with data values stored on disk.

Table G.1 R packages for accessing large datasets (*continued*)

Package	Description
ncdf, ncdf4	Provides an interface to Unidata netCDF data files.
RODBC, RMySQL, ROracle, RPostgreSQL, RSQLite	Each provides access to external relational database management systems.

The packages above help overcome R's memory limits on data storage. However, specialized methods are also needed when attempting to analyze large datasets in a reasonable length of time. Some of the most useful are described below.

G.3 Analytic packages for large datasets

R provides several packages for the analysis of large datasets:

- The biglm and speedglm packages fit linear and generalized linear models to large datasets in a memory efficient manner. This offers lm() and glm() type functionality when dealing with massive datasets.
- Several packages offer analytic functions for working with the massive matrices produced by the bigmemory package. The biganalytics package offers k-means clustering, column statistics, and a wrapper to biglm. The bigtabulate package provides table(), split(), and tapply() functionality and the bigalgebra package provides advanced linear algebra functions.
- The biglars package offers least-angle regression, lasso, and stepwise regression for datasets that are too large to be held in memory, when used in conjunction with the ff package.
- The Brobdingnag package can be used to manipulate large numbers (numbers larger than 2^{1024}).

Working with datasets in the gigabyte to terabyte range can be challenging in any language. For more information on the methods available within R, see the CRAN Task View: *High-Performance and Parallel Computing with R* (cran.r-project.org/web/views/).

appendix H
Updating an R installation

As consumers, we take for granted that we can update a piece of software via a "Check for updates…" option. In chapter 1, I noted that the `update.packages()` function can be used to download and install the most recent version of a contributed package. Unfortunately, there's no corresponding function for updating the R installation itself. If you want to update an R installation from version 4.1.0 to 5.1.1, you must get creative. (As I write this, the current version is actually 2.13.0, but I want this book to appear hip and current for years to come).

Downloading and installing the latest version of R from CRAN (http://cran.r-project.org/bin/) is relatively straightforward. The complicating factor is that customizations (including previously installed contributed packages) will not be included in the new installation. In my current set-up, I have 248 contributed packages installed. I really don't want to have to write their names down and reinstall them by hand the next time I upgrade my R installation.

There has been much discussion on the web concerning the most elegant and efficient way to update an R installation. The method described below is neither elegant nor efficient, but I find that it works well on a variety of platforms (Windows, Mac, and Linux).

In this approach, the `installed.packages()` function is used to save a list of packages to a location outside of the R directory tree, and then the list is used with the `install.packages()` function to download and install the latest contributed packages into the new R installation. Here are the steps:

1 If you have a customized `Rprofile.site` file (see appendix B), save a copy outside of R.

2 Launch your current version of R and issue the following statements

```
oldip <- installed.packages()[,1]
save(oldip, file="path/installedPackages.Rdata")
```

where *path* is a directory outside of R.

3 Download and install the newer version of R.

4 If you saved a customized version of the `Rprofile.site` file in step 1, copy it into the new installation.

5 Launch the new version of R, and issue the following statements

```
load("path/installedPackages.Rdata")
newip <- installed.packages()[,1]
for(i in setdiff(oldip, newip))
   install.packages(i)
```

where *path* is the location specified in step 2.

6 Delete the old installation (optional).

This approach will install only packages that are available from the CRAN. It won't find packages obtained from other locations. You'll have to find and download these separately. Luckily, the process will display a list of packages that can't be installed. During my last installation, `globaltest` and `Biobase` couldn't be found. Since I got them from the Bioconductor site, I was able to install them via the code

```
source(http://bioconductor.org/biocLite.R)
biocLite("globaltest")
biocLite("Biobase")
```

Step 6 involves the optional deletion of the old installation. On a Windows machine, more than one version of R can be installed at a time. If desired, uninstall the older version via `Start > Control Panel > Uninstall a Program`. On Mac and Linux platforms, the new version of R will overwrite the older version. To delete any remnants on a Mac, use the Finder to go to the `/Library/Frameworks/R.frameworks/versions/` directory and delete the folder representing the older version. On a Linux platform, it's probably best to leave well enough alone.

Clearly, updating an existing version of R is more involved than is desirable for such a sophisticated piece of software. I'm hopeful that someday this appendix will simply say "Select the *Check for Updates…* option" to update an R installation.

<h1>references</h1>

Allison, P. 2001. *Missing Data.* Thousand Oaks, CA: Sage.

Allison, T., and D. Chichetti. 1976. "Sleep in Mammals: Ecological and Constitutional Correlates." *Science* 194 (4266): 732–734.

Anderson, M. J. 2006. "Distance-Based Tests for Homogeneity of Multivariate Dispersions." *Biometrics* 62:245–253.

Baade, R., and R. Dye. 1990. "The Impact of Stadiums and Professional Sports on Metropolitan Area Development." *Growth and Change* 21:1–14.

Bandalos, D. L., and M. R. Boehm-Kaufman. 2009. "Four Common Misconceptions in Exploratory Factor Analysis." In *Statistical and Methodological Myths and Urban Legends,* edited by C. E. Lance and R. J. Vandenberg, 61–87. New York: Routledge.

Bates, D. 2005. "Fitting Linear Mixed Models in R." *R News* 5 (1). www.r-project.org/doc/Rnews/Rnews_2005-1.pdf.

Breslow, N., and D. Clayton. 1993. "Approximate Inference in Generalized Linear Mixed Models." *Journal of the American Statistical Association* 88:9–25.

Bretz, F., T. Hothorn, and P. Westfall. 2010. *Multiple Comparisons Using R.* Boca Raton, FL: Chapman & Hall.

Canty, A. J. 2002. "Resampling Methods in R: The boot Package." http://cran.r-project.org/doc/Rnews/Rnews_2002-3.pdf.

Chambers, J. M. 2008. *Software for Data Analysis: Programming with R.* New York: Springer.

Cleveland, W. 1981. "LOWESS: A Program for Smoothing Scatter Plots by Robust Locally Weighted Regression." *The American Statistician* 35:54.

———. 1985. The *Elements of Graphing Data.* Monterey, CA: Wadsworth.

———. 1993. *Visualizing Data.* Summit, NJ: Hobart Press.

Cohen, J. 1988. *Statistical Power Analysis for the Behavioral Sciences,* 2nd ed. Hillsdale, NJ: Lawrence Erlbaum.

Cook, D., and D. Swayne. 2008. *Interactive and Dynamic Graphics for Data Analysis with R and GGobi.* New York: Springer.

Coxe, S., S. West, and L. Aiken. 2009. "The Analysis of Count Data: A Gentle Introduction to Poisson Regression and Its Alternatives." *Journal of Personality Assessment* 91:121–136.

Culbertson, W., and D. Bradford. 1991. "The Price of Beer: Some Evidence for Interstate Comparisons." *International Journal of Industrial Organization* 9:275–289.

DiStefano, C., M. Zhu, and D. Mîndrilă. 2009. "Understanding and Using Factor Scores: Considerations for the Applied Researcher." *Practical Assessment, Research & Evaluation* 14 (20). http://pareonline.net/pdf/v14n20.pdf.

Dobson, A., and A. Barnett. 2008. *An Introduction to Generalized Linear Models*, 3rd ed. Boca Raton, FL: Chapman & Hall.

Dunteman, G., and M-H Ho. 2006. *An Introduction to Generalized Linear Models.* Thousand Oaks, CA: Sage.

Efron, B., and R. Tibshirani. 1998. *An Introduction to the Bootstrap.* New York: Chapman & Hall.

Fair, R. C. 1978. "A Theory of Extramarital Affairs." *Journal of Political Economy* 86:45–61.

Faraway, J. 2006. *Extending the Linear Model with R: Generalized Linear, Mixed Effects and Nonparametric Regression Models.* Boca Raton, FL: Chapman & Hall.

Fox, J. 2002. *An R and S-Plus Companion to Applied Regression.* Thousand Oaks, CA: Sage.

———. 2002. "Bootstrapping Regression Models." http://mng.bz/pY9m.

———. 2008. *Applied Regression Analysis and Generalized Linear Models.* Thousand Oaks, CA: Sage.

Fwa, T., ed. 2006. *The Handbook of Highway Engineering*, 2nd ed. Boca Raton, FL: CRC Press.

Good, P. 2006. *Resampling Methods: A Practical Guide to Data Analysis*, 3rd ed. Boston: Birkhäuser.

Gorsuch, R. L. 1983. *Factor Analysis*, 2nd ed. Hillsdale, NJ: Lawrence Erlbaum.

Greene, W. H. 2003. *Econometric Analysis*, 5th ed. Upper Saddle River, NJ: Prentice Hall.

Grissom, R., and J. Kim. 2005. *Effect Sizes for Research: A Broad Practical Approach.* Mahwah, NJ: Lawrence Erlbaum.

Groemping, U. 2009. "CRAN Task View: Design of Experiments (DoE) and Analysis of Experimental Data." http://mng.bz/r45q.

Hand, D. J. and C. C. Taylor. 1987. *Multivariate Analysis of Variance and Repeated Measures.* London: Chapman & Hall.

Harlow, L., S. Mulaik, and J. Steiger. 1997. *What If There Were No Significance Tests?* Mahwah, NJ: Lawrence Erlbaum.

Hayton, J. C., D. G. Allen, and V. Scarpello. 2004. "Factor Retention Decisions in Exploratory Factor Analysis: A Tutorial on Parallel Analysis." *Organizational Research Methods* 7:191–204.

Hsu, S., M. Wen, and M. Wu. 2009. "Exploring User Experiences as Predictors of MMORPG Addiction." *Computers and Education* 53:990–999.

Jacoby, W. G. 2006. "The Dot Plot: A Graphical Display for Labeled Quantitative Values." *Political Methodologist* 14:6–14.

Johnson, J. 2004. "Factors Affecting Relative Weights: The Influence of Sample and Measurement Error." *Organizational Research Methods* 7:283–299.

Johnson, J., and J. Lebreton. 2004. "History and Use of Relative Importance Indices in Organizational Research." *Organizational Research Methods* 7:238–257.

Koch, G., and S. Edwards. 1988. "Clinical Efficiency Trials with Categorical Data." *In Statistical Analysis with Missing Data*, 2nd ed., by R. J. A. Little and D. Rubin. Hoboken, NJ: John Wiley & Sons, 2002.

LeBreton, J. M, and S. Tonidandel. 2008. "Multivariate Relative Importance: Extending Relative Weight Analysis to Multivariate Criterion Spaces." *Journal of Applied Psychology* 93:329–345.

Lemon, J., and A. Tyagi. 2009. "The Fan Plot: A Technique for Displaying Relative Quantities and Differences." *Statistical Computing and Graphics Newsletter* 20:8–10.

Licht, M. 1995. "Multiple Regression and Correlation." In *Reading and Understanding Multivariate Statistics*, edited by L. Grimm and P. Yarnold. Washington, DC: American Psychological Association, 19–64.

McCall, R. B. 2000. *Fundamental Statistics for the Behavioral Sciences*, 8th ed. New York: Wadsworth.

McCullagh, P., and J. Nelder. 1989. *Generalized Linear Models*, 2nd ed. Boca Raton, FL: Chapman & Hall.

Meyer, D., A. Zeileis, and K. Hornick. 2006. "The Strucplot Framework: Visualizing Multi-way Contingency Tables with vcd." *Journal of Statistical Software* 17:1–48. www.jstatsoft.org/v17/i03/paper.

Montgomery, D. C. 2007. *Engineering Statistics*. Hoboken, NJ: John Wiley & Sons.

Mooney, C., and R. Duval. 1993. *Bootstrapping: A Nonparametric Approach to Statistical Inference*. Monterey, CA: Sage.

Mulaik, S. 2009. *Foundations of Factor Analysis*, 2nd ed. Boca Raton, FL: Chapman & Hall.

Murphy, K., and B. Myors. 1998. *Statistical Power Analysis: A Simple and General Model for Traditional and Modern Hypothesis Tests*. Mahwah, NJ: Lawrence Erlbaum.

Murrell, P. 2006. *R Graphics*. Boca Raton, FL: Chapman & Hall/CRC.

Nenadic, O., and M. Greenacre. 2007. "Correspondence Analysis in R, with Two- and Three-Dimensional Graphics: The ca Package." *Journal of Statistical Software* 20 (3). www.jstatsoft.org/v20/i03/.

Peace, K. E., ed. 1987. *Biopharmaceutical Statistics for Drug Development*. New York: Marcel Dekker, 403–451.

Pena, E., and E. Slate. 2006. "Global Validation of Linear Model Assumptions." *Journal of the American Statistical Association* 101:341–354.

Pinheiro, J. C., and D. M. Bates. 2000. *Mixed-Effects Models in S and S-PLUS*. New York: Springer.

Potvin, C., M. J. Lechowicz, and S. Tardif. 1990. "The Statistical Analysis of Ecophysiological Response Curves Obtained from Experiments Involving Repeated Measures." *Ecology* 71:1389–1400.

Rosenthal, R., R. Rosnow, and D. Rubin. 2000. *Contrasts and Effect Sizes in Behavioral Research: A Correlational Approach*. Cambridge, UK: Cambridge University Press.

Sarkar, D. 2008. *Lattice: Multivariate Data Visualization with R*. New York: Springer.

Schafer, J., and J. Graham. 2002. "Missing Data: Our View of the State of the Art." *Psychological Methods* 7:147–177.

Schlomer, G., S. Bauman, and N. Card. 2010. "Best Practices for Missing Data Management in Counseling Psychology." *Journal of Counseling Psychology* 57:1–10.

Shah, A. 2005. "Getting started with the boot package." www.mayin.org/ajayshah/KB/R/documents/boot.html.

Silva, R. B., D. F. Ferreirra, and D. A. Nogueira. 2008. "Robustness of Asymptotic and Bootstrap Tests for Multivariate Homogeneity of Covariance Matrices." *Ciênc. agrotec.* 32:157–166.

Simon, J. 1997. "Resampling: The New Statistics." www.resample.com/content/text/index.shtml.

Snedecor, G. W., and W. G. Cochran. 1988. *Statistical Methods*, 8th ed. Ames, IA: Iowa State University Press.

UCLA: Academic Technology Services, Statistical Consulting Group. 2009. http://mng.bz/a9c7.

van Buuren, S., and K. Groothuis-Oudshoorn. 2010. "MICE: Multivariate Imputation by Chained Equations in R." *Journal of Statistical Software*, forthcoming. http://mng.bz/3EH5.

Venables, W. N., and B. D. Ripley. 1999. *Modern Applied Statistics with S-PLUS*, 3rd ed. New York: Springer.

———. 2000. *S Programming*. New York: Springer.

Westfall, P. H., et al. 1999. *Multiple Comparisons and Multiple Tests Using the SAS System*. Cary, NC: SAS Institute.

Wickham, H. 2009a. *ggplot2: Elegant Graphics for Data Analysis*. New York: Springer.

———. 2009b. "A Layered Grammar of Graphics." *Journal of Computational and Graphical Statistics* 19:3–28.

Wilkinson, L. 2005. *The Grammar of Graphics*. New York: Springer-Verlag.

Yu, C. H. 2003. "Resampling Methods: Concepts, Applications, and Justification." *Practical Assessment, Research & Evaluation*, 8 (19). http://pareonline.net/getvn.asp?v=8&n=19.

Yu-Sung, S., et al. 2010. "Multiple Imputation with Diagnostics (mi) in R: Opening Windows into the Black Box." *Journal of Statistical Software*. www.jstatsoft.org.

Zuur, A. F., et al. 2009. *Mixed Effects Models and Extensions in Ecology with R*. New York: Springer.

index